WOMEN AND LITERATURE
An Annotated Bibliography of Women Writers

3RD EDITION

Iris Biblowitz   Ann Kautzmann
Liza Bingham   Peggy Kornegger
Frances M. Goodstein   Virginia Rankin MacLean
Julia Homer   Jane Tuchscherer
Jill Janows   Judy Wynn

published by the Women and Literature Collective

$3.50 plus 25¢ postage per single copy.
Bulk order information available.
Standard bookstore discounts also available.

**Women and Literature Collective
Box 441
Cambridge, Massachusetts 02138**

Typeset by
Elizabeth Marshall
and
Cynthia Baron

Library of Congress # 76-473-35
ISBN # 0-915052-02-4

ii

Table of Contents

Introduction

The work of completing this third edition of **Women and Literature: An Annotated Bibliography of Women Writers** has taken two years. In the long process of bringing out this 3rd edition, we have been sustained by the belief that women's literary history must be rediscovered and made known. We have sought to correct the imbalance caused by a phallocentric culture and criticism by providing information about women's writing from a feminist perspective.

We realize, through our reading and research, that our bibliography is limited in comparison to the prodigious women's writings that must be explored. We have focused particularly on women's fictional writings plus other forms of expressive prose. In order for our common literary heritage to be fully known, other reference works are needed: bibliographies about poetry, drama, and those fictional works which might have been included but which we have inevitably missed due to limitations of time, space and the resources available to us. We urge others to make these vital efforts.

Writing this edition has been an evolving process for us. Our initial reason for continuing the Women and Literature Bibliography was the wish to give the public an expanded reading list for enriching its awareness of women authors and women's experiences through literature. We also felt committed to the idea of a collective working process, a feminist criticism, and to the small press movement as an alternative to traditional publishing.

While preparing the 3rd edition manuscript we rotated the tasks of bookkeeping, distribution, and promotion of the second edition, and through this work we have learned a lot about the business of publishing.

We are wiser, too, in regard to the dynamics of collective work. Our group was not invulnerable to conflicts—ideological and interpersonal. Our attempts to integrate differences of opinion within the context of our work were often confused and unsuccessful and we could not as a group meet everyone's needs. At various stages, three members left out of an original group of ten women. Pressures from within the collective and from outside circumstances were mostly responsible.

Nevertheless, our collective is intact and alive, if fluctuating. With new input of people and ideas, we hope that the group will continue as an ongoing study/publishing collective.

We structured our working process around once-a-week meetings at the Cambridge Women's Center. Using the second edition of

Women & Literature as a foundation, we constructed additional reading lists based on our own research, other people's suggestions, and areas of personal expertise. Political judgements about the authors involved were also a consideration. As we began to read and discuss women's writings, the enormity of our task quickly became apparent. Not only could we not include every book and author that we would have liked, but our treatment of each entry would also have to be limited. So we chose to be selective, making sometimes arbitrary and sometimes political decisions about what to include. Our feeling was that having a focus on certain types of literature or authors was better than mere descriptions in quantity.

As it developed, our work became more than simply reviewing books. Many of us found areas of special interest that we personally investigated and shared with the collective: black writing, Canadian writers, lesbian literature, and 1920's and 1930's novels of the labor movement and working class life, have made up some of these areas. We also made a special effort to include books from Daughters, Inc., the Feminist Press and other feminist publishing companies. In some cases we felt an author deserved special biographical note; elsewhere we decided to stray from our fiction rule and include plays if the author (i.e., Susan Glaspell and Lorraine Hansberry) needed special attention or was relatively unknown. Sometimes we were only able to read a few books by an author, and these might not necessarily be her best-written or most appealing. With popular or genre writers like Agatha Christie, Pearl Buck, and Daphne du Maurier, we decided to give them little or no treatment—assuming that most of our readers would be familiar with them anyway. Along with writing new entries, (expanding the bibliography to twice its original size) we have evaluated all content from the 2nd edition. While much of this earlier material has been retained, we take full responsibility for editorial changes here and throughout the work.

The annotated entries themselves are highly diverse. There is a stylistic difference between the old entries and the ones that we have added. Also, we have tried to retain the individual tastes and critical styles within our collective, rather than to edit the subjective flavor on behalf of uniformity.

The bibliography is divided into sections listed in the table of contents. We have included Author and Subject Indexes at the end. Dividing the bibliography into sections according to countries and then periods was the least confusing method we could find. The Author Index lists each writer whose work is annotated with additional references to some authors mentioned within annotations who might not have been included otherwise. The Subject Index is designed to show areas of interest and insight in each book. We chose topics with feminist concerns in mind, and only referred readers to books where these topics received substantial treatment.

Some of our bibliographic information will already be outdated by the time we go to press. New books will be published; old ones will go out of print. We urge readers to use **Women & Literature** to explore on their own what books are available—and to pressure publishers and libraries for books that aren't on the shelves and should be. Throughout the period of our production process many people have made valuable suggestions about books and authors. We hope this will continue as our on-going collective work relies on your response and constructive feedback.

We would like to thank Gill Gane, Kathleen Kelley, Susan Mullins, Susan Tenenbaum, (four members of Sense and Sensibility, an earlier collective) for their contributions. Thanks is also given to Kathi Maio, Fran Taylor, Karen Lindsey, Myra Page and Tillie Olsen for their contributions and advice. A special thanks goes to the Cambridge Women's Center for providing us with space and support for our meetings, and to Second Wave magazine for allowing us to use their production facilities.

The Women and Literature Collective
November, 1976
Iris Biblowitz
Liza Bingham
Frances M. Goodstein
Julia Homer
Jill Janows
Ann Kautzmann
Judy Wynn

United States

Pre-19th Century

1. FOSTER, Hannah W. THE COQUETTE. 1797. N.Y.: Somerset. $9.50.
An unusual, tragic heroine of early American fiction, strong-willed, restless and extroverted Eliza Wharton declares she'll settle down in marriage only "when I have sowed my wild oats." Although she rebels against the New England conventions of her time, she breaks the one rule she does believe in and become pregnant by the devious, archseducer, Peter Stanton. Alone and adrift, Eliza's death parallels Hetty Sorrel's in George Eliot's **Adam Bede.** The epistolary form of the novel allows her to confess and analyze her own misconduct and win the most moralistic reader's compassion. Despite the sentimentality, ponderous language, and flowery digressions, **The Coquette** (based on a reported incident) depicted its heroine with convincing clarity.

19th Century

ALCOTT, Louisa May. *(1832-1888). ". . . publishers are very perverse & won't let authors have their way," complained Louisa May Alcott as she completed her children's classic, "so my Little Women must be married off in a very stupid style." A confirmed spinster, Alcott longed to provide a comfortable home for her beloved mother Abba Alcott, who by early middle age was worn out from endless housekeeping in a series of make-shift homes. The father, Bronson Alcott, an impoverished Transcendentalist, was too idealistic for most kinds of work, so mother and daughter toiled at various jobs: teacher, seamstress, servant, etc. Louisa's great sympathy for the poor was no doubt rooted in these early experiences and in her mother's missionary relief work in Boston slums. Although the author's personal vision limited her to finding class solutions only in individual virtues, she did support the temperance and women's suffrage movements toward the end of her life. Despite moments of sentimentality, much of her fiction remains lively and readable today, notable for its emphasis on women's strength and women's friendships.*

2. _____ **LITTLE WOMEN.** 1869. Many cheap editions.
Still the greatest nonsexist children's book ever written. While Papa March is away doing something noble in the Civil War, Mamma, her four daughters, and their beloved housekeeper form a tight little community of women entered only occasionally by the rich but humble boy next door. Jo, the heroine, rebels against the middle-class ideal of gentle womanhood, maintaining her "tomboy" independence while working to learn the best of traditional "female" virtues: compassion and gentleness. Her rejection of romantic Laurie in favor of the prosaic (but, unfortunately, paternal) Professor Bhaer allows her the unheard of (in middle-class Victorian America) combination of motherhood and career, while her less colorful sisters grow into almost equally strong women.

3. _____**AN OLD-FASHIONED GIRL.** 1870. Many cheap editions.

A cozy, old-fashioned novel about a wholesome country girl who shows her blase city cousins how to enjoy the simple things in life: home, family and friends. Alcott celebrates sincere feminine friendship, and her heroine discovers that without it, economic independence is an empty victory. In one all-too-brief episode, we see a community of women artists who live happily together in harmony and mutual support. With tongue in cheek, Alcott chaffs frivolous high society and the shallow concerns of idle fashionable ladies. "Women have been called queens for a long time," remarks one of the artists, "but the kingdom given them isn't worth ruling."

4. _____ **WORK.** 1873. Ann Arbor: University Microfilms—Xerox, 1973.

Farmgirl Christie ventures into the grueling, underpaid world of the urban working woman. "I don't want to end my life like a coward because it is dull and hard," she declares as she moves from scullery to sweatshop to the professional stage. Part one of this autobiographical novel is a good realistic portrayal of the independent woman's lot in Civil War New England; however, the middle section slips into an improbable romance with a Thoreau-type character whom Alcott apparently felt obliged to kill off before Christie and her women friends can clasp hands in unimpeded sisterhood.

5. _____ **BEHIND A MASK: The Unknown Thrillers of Louisa May Alcott**, edited and with an introduction by Madeline Stern. N.Y.: William & Morrow, 1975. $8.95.

"I will make a battering ram of my head and make a way through this rough-and-tumble world," wrote Louisa May Alcott in her journal prior to penning the four gothic thrillers in this astonishing collection. Much of her stubborn determination is embodied in fascinating heroines like Jean Muir, governess, actress, and "psychological witch," who contrives to carve out a niche for herself in the aristocracy in the title story "Behind A Mask or A Woman's Power." Writing from behind the mask/pseudonym of "A.M. Bernard," Alcott could safely (and profitably) unleash the anger that she had stored up during her years of domestic service. "Pauline's Passion and Punishment" concerns a poor woman's vengeance upon a man who has humiliated her. Editor Stern suggests that the story might have been Alcott's revenge against a former employer. All four tales are brisk and well-plotted.

6. _____ **PLOTS AND COUNTERPLOTS: More Unknown Thrillers of Louisa May Alcott.** Madeline Stern, editor. N.Y.: William Morrow & Co., 1976. $9.95.

"Fell back on rubbishy tales," reads an Alcott diary entry, "for they pay best . . . are written in half the time and keep the family cosey." This second collection of gothic thrillers features skillfully-contrived melodramas about manipulating _femmes fatales_ and resourceful orphan girls. Of special interest is "A Whisper in the Dark" with its women-and-madness theme: Sybil, a temperamental young heiress, refuses to yield control of her estate to greedy relatives and is subsequently imprisoned in an asylum, her fully-justified anger having been diagnosed as insanity. Alcott's account of how mental institutions and clinical experimentation can promote mental illness remains as gripping and relevant as it was over a century ago. Another surprise, in a lighter vein however, is "Perilous Play" in which a group of bored, middle-class young people get stoned on narcotic bonbons: "Heaven bless hashish!" concludes the hero, and thus ends the last of Alcott's sensational potboilers. "**LITTLE WOMEN**," according to editor Stern, "Brought [Alcott] the fame and fortune she coveted and set her on the path of sweetness and light from which she seldom strayed."

7. BRENT, Linda. (pseud.) INCIDENTS IN THE LIFE OF A SLAVE GIRL. Edited by Lydia Maria Child. 1861. N.Y.: Harvest Book, 1973. (paperback $3.45)
"The secrets of slavery are concealed like those of the Inquisition." Linda Brent was the assumed name of Harriet Brent Jacobs, a black woman born into slavery in the south in 1818. Her purpose in publishing her life was to expose the crimes of slavery. She presents the facts of her early life, her escape and seven years in hiding, and her subsequent life in the north. Although hundreds of "Slave Narratives" exist, editor Walter Teller points out that this is one of the few written by a woman. Linda Brent writes, "Slavery is terrible for men but it is far more terrible for women." Women lived under the double yoke of slavery and sexual exploitation. Once pregnant, once a mother, women had to live with the horror that "children of slaves must follow the condition of the mother . . . My soul revolted against the tyranny. But where could I turn for protection? No matter whether the slave girl be as black as ebony or as fair as her mistress, in either case there is no shadow of law to protect her from insult, from violence, or even from death—all these are inflicted by fiends who bear the shape of men." And "the mistress, who ought to protect the helpless victim, has no other feelings towards her but jealousy and rage." Linda Brent did rebel, her book should be included in every 19th-century American Literature course.

8. BROWN, Alice TIVERTON TALES. 1899. New Jersey: Gregg Press, 1967. $2.45, pb. This collection of New Hampshire "local color" stories was popular in its time, and although Brown's efforts to evoke nostalgia are often maudlin, there are many fine moments. "The Mortuary Chest" opens with a group of women gathered for a mid-Sunday gossip in a church. The reader is made to feel their delight in this time together and their sympathy with Isabel, the heroine, who is trying to evade the courtship of the parson. We see a woman who forthrightly chooses not to marry in "A Last Assembling." In "The Way of Peace" a woman takes on the identity of her mother, who has just died. In spite of the hair-raising implications of this, the acceptance she demands from her relatives and friends to choose her own life style is a refreshing relief from the psychoanalytic atmosphere of the 20th century. The writing in this book is not consistently good; there is much to make a modern reader grimace, yet it holds glimpses of our female heritage.

CHOPIN, Kate O'Flaherty (1851-1904) *She was born in St. Louis ("Gateway t ᵗhe West") at the beginning of its incredible boom. Kate's Irish father died when she was only four and she was raised in a household of women: her Creole mother, grand-mother, and story-telling great-grandmother. She was also educated by women at a convent school where the nuns set rigorous academic standards and provided her with a solid background in the French classics. In 1870 she married Oscar Chopin, a Louisiana Creole, and lived with him in both New Orleans and rural Louisiana until his sudden death in 1883. A*  *widow with six children, she returned to St. Louis and began to write. Like so many of her sister-writers of the 19th century, she frequently wrote about strong women, but many of her heroines are strikingly different because they are portrayed as possessing strong sexual feelings. Deeply influenced by de Maupassant and Flaubert, she was also affected by the feminism of George Sand and Madame De Stael. The American* *writers she particularly admired were Sarah Orne Jewett and Mary Wilkins Freeman, and she ranks with them as one of our finest short story writers of the late 19th century.*

9. _____ **AT FAULT.** 1890. N.Y.: Somerset, current. $7.50.
This is an inept and superficial work about a widow who makes her divorced suitor remarry his alcoholic ex-wife. Once everyone has learned the folly of such an extreme moral stand, the wife has a fatal accident and all ends "happily". The book is interesting solely because it makes us aware of Chopin's extraordinarily rapid artistic growth; **The Awakening** was written only seven years later. Chopin wrote another novel before **The Awakening.** All we know of it is that she was unable to find a publisher, and so destroyed the manuscript.

10. _____ **BAYOU FOLK.** 1894. Ridgewood, N.J.: Gregg, 1967. $9.25, $2.45, p.b.
Her first collection of short stories brought Chopin national acclaim. As the title implies, all the stories are set in rural Louisiana. They depict the aristocratic Creoles, descendants of the French and Spanish colonists; the impoverished Cajuns, originally refugees from Canada; the blacks and mulattoes. Interestingly, the editorial choice was to exclude pieces featuring independent women. The book is still worthwhile, because Chopin, with her spontaneous style and ironic wit, is a wonderful storyteller, and many of the stories collected here are gems. "La Belle Zoraide" and "Desiree's Baby" are moving commentaries on the inhumanity of racial prejudice. "A No-Account Creole" is the funny-sad story of a young man trapped between his machismo and his deeply felt love.

11. _____ **A NIGHT IN ACADIE.** 1897. N.Y.: Somerset, current. $9.50.
The "dangerous" women have been left out. Women like the wife in "Story of an Hour," who cries "free, free, free," when she learns of her husband's death. Women like the selfless mother in "A Pair of Silk Stockings," who takes an afternoon of self-indulgence, and longs for a more permanent escape. Excluded, also, are her more sensual heroines. Still, critical response to this volume was more reserved, and Chopin was accused of "coarseness." Especially recommended is "A Respectable Woman," the humorous story of the struggle waged within the soul of a pure, middle-agee when she finds herself in love with a married man.

12. _____ **THE AWAKENING.** 1898. N.Y.: Avon, 1972. also N.Y.: Holt Rineheart & Winston, 1970. $3.95. (This edition also includes some short stories).
Edna Pontellier awakens from the 19th century dream of selfless womanhood to discover independence and sexuality. Chopin's exploration of women's sexuality shocked the critics of the day, and they universally condemned the book. **The Awakening** was banned in many libraries; Chopin herself was banned from certain literary societies. Her reputation declined, and she wrote very little after this. When she died in 1904, she was almost completely forgotten. The recent rediscovery of **The Awakening** by the women's movement, and its subsequent acclamation as a minor masterpiece have probably won Chopin a permanent place in American literature. **The Awakening** is an exquisitely written book. The author is in full control of her medium; hardly a word or image seems out of place. Edna is a tragic heroine, unable to choose either of the female roles she sees. She cannot be a thoroughly domesticated "mother-woman" like her friend Adele, nor a dedicated artist like the pianist Mlle. Reisz who gains individuality at the expense of her personal life. This book crystallizes some basic women's issues and is, therefore, an excellent choice for introductory courses on women's literature.

13. THE COMPLETE WORKS OF KATE CHOPIN, ed. , Per Seyersted. 2 vols. Baton Rouge, Louisiana: Louisiana State Press, 1967. $25.00
If one is interested in understanding Chopin as an author, particularly as an author concerned with women, this book is essential. It is here that one finds the sole surviving manuscript from her youth, "Emancipation: A Life Fable," whose theme

foreshadows **The Awakening.** Here too, one can read her first two published stories: "Wiser than a God," in which the heroine chooses a career over marriage, and "A Point at Issue," the humorous tale of a liberated young couple and their "modern" marriage. Only here do her tomboys survive: the very early "Maid of Saint Phillipe"—"tall, supple and strong," dressed in buckskin and looking like a "handsome boy"; and the post-**Awakening** "Charlie," a girl under intense social pressure to be feminine—in a story that seethes with suppressed rage. "The Storm," written after **The Awakening** but before the reviewers had dealt their crushing blow, is an interesting postscript to that novel. The story, which appears in print here for the first time, is a well-written, almost light-hearted account of a woman who has a positive experience when she finds sexual pleasure outside her marriage. The editor, Per Seyersted, has done a magnificent service in bringing together all of Chopin's work, including the many fine pieces which no one would publish during her lifetime. No library should be without these two volumes.

14. _____THE STORM AND OTHER STORIES, WITH THE AWAKENING. Ed. Per Seyersted. Old Westbury, N.Y.: Feminist Press, 1974. $5.00.
This is the very best of the paperback Chopin books in print; it is worth every penny of the price that Feminist Press is compelled to ask for it. Although one might quibble over a few choices, **The Storm** pretty much lives up to the editor's claim that it "contains all her stories of interest to both general readers and to students and teachers exploring her work in American Literature or Women's Studies courses." Thirty-five stories, a novel, and a selected bibliography—enjoy.

COOKE, Rose Terry *(1827-1892) A "natural-born storyteller," Rose Terry taught school until an inheritance freed her to write full-time about her New England neighbors: flint-hearted farmers, brow-beaten wives, and sharp-tongued spinsters. By the time she was 40, she had won considerable fame as a magazinist, having sold nearly 100 stories to* **Harper's, The Atlantic,** *and other magazines. In 1873, she married a widower, Rollin Cooke, whose numerous financial difficulties soon exhausted her savings and drove her to produce many didactic potboilers as well as the realistic "local-color" stories which set the literary stage for Sarah Orne Jewett and Mary Wilkins Freeman.*

15. _____ HUCKLEBERRIES GATHERED FROM NEW ENGLAND HILLS. 1891. N.Y.: Somerset. $9.50.
Rose Terry Cooke was a great advocate of two Yankee virtues, namely "grit" and "faculty". In these lively stories, her gritty, courageous young women battle to catch a man and, when necessary, to put that man in his place. As for faculty, no one can carve out a living or stand up for a friend or tell off a pompous preacher like one of Cooke's "old maids." A sharp observer of sexual injustice, Cooke mingles grim realism with wry humor in stories like "How Celia Changed Her Mind" and "A Town Mouse and a Country Mouse," which illustrate the folly of spinsters marrying for security. Similarly, "Odd Miss Todd," after surviving an unhappy affair, develops compassion for her sister-women and a new appreciation for the single state.

16. CRADDOCK, Charles Egbert (Mary Murfree) **IN THE TENNESSEE MOUNTAINS.** 1884. N.Y.: Gregg, 1967. $8.50, $2.45 p.b. Tenn.: U of Tenn Press, 1970. $7.50.
A collection of stories about the lives of the Appalachian mountain folk after the Civil War. Each story focuses in some way on the conflict between the values of civilization and the virtues of the pioneers. Murfree was one of the first and most successful writers of American dialect stories. Her tales are enriched (rather than obscured) by the poetry and lilt of Appalachia. They restore for us, in a very immediate way, a forgotten piece of America's past. (Unfortunately, it must be noted that the past recorded is primarily a male past.)

17. DAVIS, Rebecca Harding. LIFE IN THE IRON MILLS. 1861. Old Westbury, N.Y.: Feminist Press, 1972. $2.50.
This long-forgotten short story was one of the first to depict the misery and powerlessness of American industrial workers. Although marred by sentimentality

and in parts awkwardly written, it is nevertheless a deeply felt, compelling story of wasted human potential. Years of observation and secretive writing gave Davis a gut-level understanding of the forces that oppressed the men and women who worked the mill of her West Virginia home. Her images of the iron mills and the raw ugliness the wage slaves endured as daily life are haunting. The story was her first publication and established her at 30 as an original and promising voice in American literature; few writers before her had seen anything worth recording in the lives of those at the lowest levels of society. Sadly, though, her initial promise as a writer was never fully realized. This Feminist Press edition is especially worthwhile for its inclusion of a biography by Tillie Olsen, which is sensitive to both the tragedy and value of Davis's life and writing career.

FERN, Fanny *(Sara Payson Willis Eldredge Parton) (1811-1872) was born into a well-to-do Boston family. She was educated at Catherine Beecher's Ladies Seminary, where young Harriet Beecher was one of her teachers. After a happy marriage, she found herself, at age 36, a destitute widow with two children. It was difficult to obtain work since a lady in reduced circumstances was an embarrassment in the 19th century. Barely able to survive by sewing, she finally decided to assume a pseudonym and attempt a writing career. A persistent Fanny Fern found an editor and she achieved nationwide fame on starvation wages. Only later was she paid according to the value of her work. The cruel lessons of her life ultimately made her a shrewd businesswoman and she earned a fortune from her newspaper articles and best-selling books. Restored once more to the affluent and intellectual class she had been born into, Fanny Fern displayed in her writings a lifelong sympathy for the poor and oppressed.*

18. _____ RUTH HALL. N.Y.: Mason Brothers, 1855. O.P.
The 19th century was a thriving time for the publishing industry: books, magazines, and newspapers abounded, and many of their readers were women. Many a widow, forced suddenly to support a family, found it possible to do this as a writer. This obviously autobiographical novel tells the story of one of these women. It makes fascinating follow-up readings to Papashvily's **All The Happy Endings**, a social history of the domestic novel. The sections of the book which show Ruth being rejected by ignorant and unsympathetic editors and then accepted, only to be exploited, are brilliant and witty. **Ruth Hall** is very sentimental, the story tends now and then to wander aimlessly away from the plot. Portions of **Ruth Hall** ought to be excerpted for an anthology on women's literary and/or social history.

FREEMAN, Mary Wilkins *(1852-1930) She was born and spent her early childhood in the mill town of Randolph, Massachusetts. When an adolescent, her family moved to rural Brattleboro, Vermont. These two environments, both in economic decline in the late 19th century, form the backgrounds for almost all her work. An extraordinarily prolific writer, Freeman has a dozen novels to her credit and probably wrote in the vicinity of 1,000 short stories. It was in the short story that she excelled, and her finest work ranks with the best that has been done in this genre. After the extraordinary popularity and critical recognition which she enjoyed in her own time, it is hard to understand her current eclipse. Her work, so often featuring a strong woman, and frequently one who is moved to open rebellion, is relevant to us today. Her marriage, at the age of 50, was unhappy and after it she produced almost no work of real value.*

19. _____ A NEW ENGLAND NUN. 1891. Boston: Gregg. $3.75 p.b.
The title story has been judged by many as perfect. Another classic "The Revolt of Mother," is the story of a woman finally moved to take a stand against the anti-life values of her husband (it was an inspiration to suffrage workers). "The Church Mouse" tells how a determined woman becomes sexton of her church. Almost all her characters are memorable. Unfortunately, several of the stories are marred by trite and sentimental endings, possibly because the author was attempting to satisfy the popular taste of the day.

20. _____ **THE PORTION OF LABOR**. 1901. Boston: Gregg. $3.75 p.b.
Here is a book we can leave on the shelf to gather dust. It is poorly written: the plot is contrived and boring, the characters superficial and inconsistent. While Freeman's short stories show her sympathy with individual acts of rebellion, she felt collective action was immoral. She was firmly opposed to labor unions. In working to end inequality, a condition which had existed since the beginning of time, people were setting themselves above God. The "portion of labor" was to improve the character of the laborer.

21. _____ (edited and with an afterword by Michelle Clark.) **THE REVOLT OF MOTHER AND OTHER STORIES**. Old Westbury, N.Y.: Feminist Press, 1974. $3.50.
These eight stories, taken from Freeman's first two collections, focus mainly on single women. They are women who, as Clark notes, "having lost their status, their prosperity and often their men . . . had nothing to rely on but their pride, their capacity for a frugal independence, and their sense of self-esteem." Women's relationships with each other are explored—we see both the support and the competition. In several of the stories women reject men in favor of their own independence, and in others, lose men because they are unwilling to compromise their ideals. The portraits of older women in revolt, against village prejudice and/or a man, are particularly moving. All of Freeman's women lead lives which can be called heroic. As she said of "mother": "Nobility of character manifests itself at loopholes when it is not provided with large doors." Like all Feminist Press reprints, this book is enriched by its afterword.

22. _____ **THE LONG ARM**. 1895. London: Chapman & Hall.
Impressive, haunting detective novelette from an important author. A young woman must prove her innocence of her father's murder. The male sleuth is much less interesting than the strong woman murderer. Her motivation is protection of her life-long companion—a woman.

FULLER, Margaret _(1810-1850) edited the transcendental journal_ **The Dial** _from 1840 to 1842. Her book_ **Summer On The Lakes** _was an account of her travels in the midwest and western states in 1843; it attracted the attention of Horace Greeley, who gave her a job as literary critic for the New York Daily Tribune. In 1845 she published her most important work,_ **Woman In The Nineteenth Century.** _As a critic of patriarchy and its waste of human resources, she lists the abolition of slavery and a feminist reorganization of society as keys to liberation of the human spirit. In another volume,_ **At Home And Abroad,** _can be found many of Fuller's later essays and letters from Europe. In 1847 she joined forces with the Italian Marchise Ossoli; the two of them supported the Roman Republic in the Italian revolution of 1849. They and their son were killed in a shipwreck._

23. _____ **MARGARET FULLER: AMERICAN ROMANTIC.** ed. Perry Miller. Gloucester, Mass.: Peter Smith. $5.50.
This selection of the writings and correspondence of Margaret Fuller (1810-1850) attests to her rank as one of 19th century America's unconventional literary personalities. Her rigid academic upbringing in New England left its share of psychological scars, yet fostered great intellectual abilities and a self-confidence rare

for women of the time. "I now know all the people worth knowing in America," she remarked while dining with Emerson, "and I find no intellect comparable to my own." Included in this edition are private reflections of her youth in Cambridgeport, Mass.; essays written for the **Dial**; literary criticism and reportage published in the **New York Tribune**; plus an abridgement of her famous piece, "Woman in the Nineteenth Century," in which she argues against women's limited role in the family and society. Her writings are both academic and passionate, analytical and engaging. For some, her formal elaborate 19th century style may make ponderous reading.

24. FRENCH, Alice (pseudo, Thanet, Octave). **KNITTERS IN THE SUN.** 1887. N.Y.: Somerset, current $9.50.
A popular writer of magazine ficton and short stories in the 1880s and 1890s, Alice French (1850-1934) has been considered a "local colorist." She is usually grouped with a number of her contemporaries including Rose Terry Cook, George Washington Cable, Sarah Orne Jewett, Joel Chandler Harris, Thomas Nelson Page, and Mary E. Wilkins Freeman. **Knitters In The Sun** reflects this "local color" approach with its use of dialect and its attempt to depict different classes and races in a given locale—an odd combination of romanticism and realism. One story "A Communist's Wife" is of lasting interest as a study of the American labor struggle around the time of the nationwide railroad strike of 1877. Like the countess of her story, French (siding with the men of her family who were wealthy capitalists) opposed unions and strikes. She was early a Social Darwinist and became more reactionary as she grew older. Her story "A Heidelberg Romance" shows the latent romantic attachment between two women. (It was published in **Western Magazine**, January, 1880, and mentioned in Damon and Stuart's **Lesbian In Literature**.)

25. GILMAN, Charlotte Perkins (1860-1935).
THE YELLOW WALLPAPER 1899. The Feminist Press, 1973. $1.25.
An excellent fusion of literature and feminist politics. Written in the first person, Gilman's short story portrays both the terrifyingly convincing logic of a woman going insane and the painful reality of her emotional and intellectual oppression. The story is based on Gilman's own experience of a nervous breakdown. The Feminist Press edition includes an excellent essay by Elaine R. Hedges discussing **The Yellow Wallpaper** in light of Gilman's life and political development.

HARPER, Frances Watkins (1825-1911) *Born free in Baltimore and educated in the north, Frances Watkins Harper was a prominent Abolitionist poet and orator of the antebellum period. her poetry enjoyed a large audience during the late 19th century, and her book,* **Iola Leroy**, *was the first black novel published after the Civil War. Selectons of her verse can be found in William H. Robinson's* **Early Black American Poets** *(1969).*

26. _____ **IOLA LEROY,** or **SHADOWS UPLIFTED**. 1892. N.Y.: AMS Press, 1971. $11.00.
Following emancipation, Harper traveled through the south lecturing black people on temperance, industry and morality. One of the results of this work was **Iola Leroy**, the first black novel about Reconstruction. A curious blend of melodrama and rhetorical dialog, **Iola Leroy** urges light-complexioned negroes to stand beside the black minority and not try to pass for white. Iola, legitimate daughter of a mulatto woman and a wealthy planter, is sold into bondage after her father's death and later freed to work as a nurse in the Union Army. After the war, she rejects a white suitor and marries a mulatto instead. Iola is a totally idealized character and one wonders how she managed to preserve her cheerful resolve through the horrors of slavery. Harper provides no clues, possibly because she was more concerned with the development of refined, well-educated black characters than she was with the creation of realistic fiction.

HOPKINS, Pauline Elizabeth. *(1859-1930) Born in Portland, Maine, in 1859, Pauline Hopkins moved to Boston when very young and spent the rest of her life in that area. Deeply involved in furthering the cause of American blacks, she was also an active troubadour, orator, playwright, literary editor, actor, and novelist. When these activities did not support her, she worked as a stenographer. Much of her energy was spent writing for, editing, and raising money for "The Colored American"—a publication begun in 1900 and put out by the Colored Co-operative Publishing Company of Boston. This press published her first and best known novel,* **Contending Forces.** *After its publication, Hopkins began to write biographical sketches, stories, and novel serializations for the magazine. One of the founders of the Colored American League, (which sponsored "The Colored American,") she journeyed all over the country to promote interest in the magazine. In 1903, she became its literary editor, but retired a year later due to poor health. Pauline Hopkins died in a fire in Cambridge, Massachusetts, in 1930.*

27. _____ **CONTENDING FORCES**. 1899. N.Y.: AMS Press, 1900. $12.50. Plainview, N.Y.: Books for Libraries, 1900. $13.75.
This book was largely an attempt to promote interest in and concern for black people among whites. It captures the feeling of the brutal mob violence of the South and the apathy of northern whites who either urged blacks to wait and hope for things to get better or glibly explained that someone had to be subordinate. Most of the action of the novel takes place in Boston at the turn of the century. Besides dealing with the physical and psychological effects of slavery in their own lives, the black community is incensed by reports of the cruelty of the southern whites. The romantic plot concerns a middle class black family struggling for jobs and education as well as solutions to "the Negro question." Like many books of its day, the plot is resolved through a series of coincidences and succeeds in meting out justice to each of the main characters. The book was well received—called "the book of the century" by the head of a black businesswomen's group in Chicago—yet Pauline Hopkins is now a little-known writer.

JACKSON, Helen Maria Fiske Hunt. *(1830-1885) Helen Fiske's lively personality distressed her New England Calvinist parents, but later won her many friends in eastern society, where she met and married army engineer Edward Hunt. Young Mrs. Hunt possessed literary talents, but it wasn't until after the untimely deaths of her husband and two children that she made a serious commitment to writing. She first concentrated on poetry, publishing under various pseudonyms, and, by her mid-forties, "H.H." saw her verse featured in nearly every magazine of the day. In 1873, she moved to Colorado for her health. There, marriage to W.S. Jackson, a Quaker banker, freed her from financial cares and gave her the leisure to become, as she put it: "The most odious thing in the world, 'a woman with a hobby,' "—the "hobby" being her concern for the miserable lot of Native Americans.* **A Century of Dishonor**, *her angry treatise on U.S. Indian policies, secured Mrs. Jackson a federal commission to study the Mission Indians in southern California. This study later formed the background of her most enduring work,* **Ramona.** *The author intended this novel to be the* **Uncle Tom's Cabin** *of the Indian question, and it was widely read for over fifty years—often, alas, for its romantic interest alone, although it stands today, a powerful indictment of racism. Helen Hunt Jackson died at 54 of cancer. Emerson had thought her America's finest woman poet, but, as she remarked near the end, "*Century of Dishonor *and* Ramona *are the only things I have done for which I am glad now. They will live on and they will bear fruit."*

28. _____**MERCY PHILBRICK'S CHOICE**. 1876. N.Y.: AMS Press, 1970. $9.50.
"I feel like a great ox talking to a white moth," said Jackson about her life-long friendship with poet Emily Dickinson, the model for Mercy Philbrick in this tale of small-town New England. Jackson has lovingly evoked many aspects of Dickinson: her devotion to her dying mother, her thwarted loves, and, above all, her isolation. This is a lively story of an artist's struggle to overcome her claustrophobic environment. Unfortunately, the final chapters bog down in sentiment and Jackson's imitations of

the Dickinsonian style have the effect, as one early critic put it, of "stucco ornaments."

29. _____ RAMONA. 1884. N.Y.: Avon, 1975. $1.75.
Newly-annexed California is the setting of this story about a young half-breed woman who, defying her Mexican guardians, marries a native American and goes to live among his despised and dispossessed people. Ramona's battle of wills with her foster aunt is good old-fashioned melodrama, but the central love story is perhaps a bit too idealized for modern tastes. Nevertheless, Jackson's account of the native American persecution by frontiersmen (whom the author usually portrays as gin-soaked brutes) remains as powerful as ever and well worth reading today.

30. JAMES, Alice. THE DIARY OF ALICE JAMES, edited, with an introduction by Leon Edel, N.Y.: Dodd, Mead & Company, 1964.
"The only difference between me and the insane was that I had not only all the horrors and suffering of insanity but the duties of doctor, nurse and straight jacket imposed upon me, too." Acutely aware of herself, those around her, and the limitations of her life, Alice James records her responses to the political and personal events of the last years of her life. The invalid younger sister of William and Henry James wrote because "I think that if I get into the habit of writing a bit about what happens, or rather doesn't happen, I may lose a little of the sense of loneliness and desolation which abides with me." She kept the diary from May, 1889, until the day before her death from breast cancer on March 5, 1892. Her reflections on her life and death illuminate the feelings beneath the stifling refinement of lady-like demeanor. An engrossing diary which should be re-issued in paperback.

JEWETT, Sarah Orne *(1849-1909) was born in South Berwick, Maine. Her writings deal exclusively with the inhabitants of small towns and farms in her native state. Far from being a limitation, her self-imposed restriction, to stick to what she knew and loved best, gives her work depth and richness. It was Harriet Beecher Stowe's* **The Pearl of Orr's Island**, *a novel set in Maine, which inspired her to take up writing. In the last years of her life, Jewett herself served as a model and advisor for the young journalist, Willa Cather. Called by some a New England "spinster," she made a deliberate choice. "Marriage," said Sarah Orne Jewett, "would only be a hindrance." She did, however, receive great support in her life, and in the development of her art, from her deep and loving relationship with Annie Adams Fields, with whom she lived for part of each year after 1881.*

31. DEEPHAVEN. 1877. New Haven: College and University Press. $6.50 h.b., $2.95 p.b.
This novel, Jewett's first, is a series of related sketches about two wealthy city girls who come to spend a summer in Deephaven, a decaying New England port populated mainly by widows and retired sea captains. Many of the author's basic ideas and techniques are present in this "beginning raw work," as Willa Cather calls it, for Deephaven is a matriarchal society by default: most of its male residents are swamped in nostalgia, "condemned as unseaworthy," and the women are left to fend for themselves. The two aristocratic visitors are Jewett's voice but, unfortunately, they slip into childish sentimentality at times. Nevertheless, they are true observers and we see through their eyes that Deephaven's remaining vitality glows in its self-reliant women.

32. _____ A COUNTRY DOCTOR. 1884. Boston: Gregg, $12.50. N.Y.: Somerset, $14.50. N.Y.: MSS. Information Corp., $15.95.
Nan Prince is raised by her guardian, Dr. Leslie, in a Rousseauian fashion. He thinks he recognizes a great talent in her, and wishes to do nothing to divert her from her "natural" direction. His expectations are fulfilled when Nan chooses to study medicine. After a bout with romantic love, she firmly rejects marriage and domesticity, as unsuited to her talents. This novel is not Jewett's best; one yearns for greater structure, and finds many possibilities undeveloped. Nevertheless, **A Country Doctor** possesses enough depth and richness to make it satisfying reading. There are

many delightful dialogues, observations and images relating to the conflict for women, between marriage and a career.

33. _____ THE COUNTRY OF THE POINTED FIRS and Other Stories. 1896. Garden City, N.Y.: Doubleday, current. $2.50.

The art in these stories is so delicate, so simple, and finally so moving. Rarely does Jewett focus on a character under sixty. She gives us a sense of the richness and variety of old people's lives. The stories are all so finely done that it is impossible to single one out for special praise.

34. KING, Grace. BALCONY STORIES. 1892. Ridgewood, N.Y.: Gregg, 1968. $8.00 h.b., $2.45 p.b.
King received a good deal of positive critical notice in her day, but her writing, while a cut above the popular sentimental works of the period, reflects the 19th century "cult of true womanhood." Piety, purity and submissiveness are the recommended female virtues; self-sacrifice is woman's most heroic act. King's work is of little interest today, except possibly to serve as a comparison to the more enduring art of her contemporary Kate Chopin.

35. LARCOM, Lucy (1824-1893). **A NEW ENGLAND GIRLHOOD** (1889). Corinth Books, 1961. $1.75.
"I was born with the blessing of a cheerful temperament," writes Larcom. And she cheerfully takes us through her childhood and youth as a "mill-girl" in Lowell, Mass. She grew up one of eight children in a New England still deeply influenced by Puritan religion and austerity; and her memoir—written for an audience of girls—is peppered with little moral lessons on the importance of hard work, discipline and education. Family financial problems after the death of her father forced Larcom to start work in the textile mills when she was 13. At this time (1835), the Lowell mills were still considered a noble experiment in the dignity of labor. Mill owners hired girls of "refinement and education" and cared for them in corporation boarding houses run by respectable women like Larcom's mother. Young women working to put brothers through college, because of temporary set-backs or simply for the chance to be away from home came to Lowell with high hopes and, according to Larcom, no intention of staying: "The girls there were just such girls as are knocking on the doors of young women's colleges today," she claimed. Her own circle published a literary magazine, The Lowell Offering, and attended classes and lectures. Day-to-day working conditions in the mills are incidental to Larcom's narrative; for example, she finds the regimentation of the mill work a good exercise in discipline. But in bits and pieces a picture of mill work emerges—the 14-hour workday, the noise and smell of machinery, a single summer holiday, wages of $1 a week plus board—that explains the sweatshops the mill became as immigrant labor replaced "girls of refinement."

36. PHELPS, Elizabeth Stuart. THE SILENT PARTNER. 1871. Boston: Gregg, Americans in Fiction, 1967.
Elizabeth Stuart Phelps skillfully begins this wry labor tract by contrasting the New England manufacturing middle class with the factory workers. Perley Kelso is protected by all the trappings of privilege: a carriage, season tickets to the opera, the inheritance of her father's mills, and economic naivete. When she meets the matter-of-fact, unprotected mill girl, Sip Garth, her casual curiosity about the poor becomes a vital recognition of class divisions, paternalism, and devastating factory conditions. Most of the novel describes how Perley tries to close the gap between herself and the factory workers, and how she insists on autonomy for herself as well as autonomy and respect for "the hands." Phelps' cogent statements about labor and women are weakened by an ending which directs all of us to God for change and ultimate salvation.

37. _____ **THE STORY OF AVIS.**
Boston: Houghton Mifflin, 1877. O.P.
One is amazed to find such a deliberately feminist
book written at such an early date. Many of Phelps'
sister New England authors portrayed the strength
and integrity of women, but their characters, though
often eccentric, usually adhered to prescribed roles.
Avis is a young artist trying to define a new kind of
life which will suit her own needs and talents. Her
struggles will seem vivid and modern to any woman
who has experienced the conflict between having a
family and doing serious creative work. The best of
this book is very fine indeed, and it has been excerpted in Edwards and Diamond's **American Voices,
American Women** (N.Y.: Avon, 1973. $1.75). As a
whole, **The Story of Avis** is too long, and coincidence
and cliche intrude upon, and sometimes obscure, the
moving story which Phelps set out to tell.

38. _____ **DOCTOR ZAY.** Boston: Houghton, Mifflin, 1882. O.P.
"I had learned how terrible is the need of a woman by women, in country towns," So
says Doctor Zay, who, in response to this need, practices among women and their
children in an isolated Maine township. She is, as one of her patients puts it, one of
"the women that love women". While many writers of the period (notably Freeman
and Jewett) portray characters who act in a sisterly fashion, Phelps is again unique in
actually articulating a concept of sisterhood. Doctor Zay is courageous, intelligent,
dedicated—one could not wish for more in a heroine, though somehow she is more an
idea than a real person. The plot revolves around the role reversal (very consciously
depicted) which occurs when an accident causes Doctor Zay to treat her first male
patient.

39. _____ **FOURTEEN TO ONE.** Boston: Houghton, Mifflin, 1891. O.P.
While most of the stories in this collection are extremely sentimental and not on a
level with the best short fiction of the day, they are, nevertheless, worth reading. In
Fourteen To One, we find many lives usually overlooked by literature. "Jack the
Fisherman", easily the best piece in the book, is the tragic story of an impoverished,
alcoholic fisherman and the unlucky prostitute who trusts him. Phelps also draws on
her knowledge of the poor fishing community in Massachusetts (she was a longtime
resident of Gloucester) in "The Madonna of the Tubs". "Too Late" tells of the
government's and society's neglect of Civil War veterans. A young woman endures
extreme poverty and works as a waitress and washerwoman, while struggling to put
herself through college, in "The Sacrifice of Antigone."

40. _____ **CHAPTERS FROM A LIFE.** Boston: Houghton, 1897. O.P.
Not a very introspective autobiography, and therefore not a very enlightening one.
The remembrances of New England literary figures tend to be sentimental, little
relationship to their art. This book will probably be of interest only to those with a
special concern for the author or the period.

SEDGWICK, Catharine *(1789-1867) She was born and raised in Stockbridge,
Massachusetts. Her finishing school education, while more extensive than most girls
received at that time, was still rather minimal. Like so many early women writers, she
was indebted to her father's encouragement and tutoring. She remained unmarried,
rejecting at least six proposals, and probably resembled the active, capable
"spinsters" she portrayed in her writing. Sedgwick's earliest books, written when
most Americans still imitated British and continental writers, were considered
experimental and avant garde, in their day. She rejected both European setting and
style, abandoning the extravagance of the gothic romance for greater simplicity and
realism.*

41. _____ REDWOOD. 1824. N.Y.: Somerset, $18.00. N.Y.: MSS. Information Corp. $14.75.

If you are interested in finding out what sort of country America once was, then read this novel about rural Massachusetts in 1814. Sedgwick had a deep love for the "common people." She depicts them, both men and women, as sensible and practical, with questioning spirits and a strong desire for knowledge. While the story itself is a transparent romance with a religious moral, the author obviously had fun writing it. Readers will still be able to enjoy its humor and spirit, and women will be pleased to discover the character of Deborah Lennox, a fifty year old, six foot amazon and self-chosen "old maid."

SPOFFORD, Harriet Prescott *(1835-1921) was a member of the literary sisterhood of New England short story writers. She was the social center for a group of friends which included Sarah Orne Jewett, Rose Terry Cooke and Annie Fields. Born in Calais, Maine, Spofford spent most of her life in the seaside town of Newburyport, Massachusetts. Her talent was recognized and encouraged while she was still in high school. When her father suffered financial reverses, it seemed natural for Harriet to attempt to support the family by publishing her stories. She became an instant success when her first piece was published in* **Atlantic Monthly** *in 1858. Although her marriage, in 1865, meant the end of financial pressure, the post-war enthusiasm for magazine fiction kept her writing at a prolific rate. Some critics think that this was a mistake and that her talent was spread too thin.*

42. _____ THE AMBER GODS AND OTHER STORIES. 1863. Freeport, N.Y.: Books for Libraries Press, 1969. $16.00.

Anyone who opens this volume, expecting another collection of realistic stories about the proud, plain folk of rural New England, is in for a surprise. Spofford was a romantic: her most convincing heroines, like Yone in the *tour de force* title story, are sensual, self-indulgent creatures. They are the dark ladies, the villains; they have very consciously rejected the life of the pure "ice-maiden", so idealized in a still-puritan New England. Having thus classified Spofford, one must go on to say that these stories are incredibly varied. "In a Cellar" is an intriguing mystery. Based on a true incident, "Circumstance" tells of a Maine pioneer woman who survived a night in the clutches of a panther. Symbolic and fantastic, "Desert Sands" is the story of a husband who couldn't love and a wife who couldn't do anything else.

43. _____ THE SCARLET POPPY AND OTHER STORIES. 1894. N.Y.: Somerset. $9.50. N.Y.: MSS. Information Corp. $14.50.

This collection is inferior to the previous one. Spofford obviously tried to adjust to the tastes of the time, but she just doesn't seem suited for realism. Almost all the stories are marred by improbable, but terribly happy, endings. "Mrs. Claxton's Skeleton" starts out promisingly. Mr. Claxton sees his wife as "chattel"; he resents her having a mind of her own, but he obstinately insists on having one anyway. Then a flash flood (they miraculously survive) brings him to his senses. The best selection, "The Composite Wife", proves that Spofford still excelled when drawing a flamboyant, self-centered woman. But what is really interesting is the focus on a 19th century type: the man who outlives a procession of wives—three going on four, in this case.

44. STANTON, Elizabeth Cady. EIGHTY YEARS & MORE: REMINISCENCES 1815-1897. Reprinted from the T. Fisher Unwin edition of 1898. Schocken paperback, 1971. $3.95.

Elizabeth Cady Stanton was a leading thinker and tactician of the National American Women Suffrage Association. She sketchily describes her childhood and vignettes of her life, but the bulk of her perspective "reminiscences" deal with her work, the people with whom she was involved, of the world of political and social ideas. It's interesting reading, providing a view of the spirit, humor, differences, and rationale of the suffrage movement. Valuable introduction by Gail Parker.

45. STOWE, Harriet Beecher. UNCLE TOM'S CABIN. 1853. N.Y.: Dutton, 1972. $2.95. and various cheap editions.

Most people have not read **Uncle Tom's Cabin**, but almost anyone can tell you what an Uncle Tom or a Simon Legree is. The incorporation of these two characters into our vocabulary attests to the enduring power and influence of this novel. Although the reader will find the sentimental racism offensive and an excess of Christian piety tedious, there are also pleasant surprises: an abundance of humor as well as pathos and vivid characterizations. The intricate plot and subplots trace the fortunes of the individuals caught in the curse of slavery, black women being the most victimized, both sexually and racially. The success of **Uncle Tom's Cabin** as an abolitionist manifesto is well-documented, but one should read it for more than historical interest. The book presents a dilemma and vision entirely relevant to contemporary life. When the laws sanctify immortality, then to live morally one must defy the laws or be martyred to them—or by accepting them become passive or brutalized. Harriet Beecher Stowe offers no solutions, and this perhaps explains a major flaw in the novel: its failure to reach any convincing conclusion. The view from **Uncle Tom's Cabin** is ultimately apocalyptic.

46. _____ **OLDTOWN FOLKS.** Boston: Houghton Mifflin Company, 1896. O.P.

Oldtown Folks blends history, local color, and character sketches to create an entertaining portrait of New England in the generation after the Revolution. The folks of Oldtown are second generation puritans and first generation democrats. At the center of their community are the women: genteel-poor Miss Mehitable, whose homely strength is "better than beauty"; her maid, Polly, the most partisan, articulate member of the household; and Grandmother, who dominates her household by force of intellect and will. Conversation among these women and the other well-defined members of the community form the backbone of this novel. The topics range from politics to gossip to spirituality—each debated with equal intensity and good humor. Although Stowe cannot resist interjecting an occasional lecture to the reader, she keeps the moralizing to a minimum. **Oldtown Folks** is as lively as it is informative, and an excellent introduction to the much-misjudged New England Puritan.

VICTOR, Frances Fuller. *(1826-1902) Born in New York state, Victor spent her youth in Ohio and moved to California after her marriage in 1862. She was a poet and a journalist, but it was her work as a historian of the Northwest which established her reputation. Her sister, Metta Fuller Victor, was a popular "dime novelist."*

47. _____ **THE NEW PENELOPE, AND OTHER STORIES.** San Francisco: Bancroft, 1877. O.P.

At the beginning of the long title story, Victor declares herself to be "that anomalous creature—a woman who loves her own sex." What follows does not disappoint. While "The New Penelope" is the only explicitly feminist piece in this collection, several others feature memorable and unusual women. The engrossing plots rarely rely on contrivance and coincidence. The setting, one not usually depicted in the 19th century, is the Pacific Northwest of the mid 1800s. One suspects that eastern cultural chauvinism, and the fact that the writing was a bit ahead of its time, are the reasons that **The New Penelope** never received much notice and now rests in obscurity. It deserves a better fate; someone should reprint this book.

48. WILDER, Laura Ingalls. LITTLE HOUSE series 1937, many editions.
Should be read by everyone interested in the frontier experience of white pioneers and women's perspective of it. This series of seven books traces the route of the author's pioneer childhood from a log cabin in the big woods of Wisconsin through the equally isolated prairies of Oklahoma, Kansas, and South Dakota. Wilder does not minimize the dangers and hardships the family faced; plagues of grasshoppers, raging prairie fires, an afternoon rain that could wipe out a year's crops. But melodrama and violence are relatively absent. She tells us both her parents' and her own reactions to encounters with Indians—perhaps one of the more accurate accounts from a white settler's viewpoint.

1900-1950

49. ANDERSON, Barbara Tunnell. THE DAYS GROW COLD. 1941. O.P.
Eleven-year-old Lucinda's wanderings into the mysteries of the town of Macklin in the lower South uncover the stagnant traditions and conflicts which weigh heavily upon the area. Her gnawing curiosity latches on to Castleton, the deteriorated estate next door in which two recluses, mother and daughter, survive on memory and pride. Through her perseverance in gathering information about Castleton from Mittie, the black housekeeper, from Eva Carley, her schoolteacher, and from the insinuations of her parents, Lucinda learns about the racism in the town, about W. W. II, art, and fear as a major factor in decision-making. Fantasy is woven into Lucinda's perceptions to create an imaginative view of a community divided over what to do with its poor black population, and with its children.

50. _____ **SOUTHBOUND.** N.Y.: Farrar, Straus & Co., 1949. O.P.
Laura Crane, a powerful, independent black woman, is left with the task of raising her granddaughter, Amanda, in racist Alabama. Determined that Amanda will have the same opportunities as the "best" (wealthiest) southern whites, Laura moves the child and her old mother Persy to Ohio, where a rich white woman wishes to "adopt" Amanda and raise her as her own. Amanda, who is very light-skinned, experiences the pain and sometimes the joy of both worlds. During the Ohio period, Laura is forced to act as the child's nurse, a position which forces her to restrain her real feelings for Amanda, creating a gap which can never really be overcome. Laura wants so much for Amanda to "make it" that she literally works herself to death. Persy, the great-grandmother, is one of the most loving and real portrayals of an old woman we have read. Persy is constant in her black pride.

51. ANDERSON, Margaret. MY THIRTY YEARS WAR. 1930. N.Y.: Horizon, 1969. $10.00. **THE FIERY FOUNTAINS.** 1951. N.Y.: Horizon, 1969. $8.50. **THE STRANGE NECESSITY.** N.Y.: Horizon, 1969. $7.50.
Margaret Anderson was a major intellectual figure during the first half of the 20th century. She founded the **Little Review**—the most revolutionary literary magazine of the 1920s, where, among other things, she published James Joyce's controversial **Ulysses**. She was, by her own definition, a dilettante with a passion for music, literature, ideas, and people. Her lovers were women, and though she never writes about herself in terms of lesbianism she describes the great loves she has known with unselfconscious frankness. The first volume of her autobiography deals with her struggles to become free of her family's plans for her, her interest in furthering the arts, and her relationship with Jane Heap. The second volume describes her search for something beyond art, which led her, together with her lover, Georgette le Blanc (Maeterlinck) to the Gurdjieff institute in Paris. The third volume was written after Georgette's death and is a sketchy, halting reiteration of bits of the first two volumes, plus a little information about Anderson's relationship with Dorothy Caruso. This volume reveals some new information about Georgette and Anderson's thoughts on

growing old and approaching death. Through it all, she discloses a passionately active woman, an elitist and fiercely opinionated individualist (not surprisingly, she disliked Gertrude Stein). Her great respect and love for her women friends is one of the most exciting and enduring features of the autobiography.

52. ATHERTON, Gertude. JULIA FRANCE AND HER TIMES. 1912. Folcroft, PA: Folcroft Library Editions, $15.00.
Julia France is a leader of the militant woman suffrage movement in England, in the first decade of the 20th century. She is also one of the most unpleasant heroines, feminist or otherwise, to have ever graced a novel. An elitist snob, who feels herself far above "the vast and insignificant majority of her sex," she aspires to nothing less than "perfection." Julia is also a bigot who has little understanding of racial and ethnic minorities and working class people. To some degree this is historically accurate, as the British movement was flawed by elitist attitudes and authoritarian leadership. Skip **Julia France** unless you are researching the history of the feminist novel, in which case, this book is important. Atherton, who thought herself a feminist, has her heroine say several things which many of us would applaud today. Stylistically, the writing is poor and the characterization shallow, with Atherton typically jumbling syntax and misusing fancy words.

53. _____ MRS. BALFAME. 1916. Folcroft, PA: Folcroft Library Editions, $15.00
"Mrs. Balfame had made up her mind to commit murder." This somewhat startling first sentence sets the theme as Mrs. Balfame, a strong, reserved society woman, decides to murder her lumpish, chauvinist husband, David. Atherton has a weakness for ten-dollar words and a dated bias against Germans, but the book is enjoyable and the conclusion will especially appeal to feminists.

54. _____ BLACK OXEN. 1923. Folcroft, PA: Folcroft Library Editions, $15.00.
This sensational best seller of the 1920s must offend a modern reader for its overall upper class white male white supremacist perspective. We include it here because it deals with a 58-year-old woman who has been rejuvenated by x-ray treatments to "that portion of the body covering the overies." She is now completely restored to youth, physically and mentally. What does one do, with one's whole life before her again? It's fertile ground for a novelist; Atherton posits some compelling themes: reactions to growing old, assumptions about old people, artists, sex, women, duty and desire. The novel is not illuminating in the way it deals with these questions, but noteworthy in that it raises them at all. An interesting aside is that Atherton herself underwent this treatment, and credited it with the fact that she was still writing at the age of ninety.

AUSTIN, Mary Hunter *(1868-1934). As an established writer and lecturer, Mary Hunter Austin worked tirelessly for the suffrage and birth control movements, publishing numerous essays and problem novels. Today, she is remembered mainly for her studies of Native American culture:* **The Basket Woman** *(1904), a collection of Paiute legends, and* **The American Rhythm** *(1923), an attempt to trace aboriginal song to its roots. Austin's autobiography,* **Earth Horizon** *(1932), tells of her early "picking and prying" years in the southwestern deserts, years which resulted in* **Land of Little Rain** *(1903) and* **The Flock** *(1906), nature-writing classics that are ranked with those of John Muir and Thoreau.*

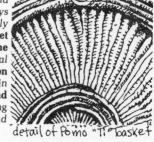
detail of Pomo "Ti" basket

55. _____ WOMAN OF GENIUS. 1912. PA: Folcroft. $25.00.
Olivia Lattimore escapes her dreary small-town lot and travels to Chicago, where, after years of struggle, she becomes the leading actress of her day. At the height of her

career, she has to choose between marriage to a childhood sweetheart and the fulfillment of her natural dramatic gift—her "genius." The novel is largely autobiographical. Through Olivia, we see Austin's struggle with her conservative mother, her resentment of an overly-solicitous brother, and her love for her sister, portrayed here as a suffragette. Although there's a lot of talk about woman's rights to personal and artistic fulfillment, **Woman Of Genius** is all tell and no show, and the characters remain two-dimensional.

56. _____ **NUMBER 26 JAYNE ST.** 1920. PA: Folcroft, $25.00.
Greenwich Village between 1910 and 1920 is seen through the inquisitive eyes of Neith Schuyler, a young woman who has spent most of her life in Europe nursing her invalid father. Neith is in the privileged position of being interested in socialist and feminist activities in the village while having enough money not to be dependent upon their consequences. Every meeting, demonstration and conversation leaves her reeling with new ideas about revolutionaries, until she discovers, within the turmoil of romance, the hypocrisy of a man who preaches "public democracy" but practices "personal autocracy." The final plea that women must find "freedom" for themselves is firm, but more didactic than convincing. (That goes for the book as a whole.) **Number 26 Jayne St.** creates an atmosphere of specific rhetoric for the village but is too vague in describing women's involvements.

57. BAKER, Dorothy. YOUNG MAN WITH A HORN Cambridge: Houghton Mifflin, 1938. O.P.
A fictionalized biography of trumpeter Bix Biderbecke, **Young Man with a Horn** is a romance of the jazz age. Like Rick Martin's career, the novel moves swiftly—from Rick teaching himself to play piano through all night jam sessions, to fame, fortune, and his premature, inevitable death at the age of 24. The doomed musician embodies the glories and pitfalls of jazz age romance. Rick's all-consuming passion for music is both the source of his genius and the cause of his death. He can play the horn better than anyone, but he cannot cope with or even recognize other facets of life, including mortality or the needs of his wife, Amy. Although Amy appears only briefly in the novel, she emerges as its most intriguing character. Her fascination with the dedication of the musicians draws her first to Josephine, a black vocalist, then to Rick. When immersing herself in his world fails, she struggles to find a work of her own. Amy's serious, desperate attempt to become a doctor, bewildering to Rick and amusing to the author, makes as compelling and poignant a story as her husband's.

58. _____ **CASSANDRA AT THE WEDDING.** Boston: Houghton Mifflin, 1962. O.P.
Written in the first person of each of the main characters in turn, this novel tells the story of Cassandra, a lesbian who feels that she is only half a person without her twin sister, Judith. When Judith decides to marry, Cassandra is forced to confront the fact that she alone must live her life. Cassandra speaks first and last; she gives a forthright, vigorous, and even humorous voice to themes of independence and responsibility.

59. BAKER, Estelle. THE ROSE DOOR. 1911. Chicago: Charles Kerr and Co. O.P.
Overly sentimental, awkward scenarios sprinkled with tongue-in-cheek passages tie together the lives of several women who have all been persuaded, through economic necessity, to become prostitutes. The women are most often portrayed as victims dehumanized by scheming upper middle-class cads. The socialist finale—the history of marriage and women as property—comes too late and too drily to save this short and dull book. Historically, it is important because it was one of the few socialist books at the time to deal entirely with prostitution.

60. BARNES, Djuna. A NIGHT AMONG THE HORSES. N.Y.: Horace Liveright, 1929. O.P.
This collection includes short prose pieces, poetry and a number of one-act plays. A recurrent theme is the inevitable and ironic danger of love. In **A Night Among The Horses**, we find a familiar Barnes figure—the aloof, upper-class woman who becomes involved in relationships in which she alternately attracts and repulses mismatched

lovers. This leads to their eventual disintegration. In "The Doves," a short play, two highly cultured, virginal spinsters cherish a vampire-like street urchin who spends most of her time caring for a collection of swords and firearms. As in **Nightwood**, Barnes' use of language is striking and compact—at times her images achieve the same haunting perfection as the later work.

61. _____ **NIGHTWOOD.** 1937. N.Y.: New Directions, current, $1.75. An extraordinary and haunting book by a highly gifted writer. The characters are exiled spirits moving around the capitals of Europe: the beautiful but remote Robin Vote inspires passionate love first in the Jewish Baron, then in several women lovers; the ubiquitous doctor, a secret transvestite, comments on life in endless implausible fables. Barnes's language has the dense richness of an intricate tapestry.

Djuna Barnes

BOWLES, Jane (1917-   ) _is an American who has travelled widely and now lives in Tangiers with her husband, author Paul Bowles. Her small literary output is highly original and bizarre; it has a high repute among a circle of devotees. Her characters seem mainly to be strange, warped people; she presents the apparent illogic of their actions and relationships with a devastating coolness and clarity._

62. _____ **THE COLLECTED WORKS OF JANE BOWLES.** N.Y.: Noonday, 1966. $2.45.
This volume contains:

_____ **Two Serious Ladies.** 1943. A novel. Christina Goering is an eccentric even as a child. As an adult she acquires a companion, Lucie Gamelon, with whom she has an ambivalent love-hate relationship; they move to an island, accompanied by Arnold, a persistent hanger-on. Meanwhile, Mrs. Copperfield and her husband are holidaying in Panama, where she falls in love with a prostitute, Pacifica. It is difficult to convey the captivating humor and pathos of this work.
_____ **Plain Pleasures.** Seven short stories, written from 1946 on, and brought together here for the first time. "A Guatemalan Idyll" shows an American man's panic at his seduction by a Latin woman. "Camp Cataract" is a masterpiece; it presents an obsessive relationship between two sisters, where insanity lurks very close to the surface. "A Day in the Open" is about two South American prostitutes, "A Stick of Green Candy" about an independent little girl who plays soldiers.

63. _____ **IN THE SUMMER HOUSE.** 1948.
In The Summer House is a derisive and witty play which was performed in New York in 1953. Irony, mockery and buffoonery serve as a bitter backdrop for the desperation, helplessness, and stagnation of the women characters.

BOYLE, Kay (1903-   ) *started her career doing freelance reviewing for* **The Dial.** *She spent many years in Europe and wrote much about the effects of World War II on France. A prolific writer, of poetry as well as prose, she is best known for her short stories.*

64. _____ **PLAGUED BY THE NIGHTINGALE.** 1931. Carbondale, Ill.: Southern Illinois University Press, 1966. $5.95.
A novel dealing with the pressures a couple face when they decide to remain childless (because of hereditary bone disease); it offers interesting insights into exclusively female experience. The style is a bit difficult.

65. _____ **THIRTY STORIES.** 1946. N.Y.: New Directions, current. $4.45.
Though these stories, set in Europe and the U.S., are highly competent and polished, few of them challenge conventional ideas about romance, femininity, etc.; a significant number are written from a male viewpoint. "Your Body Is a Jewel Box" is the one outstanding exception, a shocking, brilliant tale about two adolescent sisters. A few stories deal poignantly with the effects of racism, but without any awareness of black pride; others present unloved women servants and their pathetic little pretensions, while some others feature tougher and more enterprising women.

_____ **UNDERGROUND WOMAN** (see contemporary section)

66. BRODY, Catherine. NOBODY STARVES. Chicago: Longman's, Green & Co., 1932. O.P.
This competently crafted novel chronicles the experiences of working class people during the Depression. With masses of people needing work, strikes and individual acts of rebellion are courageous but ineffectual. They comprise only a minor part of this book; most of the dramatic action centers around the fear and desperation of a young couple whose resources are gradually drained by the demands of existence. Though the book does not attempt to suggest solutions, it makes one feel the effect poverty has on friendships, energies, and priorities. Suitable for high school classes.

67. BURKE, Fielding (pseudonym) (Olive Tilford Dargon). **CALL HOME THE HEART.** Chicago: Longmans Green and Co., 1932. O.P.
Ishma Waycaster carries the burdens of her family's failing mountain farm from her childhood into womanhood. On Sundays she escapes into the hills she loves to dream beyond the limits and isolation of her life. Finally discouraged with the endless poverty and fearing the prospects of being trapped by continual pregnancies, Ishma runs from her farm and her husband to the mill town. There she discovers another, more grinding poverty. She also discovers her own strengths as she begins to organize for

the National Textile Workers Union and learns about Communism. Despite the preachy, didactic tone and the novel's easy veering into sentimentality, there's still a good story here. Burke's descriptions of the land and mountains are evokative and loving. Ishma's relationship with her nagging, exhausted mother is well done and developed with some depth. Many of the incidents in the novel are based on the Gastonia, N.C., mill strike; and Burke renders her descriptions of the mill workers lives in considerable detail. If nothing else, the novel makes clear the straight line travelled by the mountain poor between their farmed-out land and the "slums" of company towns.

68. _____ **A STONE CAME ROLLING.** Chicago: Longmans Green and Co., 1935. O.P.
At the end of **Call Home the Heart**, Ishma had returned to the hills with her vision enlarged, but discouraged by her own inability to live out the letter of her new ideals. In this sequel, she returns to the mill towns with her husband and son and begins organizing full-time. She works to organize unemployed councils and build a region-wide textile strike, while her husband Britt maintains their farm collectively with the man who was forced by debt to sell it to them. This novel suffers the same limitations as its predecessor and, if anything, it's more propagandistic—flush with optimism and possibilities for a new world order. Yet, in many ways, it's more successful than the first. Burke deals with a much larger cast of characters and attempts to take on a large range of subjects—the colusion of businesses, the churches and city government against the workers; corrupt union leaders and misguided ones; the personal conflicts of a mill owner who has sympathy and respect for his workers; the struggles and shaky possibilities of a worker-run mill. And even if the deck is stacked from the beginning, a number of the interrelationships here are developed with considerable depth as she attempts to show the forces acting on her characters. Again, Burke has based many of the events on the strikes of the 1930s that rocked the southern textile industry and the towns it supported. The action she develops around these strikes is often genuinely exciting and a not-too-implausible account of people striving to build dignity for themselves.

CANFIELD, Dorothy (Fisher) _(1879-1957) Dorothy Canfield's mother was an artist, and her father a prominent educator. She was named after Dorothea in George Eliot's_ **Middlemarch**. _Raised in Kansas and later Nebraska, Dorothy was to meet Willa Cather and collaborate with her on an adolescent short story. Flavia Canfield (Dorothy's mother) came from a Vermont family which prided itself on having "pioneered" there. Dorothy's childhood visits to Vermont fostered a lifelong affinity with this region where she was to live most of her adult life. Having spent all of her youth surrounded by academics, it is not surprising that Dorothy joined the minority of women earning Ph.D.s In 1904, one of her professors was to typically remark, "What in the world will she do with [her degree] . . . hang it around the neck of her first baby for him to play with?" Dorothy became a prolific writer and an energetic promoter of things she believed in, like Montessori teaching. Politically, she was a liberal, somewhat paternalistic by today's standards towards blacks and working people. Her short stories, often crafted to perfection, will give her a permanent place in women's literature._

69. _____ **UNDERSTOOD BETSY.** 1916. N.Y.: Grosset & Dunlap. O.P.
This classic children's story came out of Dorothy Canfield's commitment to progressive education. After meeting Madame Montessori in 1912 at Casa di Bambini in Italy, Canfield was so impressed with the method's sensible emphasis on self-reliance and self-government that she was determined to bring this new idea to the attention of American parents and teachers. After writing three educational books on the subject, **The Montessori Mother, Mothers and Children** and **Self-Reliance**, she decided to approach it from a different angle—a children's book. In it, 9-year-old Betsy transforms from a finicky city-girl to a healthy child when she leaves the over-protective care of her Aunt Frances to say with Vermont relatives who live an example of self-reliance and independence. The liberation and variation of farm life arouses many interests and strengths in Betsy. In spite of the positive elements,

readers today will notice the sex-role playing that the laudable country-cousins project onto Betsy. Still, of its kind, **Understood Betsy** remains an enjoyable and positive story.

70. _____ **HER SON'S WIFE.** 1926. N.Y.: Harcourt Brace & World. O.P. Although slow going for the most part, this novel centers on several important themes. One is that of the mother-in-law, traditionally ridiculed in our culture. Though the novel does not go far in dispelling the underlying myths, it does get across the bitterness and waste of the traditional role of the middle-aged mother. As her self-sacrifice at home increases so does her powerlessness and invisibility. Another interesting theme of the book comes from Mrs. Bascomb's gradual consciousness of the meaning of different class backgrounds. Long a successful fifth grade teacher, Mrs. Bascomb is an arrogant classist; she views the working class mothers as hopeless and ignorant women. When her son marries the pregnant daughter of a factory nightwatchman, Mrs. Bascomb views Lottie as cheap and the ruination of her son. Although still deluded at the end and thinking that middle-class aspirations and education will save her grand-daughter, Mrs. Bascomb finally learns what Lottie's view is and comes to understand something of what she experienced growing up in poverty.

71. _____ **THE DEEPENING STREAM.** 1930. N.Y.: Modern Library. O.P.
The Deepening Stream is a novel about war, particularly about the lives of women and children in war. In the novel, Matey learns what her American privilege is. She strives to an unusual degree to escape it, or at least to share with others in war-torn Paris between 1915 and 1919. The novel's most profound message is Matey's eventual consciousness "that they [she and all the people she had lived and struggled with in Paris] had been fooled, that nothing at all would come from their sorrow except a firmer grip by the Francises [Matey's capitalist brother] of every nation on what they wanted." The novel shows how, early in the war, long before official American involvement, Matey's brother Francis had invested heavily in war-related industry. **The Deepening Stream** was based on the period of Dorothy Canfield's life during World War I when she worked in France with blinded soldiers and refugee French children while her husband was in the ambulance service.

"The Mothers" by Käthe Kollwitz

72. _____ **FABLES FOR PARENTS.** N.Y.: Harcourt, Brace and Company, 1937.
In these fables about family relationships, love conquers the conflicts that arise, and families remain together. Read today, when the nuclear family is under justifiable attack, these stories are nostalgia. Yet, the psychologically real portraits of parents and children and their conflicts present happy alternatives while narrowly avoiding maudlin sentimentality. Particularly outstanding is "Babushka Farnham," a story of a woman struggling to balance family commitments with an artistic career. She is rescued by her husband's grandmother, Babushka Farnham. Unknown to anyone but herself and the reader, Babushka Farnham sacrifices her own creative needs and independence in order to facilitate her daughter-in-law's career by relieving her of family burdens.

73. _____ **A HARVEST OF STORIES FROM A HALF CENTURY OF WRITING.** N.Y.: Harcourt Brace & Co., 1956.
This volume contains 28 selected Canfield stories, divided into the categories "Vermont Memories," "Men, Women—and Children," and "War." Particularly recommended are: "The Bedquilt," which presents a humble woman's one great achievement, in a traditional female art-form, and "Sex Education," where a woman tells, at three different points in her life, the story of a frightening girlhood encounter with a man. The highlight of the book is the prologue, "What My Mother Taught Me," a vivid, wonderfully funny description of the author's strong, unconventional mother and her own relationship with her.

74. _____ **THE HOMEMAKER.** 1924. N.Y.: Harcourt, Brace & Co. O.P.
Eva Knapp is a totally frustrated housewife. With powerful capabilities for organization and competition, she is a perfect example to all her friends in the Ladies Guild, while her own life and those of her husband and three children are miserable. Lester Knapp unhappily drags himself to work in the accounting department of a ladies clothing store. He is a dreamer who loves poetry and has a gift for nurturing children. This book is an indictment of a society that fixes women and men in rigid roles, and provides a gentle, romantic view of how things could be. Highly recommended for high school students, mothers, fathers, and grandparents.

CATHER, Willa (1873-1947). *You have probably heard of her great love of "the land," her ability to write about it vividly. That is true. It is also true that her heroines are some of the strongest women in fiction, and their struggles in a world which would have them otherwise are powerfully portrayed. As a teenager she called herself William and wore boys' clothes. Unanswered questions about her life are corollaries to the ones we ask about her books. Why do the early virtues in her characters—their strength and independence—lead them to such terrible ends, lonely or domineering? Why, although she understands so much about women, does she so often fail to draw conclusions, reach a real "consciousness?" Although lesbianism is never explicit in her writing, much of her work is directly relevant to lesbians. Read her for this, but read her also because she is a truly fine writer whose work was of consistent quality throughout her long career, and because she has left us a legacy of remarkable heroines: young Thea in* **The Song of the Lark***, Alexandra in* **O Pioneers***, and Lena and Antonia in* **My Antonia***.*

75. _____ **O, PIONEERS.** 1913. Boston: Houghton Mifflin, 1971. $2.65.
A chronicle of immigrant life and "the battle with the land" on the Great Plains in the late 19th century. Alexandra Bergstrom is an extraordinary and wonderful heroine, powerful and self-assured. And yet, when finally a successful middle-aged farmer, she feels herself to be terribly lonely and, worst of all, a "freak". Intertwined with her story is the tale of the hopeless love between her younger brother and a married woman.

76. _____ **THE SONG OF THE LARK.** 1915, revised 1937. Boston: Houghton Mifflin, 1971. $10.00.
A stunningly beautiful portrait of a girl of strength and talent who resists society's pressures to turn her into a smiling pink fluff. We follow Thea Kronborg through young womanhood and her struggle to become an opera singer. She achieves professional success, but her private life is empty.

77. _____ **MY ANTONIA.** 1918. Boston: Houghton Mifflin, 1971. $2.95.

If you attempt a rereading, you are apt to find this book quite unlike your high school memories of it. It is an autobiographical story in which Cather pays homage to the land and people of her childhood. While the author casts herself as a boy, the people who impressed her were, almost without exception, the strong immigrant women who were able to meet the challenges of a harsh land. Women readers have objected to Antonia's end as an earth mother (and a toothless leathery one), but most of the other female characters choose to lead independent lives.

78. _____ **ONE OF OURS.** 1922. N.Y.: Vintage, 1971. $2.45.

Claude Wheeler, a sensitive misfit in a Nebraska farming community, sets himself idealistic goals which he is forced to compromise one by one. Disillusioned with life, at 24 World War I gives him a sense of purpose. Written between **My Antonia** and **Lost Lady, One of Ours** won the Pulitzer Prize in 1922. A strong novel, until it becomes a watered-down war story.

79. _____ **A LOST LADY.** 1923. N.Y.: Vintage, 1970. $1.95.

The narrator shows us the "lady" through the male eyes of Niel Harding, as he grows from boy to young man. She is, for him, an image of feminine perfection, and when she proves to be human he is furious and disgusted. Her decline from perfection is itself an image for the fading of a "golden era" in the West. While the writing is powerful and vivid, the book is confusing. It is clear that Cather herself idealized the Old West, but she appears ambivalent about her hero's idealization of a woman.

80. _____ **THE PROFESSOR'S HOUSE.** 1925. N.Y.: Vintage Books, 1973. $2.45.

Professor St. Peter has spent many years upstairs in his attic study working on an immense history of the American Southwest; downstairs, in the body of the house, his wife and daughters have cooked, purchased, and entertained. When the story begins, St. Peter is middle-aged and at the height of his intellectual powers—yet bitterly out of touch with himself and with the women in his life. Drifting toward death, he recalls the wellsprings of his energy as Cather takes us on "a perilous journey down through the human house" into the past, the subconscious, of a person and a continent.

81. _____ **MY MORTAL ENEMY.** 1926. N.Y.: Vintage. $1.95.

A novella which pictures the end of the life of a strong woman. She faces death a bitter, spiteful, lonely old woman—the end to which many strong women come in a society that has no place for them. Myra Henshawe is not an appealing heroine, but the manner in which she meets her death finally compels our admiration.

82. _____ **OBSCURE DESTINIES.** 1932. N.Y.: Vintage Books, 1974. $1.95.

The 3 delicate short stories contained in **Obscure Destinies** supposedly stem from Cather's early memories of Virginia (where she lived until she was 10) and Nebraska. Two of them have the makings of a legend. "Old Mrs. Harris" (1931) is an expansive and tender portrayal of the cultural values which cyclically unite women regardless of class, age, and race differences. The reader cannot help but echo Cather's affection for the people and the land in "Neighbor Rosicky." Rosicky, a loving and observant Nebraskan farmer, tries to weave contentment into the lives of everyone he knows. As he unveils his history (from Czechoslovakia, to London, to N.Y.), he describes the comfort, security and personal dignity of farm life. Competition, money, distinctions between life in Tennessee and Colorado, and aging are important subjects in this collection.

83. _____ **SAPPHIRA AND THE SLAVE GIRL.** 1940. N.Y.: Vintage, 1975. $2.95.

Willa Cather's last novel, set in her native Virginia, examines relationships between slaves and their masters, between a jealous, aging woman (Sapphira) and her somewhat dull husband, and between mothers and their daughters. Cather has created a remarkably visual work. She confused and upset her critics though by writing the epilogue of the book in the first person to tell of the return of Nancy, a slave who escaped from Sapphira's plantation via the underground railroad before the Civil War began. Much of **Sapphira and The Slave Girl** is based on true incidents, including the beautiful epilogue.

84. COOK, Fannie. MRS. PALMER'S HONEY. N.Y.: Doubleday & Co., Inc., 1946. O.P.
Using the novel as an instructive vehicle for political and social ideas, Fannie Cook portrays the transformation of a black woman from her passive role as a maid in a white family to an active life both in the black community and as an organizer for the CIO. Focusing on the lives of her black characters, Fannie Cook's overriding theme deals with the effect of World War II on the black community who see many of their sons fighting abroad, while their daughters and sons at home begin to edge into industrial jobs, formerly segregated neighborhoods, and CIO unions. An excellent book to read in conjunction with **Mrs. Palmer's Honey** is Mary Heaton Vorse's **Labor's New Millions.** Published in 1938, it supplies needed background on the development and meaning of the CIO for millions of industrial workers in this country for whom the craft union approach of the A F of L was not sufficient. Honey Hoop of **Mrs. Palmer's Honey** echoes Vorse's conviction, "The status of the Negro worker has completely changed. Kept out of the A F of L unions, the Negro worker will never again be isolated and friendless within the labor movement, for the CIO organizes without regard to color, creed or nationality." Unfortunately many of these efforts and hopes for blacks were disappointed after the war.

85. ELLIS, Anne. THE LIFE OF AN ORDINARY WOMAN. 1929. N.Y.: Arno Press, 1974, Women in America Series. $18.00.
This autobiography is as homey and informative as letters from an old friend. Anne Ellis had never tried to write before, and expected this summary of the past 45 years of her "very ordinary" life to "be in pieces like a crazy quilt, as it comes back to me that was—all in bits." What seems at times to be an interminable string of anecdotes begins with Ellis' earliest memories of traveling by covered wagon from Missouri to Colorado with her spartan mother and unreliable father, fearful of Indians and zealous for silver. The plights and economic vacillations of life in mining camps,

particularly the burdens on women, are reflected through Ellis' child and adult eyes. **The Life Of An Ordinary Woman** is a valuable documentary of a pioneer woman's life as she saw it.

86. FAUSET, Jessie Redmon. THE CHINABERRY TREE. 1931. Westport, Conn.: Negro Universities Press, current. $12.00.
Fauset was trying for, and failed at, Greek tragedy in this story of infidelity, incest and interracial love. What we do get is a detailed look at the black middle class in a New Jersey suburb: an understanding of its interactions and of the effects the larger white society can have on it.

87. _____**PLUM BUN.** 1929. No current edition.
This sympathetically told story, of a "white colored" woman's attempt at passing, is Fauset's best novel. It is very much worth reading, for it vividly evokes a time and place: the late 1920s in Greenwich Village, a terrain we must usually view through the eyes of white male authors. In **Plum Bun**, Fauset displays a profound understanding of sexual politics, and the writing is generally well done, marred only by too many coincidences in the final chapters. It is inexplicable and infuriating that this is the only one of Fauset's novels not currently in print.

88. _____ **COMEDY AMERICAN STYLE.** 1933. Westport, Conn.: Negro Universities Press, current. $12.00.
The author again deals with the issue of passing. By presenting us with a range of characters, of differing hues, who make different choices about racial pride and identification, Fauset is attempting to show the absurdity of racial prejudice. Stylistically the novel is an interesting attempt to tell a compelling story without using a permanent central character.

89. FERBER, Edna. FANNY HERSELF. 1917. N.Y.: Grosset & Dunlap. O.P.
According to Ferber, "this my 2nd try at novel-writing, was not a well-sustained effort." Though this self-criticism is well taken, the novel is among those Ferber novels which feature tough, self-motivated women. Molly Brandeis (modeled after Ferber's mother) defies the tradition of her Jewish community earning her living "in business like a man" as a shopkeeper; and her daughter, Fanny, becomes one of the first women buyers for a giant Chicago mail order corporation. In spite of her management position and aspirations, Fanny gives some thought to the conditions of lumber mill women back home and to the women in the factory of her own employers. She resents the bootstrap glibness and sexism of her male colleague and boss. A moment of solidarity comes when Fanny witnesses a huge suffrage demonstration in N.Y.C. "What pen and tongue and sense of justice had failed to do [women] were doing now by sheer, crude force of numbers. After all, one might jeer at 10 or 50 or 100 women, or even 500, but not at 40 thousand." In spite of the inability of the young Ferber to carry through the promise of the novel's more interesting themes and its stock romantic ending this book is worth searching out for Ferber fans.

90. _____ **THE GIRLS.** N.Y.: Doubleday, 1922. O.P.
The Girls is recommended for those wanting to choose only one Ferber novel. In spite of the unfortunate title, the book focuses on women's lives (three generations of women in a Chicago family) from Charlotte's youth in Civil War days to Charley, a tough-minded post World War I working girl. This is a story that comes from her own experience, which gives it a spontaneous quality missing in some of Ferber's more self-consciously researched fiction. **The Girls** is about the subtle but astounding transition in women's lives from the Civil War to the 1920s. The novel was rejected by

several publishers when Ferber wrote it, because of its open defense of her unmarried heroine's right to maintain her pregnancy and keep her child. Her characters move away from the traditional family framework, seek paying and interesting work and develop a warm, supportive female household. A terrific book.

"Office Girls" by Isabel Bishop

91. _____ **SO BIG.** 1923. N.Y.: Fawcett World, 1975. $ .95.
The story of the successful son and the sacrificing mother. Selina Peake DeJong defies her neighbors and the little farm community and takes on the "work of a man" when her husband dies.

92. _____ **CIMMARON.** 1929. N.Y.: Fawcett Crest, 1971. $1.25.
Sabra Venable marries the flamboyant but undependable Yancey Cravat at 18 and follows him to settle the frontier of Oklahoma. She soon discovers that she is not the weak and charming girl she was brought up to be, and the book tells of her growth and transformation, along with the Oklahoma she and others like her settled. Yancey figures as the novel's romantic hero while the women are portrayed largely as either nursemaids or sex objects for men. Ferber intended this as sardonic, but it was popularly received as straight romance. The story is eminently readable and the comments about frontier life are a real addition to our history.

93. _____ **AMERICAN BEAUTY.** N.Y.: Doubleday, Doran & Co., 1931.
After writing **Cimmaron**, Edna Ferber had sworn off what she called "background"novels, only to find herself fascinated by the history of the New England countryside with its influx of immigrants and its residue of old Yankees. She

spent a year researching and writing **American Beauty** only to say later, "Perhaps I should have been stern about practicing birth control on this novel. I hadn't meant to have it. But there it was." Her second thoughts came from the book's reception: old family New Englanders resented it while at the same time it was criticized for its treatment of the Polish community. It is true that her characterizations tend toward the simplistic or stereotypic and there are elements of paternalism toward Native Americans and post-slavery blacks. In spite of all this the passion and eccentricity of the novel's female characters make for absorbing reading. The tight-lipped spinster Jude Oakes and her gypsy-like niece Tamar are interesting and memorable.

94. _____ A PECULIAR TREASURE. N.Y.: Doubleday, Doran & Co., 1939.
This first part of Ferber's autobiography begins with her experiences growing up in small towns in Iowa and Wisconsin. Ferber gives us a feeling of the strength she gained from her Jewish culture and community and also of the damage done to her by anti-semitic episodes. In spite of the limited resources of her parents (who owned a small notions store), and her own limited education, at age 17 she pushed her way onto the staff of the local newspaper, earning $3 a week. From Appleton, Wisconsin, Ferber graduated to the Milwaukee Journal and then to novels and short story writing. Theatre and movie productions of her more popular works brought her financial success and even a coveted penthouse apartment on Park Avenue in New York. Maybe because of her own reporter-to-riches story, Ferber tended to buy the American myth that hard work and talent can and/or should bring success. It was the situation of minorities (particularly women and Jews) that began to change that impression. Anti-communist, she was never able to put this knowledge into a political framework. Nevertheless, she deserves a lasting place in women's literature for those of her works which document the struggle and transition in the self-image and the work life of American women in the first half of this century. In the second part of her autobiography, **A Kind of Magic** (1963) Ferber summarizes her view of women as one who has believed in our suppressed power and potential.

FISHER, Dorothy Canfield. See CANFIELD.

95. FITZGERALD, Zelda. SAVE ME THE WALTZ. 1932. N.Y.: New American Library, 1974. $1.25.
In this autobiographical novel, Zelda Fitzgerald describes the person behind F. Scott Fitzgerald's flapper. In a flood of poetic images we glimpse a southern belle's girlhood, the emptiness of society life beneath‘ 1920s glitter, and her husband's inability to support her creative need. In ballet, Zelda attempts to find something positive and truly her own; in a studio separate from their apartment, she studies dance and feels the conflicts marriage and a family place upon her. Her need to study dance is rationally, lyrically expressed, and the passages evoking her study of the dance are the most beautiful in the novel. Another woman's attempt to fight for an independent identity, this is a remarkable achievement, particularly in view of the fact that she wrote it in only six weeks while in the hospital recovering from a complete breakdown.

96. MILFORD, Nancy. ZELDA. 1972. N.Y.: Avon, 1974. $1.95.
"She was the American girl living the American dream, and she went mad within it." An extraordinary biography, remarkable for its feminist perspective. It documents the conflicts Zelda Fitzgerald endured as a woman struggling to be an artist and to realize herself as an individual under the pressures of Scott's success. Her own writings were published under Scott's name, Scott having made free and unacknowledged use of her letters and writings in his novels. A beautifully-written book, it is highly recommended.

97. FLYNN, Elizabeth Gurley. THE REBEL GIRL: MY FIRST LIFE (1906-1926). 1955. N.Y.: International Publishers, 1973. $3.95.
Elizabeth Gurley Flynn's first volume of autobiography gives a brief but fascinating

Elizabeth Gurley Flynn addressing a rally.

summary of several generations of her Irish rebel ancestors, then settles into a fuller account of her own early life in the U.S.—from her first speech in 1906 at age 16 to her tireless efforts to save Sacco and Vanzetti in the mid 1920s. As a devoted member of the Industrial Workers of the World, "Gurley" travelled from the mills of New England to the lumber camps of the Northwest, speaking and organizing the workers. Flynn's descriptions of her actions and the forces around her—the labor organizers and workers; and the bosses, government, and police—are rich and perceptive, but her story sometimes lacks political depth. She tells of flirting with syndicalism, rejecting anarchism, working wholeheartedly with the IWW while feeling qualms about its "extreme rank and filism" or "infantile leftism," and then never really explains what she means. The book ends shortly before Flynn joins the Communist Party. Her second volume of autobiography, **The Alderson Story: My Life as a Political Prisoner**, focuses on her 2½ year stretch in the Federal Women's Reformatory at Alderson, West Virginia, after conviction under the anti-communist Smith Act in the 1950s. Flynn's plans to write of the years in her life between 1927-1951 were cut short by her death in Moscow in 1964.

98. GALE, Zona. MISS LULU BETT. N.Y.: Grosset & Dunlap. 1920. O.P.
In this ironic comedy about small-town life, Miss Lulu, a 34-year old "spinster, comes to the realization that most women—young or old, married or single—ar forced to live in perpetual childlike dependence. She is allowed a brief moment c rebellion before being sacrificed to a romantic happy ending. Gale's adaptation of he novel for the stage won the Pulitzer Prize for drama in 1921.

99. GELLHORN, Martha. THE TROUBLE I'VE SEEN. N.Y.: William Morrow & Co 1936. O.P.
Martha Gellhorn is best known as a war correspondent for her accounts covering th Spanish Civil War, the Munich pact, Czechoslovakia, and the war in Finland. Both he fiction and journalism detail the lives of ordinary people in impoverished circum stances. **The Trouble I've Seen** contains four pictures of misery during the Depression Each story is about a different part of America and a different group of people; but i all of them, human beings are reduced to perpetual hunger, exhaustion, and depen dency on relief rolls. Gellhorn documents the crippling process which forces people t prostitution, stealing, self-hatred, and "insanity". This book may be particularl good for high-school students who want to understand how generalized economi conditions affect individuals and their families. **The Trouble I've Seen** is like visitin families from one dilapidated building to another, listening to their stories of th Depression.

GLASGOW, Ellen (1873-1945) *was born and spent most of her life in Richmona Virginia. She was burdened as a child with a sickly constitution which plagued he throughout her life, as well as a nervous disability and encroaching deafness. Sh* *faced other struggles: the deaths of loved ones one after another; a lack of money in her early writing career; her audience's preference for sentimentality over an author's own vision of truth; and the dominance of wealthy old men in literary circles. She remained faithful to her artistic vision, which ebbed and flowed and changed direction as did her life. She was determined not to marry. Her works indicate great sensitivity to oppression, though she relates to the individual rather than the societal causes.*

100. _____ **THE BATTLE-GROUND.** N.Y.: Doubleday, 1902. O.P.
the Civil War through a woman's eyes. It could be used as a contrast to Crane's **Red Badge Of Courage.**

101. _____ **BARREN GROUND.** 1925. N.Y.: Hill & Wang, current. $4.50.
This novel is situated in Glasgow's South and tells the life of a strong, courageous woman, Dorinda Oakley, from adolescence to old age. The major theme is Dorinda's struggle to develop an enduring core of herself in spite of societal fantasy of romantic love. Eventually Dorinda succeeds in transcending many of the limitations of her female caste; after years of painful, hard work she becomes a successful dairy farmer. An illustration of Dorinda's character is the horror she feels for the patriotism that thinly masked the madness of U.S. involvement in World War I. she also observes the apathy and economic disintegration of the common people in post-war society. **Barren Ground** is a realistic and highly recommended portrait of a woman.

102. _____ **THE COLLECTED STORIES OF ELLEN GLASGOW,** ed. Richard Marker. Louisiana State University Press, 1963. $1.95.
Four of these stories delve into the supernatural and two evoke the decay of the South, but the real subject of this collection is romantic love and the difference between men and women. Like Dorothy in "The Difference," Ellen Glasgow observes relations between the sexes with "a look which was at once sympathetic and mocking." Her treatment of men is more mocking than sympathetic. Husbands and lovers display a degree of selfishness and vanity exceeded only by their inflated egos, and Glasgow's use of irony to dramatize these flaws does not soften her anger at men's callous abuse of the women who love them. Though critical of self-sacrificing wives and maidens who see marriage as "like Heaven, a passive and permanent state of bliss," Glasgow credits women with an integrity and sensitivity lacking in their lovers. The placement of stories in this collection allows the reader to see clearly the development of Glasgow's thought and technique. But the editor's introduction and quasi-Freudian interpretations of each story are worse than useless; one wonders what Glasgow would have had to say about him.

103. _____ **VIRGINIA.** N.Y.: Doubleday, 1929. O.P.
The tragic story of a woman reared to be a southern gentlewoman. She is betrayed by love: her parents' love which gently cripples; her husband's romantic love which dies as her beauty fades and his mind expands; and her children's love, for children grow up and seek their own lives.

104. _____ **THEY STOOPED TO FOLLY: A Comedy of Morals.** N.Y.: Doubleday, 1929. O.P.
An interesting Glasgow novel told first by a husband and then by his wife, revealing the distance between them and questioning the nature of the marriage tie.

105. _____ **VEIN OF IRON.** 1935. N.Y.: Harcourt, Brace and World, Inc., 1971. $ .95.
Ada Fincastle, a descendent of generations of pioneer women, has inherited their spirit of passive endurance and active self-sacrifice. Unfortunately, Ada lacks the independence of Dorinda, the heroine of Glasgow's **Barren Ground**; therefore, feminist readers will probably find this book of less interest. The Fincastle women are earthy and practical, and they support philosophical men less able to cope with life's realities. The novel is a soap opera chronicle of life's miseries which culminates in the

Depression. Ada, who possesses a Pollyanna-like fortitude, supports her family during its hard times and even manages to find fulfillment in her marriage to Ralph, her weak, moody childhood sweetheart. In the words of Ralph: "You're a dreamer, Ada. It's queer that a dreamer should be a rock to lean upon." Ada's dreams of happiness are complete when she and Ralph, middle-aged and impoverished, make the decision to return to the rural village they have uprooted themselves from to start anew.

106. _____ **THE WOMAN WITHIN.** 1934. N.Y.: Harcourt Brace, 1954. O.P.
This autobiography is the story of Glasgow's personal and social struggles to be a writer.

GLASPELL, Susan *(1882-1948). Susan Glaspell's mother was from Dublin and her father of old New England stock who had settled in the midwest as pioneers. She grew up in Iowa and attended college in Des Moines, where she began her career as a journalist and writer of magazine fiction. Throughout her writing career she continued to express a deep abiding interest in midwestern culture and values. With her husband, George Cram Cook, Mary Heaton Vorse, and others, she became one of the founders of the early experimental (radical?) theatre, The Provincetown Players, who performed seasonally in Greenwich Village and in Provincetown, Massachusetts. Though she worked with them from 1913 to 1922 (winning the Pulitzer Prize for her play* **Alison's House**) *she insisted that she was "a playwright by accident and a novelist by profession." Her novels strike a somewhat more conservative tone than some of the plays. In them, Glaspell explored with soul-searching honesty and compassion the consciousness of the middle-class liberal. Glaspell is also the author of* **The Road To the Temple,** *the story of her husband's life.*

107. _____ **FIDELITY.** Boston: Small, Maynard & Co., 1915. O.P.
This early 20th century novel explores a theme which recurs in later Glaspell works: the personal struggle of a young woman who chooses to defy convention and smalltown mores. Most of the book consists of descriptions of Ruth Holland's affair with a married man and the consequent ostracism of her family and friends. Glaspell, however, was attempting much more than commonplace melodrama. Her heroine is a strong woman, committed to independent decisionmaking. When, after eleven years, she finally has the chance to marry her lover, Ruth refuses: ". . . what you don't see is . . . that the thing that made me go with you then is the thing that makes me go my way alone now." Although at times overladen with tears, sighs, and sorrow, **Fidelity** has an excitingly feminist conclusion.

108. _____ **PLAYS.** Boston: Small Maynard & Co., 1920. O.P.
In the play "Woman's Honor" a man is being tried for a murder of which he is supposedly innocent. He will not say, however, where he was at the time of the murder, because he is "protecting woman's honor." In answer to this, one of the female characters says, "Did it ever strike you as funny that woman's honor is only about one thing, and that man's honor is about everything but that thing?" Glaspell is delightful reading, portrays a woman's consciousness, and has been hidden from us for too long.

109. _____ **BROOK EVANS.** N.Y.: F.A. Stokes Co., 1928. O.P.
This novel is the story of three people in three successive generations, and of their attempts to reach across time to understand each other. It is stylistically simple, yet complex in its implications. When her lover is killed suddenly, Naomi Kellogg finds herself unmarried and pregnant. She is forced by family and community pressure to marry a man she detests and to leave her home in Illinois for distant Colorado. Throughout the dreary years of her marriage, she remembers her first lover and their

meetings beside a brook in far-away Illinois. But the child of this affair, her daughter Brook Evans, cannot in her inexperienced adolescence understand the tragedy of Naomi, or her hope that Brook may realize the love that she was denied. Finally, years later, through her relationship with her own son, Evans, and a loving relationship with a man, Brook does begin to understand.

110. _____ ALISON'S HOUSE. 1930. Samuel French, Ltd. O.P.
Loosely based on the life of Emily Dickinson, this three-act play won Glaspell the Pulitzer Prize of 1930. Eighteen years after poet Alison Stanhope's death, the members of her extended family deal with the imminent sale of her house. Slowly, through the shared memories of sister, brother, niece, and nephews, Alison's character and the hidden aspects of her life are revealed. The choices and personal sacrifices she made influence decisions which each family member must make about his or her own life. Although rather over-romanticized and sentimental, the play moves quickly and leaves one with a desire to reread Emily Dickinson's poetry.

111. _____ JUDD RANKIN'S DAUGHTER. N.Y.: J.B. Lippincott Co., 1945. O.P.
A novel about liberal-leftists, and about yet another generation of sons fighting and dying in war. Frances Rankin Mitchell is the novel's central character. The daughter of a midwestern individualist, she lives in Provincetown, Massachusetts, with her husband, a literary critic. They await the return of their son Judson from a war-induced breakdown. Events in the novel cause Frances to reflect on the state of the liberal left. Lost politically, she feels bitterly betrayed by the cynicism and even anti-semitism of their acquaintants. She wonders, fearfully, what their sons are returning to and feels herself totally ineffectual to help her son, since she is a woman and war is a man's world. Though believing the war necessary, she asks "what if you don't want to kill—can you do right by doing wrong?" Since her questions remain unresolved, there is a sense of lost directions and mistakes that cannot be rectified.

112. GOLDMAN, Emma. LIVING MY LIFE. 1931. N.Y.: Dover, 1970. 2 vols., $4.50 each.
No finer account could be available of Emma Goldman's varied life than this one told in her own words. She tells of her childhood immigration to the U.S., a hasty and unsatisfactory marriage, discovering her gift for organizing and speaking, and her deep commitment to the social causes of the early 1900s and to anarchism, the philosophy which unified them for her. The story goes on through two volumes, detailing her work, her loves, the many people she knew, and, later, her imprisonments, her travels, and her disillusionment with Russian "communism".

113. HARVIN, Emily. THE STUBBORN WOOD. Chicago: Ziff Davis, 1948. O.P.
Stylistically weak but about a subject that concerns us very much, this autobiographical novel concerns a woman whose husband railroads her into a private insane asylum. The woman is middle-class and obviously a victim of the "feminine mystique;" she exhibits all the symptoms of masochism and dependency

31

which sap her strength and keep her husband in control of her fate. The book may not be good literature, but it is interesting and useful as nonfiction.

HERBST, Josephine *(1897- ?) grew up in Iowa farm country, worked her way through the University of California, and later lived with the expatriate community in Paris for three years. She worked as a reporter and often travelled abroad as a correspondent, visiting the Soviet Union, Spain during the Civil War, and was in Cuba during the General Strike of 1935. At home, she was involved during the 1930s in political actions and strikes in various parts of the country. She is considered one of the best of the so-called proletarian novelists, although she wouldn't place her own work under that category. She declined to contribute to a 1966 critical work entitled* **Proletarian Writers of the Thirties** *because of her objection to the term. The editor quotes extensively from her response in his introduction, and at one point she wrote: ". . . When I was writing my trilogy I never thought of it as 'proletarian'—in fact I hated the term, and thought it never comprehensive enough . . ." The trilogy is a fictional history of the Trexler family from Reconstruction through the 1930s, and owes much of its inspiration to Herbst's own family background. Published between 1933 and 1939 the novels attempt to portray, within a Marxist frame of reference, the splintering apart and decline of a single family set aginst periods of intense upheaval in American life. It is a complex and sweeping chronicle, for which Herbst drew on the tools of the reporter as well as those of the novelist. In order to firmly link the destiny of the Trexlers to the social and political history happening around them, she intersects the main story at various points with inserts and vignettes. In the first novel the inserts move forward in time, focussing on the lives of Anna Trexler's daughters; later they include reports of Depression's effect on people around the country.*

114. _____ **PITY IS NOT ENOUGH.** N.Y.: Harcourt Brace, 1933. O.P.
Introduces the Trexlers as a once comfortable, respectable Pennsylvania farming family now facing poverty. Most of the action revolves around Joe, his sister Anna and their younger brother David. Joe has large dreams and travels south to cash in on the fortunes being made during Reconstruction. In Georgia he becomes a scapegoat for northern industrialists exploiting the railroad industry there; he flees west, still nursing dreams of prosperity and finally becomes insane. Anna marries and moves to Iowa where she struggles to raise her four daughters against the pressures of mounting expenses and a failing farm. David—smart, self-centered, and educated with some of the first money Joe had sent home—goes into business and begins to accumulate money and power profiteering in government supplies.

115. _____ **THE EXECUTIONER WAITS.** N.Y.: Harcourt Brace, 1934. O.P.
Set against the upheavals of a growing militant labor movement and World War I, this novel follows David Trexler and two of Anna's daughters up to 1929. David continues to prosper, making a fortune on the war. Rosamund marries and struggles along while her husband goes to war and after he returns. Victoria moves to New York, marries into wealth and begins to grapple with communist philosophy. The insert pieces focus on the years of the depression and the dissatisfaction it breeds in people around the country, building the sense of impending struggle.

116. _____ **ROPE OF GOLD**. N.Y.: Harcourt Brace, 1939. O.P.

Continues the story of Victoria and her husband during the 1930s. As the novel opens they are living in Pennsylvania and trying to organize farmers. Herbst modeled many of Victoria's experiences on her own, and has her travelling around the country writing articles on the mounting depression and growing unrest. Victoria's work as a reporter gives Herbst the means to present a tapestry of the lives of farmers and workers and their attempts to organize. Another major focus of the novel is the organizing of industrial unions, and the novel ends with the auto industry strikes of 1937.

Flint, Michigan, 1937. End of General Motors Strike. Management surrenders.

HURST, Fanny _(1889-1968) was born in Ohio and grew up in St. Louis; in 1910 she left the midwest for New York City with the intention of gathering experience for writing. She worked many kinds of jobs in department stores, restaurants, and sweatshops. Her first publications appeared in 1914. She chose_ **Lummox** _as her favorite novel because she said, "it symbolized my complete breakthrough . . . from the circumscribed world in which I had been reared into a new social consciousness." A sense of social awareness characterized Hurst's work generally._

117. _____ **STARDUST**. N.Y.: Harper & Bros., 1921. O.P.

The predictability and heavy melodrama of this early Hurst novel may be a little much for 1970s readers, but there is more to **Stardust** than soap opera. Lily Becker, who leaves husband and hometown to attempt a career as an opera singer in New York, struggles against the usual sexist odds in her fight for self-sufficiency. Pregnant, unemployed, and alone, she sells her body and her own future for a clerical job and finally, years later, has money enough to send her daughter to a country boarding school. A strong, indomitable woman, Lily is nevertheless submerged in motherly sacrifice and spartanism. She wants her daughter to prevail where she was defeated. **Stardust** strongly emphasizes women's rights, particularly in marriage and career, but Hurst never points to romantic love or the traditional family as part of female oppression. The book is still well worth reading because of the author's clearly feminist perspective.

118. _____ **LUMMOX**. N.Y.: Harper & Bros., 1923. O.P.

This is the story of Bertha, who begins her life as an abandoned orphan in a waterfront boardinghouse in New York City She lives without the (dubious) benefit of schooling, without a family, a man, or any means of support other than her own brain and muscle. She works variously as a cook, waitress, charwoman, and live-in domestic. She lives from year to year, job to job, on to middle age, and never with any kind of security. Her story is an example of the kind of life lived by a sizable percentage of urban women during the first quarter of this century. The novel is well written and highly recommended.

119. _____ ANATOMY OF ME: A Wonderer in Search of Herself.
N.Y.: Doubleday and Co., 1958. O.P.
The first part of this autobiography tells how Fannie Hurst struggled to escape her overly protective St. Louis family and move to Manhattan, where she was to work alongside clerks and saleswomen, observing and writing about their lives. Later, as the "highest priced short-story writer in America," the enormously popular author got to meet such notables as Carrie Chapman Catt, whom Hurst dismissed as a colorful "zealot," and Leon Trotsky, an avid fan who declared he could recite most of **Lummox** from memory. Hurst's descriptions of her early career and her frustrating arguments with her conservative mother are absorbing; unfortunately, the second half of the book bogs down in long, tiresome paeans to her beloved husband.

HURSTON, Zora Neale (1902-1960). _Zora Neal Hurston grew up in Eatonville, Florida, a self-contained, all-black community. After her graduation from Barnard College, she traveled through the south and the West Indies collecting folklore. The poet Langston Hughes describes her as "a clever woman . . . who had great scorn for all pretensions, academic or otherwise . . . able to go among the people and never act as if she had been to school at all."_ **Mules and Men**, 1935 _(Harper & Row, $1.50) records folk tales of store porches, and_ **Tell My Horse**, 1938 _(Lippincott, out of print) tells of her explorations into Haiti. She died penniless in 1960 and lies buried near her hometown in a potter's field, "a resting place," notes biographer Robert Hemenway, "generally symbolic of the black writer's fate in America."_

120. _____ JONAH'S GOURD VINE. 1934. Philadelphia: Lippincott, 1971. $2.95.
In his introduction to the paperback edition, Larry Neale says, "This remarkable first novel is somewhat autobiographical in nature, the central characters, John and Lucy Pearson, are loosely based on Zora's own father and mother." John Pearson, a powerful, spirited young man, first hears of the all-black town of Eatonville while he is working on a railroad crew and decides to settle there with his wife, Lucy, and their children. At first Lucy is ecstatic, but after John discovers his calling for preaching, he leaves Lucy trapped at home to fade away in child raising and heartbreak while he returns to a pattern established early in their marriage of going where he pleased and pursuing other women. When he treats his second wife, Hattie, no better, she does not pine away and die—she seeks revenge. The novel is especially interesting in its depiction of the role of religion in the southern black community.

121. _____ THEIR EYES WERE WATCHING GOD, 1937. N.Y.: Fawcett World, 1972. $ .75.
The story of Janie from her first childhood awareness of what it means to be black and middle age. In reaction to the sexual exploitation that so many black women had experienced (including the experiences of her own grandmother and mother) Janie is pushed toward a marriage to a respectable property-owning older man whom she detests. She escapes from this oppressive early marriage into a long marriage with an egotistical man, Joe Starks, who becomes a leader in the all-black town where they settle. Joe relegates Janie to a secondary, supportive role throughout their marriage. Janie's first taste of real freedom comes when Joe Starks dies and, at 40, she meets a younger man, Tea Cake, and the two fall in love. The style is fast moving and perhaps the best example of Hurston's genius for recording the spoken expression of her characters. This is Hurston's most memorable work and a great novel.

122. _____ DUST TRACKS ON A ROAD. 1942. Philadelphia: J.B. Lippincott, 1971. $2.95.
In this autobiography, Hurston tells how, at the age of seven, she saw her future in twelve visions: from her beloved mother's death; through her homeless wanderings; to

her friendship with author Fannie Hurst and actress Ethel Waters. These visions, plus her "brazen" tomboy ways, marked Hurston for life. "I was not comfortable to be around," she writes. "Strange things must have looked out of my eyes like Lazarus after his resurrection." Hurston describes her voodoo initiations, gives us glimpses of the personal joys and sorrows that energized her novels, and speaks of race pride. "I have been in Sorrow's kitchen and licked out all the pots . . . I have stood on the peaky mountain with a harp and a sword in my hands."

123. _____ **SERAPH ON THE SUWANEE.** N.Y.: Charles Scribner's Sons, 1948. O.P.

It's sad to speculate on the anger that must have gone into the writing of this thoroughly unpleasant novel, Hurston's last. Janie, a withdrawn poor white woman, is forced into marriage with an arrogant ambitious man, and the author would have us believe that rape and a series of humiliations make her heroine a better person. The book also condones white paternalism at its sentimental worst, an indication of the political conservatism which poet-writer Larry Neal explores in his thoughtful essay, "Zora Neale Hurston, a Profile," **Southern Exposure**, Atlanta: Institute for Southern Studies. vol. I, nos. 3 & 4.

124. JOHNSTON, Mary. HAGAR. Boston: Houghton Mifflin, 1913. O.P.

Hagar, like the author herself, was born into an old-fashioned, somewhat impoverished, plantation family in the post-bellum South. During the course of the novel, she becomes—as Johnston in real life—a famous writer, a feminist, a socialist, and something of a mystic. This is promising material, but unfortunately, **Hagar** is a dull, flat book. Our heroine starts out as an exceptional child and simply progresses toward perfection. Never mind that her family disapproves, that she is rejecting all their values—but never experiences a conflict, never feels even slightly ambivalent. The novel was apparently written to advance the cause of suffrage, and perhaps Johnston felt it necessary to idealize. She had been known for her romantic historical novels, and her readers were astonished by the feminist **Hagar.** Despite all its shortcomings, it has been recommended in Tillie Olsen's reading list as a "classic of its own kind."

125. THE AUTOBIOGRAPHY OF MOTHER JONES, ed. Mary Field Parton. Chicago: Charles H. Kerr Publishing Company, 1974. $3.50.

Born in 1830, Mother Jones lived to be one hundred, and most of her labor organizing was done when she was middle-aged to old. Picture an old woman in the vanguard of a children's march or in prison, and the image of a thoroughly committed social activist begins to emerge. A working class woman of Irish extraction, after her iron-moulder, union-member husband and four children died in a yellow fever epidemic, Mother Jones did not stop. Instead she began to organize miners, steelworkers, mill workers—traveling from coast to coast, living wherever she was needed to organize workers. Her autobiography is an important labor history document; her life totally intertwined with the movement. Particularly active in child labor reform, Mother Jones led a band of injured mill children on a protest march, and it was largely through her efforts that the campaign for child labor reform became a public and much publicized issue. Non-violent wherever possible, her organizing tactics effectively focused media interest on the labor struggle. Politically, her primary concern was labor, and she had little sympathy with the middle-class suffrage movement of her day: "Organized labor should organize its women along industrial lines. Politics is only the

servant of industry.   The plutocrats have organized their women. They keep
them busy with suffrage and prohibition and charity . . . you don't need a vote to raise
hell."

KELLEY, Edith Summers (1884-1956) Born in Canada, Edith Summers moved to New
York City to satisfy her ambition to become a writer. Instead, she worked first at
Standard Dictionary, a job which permanently damaged her eyesight. Her second job,
as secretary to Upton Sinclair, proved more fruitful. She became involved in the
socialist/anarchist movements and formed lasting friendships with members of those
circles, including Sinclair and Sinclair Lewis. During this period she churned out a
number of pulp short stories to supplement her income, but when she and her
husband, a sculptor, could not support themselves as artists, they turned to farming.
Fifteen years in rural Kentucky and California were not much more financially
rewarding, and certainly more lonely for Edith Kelley, but they did provide the
material for her two novels. Unfortunately, the eye-strain engendered in New York in-
terfered with her writing and hindered the completion of **The Devil's Hand.**

126. _____ **THE DEVIL'S HAND.** Ill.: Univ. Press, 1974. $8.95.
Two women leave their offices in the East to farm the Imperial Valley, California. Unfortunately, the women's motives and their relationship are not explored; the details
just pile up to no apparent end. **The Devil's Hand** reads almost like a daily journal of
farming. Socialist philosophy is inserted somewhat awkwardly through the dialogues
of two male characters. Rhoda, through whom the story is told, politely listens and
vaguely agrees. A disappointment after Kelley's **Weeds**, but the published version
may be only a rough draft. As it stands, an informative chronicle of farming in
California in the 1920s.

127. _____ **WEEDS**. 1923. N.Y.: Popular Library, 1972. $1.50.
Judith Blackford would have thrived on the frontier. But for the tenant farms of Kentucky she had "too much life . . . too much life for a gal." And in this haunting novel
Kelley makes painfully clear how the forces of Judith's environment, so at odds with
her character, inexorably wear her down. From the beginning her fate is mirrored in
the haggard faces of the women around her, and later, in the already resigned eyes of
her infant daughter. The conditions of life in rural 1920s Kentucky crippled men and
women alike. Judith is bitterly aware that with the responsibility of motherhood
comes the steady erosion of strength and spirit, but she is unable to stop the process.
Edith Summers Kelley does not romanticize the hardships of this life. **Weeds** is accessible and straightforward: the reader goes through the excruciating details of farming tobacco, eating nothing but corncakes in winter, and cleaning a leaky slop
bucket. A vivid portrait of a poor white woman's struggle with her home, **Weeds** compares with other novels of country women, such as Elizabeth Madox Roberts' **Time of
man**, Ellen Glasgow's **Barren Ground**, and Willa Cather's **O Pioneers.**

LARSEN, Nella (1893-1963) belonged to the Harlem Renaissance school of writers.
Her novel **Passing** was praised by W.E. DuBois as a "studied, singular, and consummate work of art." In 1930 Larsen was awarded the Guggenheim Fellowship to enable
her to write a novel about the "different effects of Europe and the U.S. on the intellectual and physical freedom of the Negro," but for unknown reasons she never
published another work after **Passing**, and died in obscurity in New York City.

128. _____ **QUICKSAND**.
1928. Westport, Conn.: Negro Universities Press. $11.25.
Adelaide C. Hill says in her introduction that this novel "helps us to see how one black woman viewed the problem of the black community, its relation to white society, the survival of the individual black person in a totally white society abroad, and the basic problem of sex as it expresses itself for black women." The novel is probably largely autobiographical. Larson experiments with exaggeration and fantasy at the end to get her point across: Probably the most basic problem confronted in the book is that of a woman's control of her own body.

129. _____ **PASSING**. 1929. Westport, Conn.: Negro Universities Press. $9.50.
This novel seems more limited in scope than **Quicksand**. Larsen deals with only one theme, that of a light Negro passing into white society, and she does this in terms of only one group, urban bourgeois black society. The theme itself has many implications, but Larsen does not develop her characters enough. The two main characters are women: Irene Redfield, the narrator, and an acquaintance, Clare Kendry, the woman who has chosen the material advantages of white society but longs for her own people.

LeSUEUR, Meridel (1900-   ) _Meridel LeSueur chose her allies early: midwestern farm women and Native Americans, the people whom she, alienated from her own_

middle-class origins, saw as "poets". Traveling throughout the midwest with her feminist mother and itinerant preacher father, LeSueur recorded the oral histories of the people she met. After acting and directing in California and New York, she returned to Minnesota and set herself to the endless task of "social reporting," combining socialism and poetry into short stories. Before World War II, she wrote about unemployment ("Women on the Breadlines", reprinted in H. Swados **The American Writer and the Great Depression**) and farm organizing in the Dakotas. In the 1950s, she went to live with Native Americans who embodied her idea of the "cyclical rotation of time" and "communal consciousness." Meridel LeSueur celebrated her 70th birthday with peyote at the Native American Church. It is obvious in all of LeSueur's writing that she is "fierce for change, so all can live." Unfortunately most of her works are either out of print (McCarthy was a force here) or unpublished (3 novels, 130 notebooks).

130. _____ **SALUTE TO SPRING.** 1940. O.P.
Several of these proletarian stories will drive readers into libraries, searching for more. **Salute To Spring** is evidence of LeSueur's refusal to separate journalism, poetry and political radicalism. Her pro-labor feelings are the basis of her intense and sensitive descriptions of victimized people. She links despair, poverty, and anger to the economic harness which bosses keep around their workers ("No Wine in his Cart"). The exaltant hope and pride which she envisions is sometimes tied to the "mass" feeling of strikes ("I Was Marching"), at other times to children, ("Annunciation"), women, and nature. Disappointingly, **Salute To Spring** is out of print.

131. LEWIS, Janet. THE WIFE OF MARTIN GUERRE. 1941. Chicago: Swallow Press, 1973. $2.00.
The first in Lewis's three-novel series, Cases of Circumstantial Evidence, is based on an account of a remarkable 16th century French trial. It takes us into the mind and heart of Bertrande de Rols. The young wife of a wealthy peasant, she comes to denounce as an imposter the man she has accepted and loved as her husband. Initially secure in the fold of an ordered patriarchy, she must ultimately set herself against the foundation of that security to preserve her own identity. An exacting, subtle and powerful writer, Lewis has crafted a vivid reality from historical fragment. She carefully builds the intricate patterns of social and private pressures acting on Bertrande; her struggle to free herself from soul-tormenting doubt provides Lewis the focus for a provocative, unsettling examination of the nature of justice. In Bertrande herself, Lewis has given a powerful character study of a woman torn by conflicting emotions and trapped between the demands of her conscience and the expectations of those around her. A moving and beautiful novel with the intensity of fine poetry.

132. _____ **THE TRIAL OF SOREN QVIST.** 1947. Chicago: Swallow Press. $3.95.
The second of the Cases of Circumstantial Evidence is the story of a Danish minister who is viciously and cunningly framed as a murderer. As in the **Wife of Martin Guerre**, Lewis is concerned with exploring the impact of uncontrollable, inexplicable events on the individual mind. And although told in flashback, this novel shares the intensity and immediacy of its predecessor. Soren Qvist's life is structured by his religion, the love of his family and respect of his small community; yet his single enemy can build a train of events that destroys Qvist and disrupts the future of his daughter. The entire community must confront the tragedy of its leading citizen, and Lewis traces all the nuances of their disbelief and shifting perceptions. She creates the psychological reality of her characters with such skill that Parson Qvist's eventual belief in his own guilt becomes chillingly reasonable rather than incredible and contrived. Her attention to the details of his world thoroughly envelopes the reader in the life of a 17th century Danish community and the tragedy of an individual who "preferred to lose [his life] rather than accept a universe without plan or without meaning."

_____ **THE GHOST OF MONSIEUR SCARRON** (see 1950 on section)

133. LUMPKIN, Grace. A SIGN FOR CAIN. N.Y.: Lee Furman, Inc. 1935. O.P.
Disappointing in style, **A Sign For Cain** does not have the sustaining interest of Lumpkin's first novel, **To Make My Bread** (1932), which dealt with the famous Gastonia strike. Also a proletarian novel, **A Sign For Cain** deals mainly with the organizing work of two communist men, one black and one white, among black and white sharecroppers in a small southern town. Though the situations of the degenerate white upper class, the black and white sharecroppers, and black domestics are drawn realistically, characterizations tend to be stereotypic and the white male organizer is incredibly sexist. Lumpkin's own background was southern upper middle-class. Her brother was a senator in South Carolina where the family had long enjoyed first-family status. After her college days, Lumpkin moved to New York where she worked on the communist-affiliated magazine **The New Masses**. In 1953 Lumpkin was harassed by the Senate Permanent Investigating Sub-Committee for the alleged

propaganda of her proletarian works. She was to renounce her former views and in 1962 published a conservative, even religious novel titled, not surprisingly, **Full Circle.**

134. McKENNEY, Ruth. JAKE HOME. N.Y.: Harcourt and Brace, 1943. O.P.
In many ways this novel resembles its hero, Jake, the Paul Bunyon of the union organizers. Both are oversized, attempt Herculean tasks, and are definitely American in character. Through the life and career of Jake Home, McKenney examines the spectrum of American settings and classes, and at the same time provides a strike-by-strike, meeting-by-meeting chronicle of the American labor movement. The details of life in a mining town, Kansas farm country, Imperial Valley, California, and New York City receive equal attention. Some unevenness is inevitable in a novel of this scope and length, but amazingly McKenney manages to maintain a simultaneously focused and panoramic view most of the time. Unfortunately, the women in Jake Home represent the spectrum of female stereotypes so often found in labor novels: the opportunistic wife, the domineering mother-in-law; the neurotic rich girl; and the asexual comrade-who-serves-the-coffee.

135. NEFF, Wanda Fraiken. WE SING DIANA. Boston: Houghton Mifflin, 1928. O.P.
This book is a sort of tract for equal opportunity for women, especially in an academic setting. Not well written but interesting in that it raises such issues as single motherhood, socialism, free love, lesbianism, and feminism. The only issue it deals with really positively is the fact that women must have opportunities and freedom to learn, grow, and experience "just like men." Suffragettes are not really endorsed, the implication being that they're too radical, yet the main character in the novel incorporates various aspects of feminism into her life in order to fulfill herself.

_____ **VICTORIAN WORKING WOMEN** (see Works About Literature)

136. PAGE, Myra. WITH SUN IN OUR BLOOD. 1950. N.Y.: Citadel Press. O.P.
With Sun In Our Blood is the story of Cumberland mining people. It's a labor novel in which, as is so rarely the case, the will of the mining people persists and a woman emerges as an articulate and much respected leader. Myra Page wrote of her heroine: "Dolly Hawkins is the same breed as Mother Jones." The style is direct and simple, incorporating the speech of the Cumberland hills. Through the fabric of her story, Page tells us a good bit about the mountain culture, the earlier struggle of Dolly's father's generation to stop convict labor in the mines, and the danger and disaster the community constantly lived with because of the owners' concern for profit, not safety. Though slightly stereotypic in its treatment of the "evil" women Parasidy La Rue and Sal Campbell, the novel contains a gallery of complex and interesting people.

137. PARKER, Dorothy. THE PORTABLE DOROTHY PARKER. N.Y.: Vintage, 1973. $3.95.
Dorothy Parker (1893-1967) is known mainly as a wit and humorist. More closely examined, her works reveal a deep sympathy and understanding for the poor, the outcast, and particularly for women—an understanding made (barely) palatable by a light facade. Brilliantly controlled, unrelentingly intelligent, Parker fused her talent and observations into tiny masterpieces of verse and prose.

138. PESOTTA, Rose. BREAD UPON THE WATERS. N.Y.: Dodd, Mead & Co., 1944. O.P.
Rose Pesotta grew up in a Jewish Russian home where she had heard and read much about revolutionists and people's struggles. As a teenager, in 1913, she courageously set out for New York City where her sister found her a job in a shirtwaist factory.

Bread Upon the Waters is her autobiography focusing on her life as a labor organizer for the International Lady Garment Workers Union. Among her early memories she recalls May 1, 1914, "I see myself marching with hundreds of other girls like myself in the May Day parade in New York. We marched past the scene of the Triangle Waist Co. fire near Washington Square, and shudder as we look up at the windows—8, 9, 10 stories high—from which so many girls jumped to death because the exit doors were locked to keep union organizers out . . ." Pesotta's strength, courage and magnetic organizing talents come across in this wonderful autobiography, covering her years of struggle in many different cities and industries up to the 1944 convention of the ILGWU in Boston when, still fighting, she contends, ". . . that the organization ought to reconsider its old established rule of having only one woman in its high council . . ." This book should be on the "must" reading list for all those interested in the herstory of women in industrial labor.

PETERKIN, Julia (1880-) *Her mother died in childbirth and she was raised by a black nurse. From her, Peterkin, a white woman, learned the dialect and folklore of the Gullah people, who live on the sea islands and along the coastal areas of South Carolina. Always somewhat separate geographically, after the Civil War the Gullahs lived in isolated all-black communities. Here they preserved a culture and language derived from at least six African tribes and from Elizabethan England. The Gullah people are the focus of almost all Peterkin's writing.*

139. _____ **SCARLET SISTER MARY.** 1928. Dunwoody, Ga.: Berg, current. $10.95.
The story of sister Mary deals with an important theme in women's literature: a strong woman seeks to redefine her life after she loses faith in romantic love. Seen in this light, it is interesting to compare with Glasgow's **Barren Ground**, because Mary and Dorinda ultimately make such different choices. Dorinda's growth into a strong and independent woman brings with it an apparently inevitable isolation; Mary's strength and independence lead to an increased involvement with others. Both books make important contributions to the literature of woman as hero, illuminating the way society channels independence. Peterkin won the Pulitzer Prize for **Scarlet Sister Mary**. It is a well-written novel, with a simple flowing style which vividly evokes the little-known culture of the Gullah.

PORTER, Katherine Anne (1890-) *was born in Texas and educated in convent schools. For years she barely scraped by as a writer of book and theater reviews, only beginning to enjoy her first literary success when she was around 30. In an interview she advised women, "It is madness for women to try and combine home and career—you get older and tired and your faculties begin to draw in. I realized I had to make a choice, I had to be an artist—which means you work at a trade, whether it's writing or sitting at a bench making shoes."*

140. _____ **PALE HORSE, PALE RIDER.** 1939. N.Y.: Signet, current, $1.25.
While the book is made up of three separate short stories, there is a kind of unity between the different parts. This comes from the fact that Miranda, whom we meet as a young girl in the first story, "Old Mortality," is seen again in an incident of her adult life in the last story, "Pale Horse, Pale Rider." The middle story, "Noon Wine" does not deal directly with Miranda, but does give us a close-up of one family on a small South Texas farm during the same period as Miranda's childhood. Porter is particularly good at getting behind the pretension and fantasy of her characters and giving us an almost frightening sense of time and human reality.

141. _____ **SHIP OF FOOLS.** 1962. N.Y.: Signet, current, $1.75.
This book was 20 years in the making. It is the story of the transatlantic voyage of a German ship, the Vera, over the period of about a month in 1931. Porter attempts to capture a microcosm of society and does succeed in painting a picture of the complexity of pre-war European society. The character of Mary Treadwell, a 45-year-old divorcee returning to Paris, is probably at least partially a self-portrait. Porter is articulate about woman's condition, and its effects on the female psyche, though she has not considered herself a feminist.

142. PRETTY-SHIELD, MEDICINE WOMAN OF THE CROWS, as told to Frank B. Linderman. 1932. Lincoln, Nebraska: University of Nebraska, 1972. $2.45.
This is probably the first published personal account of what it's like to be a native American woman. Pretty-Shield was an elderly Crow woman when she described her life to Frank Linderman, who had asked her for "a woman's story." She used sign language and an interpreter to communicate the customs of the Crow people as well as her vivid memories of growing up in a village which was constantly on the move because of war. Pretty-Shield stops her story with the entrance of the white man and the exit of the buffalo.

ROBERTS, Elizabeth Madox *(1881-1941) was born in Kentucky, and except for her excursions to Colorado, Chicago, and Florida, she lived there all her life. Her attachment to the state and lifelong fascination with its dialects, customs and ballads are evident in all her work. In her poetry and fiction, she strove to reach the connection between "the world of the mind and the outer order". The fusion of ancestral past, personal present and place is realized in* **The Great Meadow,** *a novel based on tales of Roberts' pioneer ancestors passed down to her by her grandmother. Roberts entered the University of Kentucky in 1900 but could not complete her education until 1917, when she graduated from the University of Chicago. Her devotion to literature, music and art isolated her from her small-town neighbors. The isolation was probably chosen, but though reserved, she was not reclusive, and maintained many close friendships throughout her life. Roberts shared the imagination and intellectual vigor of her heroines, but not their physical strength. Frail and always prone to illness, she developed Hodgkins disease and died in 1941.*

143. _____ **THE TIME OF MAN**. 1926. N.Y.: Viking Press, 1963. O.P.
Though this novel takes place in Kentucky in the 1920s, the story it tells is doubtless true of the lives of farm workers and poor tenant farmers (sharecroppers) today throughout many parts of rural America. As the novel begins, Ellen Chesser's family owns nothing but their wagon of broken furniture and the clothes on their backs. For Ellen, there are no buffers hiding the reality of woman's condition. Although material deprivation is a firm common bond between men and women in her community, she learns early that woman's lot is tied to a different kind of pain than that of the men at her side. As a little girl, she sees the women gathered to help a neighbor deliver her baby. Ellen is impressed with the pain and terror of the scene. But as a woman bound to the power of this pain, she also learns to somehow keep alive an enduring vision of the person she could be. This is a great novel.

"By the time the moon was well above the trees, they were on the road, the horses stepping briskly, for they must be far from the reach of this country before the night was done..."

41

144. _____ **MY HEART AND MY FLESH.** 1927. N.Y.: The Viking Press. O.P.

Elizabeth Madox Roberts' second novel is the solemn and tedious odyssey of Theodosia Bell, a pale character compared to the ardent and intrepid women of **The Time of Man** and **The Great Meadow**. (In her notes, Roberts describes Theodosia as "a wandering spirit, a lost thing.") She is a victim of forces which tear her from the material and personal comforts and vigor of her early life into a desperate search for friendship and introspective knowledge. Although **My Heart And My Flesh** ends with the promise of rebirth and serenity through closeness with the earth, this serenity contrasts the depictions of racism, sexism and hostility which Roberts has apparently reconstructed from her memories of Springfield, Kentucky.

145. _____ **JINGLING IN THE WIND.** 1928. N.Y.: Popular Library, 1956. O.P.

Jingling In The Wind is a baffling little book, a-kind of literary experiment. The novel begins in an uncertain era which combines modern America, Medieval Europe and the distant future. In a series of myth-like conversations in which racism, the oppression of women and American class society are depicted, Jeremy—the professional rainmaker—travels to the Capital for a rainmakers convention. He and his "fellow travelers" engage in a Canterburyesque exchange of tales creating an alternative vision of love and romance.

146. _____ **THE GREAT MEADOW.** 1930. Covington, GA: Mockingbird Press, 1975, $1.50.

The straighforward external events of **The Great Meadow** (spanning 1774 to 1781) form a powerful historical backdrop for a group of pioneers moving westward from Virginia to settle in Kentucky. The journey revolves around Diony Hall, a resourceful young woman who decides to marry Berk Jarvis and go west with him to shape their lives in the wilderness. They settle temporarily at Harrod's Fort and attempt to overcome lack of food and warm clothing during the winter of 1778; the Indian invasions; Berk's vindictiveness toward the Indians for killing his mother. Through impressionistic and detailed descriptions, Roberts constructs a society of seemingly mythic settlers who go through symbolic rites of passage to learn that they can outlive their current conditions through spiritual strength. Roberts emphasizes the differences between men and women (the women concentrate on community life, the men plan revenge on the Indians) and the settlers. But she is sympathetic to all her characters in this moving novel.

147. _____ **HE SENT FORTH A RAVEN.** 1935. N.Y.: Viking Press. O.P.

Roberts' most difficult, baffling novel, and possibly her most revealing. The underlying, sometimes obscured structure of **Raven** is a recreation of the Noah myth. When his second wife dies, Stoner Drake vows never to set foot on earth again. He makes his farmhouse into an ark in which to hide from the flood outside, a symbol for World War I, whose waves encroach on the farm and roll inexorably over all. The raven, whom Noah sent forth to fly over the flood and report, is Stoner's granddaughter, Jocelle. Within the confines of the ark, a motley crew of men grapple with the contradictions of life, each arguing his own philosophy. The novel often becomes vague and murky in these sections, perhaps because the problem is. While the debate is raging inside, the daily process of farming continues, carried on mostly by Jocelle. The undercurrent of exasperation with an anger towards men in Roberts' other novels is voiced here also. In their efforts to impose a philosophical framework on life, the men are both sublime and foolish. The women maintain their dignity. Jocelle, battered by the war, emerges strong and whole, both the symbol and sustainer of life. Her cousin, Martha, the most complex character in the novel, is like the novel itself, suggestive, intriguing and ultimately frustrating.

148. _____ **THE HAUNTED MIRROR** 1932. **NOT BY STRANGE GODS.** 1941. N.Y.: The Viking Press. O.P.

In most of the 13 short stories contained in these collections, Elizabeth Madox Roberts skillfully focuses on critical situations and characters wrought with conflict. Various stories are direct and uneventful descriptions with a biblical tone, such as "Children of the Earth," a portrayal of Kentucky folk. Others are riddled with dichotomies and omens. "The Betrothed" captures the sinister monologue of Rhody's grandmother who warns Rhody about the man she is preparing to marry. In "The Scarecrow," Joan, the youngest daughter and blacksheep of the family, builds a scarecrow in her own image to protect her father's cornfield, and later decides to make an identical one in another field to ward off men (as sexual intruders) as well as crows. The stories are too cropped to explore their tantalizing implications and are not the fertile grounds of poetic symbolism and character study that her novels are.

SANDERS, Marion K. DOROTHY THOMPSON: A Legend in Her Time. (see THOMPSON, Dorothy.)

149. SCOTT, Evelyn. MIGRATIONS. N.Y.: A. and C. Boni, 1927. O.P.
Emma Goldman described her friend Evelyn Scott as "deeply socially aware." Born in Tennessee, Scott spent many years outside the U.S., first "in exile" in Brazil, and later living in Bermuda, Canada and Europe. These experiences no doubt contributed to the scope and intricacy of **Migrations**. Scott covers a lot of ground as she ties in American history and habits during the Gold Rush in 1851 with the peculiarities of her characters. She starts with superficial relationships between slave and slaveholder, between women and men, and quickly reveals deep contradictions and self-consciousness. Scott makes clear that everyone shares the illusion that life will improve once they escape their specific circumstances. The book is plodding at times because Scott never sacrifices detail for the sake of readability.

150. SINCLAIR, Jo. WASTELAND. N.Y.: Harper, 1946. O.P.
Sinclair is a novelist with a unique sense of the effect of the family on its members. This is a story told by Jake, generally considered the most "successful" member of the family, but knowing himself divided and paralyzed by self-hate. He goes into therapy, and through his eyes we see his tormented married sister, confused nephews, and his older brother, unemployed for years. We also see his liberated younger sister, a lesbian who has accepted herself as she is. In the course of Jake's therapy we see how many of the family's problems can be traced back to the hardship suffered by the parents' generation when they first arrived as poor Jewish immigrants in the U.S. The book is a revelation of family life, and a fine (though speeded up and perhaps simplistic) account of the process of therapy.

151. _____ THE CHANGELINGS. N.Y.: Putnam, 1955. O.P.
This is a fine novel, vivid with action, illuminated by unforgettable characters, and deeply enriched by the complexity of the author's vision of community, family, and individual. Characters are shown in the midst of family life; the author sees how they are affected by family structure, and what effect they in turn have on their families. The neighborhood is also fluid; it is finely drawn, with portraits of the different families on the block. Then we see it altered by black families looking for housing during a hot post-World War II summer. Few novelists have thought through the forces which affect our lives as individuals so clearly and so well. Sinclair's vision recalls the work of the Laingian psychiatrists on the family, but no one else has written such ideas into a compelling story which holds our attention from beginning to end.

152. SLADE, Caroline. MRS. PARTY'S HOUSE. N.Y.: Vanguard, 1948. O.P.
Though this novel is written in an uneven, at times slightly didactic style, it deals with a question that reflects the function and status of women in a male-dominated culture. The central character, Mrs. Party, is used as a vehicle for describing several groups of prostitutes in an average sized city. She is portrayed as a big-hearted, bewildered woman who gets into "the life" after her husband is killed in an accident, leaving her with an invalid mother and no means of support. She becomes a madam, in which position she treats "the girls" in her house with great humanity. Among the best parts of the book are the descriptions of the courts and the cops; these give clear insights into how the system works.

153. SLESINGER, Tess. THE UNPOSSESSED. 1934. Simon & Schuster. O.P.

This novel is an expansion of the author's story, "Missis Flinders," which serves as the final chapter in **The Unpossessed.** The story and the book as a whole relate a classic dilemma: the problems of so-called "intellectuals" who understand how to change the world. Here they are a group of young Greenwich Villagers in the 1930s. Despite their revolutionary fervor, they can only manage to dabble in communism, dabble in starting a magazine, dabble in relations with each other. Their lives are hectic and futile. Because Slesinger translates the flood of their thoughts and feelings so intensely, their lives become dramatic, alive, and ultimately tragic to the reader.

154. _____ ON BEING TOLD THAT HER SECOND HUSBAND HAS TAKEN HIS FIRST LOVER AND OTHER STORIES. 1935. Quadrangle, 1974. $4.50.

This short story collection deserves all the praise it can get. Comedy and tragedy are blended from a feminist point of view. The title story—about a woman's obsessional thoughts and past associations upon learning of her husband's betrayal—reveals the pain and self-control which characterize a woman determined not to fall apart. The author also depicts the pitiful efforts of a provincial young secretary trying to get ahead in New York, who disavows her office co-workers only to be exploited by her male boss. "The Friedman's Annie" is a pathetic study, parodied, yet dead serious, of the ways in which maids adopt the values of their upper-class employers without seeing their own oppression. This collection is deeply committed to exposing the plight and confusion of many women. the theme is best portrayed in "Missis Flinders," a story which deftly captures the subtle trauma of a young wife who has just had an abortion because she submitted to her husband's intellectual decision not to have a child. Slesinger's observations are acute as she shows the reality behind human pretensions over and over again. Her own promise was tragically halted when she died of cancer in 1945 at the age of 30.

155. SMEDLEY, Agnes. DAUGHTER OF EARTH. 1929. Old Westbury, N.Y.: Feminist Press, 1973. $3.00.

This autobiographical novel presents an outstanding tale of a strong woman who stepped beyond all the bounds her society and her sex imposed on her. The childhood of Marie Rogers/Agnes Smedley in the 1890s was one of poverty and hardship in rural Missouri and then in a series of small mining towns in the West. Yet, even as a child she was a fighter. She realized early that marriage was a trap, and saw that the lot of her prostitute aunt was better than that of most married women. Grown up, she went to teacher-training school, shocked her society by going on the road as a saleswoman, and worked as a radical journalist. She became deeply involved in left-wing politics, and was imprisoned for her connections with a revolutionary movement for the freedom of India. Both her husbands were political men, and theoretically prepared to treat her as an equal; yet both marriages ended because of sexism.

156. _____ **PORTRAITS OF CHINESE WOMEN**. (Edited by Jan and Steve MacKinnon, with an afterword by Florence Howe.) Old Westbury, N.Y.: Feminist Press, 1976. $3.25.
The 18 pieces in this gem of a book (six fictional, 12 journalistic) give us glimpses of the revolutionary struggle in China between 1928 and 1941. The reader is swept up into another world where both oppression and revolutionary dedication reach heights generally undreamed of in the West. Smedley introduces us to the silk spinners of Canton, women who, because of their pride and unity in the fight for better working conditions, are called lesbians, and to old Mother Tsai, an early worker for women's rights. The fiction draws on rich Chinese idioms. We are presented with a variety of heroines, both wealthy and peasant, and even with a villain: the despicable "Martyr's Widow." Memorable as Smedley's characters are, they never overshadow the larger story she set out to tell, of the Communist Revolution in China. This is a tremendously moving collection which cannot be too highly recommended. (Readers may also be interested in Smedley's **Battle Hymn of China**, 1943.)

157. SMITH, Betty. A TREE GROWS IN BROOKLYN. 1943. N.Y.: Harper & Row, current. $1.25.
This long-time best seller is set in a Catholic working-class community at the turn of the century. It shows Francie Nolan, a sensitive girl who wants to become a writer, struggling through childhood and adolescence. The book can be criticized for the sentimentality that colors its treatment of poverty and of family life. Nonetheless, it presents many good insights. See for instance Chapter XXX, where Francie starts to menstruate.

STEIN, Gertrude (1974-1964). _The brilliant daughter of Bavarian immigrants, Gertrude Stein read copiously while growing up in California. She studied under William James and Santayana at the Harvard Annex (later called Radcliffe). After a stint at Johns Hopkins Medical School, she headed for Paris, where she formed a salon for the unknown and struggling artists of the period: Picasso, Matisse, and the like. She also began the lesbian relationship which was to last for the rest of her life with Alice B. Toklas. Her writing is experimental. Some have praised it as a presentation of the "immediate existing," the "continuous present;" some have called it unreadable. The books listed below are definitely worth trying._

Gertrude   Gertrude   Gertrude / Stein

158. _____ **FERNHURST, Q.E.D., AND OTHER EARLY WRITINGS**.
N.Y.: Liveright, 1973. $3.95.
If you like Gertrude Stein, you will love this book. If you have never read anything by her, this is a good place to start, as it is much less abstract than her later writings. It

contains three of her earliest pieces, written between 1903 and 1905. Leon Katz has written an excellent introduction in which he describes Stein's life at the time she wrote them, and also discusses what she attempted in her writing. Readers are thus offered both a personal look at Gertrude Stein and a glimpse of her literary beginnings. A wonderful book.

159. _____ **THREE LIVES.** 1909. N.Y.: Vintage, 1970. $1.95.
Stein's first work, one of the most easily accessible, and probably the most interesting to the common woman: the lives of three simple women, recounted in simple words, yet in such a way as to give a real sense of their complex realities. **The Good Anna** and **The Gentle Lena** are German immigrant servants; **Melanctha**, whose story is the longest (also included in **SELECTED WRITINGS OF GERTRUDE STEIN**. N.Y.: Vintage, 1972. $2.95), is a black woman. Stein shows the fragile means by which these women survive, focusing in particular on their personal relationships. The natural, speech-like cadences of Stein's style here were revolutionary at the time of publication; the use of repetitions foreshadows Stein's later techniques.

160. _____ **THE AUTOBIOGRAPHY OF ALICE B. TOKLAS.** 1933. N.Y.: Vintage, current. $2.45.
Stein wrote this book in Toklas's conversational style, which, it would seem, is quite witty and lucid. She has Toklas say of Stein, "She always liked knowing a lot of people and being mixed up in a lot of stories." This book is full of people and their stories. Most of the great painters, many of the great writers, and several great composers of early 20th century Paris are here. The picture she gives us of that artistically revolutionary time, coupled with the picture she gives of herself (an external portrait, since it is supposedly through Toklas's eyes), make this a book which is both interesting and entertaining.

161. SANDERS, Marion K. DOROTHY THOMPSON: A Legend in Her Time. 1973. Avon, 1974. $1.95.
Anyone interested in media and public affairs will enjoy this thoughtful account of the life of Dorothy Thompson. Marion Sanders treats her subject with insight and intelligence, making sure to underline the conflicts between Thompson's globetrotting journalistic career and her often-slighted private life, including a marriage to Sinclair Lewis and motherhood. Thompson was a European foreign correspondent in the 1920s; in the 1930s she became a renowned columnist and radio commentator. She and Eleanor Roosevelt were said to be the most influential women in the U.S. at the time. Despite her conscientious, brilliant journalistic work, Thompson was less organized in her emotional affairs, often failing to analyze problems in her relations with friends and family. This biography poignantly reflects both the public and privately vulnerable sides of a gifted and influential woman.

162. VORSE, Mary Heaton. THE AUTOBIOGRAPHY OF AN ELDERLY WOMAN. 1911. N.Y.: Arno, 1974 (Women in America Series). $15.00.
This testimonial of frustration and anger comes from an elderly woman who laments the position of uselessness which she and most elderly people are forced into by their children. Mary Heaton Vorse used her mother as a model: "I knew exactly how my mother felt about age—or rather about growing old, for she never was old except in years and retained her gusto for life until shortly before her death." This is a short and readable protest against the dictatorship of younger people who curb the impulses, spirit and courage of the elderly.

163. _____ **I'VE COME TO STAY. (A LOVE COMEDY OF BOHEMIA).** N.Y.: The Century Co., 1918. O.P.
A parody of Greenwich Village, **I've Come To Stay** exhibits the frivolity and absurdities of stereotypic village inhabitants. Ths humorous plot centers around a befuddled romance and a feisty 14-year-old girl.

164. _____ **STRIKE!** N.Y.: Liveright, 1930. O.P.
Written during the influx of "proletarian" strike novels, Vorse fictionalizes the details of the 1929 National Textile Workers strike in Gastonia, North Carolina. Never

faltering in her commitment to labor, Vorse presents the dramatic vacillations of the strike: the evictions of 300 people, the makeshift tent colony for strikers and their families, the relentless violence of the "Mob" and the police against strikers. The strength and leadership of women in keeping the strike going is evident throughout the novel, as is the analysis of the lives of textile workers stuck in a system of paternalism. The political depictions in **Strike!** are informative and important for an understanding of the repression of labor in the 1930s. Its dogma makes it predictable in plot and lack of character development.

165. _____ FOOTNOTE
TO FOLLY. N.Y.: Farrar & Rinehart, Inc., 1935. O.P.
"Indeed, my book is the record of a woman who in early life got angry because many children live miserably and died needlessly." **Footnote To Folly** is an unusual documentary of the labor movement between 1912 and 1922 as well as a down-to-earth account of Vorse's development as a journalist. The textile strike in Lawrence, Massachusetts, in 1912 marked the final transition from her intellectual support of labor to constant personal involvement. She tells of the struggles of the unemployed in North Carolina (1914), the Ludlow Massacre, the Sacco and Vanzetti frame-up, the steel strikes (1919), "Red" raids, World War I and anti-war women's groups. Vorse's inclusive reporting gives readers not only a sense of specific events, but also a view of economic causes and repressive tactics ruthlessly used by business and government.

"Things I saw in Lawrence aroused in me an indignation whose fire has never gone out."

166. **WARD, Mary Jane. THE SNAKE PIT.** 1946. N.Y.: Signet, current. $1.25.
An exceptionally fine account of one woman's experience with mental health professionals and with the horror of institutionalized treatment. Her graphic accounts of hydrotherapy and electric shock treatment seem to corroborate Thomas Szasz's theory that mental patients are persecuted in modern society as supposed witches were in the past. The style is simple and flowing as Virginia struggles to regain conscious control of her life, finally realizing that the hospital is a prison, and that her therapist is wrong in his analysis of her (and probably in his basic assumptions about the nature and treatment of the problems that bring people to him).

167. **WEATHERWAX, Clara. MARCHING! MARCHING!** 1935. O.P.
The revolutionary zeal suggested in the title is a consistent factor throughout the novel, but it does not obscure the often inventive and compelling style and diversity of characters. Weatherwax simultaneously unfolds the personalities of different men and women with various ethnic backgrounds (most with a strong Communist Party stance) and the trying preparations for a strike of lumber workers in the Pacific Northwest. Her focus shifts from internal observations to external dialogues, from physical descriptions of people to the details of lumbering, clam digging, stevedoring, and the cutting up of whales. Each character provokes interest but the book emphasizes the strength of collectivity, and no individual stands out as hero. **Marching! Marching!** won the **New Masses-**John Day Company award for the best novel on an American proletarian theme in 1935.

168. WEST, Dorothy. THE LIVING IS EASY. 1948. N.Y.: Arno, 1970. $14.00.
This novel is recommended especially for the relationship between Cleo, a southern black woman who is striving to be accepted in Boston black society, and her three sisters Lily, Charity, and Serena. West is impartial, showing both the grubbing and conniving side of Cleo and her enduring creativity and strength. West's brilliance is reflected in the fact that the reader feels both drawn to and repelled by the character of Cleo. It is clear that part of Cleo's manipulation of the people closest to her is the result of the racism, poverty and insecurity in which she grew up, still specters haunting her adult life.

WHARTON, Edith *(1862-1937). Born into New York upper-class society, Wharton wrote as a girl, married into her class, became disillusioned with her marriage, and was separated for many years before her divorce in 1932. Her family doctor advised her to take up writing again to relieve the nervous strain of the early years of her marriage. Her novels are marked by understatement, a subtle code of personal and social honor and a sense of the futility of struggle against social circumstances. While some of her novels seem mere escapes into a world of fantasy characters, her successful novels boldly depict her experiences.*

169. _____ THE HOUSE OF MIRTH. 1905. N.Y.: Signet, current. $1.50.
A devastating account of the rise and fall of Lily Bart, beautiful, unprotected, and possessed of too much integrity to allow herself to succeed in a social world which half the time she sees as tantalizingly attractive and half the time recognizes as shallow and tawdry.

170. _____ ETHAN FROME. 1911. N.Y.: Scribners', 1970. $1.95.
Wharton's best-known work, and one of the few with a man for a central character—a poor man trapped by custom and ignorance and above all by his own misguided integrity into a life of self-destruction.

171. _____ SUMMER. 1917. Saint Clair Shores, MI: Scholarly Press, 1970. $14.50.
The central character in this novel could well be compared to Ethan Frome. Like him, she is dependent, poorly educated. She lives in a similar setting of northern rural poverty, yet her adaptation to the limits and necessities of her life is very different. She is one of the few Wharton characters ever to yield to the inevitable.

172. _____ THE AGE OF INNOCENCE. 1920. N.Y.: New American Library, 1962. $ .95.
This is perhaps the most complex of Wharton's good novels; it is about a man and a woman, both trapped by the inflexibility of their upper-crust New York society. Wonderful characterizations, fine timing and story line.

173. _____ OLD NEW YORK. 1924. O.P. (See **THE PORTABLE EDITH WHARTON**)
A collection of short novels; these stand among Wharton's most memorable works.

174. WILHELM, Gale. WE TOO ARE DRIFTING. 1935. N.Y.: Arno, 1975. $9.00.
This is a novel about Jan, a successful artist and lesbian. Her lesbianism (the word is not used) is simply and completely accepted. The book tells of the end of her affair with one woman, and the beginning of her love for another.The cool, spare lucidity of Wilhelm's experimental style is a delight.

175. _____ THE STRANGE PATH. Originally published as **TORCHLIGHT TO VALHALLA.** New York: Random House, Inc., 1938.
Morgen lives in a fairy tale world . . . however, in this case Prince Charming's rescue attempt fails. Isolated in the hills with her father, Morgen's life is the world they have built together. Her father paints, Morgen writes; and they are self sustaining in their isolation. When Morgen's father dies, her suitor, Royal St. Gabriel fails to replace

Daddy as the central figure in Morgen's life. Royal simply cannot compete, not even with Daddy's ghost. Suddenly, deus ex machina, Toni, a girlhood friend of Morgen's returns; and in Toni, Morgen finds the sexual and spiritual fulfillment lacking in her relationship with Royal. Morgen remains an enigmatic woman throughout the novel—strangely non-verbal for a writer—she is scarcely able to define her emotional needs, even to herself. Regressively infantile in character, Toni and Morgen's lesbian relationship reinforces the myth of the lesbian as a Daddy's girl, who, unable to achieve a well integrated relationship with another man, turns to women by default. Imprisoned in a fairy tale kingdom, this princess chooses not to escape, and Daddy remains central to her life.

176. WOLFF, Maritta M. WHISTLE STOP. N.Y.: Random House, 1941. O.P.
The work of an obviously talented writer, **Whistle Stop** is the story of a working-class family in a small midwest town. Major characters include a dominant, loving mother, who attempts to keep order in the family; Ken, the mother's admitted favorite, who is charismatic, somewhat tragic, jobless, and hopelessly in love with his sister Mary; and Mary herself, elegant, involved with all the raunchiest characters in town but somehow above it all, watching, caring, quietly intervening wherever help is needed. The reader is introduced to the rest of the clan, each of whose story is a compelling one. Wolff has brought the characters to life so that long after the book ends, one finds oneself wondering what they're all doing these days.

177. _____ NIGHT SHIFT. N.Y.: Random House, 1942. O.P.
Maritta Wolff wrote **Night Shift** (her second novel) at age 23. She was acclaimed at the time as a "female Steinbeck." The novel is an excellent, tough account of lives in an industrial factory town in the midwest. Two of the women in the novel are of special interest. Sally, whose husband is incarcerated in a state hospital, earns the family income through waitressing. She is a magnetic center around whom disappointments, joys and injuries accumulate. The other outstanding character is Petey, Sally's sister, an entertainer and hustler. Admired for her nerve, she remains undefeated—an unusual character in the fictional depiction of working class women. Wolff has drawn us a model of a cooperative household arrangement, shared work and child care responsibilities and a strong acceptance of the unique needs of women as well as men. It is a highly recommended book.

YEZIERSKA, Anzia (1885-1970) was one of many Russian Jewish immigrants who arrived at Ellis Island in the 1890s. She rejected her mother's despair and defeat, and left home at age 17, escaping her authoritative father. She worked in sweatshops, laundries, and kitchens, and developed a deep hatred of the rich. Insisting on her independence (her two marriages were shortlived) Yezierska lived alone and continued to write short stories and novels about ghetto life. In 1920, her cycle of poverty was broken when Sam Goldwyn bought the screen rights to **Hungry Hearts** for $10,000. Famous now as the "rags to riches" writer, she rubbed elbows in Hollywood with "eminent authors" and enjoyed the luxuries of wealth. Of this time she wrote: "And here I was, losing the very soul that my security was giving me." When Yezierska's books went out of vogue in the 1950s, she was reunited with poverty and her origins.

178. _____ HUNGRY HEARTS. 1920. N.Y.: Arno, 1975. $18.00.
Anzia Yezierska recorded New York's lower east side, the community she knew best. These effective nine short stories overlap: they are about poverty in the Jewish ghetto and the grueling work in shirtwaist factories. Yezierska's characters are constantly assaulted by the American emphasis on competition and profit-making, values which they try to accept in order to keep alive the promises of America as "golden country." The tedium of their struggles comes through in the repeated themes of back-breaking work and alienation from the "New World."

179. _____ BREAD GIVERS. 1925. N.Y.: Braziller, 1975. $3.95.
In what is considered to be her early autobiographical novel, Yezierska shows Sara Smolinsky caught between the two worlds in which many Jewish immigrants found themselves: the Old World of Russia, where men were revered as scholars and women as their servants, and the new World of independence and "Americanization"

(American jobs, money and men). Sara watches her tyrannical father map out the unhappy lives of her older sisters and decides to leave her family. Her tactics for survival are common: working in a laundry to buy a meager meal, and going to night school to buy acceptance as an American. **Bread Givers** is a realistic account of the loneliness and conflicts of immigrant women in the 1920s. Includes a good introduction by Alice Kessler Harris.

In 1912, the disastrous fire in the Triangle Shirtwaist factory in New York City left 146 women employees dead. All exits were barred and there were no fire escapes. Most employees were forced to jump from the 8th, 9th, and 10th floors.

Contemporary: 1950-Present

180. ADAMS, Alice. FAMILIES AND SURVIVORS. 1974. N.Y.: Warner, 1976. $1.50.
The scene is Virginia, 1941. Two young girls, Kate and Louisa, lounge nude beside the swimming pool and joke about the world of sexual competition that they are about to enter. Abruptly the story pace speeds up as the author flashes us X-ray visions of her characters' futures and the accuracy of their present perceptions. The years slip by in witty, telling scenes, and Adam's wistful women and men stumble into the 1970s toward a realization of who they actually are and what they actually want and can have in life. Often funny, always compassionate, **Families and Survivors** will leave you with the feeling that there is hope for love and friendship in this hectic, role-infested society.

181. ALTA. MOMMA, A START ON ALL THE UNTOLD STORIES. Albion, California: Times Change Press, 1974. $2.00.
Alta's prose is as uncontrived and free-flowing as her poetry. **Momma** is her own story, told in anecdote/diary, disjointed yet unified form. It runs up-and-down, on-and-off as does her life, her life as a mother of two daughters and occasional foster children, struggling to be a writer in between babies, dishes, lovers, and endless demands for her attention and energy.The immediacy of her experiences is all there on paper, undiluted, for each of us to live with her. "Why bother to tell all this anyway? because i know every woman in every house has her story & they're not in books & we must begin to tell how it is, to tell & share our lives with each other . . ." A potent and essential book.

182. ALTHER, Lisa. KINFLICKS. N.Y.: Knopf, 1976. $8.95.
A new writer, Lisa Alther is already being likened to Doris Lessing for her energetic drive to explore large areas of philosophy, science, and politics in her fiction. This first novel concerns a young woman's quest for liberation. When the book opens, Virginia Babcock Bliss is flying home to Tennessee, where her mother lies dying of a gruesome, mysterious disease. Virginia has already been through a series of adventures that echo Shulman's **Memoirs of an Ex-Prom Queen** and Piercy's **Small Changes,** and much of the story is her flashback to former roles: cheerleader, philosophy student, women's commune member, and unhappy wife. In this respect, **Kinflicks** breaks no new ground, although the wild, often grotesque humor, is entertaining: "She had me laughing at four in the morning," attests Lessing on the bookjacket. Between Virginia's reminiscences, however, we enter the mind of her disintegrating mother, and the reflections that we find there on motherhood and self-sacrifice are among the best ever written.

ANGELOU, Maya. *(1928-   ) Actress, poet, journalist, Maya Angelou was the Northern Coordinator for the Southern Christian Leadership Conference in the 1960s and later traveled to Africa, where she taught at the University of Ghana. Her latest collection of poetry is* **Oh Pray My Wings Are Gonna Fit Me Well** *(Random House, 1975). She now lives in California, where she produces television features and writes film screenplays.*

183. _____ I KNOW WHY THE CAGED BIRD SINGS. 1970. N.Y.: Bantam, 1971. $1.50.
An autobiography of the author's Arkansas childhood and her adolescence (mostly in San Francisco). It is written with a wonderful tone of irony and seriousness combined, a fine combination of black consciousness and the special experience of being a black woman. There are many brilliant descriptions, from the farce of hypocritical pompous white speakers at a high school graduation to adventures with a group of drop-out teenagers on the road in California and a job as the first black streetcar conductorette in San Francisco.

184. _____ GATHER TOGETHER IN MY NAME. 1974. N.Y.: Bantam, 1975. $1.50.
A continuation of **I Know Why The Caged Bird Sings**, this book encompasses such an astonishing range of experience that it's startling to discover that, by the story's end, the author is still in her teens. From cook to manager of her own brothel, from professional dancer to prostitute, Angelou endures a shattering series of disappointments and rejections (even the U.S. Army refuses her application, in 1946, because she once studied dancing at the California Labor School, an alleged "Communist organization"). Yet the author always springs back, ever confident of her own "sterling attributes." A nearly disastrous visit to Arkansas reveals how much she has grown in black pride and consciousness, and the book as a whole gives a grim picture of a post-war economy casting off the black workers, soldiers, and hangers-on that it no longer needs. Exceptionally good autobiography.

185. ARNOLD, June. APPLESAUCE. N.Y.: McGraw-Hill, 1966. O.P.
To the matriarchal tribe the tree was a symbol of fertility, but since then we have gone from Genesis to genocide. As a result of this, the tree in patriarchal culture is another phallus and the apple that Adam usually consumes (according to Liza, the heroine of **Applesauce**) is woman's energy. Originally an innocent, Liza offers her sexuality to a man, Gus. She marries him and has several children only to realize that the core of herself has been consumed. Taking over the persona of Gus, Liza reclaims the lost parts of herself: Eloise, a young upper-middle class girl trapped by her sexuality; Rebecca, a mother of small children, trying to be taken seriously when she returns to graduate school; and, lastly, Lila, pregnant and left "spread-eagled"—feet in exam-room stirrups, waiting for the doctor to come in "like the bird which prayed on Prometheus and peck away at her." The novel is somewhat difficult to follow, but is a moving account of a woman's struggle to love and accept herself.

186. _____ **THE COOK AND THE CARPENTER By the Carpenter**. Plainfield, Vermont: Daughters, Inc., 1973. $3.00.

Don't be sidetracked or confused by the use of neuter pronouns ("na", "nan") in this experimental novel. It's a woman's book, about women. The setting is a Texas commune where the cook, the carpenter, and various others struggle with age, race, and class differences while attempting to break power, role, and sexual expectations forced upon them by male society. **The Cook and the Carpenter** chronicles a whole chunk of women's movement herstory through the personal relationships and political activities of its characters. The author's multi-level focus allows the reader a vision of the past, present, and a possible future as women work together to share both anger and love for one another in non-destructive ways. Difficult reading at first (because of the pronouns) but well worth the initial effort.

187. _____ **SISTER GIN.** Plainfield, Vermont: Daughters, Inc., 1975. $4.00.

The most accessible and probably the best-crafted of June Arnold's novels, **Sister Gin** is the story of Bettina (46), Su (50), Mamie Carter (77), and their friends. More than anything else, it is a celebration of age. The women in **Sister Gin** are growing old: they have hot flashes, get drunk, cry, are lonely; but they also make love with each other, run for office, write plays, and form a "gang" to deal with rapists and other male troublemakers. Arnold's characters are incredibly real: the love affair between Su and Mamie Carter, the isolation of Su's mother, and the antics of the "Temple Gang" are all portrayed vividly with sympathy and humor. **Sister Gin** is a beautiful, painful, funny book, a tribute to the resiliency of all women, of all ages.

188. ARNOW, Harriette. THE DOLLMAKER. 1954. N.Y.: Avon, 1972. $1.50.

Set in the hills of Kentucky and war-time Detroit, this powerful and moving novel gives us an honest and intimate glimpse into the lives of the urban poor as they are exploited by landlords, public schools, unions, anti-communism, and each other. Gertie Nevels is a magnificent heroine, strong, capable, and wise. Her hopes and the creative spirit represented by her woodcarving are systematically destroyed by social forces that are too big for her when she yields to family pressures not to buy a farm independently and leaves the land to follow her husband to Detroit. In the transition from rural life to an urban industrial economy, the quality of everyone's life is altered dramatically. This book shows how the lives of women and children are particularly affected.

189. _____ **THE WEEDKILLER'S DAUGHTER.** N.Y.: Knopf, 1969. $6.95.

Arnow's first novel since **The Dollmaker** does not approach the greatness of its predecessor. Although it is less satisfactory artistically, it does present a strong and ingenious young heroine, and it is imbued with Arnow's acute consciousness of oppression. Fifteen-year-old Susie is the victim of both a regimented school system and a tyrannical father who hates communists, blacks, and all forms of natural growth. She resists dissimulating rather than rebelling: escapes for secret visits to the beloved relatives her father has broken with and conspires with kindred spirits at school.

190. BAMBARA, Toni Cade. GORILLA, MY LOVE. 1972. N.Y.: Pocket Books, 1973. $1.25.

Fifteen short stories, most of them excellent portrayals of black life, particularly the lives of black women of all ages. Many portray superbly tough and rebellious girls growing up in the ghetto, resisting the world in general and creeping femininity in particular. In "Basement" two women warn two little girls against men then go on to take their revenge against the super, who exposes himself. In "The Johnson Girls" a group of young women candidly discuss men. "The Survivor" is the complex, haunting story of an actress on the brink of madness, having a baby after the death of her husband.

191. BANNING, Margaret Culkin. THE VINE AND THE OLIVE. N.Y.: Harper & Row, 1964. O.P.

Stylistically weak, this is the story of a Catholic woman who is "successfully" married to a prominent corporation man, but who becomes involved in the birth control movement. This involvement becomes a major conflict between Clare and her husband, who feels that her speechmaking on this topic will ruin his career. In contrast to the rest of the book, the end is a total capitulation.

192. BASSING, Eileen. HOME BEFORE DARK. N.Y.: Bantam, 1958. O.P.

Ever since she was a teenager, Charlotte has imitated her popular stepsister in order to become socially acceptable. This has catastrophic results when she marries Arnold Bronn, a 40-ish college professor who wants a pretty, young wife who know her place and is an asset to his career. The difference between the real Charlotte (intelligent, aggressive, and unconventional) and Arnold's ideal finally causes Charlotte to break down. On the road back to health Charlotte forces herself to realize who Arnold really is (a pompous and egotistical bore) and who he really loves (her stepsister).

193. BERKMAN, Sylvia. BLACKBERRY WILDERNESS, 1959. Plainview, N.Y.: Books for Libraries Press. $11.25.

Eleven delicately-crafted short stories, often presenting lonely people in search of themselves in a world where human response is hard to find. "Et Encore Il Pleut" shows a Parisian waiter's shocking anti-woman malevolence; the title story traces a young woman writer's unhappiness back to the way she was let down as a child; "October Journey" is about an abandoned wife recovering from an illness.

194. BOWEN, Elenore Smith (Laura Bohannon). RETURN TO LAUGHTER: AN ANTHROPOLOGICAL NOVEL. 1954. N.Y.: Doubleday, current. $2.50.

Laura Bohannon, an American anthropologist, has given us an introspective view of her profession in this fictionalized account of a young woman's first field experience. Written in the first person, the book starts with details of life with a West African tribe and, for a while, it reads like a journal or autobiography. But soon we are drawn into the dramatic tensions of the plot. The anthropologist finds her own values coming into conflict with those of the culture she is supposed to analyze. We are given much fascinating information about women's lives in a pre-technological culture and we learn about the special problems which arise when an anthropologist is female.

195. BOYD, Blanche M. NERVES. Plainfield, Vermont: Daughters, Inc., 1973. $3.00.

The frightening downward spiral of four women's lives—mother, daughter, aunt, and family friend. Each is trapped within her own nameless misery, unable to share pain or confusion with those women closest to her. Thoughts are never fully spoken aloud, and the need to connect is never satisfied for any of the four. They seem incapable of reaching past husbands, lovers, and stepfathers to save each other. **Nerves** is a book about women in isolation, with no words to pinpoint their common oppression. It is depressing in that it offers not alternatives, but otherwise clearly written and undeniably "real".

196. BOYD, Shylah. AMERICAN MADE. 1975. Greenwich, Conn.: Fawcett, 1976. $1.95.
A real disappointment, this one, and it could have been terrific. After her mother's suicide, teenage Shylah goes to the Florida Keys to live with her Daddy, a racist bully who loathes all forms of female sexuality. Shylah is a born fighter, though. At least at first. From oppressive classrooms to hectic New York artist scene to fashionable insane asylum, Shylah, with the help of her women friends, asserts herself against the men who would convince her that she's worthless. Unfortunately, in the last quarter of the book, she's called back to Florida for a reunion with Daddy, who's now conveniently broken by terminal illness. Plot and prose nosedive into semi-coherent sentimentality. All is forgiven and Shylah marries Mr. Right, a faceless character twice her age—Hmmmm.

197. BOYLE, Kay. THE UNDERGROUND WOMAN. N.Y.: Doubleday, 1975. $7.95.
Kay Boyle deftly links contemporary history and the archetypes of myth to this very personal story of one woman's self-discovery. Athena, a professor of mythology, typifies a distinct class of women: liberal middle-aged, professional, she is also a mother whose one anguish concerns the loss of her daughter to a fanatic-led commune. Athena, outraged by the Vietnam war, goes to jail for demonstrating against it. The day-to-day realities of prison challenge her insular, academically detached concepts of life. In working with the other prisoners, she develops a sense of sisterhood beyond their well-marked differences. On leaving the jail, Athena still craves Dubonnet with a twist of lemon, but her contempt for her male counterparts who passed the time by conducting seminars on esoteric subjects, signals a change. Only two jarring descriptions mar this otherwise excellent novel: repeated references to the color of her black neighbor, and a pointlessly vicious media-caricature of a feminist. Both betray the prejudices of the nice liberalism that Kay Boyle was hoping to transcend.

198. BROOKS, Gwendolyn. MAUD MARTHA. N.Y.: AMS Press, 1953. $11.00.
The story of a black woman who grows up in Chicago. The novel begins when Maud Martha is six and ends when she is a married woman expecting her second child. there is a wonderful account of Maud Martha's first pregnancy and childbirth. Brooks's style is both poetic and humorous, and contains insights into what happens when love and marriage become substitutes for self-development, as well as into the effects of American racism on black people.

Courtesy Broadside Press, Detroit.

199. BROWN, Rita Mae. RUBYFRUIT JUNGLE. Plainfield, Vermont: Daughters, Inc., 1973. $4.00.

Poet Rita Mae Brown's first novel is unclassifiable. Within the space of its 217 pages, it is possible to experience everything from outright laughter to anger to tears. The assumption is that the book is autobiographical, and, although one sometimes doubts the plausibility of Brown's pre-pubescent radical lesbian politics, the narrative, if not every incident, is believable. From Pennsylvania to Florida to New York City, Molly, the "heroine," moves from audacious child to "outrageous," uncompromising adult in a series of funny/sad adventures which make **Rubyfruit Jungle** impossible to put down until the end. In much of the book, there seems to be a lack of sympathy for the oppression of many women (e.g. secretaries, mothers, wives), but the final chapters about Molly and her stepmother reveal a deep love and compassion for women, undiluted by the flippant humor of previous sections.

200. BROWN, Rosellen. STREET GAMES. N.Y.: Doubleday, 1974. $6.95.

this story collection might be likened to E.L. Master's **Spoon River Anthology**, that midwestern village having been transformed into Brooklyn's teeming, "semirenovated" George Street, where welfare mothers and junkies live side-by-side with social workers, "professional humanists," and affluent hip liberals. Nobody, with the exception of Grace Paley, can capture American urban voices like Rosellen Brown does. The addict's wife, the bewildered Lindsay appointee, the upwardly-mobile former street-lord—all pass before us in living, breathing color until it seems like **Street Games** is the work of not one author, but of many authors. Most of the stories are written in an immediate, straightforward style. One experiment, and a very entertaining one, is "Questionnaire to Determine Eligibility," a deceased woman's application form for admission to heaven. Don't miss this wonderful book.

201. _____ THE AUTOBIOGRAPHY OF MY MOTHER. Garden City, N.Y.: Doubleday, 1976. $7.95.

Once again Rosellen Brown gets thoroughly into her characters' voices and heads, and readers may find it hard choosing sides in this intricate tale of mother/daughter conflict. Renata, an obsolete flower-child, and her baby girl are forced by economics to go home to Renata's mother Gerda, a famous German-Jewish civil rights lawyer. The two women are total opposites: Gerda is cold and endlessly busy with abstract legal issues; Renata is passionate but ineffectual and inert. They haven't spoken to each other in eight years, but they immediately begin hurling accusations and judgments at each other once reunited. Like opposing lawyers, they present their lives as arguments, and the battle finally degenerates into a grim struggle over Renata's child. Complex and compelling reading.

202. BRYANT, Dorothy. ELLA PRICE'S JOURNAL. 1972. N.Y.: Signet, 1973. $1.25.

This is the diary of a woman who goes back to school after 15 years of marriage and begins to see her carefully-structured world in quite a different light—a development both unexpected and unwelcome. The tale contains everything from the struggle with her husband and family to the exploitative professor who stimulates her thinking and starts an affair with her, then drops her as she moves ahead. Ella is too self-aware to be real, but her confusion and her efforts to recreate herself are familiar and important.

203. BURCH, Pat. EARLY LOSSES. Plainfield, Vermont: Daughters, Inc., 1973. $3.00.

Freda Zax eats her way through adolescence. Her father is dead. Her mother and girlfriend are her pizza eating, potato chip munching sidekicks. Food as sublimation, the result is predictable: overweight. When Freda enters college and begins to de-sublimate, she experiences some early losses: weight, virginity, and her close, sisterly relationship with her mother. Burch does not give us in-depth psychological portraits of her characters, but she has a sense of humor, and the novel is a light and readable one that focuses on the surfaces of her characters' lives. The first portion dealing with the all girl mother/daughter/girlfriend eating triad is the best.

204. CALISHER, Hortense. HERSELF 1972. N.Y.: Dell, 1974. $1.75.

This experimental autobiography abandons strict chronological information in favor of

American 1950-present

issue-oriented concerns. Now middle-aged, the noted novelist, short story writer and critic relates her struggles as a writer in a style ranging from journalistic to metaphorical. Along with a self-conscious regard for sexual roles, Calisher talks about her Jewish background, two marriages, motherhood, anti-war activities in the 1960s, teaching, and her travels to the Far East. Though sometimes dogmatic on the subjects of literature and writing, her book will be compelling for those women caught between marriage and family and the desire for an adventurous literary/intellectual career.

205. _____ STANDARD DREAMING. 1972. N.Y.: Dell, 1974. $1.50.
An ongoing New York encounter group formed by parents of rebellious and/or self-destructive children is seen through the eyes of one of its members, Dr. Berners, whose own son is slowly starving himself to death in a mental hospital. The gaps between parents and children and among the adults themselves are explored realistically, at times even poignantly. Yet the novelistic style is so abstruse that separate circumstances and actions become obscured.

206. _____ QUEENIE. 1971. N.Y.: Arbor House. $6.95.
A slick stylish book about a precocious teenager whose only questions about sex are when and where to first have it. Queenie is raised in a Manhattan penthouse by her unmarried Aunt Aurine and her aunt's lover Oscar, whose unconventional middle-age lifestyle and indulgent love for Queenie give her nothing against which to rebel. Most appealing are the portraits of Aurine and Oscar and the comic antics of their social set; otherwise Queenie is an unbelievable, superficial character whose circumstances should have created a more complex character than this.

207. _____ IN THE ABSENCE OF ANGELS. 1948. Boston: Little, Brown, 1951. O.P.
Believed by some to be preeminently a writer of short stories, Calisher proves her skill in these superb, delicately-crafted vignettes. Compassionate, wry, deeply moved by the brief encounter, the author renders the pathos of contemporary life without sentimentality. Her tragedies are prosaic ones—an unfulfilled or unappreciated human life; the pain and disappointment inherent in family relations. Several of the stories involve the same character, a young girl named Hester raised by immigrant Jewish parents in New York, and her relationship with her mother. Its rich language and subtle moods make this collection well worth reading.

208. CARRIGHAR, Sally. HOME TO THE WILDERNESS. 1973. Baltimore: Penguin Books, 1974. $1.95.
When Sally Carrighar was five years old, her psychotic mother tried to strangle her. Narrowly escaping death, the girl grew up with a deeply disturbed parent who had been traumatized by the author's long, agonizing birth. Carrighar's story is a triumphant one, however. Never overdramatizing, she seeks out the reasons for her persecution and tells how she survived, built a radio-movie career and—after renouncing Hollywood—developed her near-mystical perceptions of the animal kingdom into a brilliant writing talent. Author of **One Day At Beetle Rock** and **Wild Heritage**, Carrighar is a widely-read naturalist today. Her autobiography is an amazing story of a sad and joyous life.

209. CHILDRESS, Alice. A HERO AIN'T NOTHIN BUT A SANDWICH. 1973. N.Y.: Avon, 1974. $ .95.
Benjie Johnson, 13, is nearly hooked on skag. Harlem pushers eased him into his first skin-pop, "I like how they watchin me and paying their respeck, lookin at me like they know I'm somebody fine." Dramatist Alice Childress centers on Benjie's network of relationships from Butler (his 'step-father' who cares but withdraws help and love because Benjie isn't his real son) to Nigeria Green (the Black Nationalist teacher at Benjie's grade school who struggles against passivity and desperation to make his class understand how, "they makin big profit from openin your veins & makin small profit trying to close them shut again. Y'll better learn to defend yourself.") The book is highly recommended for adolescents and could easily be adapted into a dramatic performance.

CROSS, Amanda *(pseudonym of Carolyn Heilbrun) The style of these mysteries (featuring Professor Kate Fansler) is lifted, almost directly, from Dorothy L. Sayers. Still, mystery fans should enjoy their comedy-of-feminist-manners appeal.*

210. _____ **IN THE LAST ANALYSIS** N.Y.: MacMillan, 1974. O.P.
Kate sets out to solve the murder of one of her female students in an attempt to protect the prime suspect—her ex-(male) lover.

211. _____ **THE JAMES JOYCE MURDER**. N.Y.: McMillan, 1967. O.P.
Kate ponders the sexual proclivities of academics and country-folk alike. Her friend Reed is in pursuit of Kate as well as killer.

212. _____ **POETIC JUSTICE**. 1970. N.Y.: Warner, current. $ .95.
After much soul-searching, (and contemplation of W.H. Auden) Kate agrees to marry Reed. Their engagement party features an aspirin murder.

---

213. DAVIS, Angela. WITH MY MIND ON FREEDOM: AN AUTO-BIOGRAPHY. 1974. N.Y.: Bantam Books, 1975. $1.95.
From her arrest, in 1970, on charges of murder and con-spiracy, to her acquittal 16 months later, Angela Davis was a victim of "correctional faci-lities" in both the New York City Women's House of Detention and the California prison system. Her autobiography is an intense statement linking these institutions of "justice" and her childhood in Birmingham, Alabama, with a government and economic system which thrives on class, race and sex hatred. Davis describes the

experiences of women in prison with compassion and honesty.
She tells how mutual support combats the isolation and apathy which prison autho-rities encourage. While most women prisoners are kept invisible, Davis' political commitment brought her media attention and public visibility. Her autobiography is also an engrossing account of her involvement with the black movement, her belief in socialism, and her eye-opening visit to Cuba. Unfortunately, her membership in the Communist Party is not explained enough. A valuable and related book is Kathryn W. Burkhart's **Women In Prison** (N.Y.: Popular Library, 1973. $1.75.)

214. DEMING, Barbara. PRISON NOTES. 1966. Boston: Beacon Press, current. $1.95.
This is a well-written chronicle which echoes the screams of many others, that "people don't belong in jail." Barbara Deming and 34 other Peace and Freedom Mar-chers were arrested in Albany, Georgia, in 1964. **Prison Notes** is a poignant account of the racist, sexist and coercive tactics within and outside of prison. It is enveloped in the philosophy and practice of nonviolent resistance. Deming's gentleness in no way obscures the violence and destructiveness of jails, city officials, and poverty.

215. _____ **WASH US AND COMB US.** N.Y.: Grossman Publishers, 1972. $8.95.

This collection of short stories is Barbara Deming's first book of fiction. A political activist and feminist, Deming emphasizes life-affirming attitudes and human contact. Her characters struggle to meet across barriers of age, sex, and nationality. The relationships between the young woman and her grandmother in "Death and the Old Woman" and the middle-aged woman writer and the young male sculptor in the title story are particularly well-developed and moving. Deming's style is very clear and uncluttered; her words have an impact and significance beyond the specific events of the stories. Yet it is not so much the events, but rather the human beings she has created which linger long after one has finished the book.

216. DIDION, Joan. PLAY IT AS IT LAYS. 1970. N.Y.: Bantam, current. $1.25.

If life is a crap game, a rattlesnake under every rock, "Why play? Why not?" Sizzling heat, coca cola, and cigarettes, sleeping poolside, up every morning by ten o'clock to drive aimlessly back and forth on the freeways, raped by a motorcycle gang in one of her husband's pictures, mother of a retarded child, casual fuck—ex-actress-model Maria breaks down on the set of Beverly Hills culture. The terse sentence-chapter style synchronizes the momentum of Maria's mind with L.A. A vision of women totally exploited, as compelling as it is defeating. The best novel about Hollywood since Nathaniel West.

217. _____ **RUN RIVER.** 1963. N.Y.: Astor-Honor, $7.95.

A novel about an upper-class southern family, somewhat in the Faulkner tradition. It is the story of Lily, a woman always associated with wealthy men. She herself has had few, if any, alternatives in her life.

218. DILLARD, Annie. PILGRIM AT TINKER CREEK. 1974. N.Y.: Bantam, 1975. $1.95.

For the past ten years, city-born Annie Dillard has lived in Virginia's Blue Ridge Mountains. This book chronicles one year in her life on the banks of Tinker Creek, where she writes about the beauty and violence of nature "in the raw." The questions she asks herself are philosophical rather than socio-political so one never learns how she sees herself in relation to those who have neither the money nor the leisure to be a latter-day Thoreau. The detailed descriptions of animal and plant organisms are at times quite interesting, but Dillard's writing style has a tendency toward distracting choppiness. All in all, the book is recommended only for those with an unflagging naturalist bent.

219. DI PRIMA, Diane. MEMOIRS OF A BEATNIK. N.Y.: Olympia, 1969. O.P.

This is a pornographic novel about a young female poet involved in the 1950s Bohemian scene. Di Prima tells us a lot about her bisexual development, but, sadly, very little about her art. The sex is a mixed bag of positive experience and living out male fantasy.

220. DISNEY, Doris Miles. SHADOW OF A MAN. 1965. Manor Books, 1975. $1.25.

Maggie Thayer has a seemingly ideal nuclear family/ marriage. Her husband is clean-cut, good-looking and successful. But is he really a rapist-murderer? Chilling revelations from America's finest writer of grisly suspense.

221. DIZENZO, Patricia. PHOEBE. N.Y.: Bantam, 1970. $ .95.
Although this book is written in language which is very accessible to teenagers and presents an accurate picture of many aspects of young people's lives, it is not one that we would recommend to teenagers. Dizenzo's portrayal of a young girl "in trouble" is a picture of inescapable horror which seems expressly designed to frighten young women away from sex.

222. _____ AN AMERICAN GIRL. 1971. N.Y.: Holt, Rinehart & Winston, 1974. $4.95.
The first-person story of a middle-class girl living through early adolescence in the early 1950s. The many brief, journal-like entries gradually recreate a 1950s atmosphere. A particularly skillful device is the girl's re-tellings of movie plots which allow us to see, in a participatory way, the interaction between a child and her culture and the messages it gives her. The girl is depicted as absolutely real, moving, and worth caring about.

223. DREXLER, Rosalyn. THE COSMOPOLITAN GIRL. 1974. N.Y.: Warner, 1976. $1.75.
Love, sex, romance, marriage . . . Are they dead? A woman bored with the singles scene forms a lasting relationship with her talking dog, Pablo. Though certainly not to everyone's taste, the novel is a hilarious spoof on relationships parental and heterosexual.

224. _____ I AM THE BEAUTIFUL STRANGER. 1965. N.Y.: Dell, 1966. O.P.
the naively-wise diary of a young girl growing up in the 1960s, describing with equal solemnity the dramas in her Jewish family, her crush on a schoolfriend's brother, and interludes where she plays nymphet to older men.

225. _____ ONE OR ANOTHER. N.Y.: Dutton, 1970. O.P.
A strange book, we don't claim to understand the author's viewpoint or design. Reality and fantasy merge and separate as the story unfolds: a woman married to a teacher who is a jealous right-wing sadist, has affairs and longs to be free. The writing is experimental, there are numerous word games; madness and sanity lose their polarity in a kaleidoscopic whir.

226. _____ TO SMITHEREENS. N.Y.: Norton, 1972. $5.95.
This is the story of a woman who becomes a wrestler to satisfy her boyfriend's fantasy life and because she hasn't much else to do. The book is a curious blend of feminism and male-oriented language and behavior. This is at least partly due to the fact that a woman and a man alternate as first-person narrators. It does seem that in many ways Rosa, the main character, is struggling towards a self-definition.

227. DURHAM, Marilyn. THE MAN WHO LOVED CAT DANCING. 1972. N.Y.: Dell, 1973. $1.75.
In this novel described by some as a "feminist western," a woman fleeing her husband becomes hostage to bandits fleeing the law. Whether the description as feminist is merited depends on one's definition. The book doesn't advocate separation from men, changing society, or even sisterhood; one has to be satisfied with a realistic picture of the oppresion of women in the Old West, and a main character who has insights into her own and other women's oppression. Their land stolen, the buffalo killed—the Plains Indians are accurately and sympathetically described.

228. EMSHWILLER, Carol. JOY IN OUR CAUSE. 1974. N.Y.: Harper & Row. $6.95.
Carol Emshwiller is an innovative writer. Her life is the raw material for several of her stories—as wife, mother, writer—roles viewed separately and in conflict. These pieces are a delightful blend of wit and surrealism. In the second half of the collection, the stories become more fantastic and the link with her own life less obvious. In "Methapyrilene Hydrochloride Sometimes Helps," a woman has been operated on so many times that she is a mass of artificial organs. And then there is a fable about a

middle-aged, middle-class woman's enthusiasm for, and ambivalence toward, the women's movement. She is marching with thousands of others, baby strapped on her back, toward a women's paradise.

229. FOX, Paula. DESPERATE CHARACTERS. 1970. N.Y.: Harcourt, Brace, Jovnovich, 1974. $4.95.
Sophie and her husband live elegantly while New York City disintegrates around them; they feel besieged as the chaos of the 1960s erupts. A well-written novel about the "quiet desperation" of middle-class lives.

230. GIOVANNI, Nikki. GEMINI. N.Y.: Viking, 1971. $1.95.
Giovanni calls this book "an extended autobiographical statement on my first twenty-five years of being a black poet." Each chapter can actually stand on its own, which makes this a good book to use in the classroom. Of special interest to women is "Don't Have a Baby Til You Read This." In this chapter Giovanni recounts her experience of giving birth to her son with a type of detail rarely seen in literature.

231. GODWIN, Gail. THE PERFECTIONISTS. N.Y.: Harper & Row, 1970. O.P.
When Dane marries, she takes on not only a husband who is an intense and demanding English psychotherapist, but also his three-year-old son who refuses to speak or to respond to her. The novel perceptively explores Dane's relationship with her husband, her stepson, and several other women. The book offers real insights into the grimness of the female condition, but its ending is something of a shock.

232. _____ GLASS PEOPLE. 1972. N.Y.: Dell, 1975. $1.95.
Francesca is a beautiful woman. Cameron Bolt, a ruthlessly ambitious and ultra-conservative Californian politican, marries her simply for her perfect image. Realizing the emptiness of her life, she tries to break away; she has an affair, flounders helplessly in search of a job in New York City, and discovers soon enough that she has absolutely no resources to aid her in surviving on her own. A novel with a strong, sad message, though its insights are perhaps sparser than those presented in **The Perfectionists.**

233. _____ THE ODD WOMAN. 1974. N.Y.: Berkeley Medallion, 1976. $1.95.
An insomniac professor of Victorian literature, Jane Clifford lives with one foot in 19th century fantasy, the other in 20th century reality. Thirty-two years old and unmarried, she empathizes with the predicaments of the five odd women—women without husbands—in George Gissing's novel, **The Odd Women**, written at the turn of the century. Gissing's odd women, like Jane, have certain choices to make about how to integrate love, economic security, and independence in their lives and are often lonely and anxious in the process. Godwin's novel focuses on Jane's anxieties and her relationships with her lover, family, and friends. Particularly interesting are the personal histories of three generations of women in Jane's family: grandmother, mother, and daughters (Jane and Emily)—all (with the exception of Emily) insomniacs.

234. GOULD, Lois. SUCH GOOD FRIENDS. 1970. N.Y.: Dell, 1971. $1.25.
Julie is keeping watch at the hospital during the grave and sudden illness of her young husband. During this time she learns more about his life than she can handle and gets involved with "friends" all too willing to prey on her misery. Some readers are alienated by the chatty tone, the destructive sexuality found in these pages; others find it justified by the sympathetic portrayal of a woman in crisis.

235. _____ NECESSARY OBJECTS. 1972. N.Y.: Dell, 1973. $1.75.
The tale of four Jewish princesses, daughters of a department-store dynasty, and the objects necessary to their super-rich, soul-destroying lives. A boring and gossipy book, unredeemed by the larger vision of Gould's earlier work.

236. _____ FINAL ANALYSIS. 1974. N.Y.: Avon, 1975. $1.75.
The author again writes about chic, zany, neurotic New York lifestyles, and, despite

some superficial parodies of women's consciousness-raising, psychotherapy, and the Manhattan publishing scene, manages to present insights into male-female relationships. She features a young woman who is sensitive, talented, attractive, and highly insecure while struggling with a writing career and her resistant lover-ex-psychiatrist. Unfortunately, the author has chosen to let her heroine remain nameless throughout the book, making it harder for the reader to grasp her wholeness as a character and as a woman.

237. GRAU, Shirley Ann. THE KEEPERS OF THE HOUSE. 1964. Greenwich, Conn: Fawcett, 1971. $1.25.
a novel about a southern white woman reared in the tradition of southern gentility and filling the roles expected of her by her husband, family, and town. Ultimately, a revelation from her family history forces her to stand alone against them all. This novel dealing with troubled race relations in the South won the Pulitzer Prize for 1964.

238. GREEN, Hannah (Joanne Greenberg). I NEVER PROMISED YOU A ROSE GARDEN. 1964. N.Y.: Signet, current. $1.25.
Already something of a classic, this book gives a powerful but unsentimental picture of the experience of mental illness which includes its strengths as well as its nightmares. Deborah, an institutionalized teenager, works with her therapist (a woman doctor) to return to a reality which is acknowledged to have its nightmares, too.

239. GREENBERG, Joanne. IN THIS SIGN. 1970. N.Y.: Avon, 1972. $1.50.
Writing here under her own name, the author of the previous book focuses now on a deaf couple. She tells of their long climb from abject poverty and horrifying ignorance (taken by every shyster, used by courts and landlords, unable to communicate even to the midwife who comes to attend at births) to a life of decency, and of the effect of this struggle on their "hearing" daughter.

240. GUY, Rosa. BIRD AT MY WINDOW. 1966. O.P.
Bird At My Window is a powerful and unforgettable novel. At age 38, Wade Williams, who has grown up on Harlem's Lenox Ave., has felt the effects of every kind of discrimination. Wade is confronted with the insanity of white racism throughout his life: in an early losing battle to desegregate a school, trying to find work, and even as a soldier in World War II. His rage finally leads him to destroy the people he is closest to, including his sister Faith, the one person he truly loves. Guy is telling about a common situation: people's violent reaction to oppression. Wade had gradually become obsessed with the need to stop his tragically parasitic mother and his exploitative brother. Turning from the burden he had always felt to be his, that of filling his father's shoes by supporting the family, Wade begins to see his mother as the one who has killed his dreams. "To have a dream you have to have an image and she never had one except of a man pinned to a cross." Clearly the crime that causes all others in this novel is that of racism.

241. _____ **RUBY**. N.Y.: Viking Press. 1976.

In spite of its disappointing conventional ending, **Ruby** is a fine novel about a lesbian relationship between two black women. Ruby, who is under the thumb of her old-fashioned West Indian father, falls in love with Daphne, a woman in her Harlem high school class. Ruby finds that she has much to learn from Daphne. For one thing Daphne's dead father had been a self-educated passionate man who was a leftist and black nationalist. After his accidental death, Daphne had vowed to realize his ideals in herself and she shares these ideas with Ruby. Ruby and Daphne's affair is circumscribed by their youth and their dependence on parents for survival. **Ruby** is highly recommended for high school readers.

242. HAGGERTY, Joan. DAUGHTERS OF THE MOON. N.Y.: Bobbs-Merrill, 1971.

This book tells of a friendship growing into a love affair between two women, both pregnant and taking refuge from unhappy lives on an island off Spain. The structure of the book is as innovative as its content. Much of the story is recalled during labor. The handling of switches in time and the occasional imagistic quality of the style can be disconcerting, but the book can be highly recommended for its bold content, its richness in feelings for women, and its strong feminist identification.

243. HANSBERRY, Loraine. TO BE YOUNG, GIFTED, AND BLACK. Adapted by Robert Nemiroff. 1969. N.Y.: New American Library, 1970. $1.25.

In 1959, Lorraine Hansberry was "the youngest American playwright, the fifth woman, the only black writer ever to win the New York Drama Critics Circle Award for 'The Best Play of the Year.' Six years later, at the age of 34, Lorraine Hansberry was dead of cancer." (from the Foreword) In this "autobiography"—a posthumous collage of Hansberry's speeches, plays, letters, pictures, interviews, and even a note to the postman—her attitude is consistently one of hope, encouragement, and pride in the struggles of black people, a really determined faith in humanity. this is an excellently crafted collection; it gives the reader a real sense of the vibrant, struggling artist that Lorraine Hansberry was. If you ever get a chance to see the stage production, do so; it's wonderful.

244. HELLMAN, Lillian. AN UNFINISHED WOMAN. 1969. N.Y.: Bantam, 1974. $1.50.

It's a short book for such a long, full life, but what's talked about seems to be what mattered, and it's talked about in a remarkably open manner. Lillian Hellman is a first-st-rate playwright (**The Children's Hour, The Little Foxes**). She has also been involved in left-wing politics. She writes of her experiences in Spain during the Civil War, in Russia during World War II, and in the U.S. during the McCarthy period. Of particular interest to women is a chapter on her relationships with two black women.

Lillian Hellman E.GM.

245. _____ PENTIMENTO. 1973. N.Y.: Signet, 1974. $1.95.

When old paint on canvas ages, it sometimes becomes transparent—uncovering the original picture as conceived by the artist, often quite different from the surface design. This process called "pentimento" is Hellman's way of describing her literary journey backward, uncovering the meanings in past relationships with people and places. In simple, sharp, beautiful prose these memoirs supplement **An Unfinished Woman**, describing characters from the author's childhood and adulthood, all of whom are dead. Especially memorable is the story of Julia, a longtime friend who was to die tragically at the hands of the Nazis for her underground activities in Europe. Hellman's ties to individuals and to the theater are so profound that the episodes in **Pentimento** will linger in the reader's memory. Hellman's unspoken acceptance of life is not without sadness and indignation at the course of events she has witnessed—hence the book's moral as well as literary value.

246. _____ SCOUNDREL TIME. Boston: Little, Brown & Co., 1976. $8.50.

Hellman's memoir of her experience during the McCarthy period and its aftermath. Admitting a sense of resistance to writing about the subject, she focusses on "what happened to me and a few others." The result is a chronicle of personal courage and determination and at the same time a striking analysis of the climate that fed the "Red Scare" and led so many people to sell out their consciences. Her recollections are clear, moving and angry, although the anger is directed less at McCarthy, Nixon, and the rest who tried to make political fortunes from cheap intimidation than at the intellectuals who caved in so easily to their threats. She feels that if a few more people had faced down the blacklist when it was first threatened, it might not have become so destructive a reality.

247. HENDERSON, Zenna. PILGRIMMAGE, THE BOOK OF THE PEOPLE. 1961. N.Y.: Avon, current. $ .95.

These stories tell of "The People," who are stranded when their space ship crashes on earth. They come from a culture which had rejected materialism and chosen, instead, to cultivate mental powers. They know how to do magical things, like fly, and profoundly important things like heal and communicate. But on Earth they are different, and, on Earth, "different is dead". Some respond by concealing their powers and using them in secret, others grimly try to repress and deny. Each story deals with a different aspect of the problem of identity and conformity; each new tale slightly upsets and rearranges the conclusions of the previous one.

248. HOBSON, Laura Zametkin. GENTLEMEN'S AGREEMENT. 1947. N.Y.: Avon. O.P.

A novel of anti-semitism in Post-World War II. It is a good story and a sensitive one as far as it goes, but it lacks insight into more subtle effects of discrimination, such as self-hatred. It is remarkable today, in that it examines only one facet of prejudice, making no connection between anti-semitism and the oppression of other minorities or of women.

249. _____ THE TENTH MONTH. 1971. N.Y.: Dell, 1972. $1.25.

The convincing account of a professionally established single woman who learns at the age of 40 that she is pregnant. She has wanted the pregnancy for years but never expected it would happen. She decides to have the child, but keeps her pregnancy secret and eventually presents the baby as adopted. Along with its theme of the single mother, this is a uniquely honest account of the importance of sexuality in a woman's life.

250. HOLIDAY, Billie. LADY SINGS THE BLUES. N.Y.: Lancer, 1965. O.P.
This oral history of a great black female artist clearly documents the oppression of poor black women in America. Billie Holiday's life was a struggle against racism, drugs, poverty, and men; yet she still managed to sing. Holiday's verbal style, aside from being extremely readable, permits her to present the truth about her life with vividness and perception: "You can be up to your boobies in white satin, with gardenias in your hair and no sugar cane for miles, but you can still be working on the plantation."

251. HOWARD, Jane. A DIFFERENT WOMAN. N.Y.: Avon Books, 1974. $1.95.
Former Life staff writer Jane Howard has perfected the art of personal narrative. Her new book, a collage of capsule portraits of American women from Arizona to New Hampshire, maintains an excellent balance between anecdote, information, and personal herstory. Anyone who grew up midwestern will especially enjoy the description of her Illinois roots and family ties. She writes of her own and other women's lives with great humor and insight. Unfortunately, however, she seems to regard vocally feminist women as "abrasive" and extreme. Her bias is in favor of "those Closet Feminists", as she calls them, "who wrest sap from trees, fish from the seas, . . . fashion quilts from scraps of cloth . . . [and] yoked to their menfolk, . . . flourish on a fraction of the options granted most of us." These are the subjects of her book. Although one would have hoped for a more sympathetic attitude toward the women's movement, **A Different Woman** does give a varied and immensely readable presentation of some aspects of American womanhood.

252. HOWARD, Maureen. BRIDGEPORT BUS. 1965. N.Y.: Curtis Books. O.P.
Mary Agnes Keely, a 35-year-old virgin working for a zipper factory, suddenly decides to leave her old mother and seek freedom. In New York City she finds a job, Bohemia, friends, and a lover before falling pregnant after a casual encounter. She is an unconventional and highly likable heroine. The book is well-written and extremely entertaining, and positive.

253. HOWE, Fanny. FIRST MARRIAGE. N.Y.: Avon, 1974. $2.95.
An insightful and poignant book about growing up to be a woman. It's well-written in a very terse, modern style; Howe constructs a series of scenes, each of which stands for a short time, then fades into the next one. Though the narrator's voice, like those of the characters, is flat, and understated, the result is dramatic, exposing the myriad pains, conflicts, and bittersweet emotions life offers against a backdrop of gray, everyday existence. Though not a very cheerful book, its style is unusual and very readable, its characters are familiar and real.

254. HULME, Kathryn. THE NUN'S STORY. 1956. N.Y.: Pocket Book, 1974. $1.25.
This once-controversial book, the fictionalized biography of an ex-nun whom the author befriended in postwar Europe, tells of a woman's 17 years in a Catholic sisterhood and how her conflicting roles of worldly nurse and unworldly nun finally drove her to leave the convent in 1944 and work for the Belgian underground. Step by step, we follow Sister Luke through the rigorous, depersonalizing novitiate then on to her mission assignments: the first at a women's insane asylum where she sees an in-

mate stab a sister-nurse, the second at a "white" hospital in the Belgian Congo where another nun is murdered by a black man. Although this book was never intended to be political, it leaves a vivid impression of how altruistic women, having surrendered their autonomy, can become the tools of repressive institutions and the random victims of rebellion.

255. HUNTER, Kristin. GOD BLESS THE CHILD. 1964. O.P.

Three generations of black women, Rosie (age 10 when the novel begins), Queenie (her mother), and Lourinda (her grandmother), desperately cling to their conflicting tactics of survival. Rosie is a combination of her mother's cynicism and her grandmother's belief that money buys dignity and acceptance into the white world. Rosie's audacity and energy enable her to take on two full-time jobs and to cut through the competitive threats of the underworld. She becomes a "financial success", drowning in bills, illusions and exhaustion. **God Bless The Child** is a poignant and compelling story about poverty and racism, and how people in the same situation are pitted against each other because the controlling world of the "white machine" is always breathing down their necks.

256. ISABEL, Sharon. YESTERDAY'S LESSONS. The Women's Press Collective, 5251 Broadway, Oakland, Calif. 94618, 1974.

Growing up in a poor community in California in the 1950s, Sharon survives the deprivation of her home, neighborhood and school through a painful system of balancing self-denial and overwhelming need—balancing the self-hatred of the oppressed with the sense of pride that is the code of her community. High school actually becomes a happy time for Sharon as she gains awareness of her own strength, gets a glimpse of the possibilities of sexuality and (at least for the length of her senior year) manages to block out the reality of a careerless and difficult future. Sharon's recognition of her love for Jan, her closest friend, leads her to know that this is a part of herself that she cannot and will not deny. The strength of her lesbian identity—even through troubled times, personal depression and the upheaval of relationships—is real and moving. Of special interest (because so little explored in literature) are Sharon's experiences in the Army, which she, like many working-class kids, saw as her only job opportunity after high school and her very positive experiences with a women's ball team. Reading **Yesterday's Lessons** is like talking to a friend across your kitchen table. It is an important book.

Wendy Cadden from "Yesterday's lessons." Courtesy Women's Press Collective.

JACKSON, Shirley (1919-1965)**Life Among The Savages** and **Raising Demons** *amused a wide audience with autobiographical accounts of "womanly" pursuits. Then she wrote* **The Witchcraft Of Salem Village** *for children; virtually all the rest of her short stories and novels bring into sharp focus the hell under the commonplaces of life, the cruelty, terror, morbidity, alienation, and the surreal inherent in the human, especially the female, condition.*

257. _____ **LIFE AMONG THE SAVAGES**. 1953. Included in **THE MAGIC OF SHIRLEY JACKSON**. N.Y.: Sunburst, 1971. $5.95.

A very funny book about mothering young children in the late 1940s/early 1950's. It is not written with feminist consciousness, but Jackson is a true and thorough observer. A conversation between two mothers is shown to be a contest. Parental sex roles are unconsciously divided. There is a chilling moment when a son has been naughty and his sister whines, over and over, "I'm good, aren't I? I'm good." The same sister is later transformed (temporarily) from a gun-toting cowgirl to a prissy "little lady" by a first grade teacher.

258. _____ **THE HAUNTING OF HILL HOUSE.** 1959. N.Y.: Popular Library, current. $1.25.
The gothic horror story of four people who come to live in an "evil" house for "experimental purposes." Often one is not sure if what seems to be happening on the surface is "real." Is one woman paranoid, or are the others conspiring to drive her over the brink, their acts of caring really calculated to drive her crazy? Not a "scary" book that evaporates after reading, but one whose horror remains and leaves one with a thousand questions.

259. _____ **WE HAVE ALWAYS LIVED IN THE CASTLE.** 1962. N.Y.: Viking, current. $2.45.
The story of a deep love relationship between two sisters. One of them poisoned their entire family six years earlier, and now lives in seclusion with the only survivor of that episode. The world outside is too horrible. Paranoia—or is it? In the story, their only encounters with the "outside" are terribly destructive. Beautifully told through the eyes of the "mad" sister.

260. _____ **Short Stories.** In **THE MAGIC OF SHIRLEY JACKSON.** N.Y.: Sunburst, 1971. $5.95, and **THE LOTTERY.** N.Y.: Avon, current. $ .95.
(Many of the stories appear in both collections.)
Jackson's skill here lies in creating ordinary characters, most often housewives and young "working girls," who do ordinary things, and who are believable and interesting. She focuses on their alienation and "quiet desperation," and on the relationship between these feelings and a person's capacity for cruelty. The collections contain some humorous stories which remind us how fine the line is between comedy and tragedy.

261. JAFFE, Rona. MR. RIGHT IS DEAD. N.Y.: Simon & Schuster, 1960. O.P.
A collection of short stories of varying quality. At her best, Jaffe is very insightful about people's fantasy lives and the part that they play in creating female and male roles; at her worst, she presents us with elitist and decadent characters one can care little about. "Rima and the Bird Girl" is a potentially consciousness-raising tale about a woman who changes her identity with every man she meets.

262. JOHNSON, Diane. THE SHADOW KNOWS. 1974. N.Y.: Pocketbooks, 1976. $1.95.
This compelling (often comic) novel is a real murder mystery. There is no solution and no dashing male sleuth. There is only N., a real Everywoman, autonomous and fighting to stay alive. The book closes with a violence that is both our tragedy and our vindication. Women are not paranoid: our recognition of male threat and our fears are fully justified. Important reading.

263. JONES, Gayle. CORREGIDORA. 1975. N.Y.: Bantam, 1976. $1.75.
A terse, tightly-controlled vision of how the memory of slavery plagues black women and men long after legal emancipation has taken place. Blues singer Ursa has been charged by the women in her family to "make generations" in order to bring eternal witness against Corregidora, the 19th century slavemaster-pimp who fathered Ursa's grandmother and mother. However, during a fight with her possessive husband Ursa is made sterile by a terrible fall down a stairway. **Corregidora** raises many disturbing, often infuriating, questions: Is male tyranny best met with love and forgiveness or with rage and withdrawal? How can a woman break out of the injury/revenge cycle? And finally, Jones asks, are the slavemaster's crimes any worse than the pain that black people inflict upon one another? Whether you are convinced

by the hasty, conciliatory ending, you are sure to find Gayle Jones a unique new voice speaking on blackness, sexuality, and the ways in which oppression twists love and hatred until they are nearly indistinguishable from each other.

264. _____ EVA'S MAN. N.Y.: Random House, 1976. $6.95.
This is an eerie companion to Jones' first novel. **Corregidora** ends with an act of fellatio; **Eva's Man** begins with an act of sexual mutilation. Eva Medina Canada has been in a psychiatric prison five years for poisoning a casual pick-up and then biting off his penis. Doctors, officials, and Eva's lesbian cell mate question her relentlessly: "Did you love him? . . . You're a very lonely woman, aren't you? . . . It's like a bad dream, isn't it?" Meanwhile, Eva's thoughts range dizzily back over her past: a childhood crushed between sexual abuse and fear of punishment; marriage to a jealous older man; street-life where all the men breezily assume that Eva must be a whore since she isn't attached to any one man. Eva fights against being defined by the hostile and/or the ignorant. Jones' stream-of-consciousness style is more intricate here than in **Corregidora**, the complexity pulling the reader right into a life that might have been too strange and painful to approach in a straightforward narrative.

265. JONG, Erica. FEAR OF FLYING. 1973. N.Y.: Signet, 1974. $1.95.
Fear of Flying is a funny book. Erica Jong's wit and caustic humor make her descriptions of people and places the novel's best asset, and there are many who may agree that it is the modern woman's erotic novel. Unfortunately, however, Jong's feminism almost gets lost amid the actual and imaginary sexual exploits of her cosmopolitan heroine, Isadora Wing. Isadora's sexuality seems to take up where Helen Gurley Brown left off, and although she eventually comes to recognize the emptiness inherent in her fantasy "zipless fuck," the alternatives she then considers seem limited, i.e. exclusively in terms of men (except for one brief allusion to a dream about Colette.) Undoubtedly, **Fear of Flying** will engender a variety of responses among readers: it is possible to both appreciate the author's writing ability and question her rather male-biased presentations of female sexuality.

266. KAHN, Kathy. HILLBILLY WOMEN. 1973. N.Y.: Avon, 1974. $1.25.
Hillbilly Women is so informative and personal that the reader may feel like she has just had coffee with a waitress from North Carolina or just overheard conversations on a picket line. Eighteen Southern Appalachian women talk about their lives, be it in the coal mining camps of Goose Creek, Kentucky, or the factories of Cincinnati, Ohio. Their analyses are straightforward, and their anger is not seen apart from the historical, economic, and cultural circumstances which pervade their lives. The details of hillbilly life are trying and grim, but the determination and energy with which these women talk about their organizing efforts (in health clinics, a sewing factory, food and craft coops), their religion and their music are exhilarating proof that they will not be "walked on" anymore.

267. KALLEN, Lucille. GENTLEMEN PREFER SLAVES. 1964 as **OUTSIDE THERE, SOMEWHERE—!** N.Y.: Beagle, 1972. O.P.
This fast-paced and witty novel about a suburban housewife's struggle for a meaningful life has a surprisingly high level of consciousness about the nature of male-dominated society. Angry and bored, Ruth decides to tackle a TV writing career. It turns out to be big stuff, both salary- and time-wise. Although her neighbors and her husband give her a hard time, Ruth fights off both guilt and submissiveness. With the help of her friend Vicki, a woman doctor who seems almost too perfect to be real, our heroine becomes a role model for other housewives in her community.

268. KARP, Lila. THE QUEEN IS IN THE GARBAGE. 1969. N.Y.: Belmont, 1971. $ .95.
Seven months pregnant, Harriet goes into labor. In the hospital, real events alternate in her mind with dreams and flashbacks: to her Jewish family and the mother who hated her; a childhood peppered with sexual experimentation, molestation, and repression; then marriage, miscarriage, abortion, divorce; a lover who turns sadist. The whole book, with its brusque, brutal style, is a bitter catalog of a woman's pain. In her foreword, Kate Millett hails it as a new and unfeminine kind of book.

269. KAUFMAN, Sue. THE HAPPY SUMMER DAYS. N.Y.: Scribner's, 1959. O.P.
An ambitious attempt to expose not just one but a whole group of posturing adults brought together while spending the summer on a resort island. While some portraits are well done and create life-like, moving human beings, the book falls short of its larger objective and cannot make sense of the whole group Kaufman has set out to study.

270. _____ DIARY OF A MAD HOUSEWIFE. 1967. N.Y.: Bantam, 1975. $ .95.
An honest account of a troubled woman struggling within the confines of her role, her lifestyle, and her husband's unreasonable demands to find some sense of her identity. Tina plays with the idea of resisting her psychiatrist-approved "feminine role," but decides that for her there are no other options. Many readers will probably consider the ending unsatisfactory. The movie based on the book robs Tina of any integrity.

271. _____ THE HEADSHRINKER'S TEST. 1971. N.Y.: Bantam. O.P.
Kaufman excels at revelations of self-deluded characters. This long and colorful monologue reveals the sick insecurities of a neurotic man, but offers little in the way of universal experience or insight.

272. KELLOGG, Marjorie. TELL ME THAT YOU LOVE ME, JUNIE MOON. 1968. N.Y.: Popular Library, 1975. $1.50.
This is the story of three ugly, physically handicapped and psychically damaged human beings who decide to try and make it together in a hostile world. Junie Moon, the female of the trio, is developed as a unique and beautiful individual, and the two men are suitable complements to her. The book portrays them with great dignity and sensitivity, and stresses the idea that persons rejected by social norms are in fact unique and complex people.

273. _____ LIKE THE LION'S TOOTH. N.Y.: New American Library, 1973. $1.25.
A bloodcurdling, heartbreaking book about the lives of children—the bruised and battered children of the poor and desperate of New York City, brought together in a school for problem children.

274. KROEBER, Theodora. THE INLAND WHALE. 1959. Berkeley: University of California Press, current. $2.45.
This remarkable volume contains retellings of nine stories from the American Indian literature of California. Each focuses on a woman. the author tells us: "I have tried not to revalue, not to judge the women whose stories I tell, but to bring them to you, to whom they are strange, as they were seen by their peers." As beautifully written and engrossing as the stories themselves, is the 60-page section at the end of the book, which gives us background on the individual stories and makes stylistic and thematic comparisons with the literatures of non-native cultures. A bibliography of sources is also included.

275. KUMIN, Maxine. THE DESIGNATED HEIR. N.Y.: Viking, 1974. $6.95.
Pulitzer-Prize winning poet Maxine Kumin has failed to move beyond stereotypes in this story of an independent Boston-Brahmin woman and her involvement with a politically-committed Jewish man from New York. Jeff Rabinowitz becomes the more interesting character as his deep personal values are the ones most vividly expressed.

Robin Parks, less substantially drawn, declares, "I want to come into my own," but the reader never finds out exactly what this statement means. Robin pursues a vague self-liberation, rarely analyzing her feelings as a teacher, for example, and there is little psychological exploration of what one would guess to be strong emotional reactions to her mother's alcoholism and discovered lesbian affair. Appealing, however, is the author's funny, sensitive depiction of the personality clashes between Robin's two dowager guardians, Gran and Tante, who are lovable yet manipulative vestiges of old-guard Boston society.

276. LEE, Harper. TO KILL A MOCKINGBIRD. 1960. N.Y.: Popular Library, current. $1.50.
If you read this book in high school, as most of us did, you may be surprised to find paternalism toward blacks and women in it upon rereading. Still it remains a classic—beautifully written, human, warm; it generally speaks of all that is most good and most evil in people and of the compromises that most people live in order to survive.

277. LEFFLAND, Ella. MRS. MUNCK. 1970. Boston: Houghton Mifflin. O.P.
In her first novel, the story of a middle-aged woman who lots revenge against the elderly man who, 20 years before, exploited and betrayed her, Ella Leffland displays a formidable literary talent. Like Joyce Carol Oates, Leffland is adept at portraying obsessive states of mind. Her characters are complex, yet unglamorous individuals; both men and women are compelling without being entirely sympathetic figures. The California environment—expansive, sultry, but arid as well—is especially well-drawn.

278. _____ **LOVE OUT OF SEASON.** N.Y.: Atheneum, 1974. $8.95.
The 1960s counterculture/protest movement in Berkeley-Haight-Ashbury forms the backdrop for this unsettling drama about two unsuited lovers. Johanna is a withdrawn and impoverished painter, strongly independent; Morris is a gambler and shameless philanderer, but a man with strong political convictions. Their story relationship—ultimately doomed—and the fates of those around them are equally caught up in the turgid happenings of the time. Telling discrepancies exist between their idealized and actual lives. Again Leffland has written an engrossing, disturbing novel about characters who find it difficult to achieve their personal goals, however passionately they try to live.

279. LeGUIN, Ursula Kroeber. THE LEFT HAND OF DARKNESS. 1969. N.Y.: Ace, 1974. $1.75.
Imagine a world of androgynous humans, absolutely without sexuality except for four days out of every twenty-six, when they are "in kemmer." Imagine that no one is ever consistently male or female in kemmer. Everyone may bear a child. ". . . no one is quite so thoroughly 'tied down' here as women elsewhere are likely to be—psychologically or physically. Burden and privilege are shared out pretty equally, everybody has the same risk to run or choice to make. therefore nobody here is quite so free as a free male elsewhere." This book will tax your imagination, and the task is made harder by LeGuin's choice of the male pronoun over a neuter one. **Left Hand Of Darkness** is a beautifully written book with profound political and social implications. No one should miss reading it.

280. _____ **THE DISPOSSESSED.** 1974. N.Y.: Avon, 1975. $1.75.
An amazing book. Subtitled "an ambiguous Utopia," it presents two worlds: Annares, a libertarian society based on anarchist principles, and Urras, a hierarchical society based on "profiteering." Shevek, the Anarresti physicist who travels to Urras, challenges the existing socio-political structures of both planets through his unswerving commitment to nonauthoritarian relationships and organization. In addition, his Theory of Simultaneity (time as circular rather than linear) calls into question all arbitrary divisions in human thought and experience (past/present/future, being/becoming). **The Dispossessed** is a multi-dimensional achievement; LeGuin's

genius is in her ability to create a convincing, workable utopia while at the same time dealing with specific ways in which revolutionary communities can cease to be "revolutionary".

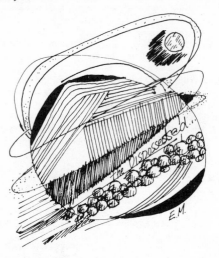

281. LEWIS, Janet. THE GHOST OF MONSIEUR SCARRON. 1959. Chicago: Swallow Press, 1965. $1.95.
The third of Lewis's series is set in 17th century Paris. Here she has enlarged the scope of the story beyond a single community and tied the fate of her central characters to the politics of a nation. Marianne, a bookbinder's wife, falls in love with her husband's young assistant; pamphlets slandering the king and his mistress have flooded Paris. An accidental configuration of events makes the consequences of Marianne's affair converge with the organized wrath of Louis XIV, and Marianne's husband is punished as the author of the pamphlets. Perhaps because of its length and broader scope, this novel lacks the striking emotional power of **Martin Guerre**, and the immediacy of **Soren Qvist**. Yet is is no less involving. Lewis's portrait of Marianne, a middle-aged woman re-experiencing love, is built of compassion and beautiful detail. Even minor characters stand vivid and memorable. Contrasts between the bitter cynicism of the court and Versailles and the anger of the Paris poor are superbly drawn. And, like the other two novels, **M. Scarron** offers us a credible history of ordinary people coping with extraordinary experience.

282. LURIE, Alison. IMAGINARY FRIENDS. 1967. N.Y.: Avon, 1975. $1.65.
The central character is one of the most believable males created by a female author. The plot is concerned with the potential madness of participant-observer sociology. Two university professors study a small-town spiritualist group which believes it is in touch with other planets. Our hero questions how much the professors' presence becomes a controlling and destructive influence in their own lives as well as the lives of their subjects.

283. _____ THE WAR BETWEEN THE TATES. 1974. N.Y.: Warner, 1975. $1.95.
Erica Tate is a faculty wife who believes in doing the "right thing" for no reward other than the simple knowledge that she is a "superior person," but as middle age approaches she finds her moral landscape eroding. Overnight, her adorable children turn into obnoxious teenagers; suburbia encroaches on her country home; her unfaithful husband becomes nationally ridiculous when he tries to use local feminists to further his career. Lurie's witty book taunts bourgeois lifestyles and just about every campus trend of the past decade. Good lightweight entertainment.

284. McCAFFREY, Anne. THE DRAGONRIDERS OF PERN. N.Y.: Ballantine, 1973.
Dragons carry their riders between time and space to fight the burning spores that endanger life on Pern. Between crises, dragonfolk mediate political issues. Unfortunately, Pernian society is decidedly medieval, and the earnest debates about tithes and classes become tedious, if not offensive. McCaffrey's depiction of human sexuality is worse than medieval—close to the Love Comics version. Several exceptinal women do surpass the men in telepathic power, and in **Dragonflight** Lessa's strong-willed courage saves the planet, but in general the women flirt with the men and compete jealously with each other. Fortunately, dragon society is much more interesting. In fact the dragons redeem this otherwise conventional extraplanetary-invasion thriller. Dragon society is matriarchal, dominated by great golden Queen dragons. At birth, dragons choose their riders, initiating a telepathic love bond that lasts until one or the other dies. This dragon-human pairing is the primary relationship on Pern, and in human love affairs. When the battles and intrigues are well-forgotten, the dragons of Pern, by far the most outstanding aspect of these novels, continue to hold one's imagination.

285. McCARTHY, Mary. THE COMPANY SHE KEEPS. 1942. N.Y.: Harvest, 1967. $2.15.
This collection of short stories was Mary McCarthy's first attempt at fiction. Together, they form a series of six chapters in the life of a young woman writer/intellectual in the 1930s (probably based on the author's own life). Each segment focuses on a different person among her acquaintances—"The Genial Host," "Portrait of the Intellectual as a Yale Man," etc. McCarthy's eye for detail and her ability to sketch in the fine lines of personality give her characters a reality in which human flaws are viewed with both shrewdness and humor.

286. _____ CAST A COLD EYE. 1950. N.Y.: Signet, 1972. $2.95.
Glittering, brilliant, brittle stories of women making, or spectacularly failing to make, their way. This is a gem among McCarthy's early works.

287. _____ A CHARMED LIFE. 1955. N.Y.: Harcourt, Brace, Jovanovich, current. $7.95.
In New Leeds, a small New England coastal community, a group of artists and intellectuals have escaped the big city "rat race" only to become enmeshed in the complexities of small-scale Bohemia. McCarthy focuses a penetrating and knowledgeable eye on the social and sexual games they play as well as their genuine human emotions. Both the male and the female characters are depicted with clarity and insight, giving the reader an acute sense of each one's individuality. A tightly constructed, fast-paced novel.

288. _____ MEMORIES OF A CATHOLIC GIRLHOOD. 1957. N.Y.: Harcourt, Brace, Jovanovich, 1972. $3.25.
These eight connected episodes deal with the influence of cruel Catholic guardians and Catholic schools on McCarthy's early life. The final chapter is about her Jewish grandmother and gives a fine commentary on the aging woman.

289. _____ THE GROUP. 1963. N.Y.: Signet, 1972. $1.25.
Don't let the Hollywood version of **The Group** prevent you from taking this novel seriously. It is a finely written and well-constructed work, one of McCarthy's best. In it, eight Vassar graduates (class of '33) explore virtually all the options open to well-educated middle class women: careers, marriage, motherhood, affairs, divorce, political involvements, etc. The limitations of these choices and the oppression the women experience at the hands of the men in their lives are clearly delineated. It is to Lakey, the lesbian in "the Group," that McCarthy gives the last word. An absorbing and detailed look at the day-to-day reality of eight women's lives.

290. _____ BIRDS OF AMERICA. 1965. N.Y.: Signet, 1972. $1.50.
Set in America and the capitals of Europe, this novel is largely the story of a young man's search for identity. It deals with changing values, a decline in the quality of

contemporary life, and the death of nature. Most of McCarthy's work is more readable than this novel. From a feminist point of view the book suffers from an underdeveloped portrait of the mother, a fascinating person of great significance early in the book.

291. McCAULEY, Carol Spearin. HAPPENTHING IN TRAVEL ON. Plainfield, Vt.: Daughters, Inc., 1975. $4.00.
Another experimental novel from Daughters. Seven middle-class women charter a plane which then crashes on the side of a mountain in mid-winter. Surviving the crash, they attempt to endure weeks and months in an abandoned cabin waiting for rescue. **Happenthing** is about women learning together how to survive both physical hardship and interpersonal friction. The characters could have been developed more fully, but their relationships with each other seem quite real, and Carol McCauley's style works well, with action, thought, and dialog flowing quickly, uninterrupted by explanatory transitions or excess words. The author has used a computer to insert various word plays and letter patterns throughout the text, but these seem fairly irrelevant to the rest of the book. Otherwise, an absorbing first novel.

McCULLERS, Carson *(1917-1967) Born in Columbus, Georgia, Carson McCullers was always considered an odd child and something of a prodigy. She suffered from extremely poor health throughout her life. At 18 she traveled to New York to study at the Juilliard School of Music, but lost all her money, and ended up working at odd jobs and writing. She wrote* **The Heart Is A Lonely Hunter** *at age 22. Problems of health and in her personal life (she was married to an abusive husband who eventually committed suicide) may have limited her literary output. McCullers kept journals and notes on her life which are as yet unpublished, and may eventually give us a more nearly complete of her unique vision.*

292. ._____ THE HEART IS A LONELY HUNTER. 1940. N.Y.: Bantam, current. $1.25.
In a tight and completely believable pattern, Carson McCullers weaves together the separate lives of young and old, men and women, black and white in a small southern town. Some of the novel's brilliant portraits include: Mike Kelly, an adolescent girl who insists on taking mechanics instead of stenography at Vocational High; Mr. Singer, a mysterious deaf mute for whose listening eyes each of the main characters explains his or her deepest hopes and fears; Benedict Mady Copeland, a black physician who gives his life in the service of his people; and Jack Blount, an alcoholic, frustrated revolutionist who dreams of leading the poor whites and the mill workers in rebellion against the owners. highly recommended for its portrayal of black and working-class life in the pre-World War II south.

293. _____ REFLECTIONS IN A GOLDEN EYE. 1941. Boston: Houghton Mifflin. $4.95.
A haunting, macabre novel set in a southern army post. Violence, adultery, and cowardice weave in and out of this controlled and powerful novel as the author exposes the bizarre and destructive relationships among two officers, their wives, and a disturbed enlisted man who intrudes on their dangerous and shifting battleground.

294. _____ THE MEMBER OF THE WEDDING. 1946. N.Y.: Bantam, 1969. $ .95.
McCullers recreates a few months in the life of a 12-year-old girl, Frankie. The reader is taken back to the pre-teen years when we first develop that painful awareness of the larger world outside of ourselves. Frankie's struggle is that of creating an identity and collecting experiences on which to base a new, adult perception of reality. The friends to whom she can come for help and compare notes about the world are: Bernice, a black woman who works for her father, and John Henry West, a six-year-old cousin and playmate. For many readers Frankie (or F. Jasmine, as she decides to call herself) will recall long-buried images of their former selves. Recommended for adolescent readers.

295. _____ **CLOCK WITHOUT HANDS.** 1961. Excelsior, Mich.: M. McCosh. $10.00.

While not giving us any female characters of interest, **Clock Without Hands** is perhaps a very important book from a feminist point of view. It is the portrait of a southern patriarch, Judge Clane, whose bigotry is based on white and male supremacy: he sees women and blacks as beings who exist to service his needs. There is also a very fine and sensitive relationship between two men in the book: old Clane's grandson Jester feels a deep and abiding love for Sherman Pew, a black man.

296. MANNES, Marya. OUT OF MY LIFE. N.Y.: Doubleday, 1971. O.P.

A self-proclaimed "spiritual hermaphrodite," noted writer-critic-commentator Marya Mannes recounts her struggle to lead an independent, career-oriented life while managing sexual and domestic affairs. Taught by her musical New York family to value culture and intellect, she produced sculpture, plays and poetry in addition to prose. Three husbands, many lovers, and a poor attempt at motherhood caused her to reject marriage as a personal mode of existence. Believing that individuals should acknowledge both male and female instincts, Marya Mannes often addresses a fictitious male persona in this engrossing autobiography.

297. MARSHALL, Paule. BROWN GIRL, BROWNSTONES. 1959. N.Y.: Avon, current. $ .95.

Paule Marshall's first novel is so involving that the reader is immediately drawn into the lives of immigrants from Barbados, in Brooklyn, New York, during the late 1930s and 1940s. Selina Boyce, a passionate and observant young black girl slowly comes to understand the divergent choices of the people she knows: her mother Silla who "hacks her way through life" toward upward mobility; her father Deighton, a cavalier dreamer, defiant of the white man's meager plans for him; Suggie, the cheerful boarder upstairs who is scorned because she is reputed to be a prostitute; Clive, Selina's cynical lover who absorbed the effects of racism long ago. Marshall's writing is clear and moving as she develops Selina's awareness of racism and power. Her ideas about how she, as a black woman, will survive stem largely from her intense, ambivalent relationship with her resilient mother.

298. _____ **THE CHOSEN PLACE, THE TIMELESS PEOPLE.** 1969. N.Y.: Avon, 1976. $1.95.

This is, above all, the story of a people, the black people of Bournehills. Living in the poorest section of a tiny West Indian island, they are seen as hopeless by the rest of the island. Aid and development projects flood the area, but they are all doomed to failure; nothing ever changes in Bournehills. Marshall sees Bournehill's people as possessing a tremendous integrity: they will settle for nothing less than a revolution which gives them actual control of their lives. The island, its people, and its history are lovingly and feelingly described.

299. MATHIS, Sharon Bel. LISTEN FOR THE FIG TREE N.Y.: Avon, 1974. $ .95.

Kwanza, and African harvest celebration, provides a background of hope and nationhood in this novel about blind, 16-year-old Muffin. The celebration, held at the Black Museum during white culture's Christmas week, is particularly important to Muffin because it marks the anniversary of her father's murder. Mathias is highly recommended for her portrayal of the world of the blind: some of the best moments come when the self-sufficient, resourceful Muffin goes about her orderly daily routine. The tension between Muffin and her lonely, nearly alcoholic mother and the beauty of Muffin's friendship with neighbor, Mr. Dale (who teaches her how to design and sew her own clothes, are also well done. One flaw in this book relates to the view of sexism in our society. When Muffin is assaulted in her hallway by an intended rapist, Mr. Dale's explanation to her is "This happens to black women because they are incredibly, profoundly beautiful," and her doctor advises, "Everything's all right, your bruises will be gone long before summer, so don't throw your bikini away." Still the novel has important things to say to the blind and to adolescent readers.

300. MERIWETHER, Louise. DADDY WAS A NUMBER RUNNER. 1970. N.Y.: Pyramid, current. $1.25.

Twelve-year-old Francie Coffin is growing up in Harlem in the 1930s. Poverty, crime, drunkenness, prostitution, and police brutality are basic facts of life for her. Her brother is jailed on a murder charge; her best friend's sister is a prostitute who ends up killing her pimp. Francie, barely adolescent, accepts sexual molestation as an everyday event. Meanwhile, the whole neighborhood bets obsessively on the numbers, dreaming of a big win and escape from these tawdry lives . . . In his foreword, James Baldwin suggests that a comparison of Francie Coffin's life with that of Francie Nolan in Smith's **A Tree Grows In Brooklyn** shows "to what extent poverty wears a color."

301. MERRIL, Judith. THE BEST OF JUDITH MERRIL. N.Y.: Warner, 1976. $1.25.

With the publication of a science ficton story in 1948, Judith Merril became one of the first women to break into this male-dominated field. The feminine mystique reached its apex in the 1940s and 1950s, yet all the while Merril was writing stories which featured strong women and which seriously probed many aspects of sex roles. The novella "Daughters of Earth," a history of a six generation dynasty of female space pioneers, is an interesting exploration of mother-daughter relationships. "Wish Upon a Star" is about a sexist society where women dominate and men are socialized and educated for limited roles; a boy's wish?—that he had been born a girl. This is an excellent collecton; the stories are well written, combining exciting plots with serious philosophical and political questions.

302. MEYER, Lynn. PAPERBACK THRILLER. N.Y.: Random House, 1975. $6.95.

Sarah Chayse, woman sleuth, is a self-proclaimed "vegetarian feminist psychiatrist." Although her detecting is rather obvious and her feminism rather upper-class, she is still a bright spot in a world of macho mysteries.

MILFORD, Nancy. See under Fitzgerald.

303. MILLER, Isabel. PATIENCE AND SARAH. 1969 as **A PLACE FOR US.** Greenwich, Conn.: 1973. $ .95.

A simple and moving story of the love between two 19th century women who finally overcome all obstacles in their way and move into new country to start their own farm. The book is of major interest for its open and honest treatment of a lesbian relationship.

304. MILLETT, Kate. FLYING. 1974. N.Y.: Ballantine, 1975. $2.25.

Millett's bisexuality is the prime issue in this copious personal statement recounting her sexual and political confusion following the publication of **Sexual Politics**. She relentlessly articulates her lesbian conflicts, the private chaos of a successful public figure. Although admirable for its painful honesty and intense idealism, so much written excess may bore some readers. Although Millett attempts to evoke feminist experience beyond the academicism of **Sexual Politics**, it is questionable whether this work is self-expression or self-defense. The book's best passages are those expressing her lesbianism.

305. MOODY, Annie. COMING OF AGE IN MISSISSIPPI. 1968. N.Y.: Dell, 1971. $1.50.

The autobiography of a black woman who was a child of poverty in the 1940s, a high school student in the 1950s, and a movement organizer in the 1960s. She never imposes a later consciousness on her experiences, but shows us her perceptions as they were at the time. The result is a moving book which cannot be too highly recommended. Of special interest to women: her feelings about her constantly pregnant mother, her observations on the job opportunities for black females (as domestics) and the sexual role of black women as mistresses to their oppressors, her own alienation from the "dating game," and her tallying of the sufferings of women civil rights organizers.

306. MORGAN, Claire. THE PRICE OF SALT. 1953. N.Y.: Bantam Books. O.P.

Therese, a would-be stage set designer, works in the doll department of a large New York City department store during the Christmas rush. Carol meets Therese while buying a doll for her daughter, and it's love at first sight. Unfortunately, their idyllic affair is interrupted by external pressure from the straight world. Carol is in the process of a divorce. Carol's husband has the two women followed and his underhanded techniques win him the custody of their child after an ugly courtroom battle. Although the plot is melodramatic, the characters are quite believable (particularly, the process of Therese's coming out), and the ending, surprisingly, is a happy one. Despite all obstacles, Carol and Therese's love endures, and neither gay character permanently breaks down or dies as is the case in many "gay" novels. Particularly noteworthy is Morgan's sympathetic attitude towards lesbian mothers. Morgan's writing is at its best when she gives us brief glimpses of the lives of women working permanently in the department store. **The Price of Salt** should be reissued.

307. MORRISON, Toni. THE BLUEST EYE. 1970. N.Y.: Pocket Books, 1974. $1.25.
This novel deals with the theme of how white standards of beauty and normality have affected the identities of black people, particularly children. Throughout the book, chapters are headed with short excerpts from Dick and Jane primers. Against this backdrop are the lives of Frieda and her sister Claudia, adolescent girls, and their friend Pecola, who in the end is tragically destroyed—a classic victim of poverty, racism, and that form of madness which appears in the oppressed. Morrison, herself a daughter of a laborer, has been a university instructor, editor, and author. Her novel is a searching and often brilliant study of individual black women, men, and children. Beyond these individual portraits, Morrison elucidates the way our society perpetuates racism.

308. _____ **SULA.** 1974. N.Y.: Bantam, 1975. $1.50.
Sula and Nel are inseparable friends growing up in a rural black community. When Nel marries, Sula leaves town; ten years later, after college and city life, she returns seeking "the other half of her equation," more restless than ever. "And like an artist with no art form, she becomes dangerous." She flouts local taboos, drawing the townspeople together against her. Nel feels herself betrayed by her former friend. A compelling look at the joys and risks of women's friendships. Morrison has a genius for dialogue; she depicts the emotional tactics of the oppressed with quick, deft strokes.

309. NACHMAN, Elana. RIVERFINGER WOMEN. 1974. Plainfield, Vt.: Daughters, Inc. $3.50.

Inez Riverfinger, the narrator, combines the elusiveness of legend and the harshness of reality. From her first description of herself, we are confronted with the honesty and irony which pervades this lesbian-feminist biography of Inez and her Riverfinger friends. Inez shuttles through views of herself (at a New England boarding school; carrying a drug deal from Tangiers, $18,000 in a tampax inserted in her vagina), her friends, her teachers, her middle-class background, and the inescapable context of the U.S. in the late 1960s and early 1970s. **Riverfinger Women** has no linear divisions in time and space. The situations shift as rapidly as does Elana Nachman's style in creating them, but the changes are absorbing rather than distracting. What remains constant are the rigid assumptions which lesbians confront. ". . . in being faceless unmentionable nameless lesbians, unapproved by Ann Landers or Jerry Rubin, in being unable to find catch words in newspapers or the books we read in our dormitories, for that, for what that meant, women loving women—in that we could have no fads. That was where some of us began our resistance, learned to change (acid on stone) who we thought we were doomed to be into who we are. Tough, strong, proud: free women."

310. NEGRIN, Su. BEGIN AT START. Albion, Calif.: Times Change Press, 1972. $2.75.

This is a wonderful collage of the author's personal reactions to her experiences in various movements of the 1960s, from free schools and mysticism to women's and gay liberation. She writes of her own life in a way that makes what she has to say about personal/political change both accessible and inspiring. Her mistrust of "political umbrellas" and her determinedly positive vision of Utopia as "necessary" make this essential reading for anyone disillusioned with left sectarianism and traditional conceptions of Revolution. Especially recommended for those interested in libertarian or anarchist perspectives.

OATES, Joyce Carol (1938-   ) *Coming from a rural working class background, Oates portrays vividly and with startling depth a wide range of Americans of all classes and ages. Her most notable achievement is her presentation of the nausea of American life and the powerlessness of the individual caught up in the "stampede of history." Yet readers often object to the passivity of Oates' female characters; they just let things happen to them, and the occasional rebellious woman is usually shown to be sick, hateful and doomed to frustration. Despite the abundant violence that characterizes Oates' fiction, feminist critics have complained that she's too timorous when it comes to dealing with the realities of female life in sexist society; and, indeed, in a recent article defending Norman Mailer against "The fiercest and cruelest of Women's Liberation attacks," Oates declared that "Somehow, in spite of all the exploitation and oppression . . . there are things about the private lives of men and women that should not be uttered, or at least we think they should not be uttered, they are so awful."*

311. _____ BY THE NORTH GATE. 1963. Greenwich, Conn.: Fawcett, 1973. $1.25.

Fourteen fine short stories, though few have any specific relevance to women. Two that do are excellent. "Pastoral Blood" shows a woman who has been raised to fit into the feminine role as neatly as she fits into her immaculate pink and white clothes; on the day before her predictable, perfect marriage, she flees in a wild search for degradaton and death. "Images" presents a series of flashes from the life of a girl struggling against the claustrophobic environment of her Catholic home.

312. _____ A GARDEN OF EARTHLY DELIGHTS. 1966. Greenwich, Conn.: Fawcett, 1974. $1.50.

Carla, a migrant worker's daughter, runs away. She tries for "something more," first finding pleasure in her initial independence with a room of her own, and later a kind of idyllic joy in solitary motherhood. These positive moments are counterpoints to the loss and pain of a disappointing romantic love, and the attainment of a security, sought after love failed, which ultimately destroys Carla and her child.

313. _____ **EXPENSIVE PEOPLE** 1968. Greenwich, Conn.: Fawcett, 1974. $1.25.

Oates turns her hand to black comedy and anti-Momism in this tale of the child-hero's murder of his manipulating mother. A strange blend of Dostoevsky and J.D. Salinger, the book is an indictment of the upper-class nuclear family and an effective statement of the integrity of childhood.

314. _____ **THEM.** 1969. Greenwich, Conn.: Fawcett, 1974. $1.50.

Based on an account of one of the author's former students, this excellent novel is about a Detroit working-class family: Loretta Wendall and her children Jules, Maureen, and Betty. Loretta survives episodes of male violence, but can't escape poverty, having many children and usually no man. Though most of her support comes from her women friends, Loretta keeps stumbling after the American dream, waiting in vain for her "real" life to begin. Her children struggle against this debilitating beginning: brother Jules does elude the slums via pimping and political opportunism, but the only escape Maureen can see is to use her body first as a prostitute and then, after a nearly fatal beating from her stepfather, to "steal" another woman's husband. Oddly enough, Betty's story is scarcely touched upon even though she defies her mother's racism by having black friends and vows that "no son-of-a-bitch is going to beat up on *me*!" In general, **Them** examines in a sympathetic way the complexities of social injustice and violence. Its conclusion—a surrealistic portrayal of the 1967 Detroit riots—is truly unforgettable.

315. _____ **WONDERLAND.** Greenwich, Conn.: Fawcett, 1971. $1.50.

This novel calls to mind the photographic work of Diane Arbus; both Oates and Arbus are drawn to and must illuminate the grotesqueries of life. The author is preoccupied here with a theme which runs through all her writing, "the heavy sorrow of the body." What does it mean to live in a body? What is its relationship to our mind, our personality? The other main focus of **Wonderland** is on the politics of families. The complex plot has a central male character, but Oates includes female interior monologues, which serve as striking counterpoints to his life.

316. _____ **THE WHEEL OF LOVE.** 1972. Greenwich, Conn.: Fawcett, 1974. $1.50.

A fine collection of stories. Most deal with the violence of love and with the failure of educated, middle-class people to connect on an emotional level. Some of Oates' most powerful stories are here including the hauntingly sad "Four Summers" and the oft-anthologized "Where Are You Going, Where Have You Been," a devastating, surrealistic vision of female vulnerability.

317. _____ **MARRIAGES AND INFIDELITIES.** Greenwich, Conn.: Fawcett, 1973. $1.50.

More tales about people from all walks of life living drab little lives full of seams that threaten to split apart and let in a tidal wave of violence. In "Normal Love," a wife's energies are gobbled up by family routine; the young mother of "The Children" develops a fearful hatred for her little girl. Several stories are take-offs on Chekov, Kafka, and Joyce: "The Dead," for instance, offers a grim portrait-of-the-artist whom Oates has called her own "alter-ego," while "Nightmusic" gives a more positive image of artists: Mozart and his sister Maria Anna, an accomplished pianist who won fame performing her brother's compositions.

318. _____ **THE HUNGRY GHOSTS.** Los Angeles: Black Sparrow Press, 1974. $4.00.

In Buddhist cosmology a ghost is a creature driven by hunger, i.e. desires of one kind or another. These seven stories cast a caustic eye on the hungry world of writers, critics, and academics as they slug it out for prizes and power. A scathing satire of the literary jungle though the irony wears thin in places and the women characters are, for the most part, a dreary collection of wimps and losers.

319. _____ **DO WITH ME AS YOU WILL.** 1974. Greenwich, Conn.: Fawcett, 1975. $1.95.

At the behest of her ambitious mother, beautiful Elena marries a big-time criminal lawyer and sleepwalks through her high-society role. An adulterous affair awakens her to physical passion ". . . her body used as a vessel to accommodate him." Elena decides to change her vapid life. Her act of self-assertion (running off with another woman's husband) will hardly rouse feminist hearts, but then it wasn't intended to. As Oates herself has remarked in interview: "I hope this book won't irritate Women's Liberation women who are somewhat anti-male because it is, in fact, a celebration of love and marriage . . . since I believe that for most women this path leads to a higher freedom through the awakening of love, is the pathway. There are women who must be independent . . . I honor them and I will write about them another time." Weigh it for yourselves.

320. _____ **THE GODDESS AND OTHER WOMEN.** 1974. Greenwich, Conn.: 1976. $1.95.

"The woman was a man's goddess, trapped in that body." This is the essential problem of the women portrayed in these 25 stories. Once again Oates deals with lives constricted and, more often, pulverized by modern society. Here we find women of zero consciousness being violently betrayed by fathers, lovers, co-workers, thugs, each other, and, above all, by their own secret cravings for violation and annihilation. The stories are, for the most part, of a very high literary quality—Oates' re-creations of deranged mental states become more powerful with every book—however, one may chafe at this relentless series of defeated women. For that reason, the stories are perhaps better taken in small doses.

O'CONNOR, Flannery. _(1925-1964). A brilliant writer with a grim vision of reality. Much of her work is set in her native South, and shows up the small-mindedness of racists and liberals alike. She also deals frequently with religion, often in the form of fanatical evangelism, though she herself was a deeply-committed Catholic. She exposes human weaknesses pitilessly; no one in her world is admirable—and yet her characters manage to arouse our compassion. Both characters and dialogue are captured with stark immediacy. Her early death from the horrible disease of lupus deprived this country of a great writer. Two short novels and a number of short stories represent her entire production; they are published in various combinations besides those listed here._

321. _____ **WISE BLOOD.** 1952. Included in **THREE BY FLANNERY O'CONNOR**, N.Y.: Signet, current. $1.25.

The author described this as a "comic novel about a Christian _malgre lui._" Hazel Motes is on the run from Jesus, obsessively protesting his lack of faith, preaching a new "Church Without Christ," and convincing no one. His tale is set in a small southern town with a cast of weird, intriguing characters. Whatever your views on religion—and the book is open to diametrically opposite interpretations—you are likely to be gripped by its macabre humor and compelling force.

322. _____ **THE VIOLENT BEAR IT AWAY.** 1960. Included in **THREE BY FLANNERY O'CONNOR**, N.Y.: Signet, curent. $1.25.

This, too, is a story of religion's strange power. Young Tarwater has been raised by a great-uncle who is a self-proclaimed prophet. When the old man dies, the 14-year-old boy is destined to succeed him and, in particular, to baptize the retarded son of a supposedly enlightened and atheistic uncle. Another superb, haunting story.

323. _____ **THE COMPLETE STORIES.** N.Y.: Sunburst. 1972. $5.95.

This volume contains all O'Connor's published short stories as well as some which were previously unpublished; a few of these were the first versions of chapters of her novels. O'Connor's stories are gems of horror and humor. In them we find more female characters than in the novels. There are women running farms, exasperated at the ineffectualness of their weak sons; there are unpleasant small girls making faces at the world. Read "Everything That Rises Must Converge" for a clash between a white woman and a black woman, seen from the point of view of the white woman's son, who uses his self-righteous liberalism as a weapon against his mother. Also read "Good Country People" for the grim tale of how Hulga, 32, with a wooden leg and a Ph.D. in philosophy, is victimized by a Bible salesman. But read them all for their sharp evocation of the South, for their technical brilliance, for their fierce vision.

O'DONNELL, Lillian *A concern for women (and for the crimes committed against us) is always evident in O'Donnell's mysteries, especially her three police thrillers featuring Norah Mulcahaney.*

324. _____ **THE PHONE CALLS.** 1972. N.Y.: Dell, 1973. $ .95.
A particularly vicious obscene phone caller drives several women to suicide and murders at least one Norah tracks his down . . . and vice versa.

325. _____ **DON'T WEAR YOUR WEDDING RING.** N.Y.: Putnam, 1973. $4.95.
Suburban housewives form a prostitution collective and Norah seeks to solve the brutal murder of one of their numbers. As Norah is a NYPD detective, the book's conclusion is not as satisfying as it could be.

326. _____ **DIAL 577-R-A-P-E.** 1974. N.Y.: Bantam, 1976. $1.25.
Norah works with an all-woman rape squad in uncovering (and convicting) the attacker of a young Chicana neighbor. In so doing, she finally connects her quest for justice with her position as a woman. Not a radical feminist approach but powerful just the same.

327. OLSEN, Tillie. TELL ME A RIDDLE. 1960. N.Y.: Dell, 1971. $2.45.
The title story in this collecton of four stories tells of an old woman dying; it is a wrenching portrayal of the aging woman and the problems she faces in our society. In "I Stand Here Ironing" a mother reflects on the life of one of her daughters, whom she has never had enough time for. "Hey Sailor" presents a family's relationship with a middle-aged alcoholic who has spent most of his life as a professional sailor and finds that he has no genuine human contacts. "Oh Yes" vividly describes the painful ending of a friendship between a black girl and a white girl as they are tracked for totally different lives due to their racial and economic circumstances. These superbly-crafted, compassionate storeis contain vital insights into the nature of marriage, woman's role as wife and mother, and the deprivations of over-work.

"To smash all ghettos that divide us—
not to go back, not to go back . . .
. . . Tell them to write:
Race, human; Religion:"

328. _____ **YONNONDIO: From the Thirties.** 1974. N.Y.: Dell, 1975. $1.25.
A Depression family migrates from one impoverished environment to another in this haunting, lyrical story. First in a bleak Wyoming mining town, the tenant farming in South Dakota, and finally in a grim midwest industrial city, Jim and Anna Holbrook and their five young children battle with poverty and its scars on their family unit. Daughter Mazie typically escapes the bleakness through fantasy; son Will lusts for the

streets. Most attention is paid to Anna, whose life is devoted to preserving the home and to "find more necessities the body can do without." Despite a miscarriage, endless fatigue and worry, she persistently fights bitterness with hope. The book was written by Tillie Olsen as a young girl and only recently recovered and reconstructed after forty years. **Yonnondio** evokes tragic characters and circumstances with remarkable feminist insight.

329. OZICK, Cynthia. THE PAGAN RABBI AND OTHER STORIES. N.Y.: Knopf, 1971. $6.95.
The author is widely respected for her short fiction; this collection of tales displays her storytelling gifts. Ozick's themes encompass art and the intellect, the family and sexuality, guilt and redemption. She uses wit and imagination to convey the spiritual conflicts of her characters. It should be noted that main characters are usually male, with females often drawn as vehicles through which men enact symbolic struggles. Despite this orientation, stories such as "The Pagan Rabbi," about a Rabbi's sexual quest for transcendance, and "Virility," which describes a male poet's exploitation of female creativity, are both humorous and enlightening.

330. PALEY, Grace. THE LITTLE DISTURBANCES OF MAN: Stories of Men and Women at Love. 1959. N.Y.: New American Library, 1973. $2.95.
Ten lovely, funny, tender short stories, most about Jewish life in New York City, many about women. Even as teenagers, these lovingly drawn women pursue their men with a lust avidity; nor, as they grow older, do they lose their capacity for love. Paley works wonders with words, twisting the familiar into new forms, startling the reader with fresh phrases.

331. _____ ENORMOUS CHANGES AT THE LAST MINUTE. 1974. N.Y.: Dell, 1975. $1.25.
Warmth, humor, and pathos characterize these brief stories, written with a particular Jewish sense of comic dialogue and irony. Paley draws her subjects from among New York City's ethnic lower classes, painting affectionate portraits of their tough-minded struggles to survive in the urban jungle. Many stories depict women independently striving to manage their relations with children, fathers, lovers, and other women. What lingers in this collection is the author's unique blend of wit, realism, and poignancy: her sensitive grasp of the tender and tragic.

332. PETESCH, Natalie L. THE ODYSSEY OF KATINOU KALOKOVICH. Tampa, Fla.: United Sisters, 1974. $3.95.
From the first page of the book, the life of Katinou Kalokovich unfolds with compelling intensity: "Kate" is so real that the usual distance between reader and character almost disappears. Her determination to be self-sufficient and a painter wavers again and again before the tyranny and desperate need of her Russian immigrant family, the seductive pitfalls of romantic love, and the economic realities of American society. Kate experiences almost all of the physical and psychological variants of woman's oppression, yet her story is not at all overdramatized. Natalie Petesch has made Katinou Kalokovich both a victim and a survivor and therein lies the **Odyssey**'s believability. A tightly constructed, excellent novel.

333. PETRY, Ann. THE STREET. 1946. N.Y.: Pyramid, current. $ .95.
This novel is about a young woman in Harlem, Lutie Johnson, who is raising her child Bub and trying to survive. Not only is Lutie a well-drawn character, but so are the minor characters who live jammed into the rundown, overcrowded apartments of Harlem. The novel gives us insights into their personal motivations and needs. Petry does not paint a rosy picture; by the end of the book, Lutie has not escaped. Reading the novel is painful at times, but certainly worth it.

334. _____ **THE NARROWS**. N.Y.: Pyramid Publications. $1.25.
A submerged classic of the 1950s exploring the interrelationship between the poor black and wealthy white communities in a small New England town. The novel contains the seeds of a screenplay. Dramatic tension slowly builds around the everpresent issues of sexism and racism. An interracial love affair between a wealthy white woman and an educated, but financially insolvent black man has consequences which snowball into a tragedy engulfing the entire community in guilty responsibility.

335. _____ **MISS MURIEL AND OTHER STORIES**. Boston: Houghton Mifflin, 1971. O.P.
Petry's only collection of stories spans approximately 20 years, from the late 1940s to the late 1960s. Almost all the stories focus on relationships between blacks and whites. Within the common theme, the situation varies from the often very subtle problems of isolated blacks in predominantly white towns to the oppressions of the ghetto, which are at the same time more brutal and more impersonal. Especially recommended: "Has Anybody Seen Miss Dora Dean?"—a beautiful telling of a tale.

336. PIERCY, Marge. DANCE THE EAGLE TO SLEEP. Greenwich, Conn.: Fawcett, 1971. O.P.
This novel is a somewhat surrealistic description of an aborted revolution, based on the Weatherman movement and the political situation of the 1960s. The failure of the movement described in the book seems to be due largely to the ego-tripping of the male leadership and the fact that women are never allowed a chance to participate equally. Piercy chooses to lead the reader through the oppressiveness of male domination rather than directly building for us a new model of a movement which could achieve human liberation.

337. _____ **GOING DOWN FAST**. 1969. Los Angeles: Trident. $6.95.
Set in Chicago of the late 1960s, **Going Down Fast** depicts the rawness and urgency of an emerging white movement and an embattled black community. Relationships between black and white characters give a believable range of attraction and withdrawal, offensive mistakes, constant need to test and retest personal needs and boundaries. The issue central in the novel is the redevelopment conspiracy of university and city planners and greedy businessmen—eating away at the housing and space of the poor community. Piercy, herself active in the movement for many years, centers on movement people, their motives, disappointments and commitment to change. The format is strikingly similar to the later **Small Changes**. We find characters who could be earlier (pre-women's movement) versions of the later cast. Though the males are the most developed characters and the macho-factor is abrasive, Anna has the tenacity of a tough woman and Vera, who is black, is both heroic and memorable.

338. _____ **SMALL CHANGES**. 1973. Greenwich, Conn.: Fawcett Crest, 1974. $1.75.
Small Changes is a controversial book. Many women feel that Marge Piercy has written an exciting, comprehensive novel about the women's movement; others feel that her characters are one-dimensional, her dialog rhetorical. Our own collective was split between praise and criticism, yet each of us was stimulated in some way, and often haunted by after-images of Miriam, Beth, and other characters in the book. The many levels of female oppression are depicted through the slow, painful changes in the women's lives, as they move from isolation to community, from paralysis to action. Even if some of the characterizations lack depth, the diversity of the women portrayed and the insights into women's consciousness as it is affected by personal/political breakthrough make **Small Changes** a unique and strongly feminist novel.

339. _____ **WOMAN ON THE EDGE OF TIME**. N.Y.: Knopf, 1976. $10.00.
In New York mental hospitals and Spanish Harlem, Consuelo (Connie) Camacho Alvarez Ramos remembers a past of deprivation and abuse, and goes into a future in Mattapoisett, an idyllic Cape Cod village in 2137. Juxtaposed with the life of this poor

Chicana, the vision of Mattapoisett provides startling contrast. Though the novel begins to read like a catalogue of bad and sometimes cloying good, each facet of the present and the future is convincing. Especially harrowing are Connie's experiences in mental hospitals where she is selected for behavior-modification experiments and her wrong turn into another future where human organ banks provide long life for the Rockemellons and the DukePonts. Do the two futuristic visions exist together, in combat, or does each represent a possible extension of today? Can the future be affected by Connie's actions? Piercy's book shows a firm awareness of the ways in which poor people, women, mental patients, blacks and latinos are starved, doped up, caged in, and killed—she fills out the vague and ungraspable term "oppression."

340. PLATH, Sylvia. THE BELL JAR. 1970. N.Y.: Bantam, 1975. $1.75.
Plath's level of consciousness here is painfully high, especially for something written in the 1950s, before the re-emergence of a visible women's movement. The book exposes the Madison Avenue dream of every American girl. Esther barely survives a summer in New York working for *Mademoiselle*, a suicide attempt, and shock therapy in a mental hospital. Her techniques of survival are fantasy, accommodation, and manipulation, all of which devastate her. She does not want security, marriage, and a family; she wants to be a poet. The limited options available even to this exceptional woman are shown dramatically.

341. POLITE, Carlene Hatcher. THE FLAGELLANTS. 1967. N.Y.: Farrar, Straus & Giroux.
First published in France, **The Flagellants** is a novel about the oppression of racist stereotypes in the lives of a black couple, Ideal and Jimson. Because so much has been internalized, they must continually fight the hated images both in themselves and in each other. These images, 'matriarch,' 'good for nothing,' encumber every plan or creation not already blocked by the external barriers of white society. These latter are clearly encountered when Ideal searches for a job. In a street corner debate, she listens to the black 'stockboys' argue non-violent vs. militant philosophy. There is a special anger for white movement people who "envy us these soulful, suffering experiences. They are in search of contrition, challenge, protest . . . all that is touching but it is coming too late. How dare they suck our essence now in the name of brotherhood?" For the most part the novel sustains a beautiful precision of language and wonderful flow of monologue and dialogue by the two characters.

342. RASCOE, Judith. YOURS, AND MINE. Boston: Little, Brown, 1973. $6.95.
Rascoe has been acclaimed as an extraordinarily promising new talent, and this, her first published book, shows why. The novella "Yours, and Mine" and many of the short stories in this collection capture magnificently aspects of Californian life. Broken marriages, divorces, remarriages, are a recurrent theme. In two stories we see the world from the point of view of small girls: "A Line of Order" presents a repressive school through the eyes of the child who is too young to articulate its horrors; in "The Mother of Good Fortune," we get the 6-year-old daughter's perspective on the desperate insecurity of her divorced mother. Technically, Rascoe is marvelously accomplished and innovative, a joy to read.

343. RODMAN, Bella. LIONS IN THE WAY. N.Y.: Avon Books, 1966. O.P.
This only novel by a Polish-born author deals with the question of school desegregation in the American south. Well-written and fast-moving, it could be recommended for adolescent readers if it were not out of print. As the novel opens, eight black students have been selected to integrate the all-white high school in their city. A white racist group begins to organize the poor and working class white elements, playing upon their powerlessness, and general despair about their lives. the white liberals stand in the middle, unable to make decisions because of their own greed and underlying racism. Because of the selfishness of these white leaders, the black parents and students go unsupported into daily situations of harassment and violence. It is the mugging and blinding of the first white liberal to march with the black students that finally moves the white majority to act against the fascism that has been

thriving unchecked. Because the fight for integrated, first rate education is a national and not just a southern question, much of **Lions In The Way** is as current as today's newspaper.

344. ROIPHE, Anne Richardson. UP THE SANDBOX. 1970. Greenwich, Conn.: Fawcett, 1972. $ .95.
A novel counterpointing the real and fantasy lives of a New York City housewife, and dealing in a very real way with this ordinary woman's dreams of liberation. In the end she is again pregnant and her fantasy life of freedom stops. Although somewhat limited by dealing so exclusively with fantasy, this is good consciousness-raising.

345. _____ LONG DIVISION. N.Y.: Fawcett, 1974. $1.25.
The narrator is traveling across America with her 10-year-old daughter to get a Mexican divorce. Flashbacks to her painful marriage to an arrogant artist break up the tale of the bizarre adventures this "Wandering Jewess" has on the road. Roiphe is conscious not only of her womanhood, but also of the oppression of other people; this is a fine, funny book.

346. ROSSNER, Judith. TO THE PRECIPICE. N.Y.: William Morrow, 1966. O.P.
Judith Rossner's first novel is the first-person account of a Jewish woman's life. Ruth comes from a poor Jewish family living on New York's Lower East Side; in the 1950s she goes to college and dates the boy from upstairs. Her brother's suicide precipitates a break with her family and with the boy; and she ends up marrying her old, rich employer. By the end of the book, Ruth sees this man as human and vulnerable, and chooses to stay with him and their three children.

347. _____ NINE MONTHS IN THE LIFE OF AN OLD MAID. N.Y.: Popular Library, 1976. $1.50.
Beth, the narrator, has a history of mental illness; now, close to 30, she lives a sheltered life with a protective sister and brother-in-law. Periodically, their lives are invaded by other family members—a pretty, irresponsible mother, a wandering father, a half-brother angry at the world. This novel has some fine, evocative passages, and gives a vivid and tender portrait of Beth.

348. _____ ANY MINUTE I CAN SPLIT. 1972. N.Y.: Warner, 1973. $1.25.
Eight months pregnant with twins, Margaret one day splits from her suburban home on her husband's motorcycle, to end up on a commune in Vermont. When her husband eventually joins her there, we see him changing as well as her. A fine, fine novel, showing, in realistic and human perspective, new lifestyles and one woman's search for a reasonable life.

349. _____ LOOKING FOR MR. GOODBAR. 1975. N.Y.: Pocketbooks, 1976. $1.95.
"Someday my prince will come"—but where to find love while waiting for him? A singles bar perhaps? All the warnings about the bad end that awaits women addicted to picking up one-nighters come true in this novel. Theresa, a habitual frequenter of singles bars is murdered by a man she picks up one night at Mr. Goodbar's. The narrative begins with this fact as confessed by her murderer ; it then proceeds to humanize the victim by taking us back through her life. We usually perceive victims as statistics, strangers, but this novel jars our perceptions by involving us in a "statistic's" life. Theresa's Catholic background, her sickly childhood, and her relationship with her family, lovers, and colleagues are explored in grim, naturalistic detail, and by the time the novel ends with Theresa's murder as she experiences it, the reader knows her well and understands the reasons behind her choices.

350. RULE, Jane. THIS IS NOT FOR YOU. 1970. N.Y.: Popular Library, 1972. O.P.
A finely written and sophisticated novel. Kate, the narrator, who has been a lesbian since high school, falls in love with Esther at college. The story of this love, which Kate chooses never to fulfill, is interwoven with the lives and loves, gay and other-

wise, of several other characters. Particularly poignant aspects of the book are the social guilt which traps Kate, and her rejection of the early lesbian rights movement.

351. _____ **DESERT OF THE HEART**. 1964. N.Y.: Arno, 1975. $10.00.
After sixteen years of marriage, Evelyn Hall flies to Reno to get a divorce. During the six weeks of waiting for residency, she lives in a boarding house where she meets Ann, a young woman 15 years her junior, who works in a gambling casino. These two gradually come to love each other and then learn acknowledge and trust this love. This is a steady, serious, thoughtful book. There are no really soaring moments, yet there is nothing careless or hasty in the writing. It's a good story, a positive account of lesbian love set in the real world.

_____ **LESBIAN IMAGES**. (See Works About Literature)

352. RUSS, Joanna. PICNIC ON PARADISE. 1968. N.Y.: Ace, 1974. $ .95.
This is a fast-paced adventure. An ancient Greek woman—tough and dirt poor—time-travels to rescue a band of giant super-humans on a technologically advanced planet. There is some sharp social criticism of cultures addicted to drugs and to psychoanalysis, but the perspective is not particularly feminist. You'll be interested in this if you're a science fiction fan and prefer your heroes female.

353. _____ **THE FEMALE MAN**. N.Y.: Bantam, 1975. $1.25.
Contrary to what the title implies, all the characters in this book are women. At times they appear to be not different from women, but different aspects of a single woman. Jeannine is a pre-World War II "babe". Joanna is a 1970s feminist who doesn't always let her consciousness show. Janet is from a future earth where only women exist. Jael is from an earth, not quite so far in the future, with separate female and male societies. Laura Rose is an adolescent in a not quite precise "now"—she is a mathematician and a lesbian. And there is "I" who sees, at different times, from each of their perspectives and from her "own". In **The Female Man**, Russ has expanded the possibilities for both what a science fiction book can be and what a feminist novel can be. The writing is a bit uneven, but the brilliance more than makes up for the dry spots. This book is recommended for all feminists. Lesbian feminists searching for a positive book should be especially pleased.

354. SAMUELS, Gertrude. THE PEOPLE VS. BABY. 1967. N.Y.: Avon. O.P.
Recommended only for Samuels's account of the life of Baby (Josephine Gomez), a young Puerto Rican woman in New York City who, like many others, has no alternative to the bitter street life of heroin, prison, and prostitution. While Samuels herself seems to lack any political understanding of Baby's experience, she is an honest journalist and is able to give us the benefit of scrupulous observation. Her greatest drawbacks seem to be her extreme fear of lesbianism, her unquestioning co-operation with the D.A.'s office, and her tendency to see as exceptions both the case of Baby and that of her own daughter and her friends when these "nice kids from good homes" get involved with dope.

355. SANDOZ, Mari. CHEYENNE AUTUMN. 1953. N.Y.: Avon, 1969. $1.25.
This historical narrative tells of the 1878 flight of 278 Cheyenne out of the government-established "Indian Territory" in Oklahoma back to their homeland in Montana. The native Americans, pursued by thousands of soldiers, traveled for 1,500 miles over six months. The book is semi-fictional because it contains conversations and inner thoughts. However, it has been thoroughly researched and Sandoz cites her sources. In addition to using libraries, museums and government records, she got much of her material from Old Cheyenne Woman, who was one of the few survivors. The fleeing band contained many more women than men, and **Cheyenne Autumn** does not neglect their part of the story—it celebrates the bravery and heroism of these women. Sandoz's careful and effective use of language creates for us a Cheyenne world view.

356. SARTON, May. THE SMALL ROOM. N.Y.: Norton, 1961. O.P.
A novel of academic life, its many conflicts and few triumphs. The book's philosophy seems dated, but the characters and situations are convincing, and the prose is clear and lovely. There is a particularly fine description of a love relationship between two aging women, endangered after many years' duration by the events recorded in the novel.

357. _____ JOANNA AND ULYSSES. N.Y.: Norton, 1963. $3.95.
The brief and deceptively simple story of Joanna, a self-effacing, dutiful daughter who, through her relationship with Ulysses, a donkey, grows to respect herself as a person and an artist. While the metamorphosis may be disappointing in feminist terms (her father's approval is needed to finalize it), it is quite believable in terms of Joanna's own life.

358. _____ MRS. STEVENS HEARS THE MERMAIDS SINGING. 1965. N.Y.: Norton, 1975. $2.45.
In her 70s, Hilary Stevens is a successful poet and novelist. An interview causes her to think back over her life and work and the women and men she has loved; she concludes that the Muses who have inspired her best work have in fact always been women she has loved. Back in the present, her life is touched by a young man who has been bitterly hurt in the course of a homosexual love affair, and she advises him as best she can.

359. _____ KINDS OF LOVE. N.Y.: Norton, 1970. $6.95.
Willard, a small New England town, is celebrating its bicentennial. It is a town with a history of strong women, a town now split between two classes, the wealthy summer visitors and the poor year-rounders. The central characters are two women, now in their 70s, whose friendship transcends the class barrier between them. Despite such promising content, this is a book rather shallower in style and substance than Sarton's best work.

360. SAUNDERS, Rubie. MARILYN MORGAN, R.N. 1969. N.Y.: New American Library, Signet. O.P.
A fast-paced nurse novel geared especially to younger readers. The novel presents a positive account of a young black pediatric nurse in a large city hospital. Though Nurse Morgan's dating life is glamorized, the book is generally a realistic portrait of the prejudice that young women have encountered when seriously choosing a career. Her parents, who feel that she should marry young, oppose Nurse Morgan's moving out of the family apartment to one of her own. She meets a series of men who also agree that marriage and serving them should be her main concern. Rising above all these pressures, Marilyn wins the admiration of her colleagues at the hospital for her dedicated work in a profession that she loves.

361. SCHOONOVER, Shirley. SAM'S SONG. 1969. N.Y.: Pyramid, 1972. O.P.
Sam, at 32, has just left her husband and three children. She hates herself and is desperately confused about who she is. Her greatest obsession is with sex and emotion; she wonders if she is a male homosexual in a female body. She sees a shrink, works as a copywriter and a model, and tries to figure things out. Though much of her consciousness is limited, she is an intriguing individual bound to provoke strong reactions. Schoonover's style is intense, direct, emotion-laden; her sexual descriptions are more than frank.

362. SCHRAM, Irene. ASHES, ASHES, WE ALL FALL DOWN. N.Y.: Simon & Schuster, 1972. $5.95.
A strange, terrifying novel about a concentration camp for children and their struggle to survive in an environment bent on their mental and physical destruction. The analogy is to our present-day world and the horrors of pollution, authoritarianism, etc., which all children face daily. Throughout the book, the tension between death and survival is almost unendurable, and although it is compellingly written, by the end, one feels exhausted, as by a too-long nightmare.

363. SEGAL, Lore. OTHER PEOPLE'S HOUSES. 1958. N.Y.: Plume Books, 1973. O.P.
This fictionalized autobiography is a must for anyone interested in World War II
Jewish immigrant experience or simply in childhood and young adulthood from a
female point of view. Lore Segal has written a vivid, sensitive account of her flight
from Austria and the Nazis—first to England, then the Dominican Republic, and
finally to New York City, first alone and later with her family. She not only speaks
with insight and a sense of humor, but manages to describe fear, loneliness, and insecurity without self-pity. Her relationship with her mother is especially moving, as is
her struggle to mature intellectually despite many obstacles. The story is beautifully
written.

364. SETON, Cynthia Propper. THE SEA CHANGES OF ANGELA LEWES. 1970. N.Y.:
Signet, 1973. $ .95.
Angelina Porter came to America from Czechoslovakia, founded an extensive and
prosperous family, then, after her husband's death, walked out on them all to return
to Europe at the start of World War II. In the 1960s, the same urge for independence
comes to her granddaughter, Angela, now 40 and a mother of four. The tale of how
she follows in her grandmother's footsteps is a positive one and is told with a good
deal of consciousness. Some readers may be put off by Seton's rather elaborate and
literary style.

365. SHEEHY, Gail. LOVESOUNDS. 1966. N.Y.: Berkeley Medallion, 1972. O.P.
Part of this book is full of cheap, stock, literary devices, part of it is rather interesting—the story of a young wife obsessively trying to save her marriage and finally
realizing the value of her own life. The marriage ends positively in divorce.

366. SHULMAN, Alix Kates. MEMOIRS OF AN EX-PROM QUEEN. 1972. N.Y.: Bantam, 1973. $1.75.
Written with a feminist consciousness, this is a worthwhile book describing the life of an
attractive, middle-class, American white woman. Sasha functions as half human, half
doll. She tries desperately to be beautiful, please men, be a good listener, etc., etc.,
while at the same time developing her secret self—her intellectual self. At 24, Sasha
finds herself faced with the problems of aging, of losing her beauty (a big part of her
identity), and thus her ability to please men.

367. SLUNG, Michele. CRIME ON HER MIND. N.Y.:Pantheon, 1975. $3.95.
Detective fiction anthology featuring fifteen examples of the female sleuth. The introduction and "descriptive catalogue of Women Detectives" make the book important regardless of the fact that over half the stories are by men.

368. SMITH, Lillian. STRANGE FRUIT. 1961. N.Y.: Harcourt, Brace, Jovanovich.
$7.95.
Lillian Smith presents us with the bitter lot of Nonnie Anderson, an educated black
woman. **Strange Fruit** is basically the story of the repercussions of a clandestine affair
between Nonnie and a white man, Tracey Dean, in a racist southern town during the
late 1940s. The power relationship between the two is so corrupt and unequal that
Tracey despises Nonnie and himself any time he has a semi-affectionate feeling for
her. Although Smith is white and not a particularly skillful writer, she seems to have
a good analysis of racial and sexual dynamics at work.

369. SPENCER, Elizabeth. THE LIGHT ON THE PIAZZA. N.Y.: McGraw-Hill, 1960.
$4.95.
Due to a childhood accident, Clara Johnson has a mental age of ten. She is now a
beautiful woman of 26. In her American home she has never fit in, but in Italy, where
she is traveling with her mother, she seems suddenly to belong. A young Italian begs
to marry Clara, a marriage she wants desperately. At first her mother dismisses this as
impossible, but slowly she begins to wonder if Clara could not fit in here. Will
anything be required of her that she cannot do? Through the story the question is subtly raised: what does our own society demand intelligence for? For living, or for the
repression of our impulses and ourselves?

STAFFORD, Jean. (1915-   ) *Henry James and Mark Twain are her favorite authors, and her own writings include elegant psychological vignettes as well as rambunctious comic stories. Although Stafford is best known as a fiction writer, her non-fiction work,* **A Mother in History** *(New York: Farrar, Straus & Giroux, 1966), is an engrossing study of Lee Harvey Oswald's mother.*

370. _____ **BOSTON ADVENTURE.** 1944. N.Y.: Harcourt Brace, current. $ .95.
Behind the frivolous title is the dark, often depressing story of a girl growing up in the 1930s. The child of immigrants (her father deserts the family; her mother goes mad), she works as a servant all through childhood. After high school she achieves her dream when she becomes a secretary/companion to a wealthy and domineering old lady. There is much to interest women in this book, particularly the exploration of mother-daughter relationships, and the power struggles and dependency which occur in them.

371. _____ **THE CATHERINE WHEEL.** 1952. N.Y.: Manor Books, 1974. $1.25.
We see a summer vacation in Maine in the 1930s through the eyes of Andrew, a child, and his cousin Katharine, a middle-aged woman who has never come to terms with her own childhood. Both struggle, in isolation, with the demons of loneliness and jealousy. Katharine is a beautiful and independent single woman (no one ever calls her a "spinster"). A crisis occurs in her life when she finds herself faced with the decision of whether to marry, a question she thought she had put aside forever in her youth. This is a brilliant book, beautifully written, and engrossing.

372. _____ **COLLECTED STORIES.** N.Y.: Farrar, Straus & Giroux, 1969. $2.95.
Stafford excells when writing about the very young and the very old. Many of the stories in this Pulitzer Prize-winning collection will be of special interest to those who want to read about the various ages of women. The final story "The End of a Career" is a heart-breaking account of a beautiful woman who is psychically crippled and finally destroyed by her fear of growing old and plain.

373. **THOMAS, Audrey Callahan. MRS. BLOOD.** N.Y.: Bobbs-Merrill, 1970. O.P.
"Some days my name is Mrs. Blood; some days it's Mrs. Thing," this book starts. The narrative switches between these two voices as Mrs. Thing/Blood has a protracted miscarriage in the West African country where her husband has gone to teach. As Mrs. Blood, she recalls bloody memories, indulges in fantastic word-play, and explores such themes as that of woman as sacrifice. A brilliant, compelling book, though not for the pregnant or those who have weak stomachs.

374. **UHNAK, Dorothy. THE BAIT.** N.Y.: Simon & Schuster, 1968.
The first and best of a three-book series of police-procedural mysteries featuring Christie Opara. The politics of the street and her (detective-squad) working place are vividly portrayed. She fights constantly, if unsuccessfully, for her humanity, even while being used as "bait" to catch a rapist-killer.

375. **VROMAN, Mary E. HARLEM SUMMER.** 1967. N.Y.: Berkeley Publications, 1968. $ .95.
When John Brown, a high school student from Alabama, comes to Harlem to spend a summer, he is excited by sights and sounds of the theater and the street speakers. He is also challenged for his basically non-violent position, mystified by the effects of poverty he sees around him. **Harlem Summer** describes a summer in which John grows toward adulthood—aware of contradictions, beginning to sort out many complexities in his life, learning about black history and discovering how it differs from what is taught in schools. A short, swift-reading novel, this book would be very good for high school boys, because of the diverse male characters presented. Unfortunately, the few females are not drawn as carefully.

376. WALKER, Alice. THE THIRD LIFE OF GRANGE COPELAND. N.Y.: Harcourt, Brace, Jovanovich, 1975. $7.95.
This novel shows three generations of a black family in the rural   south and presents with horrifying realism the dehumanizing conditions of their lives. It shows how brutalization turns black men against black women, how they resort to the tactics of making a woman pregnant to weaken her, or even, finally, of murder. In the end Grange Copeland becomes human largely through his love for his granddaughter, Ruth.

377. _____ IN LOVE AND TROUBLE. 1973. N.Y.: Harcourt, Brace, Jovanovich, 1974. $2.65.
These stories, first published from 1967 to 1973, present a diverse portrait of black women's lives. One of Alice Walker's themes concerns people who are pulled into (or who are changed with) the black movement. In "Everyday Use," Wangero claims a heightened consciousness of black culture—but forgets to be sensitive to her own mother and sister. In "Her Sweet Jerome," a revolutionary man ignores the desperate need of the woman he married. In contrast the "Revenge of Hannah Kemhuff" portrays a racist woman who brings about her own destruction through her bigoted fear of the black "root-worker's" curse. Class differences within the black community are brought out in other stories. "Roselily" illustrates the dawning misgivings of a strong, working mother "discovered" by an urban brother who wishes to "free her from her present condition;" instead he makes her feel "ignorant, wrong and backward." This is a great collection of stories.

378. _____ MERIDIAN. N.Y.: Harcourt, Brace, Jovanovich, 1976. $7.95.
Meridian cuts through glib revolutionary rhetoric to get at the core of being a black revolutionary in the 1960s and 1970s. It is the history of the Civil Rights movement in America as well as the biography of Meridian Hill, an earnest woman who believes that she needs knowledge before she can answer the question put to her by radical black friends: "Can you kill for the revolution?" Nothing comes easy in Meridian's life. She lives in the South canvassing for voter registration and becomes a symbol of defiance against the white power structure in black communities. She is raw to everything she learns and absorbs the horrific history of her relatives which give her no other choice but to be a revolutionary. **Meridian** is a beautifully written book which goes fully into the emotions as well as the political actions of its characters.

379. WALKER, Margaret. JUBILEE. 1966. N.Y.: Bantam. $1.50.
Jubilee is the story of Margaret Walker's great-grandmother—a vivid re-creation of slavery on a Georgia plantation. It traces the life of Vyry, a stoic and compassionate house slave who waits patiently for freedom while she daily watches and endures the inhuman treatment dealt to slaves in the name of christianity and economic necessity. After the Civil War, freedom for her means endless toil for someone else's profit. This wonderful inclusive novel is a woman/slave's personal view of the pre- and post-War South. Through extensive research and remarkable sensitivity, Walker presents a wide range of well-developed characters. Everyone should read **Jubilee** to challenge **Gone With the Wind** stereotypes.

Dorothea Lange, "Ex-Slave with a Long Memory," Alabama, 1938.

380. WEINGARTEN, Violet. MRS. BENEKER. 1968. N.Y.: Signet, 1970. O.P.
A sympathetic portrait of a suburban middle-class woman in her 50s, a good woman who has always worked to do what's right. Small incidents in her life are sketched: her relationship with her husband, with her children, with a young girl whom she dislikes but who needs her, with older people dependent upon her. Each incident ends with her feeling guilty for some lack, some flaw, some accident of society. An excellent and realistic portrait.

381. _____ A LOVING WIFE. 1969. N.Y.: Signet, 1970. O.P.
The moving story of a wife who takes a look at herself in the mirror and says, "You are forty-two years old, and nothing is going to be. It is." She looks at her husband and sees how much more he is enamored of his work than his life. She sees her son growing up and away from her. Her job suddenly means little to her. This dispassionate look results in a brief affair which further shakes her faith in the life she has, and she considers leaving it to live alone. Her mother tells her, "At your age. You're a drug on the market. If you were a man, women would be stopping you and begging you to come

91

and see them . . ." A trip to Italy raises further questions about living alone. The story is beautifully told, and the fact that it is about a relatively commonplace experience makes its conclusions all the more tragic.

382. WELTY, Eudora. THIRTEEN STORIES. 1965. N.Y.: Harcourt Brace, current.
This collection shows the scope and variety of Welty's talent; the only generalization that can be made about these stories is that virtually all of them are set in Mississippi. They range from a brutal satire on vicious, petty, gossiping women ("The Petrified Man") to the heartbreaking tale of an old black woman's long and arduous trip to town to fetch medicine ("A Worn Path"); from "Why I Live at the P.O.," a flippant tale of family conflict, to "Moon Lake," a fine, long story about pre-adolescent girls at a summer camp.

383. _____ THE OPTIMIST'S DAUGHTER. 1972. Greenwich, Conn., Fawcett, 1973. $1.25.
The McKelvas are a prominent family in a small southern town. When old Judge McKelva dies he leaves a much younger wife, Fay, and a middle-aged daughter, Laurel. The story is told from Laurel's point of view, and focuses much on Fay, who is portrayed as shallow, insensitive, and self-centered. Fay is working-class, and it's hard not to feel that Welty is guilty here of gross class bias.

384. WILLIAMS, Joy. STATE OF GRACE. N.Y.: Doubleday, 1973. O.P.
An impressive first novel, plumbing the depths of a woman's consciousness in a rich, innovative style. Kate's life has been overshadowed by the grim hold her fanatical minister father has over her; her marriage to Grady seems to offer an out, until he is struck down in a car accident. Even the humor in this book has a grimness.

Elizabeth Catlett "Homage to My Young Black Sisters," 1968. Courtesy of Elton C. Fax, author of Seventeen Black Artists (Dodd Mead & Co.).

385. WRIGHT, Sarah E. THIS CHILD'S GONNA LIVE. 1969. N.Y.: Dell, 1975. $1.25.
Violence and starvation loom as constant threats to the lives of Mariah and Jacob Upshur in Tangierneck, a black ghetto in Maryland. Jacob tries to scrape together whatever he can from the farm and the sea. (The neighborhood mills don't hire blacks.) Mariah, who is pregnant, determines to pull herself and her children out of their daily misery. Sarah Wright powerfully shows how powerless people respond to the economic sexual and emotional effects of racism. A wonderfully written book that makes the reader feel directly vulnerable to the poverty and futility facing the Tangierneck community.

386. YGLESIAS, Helen. HOW SHE DIED. 1972. N.Y.: Warner, 1973. $1.25.
Mary's breast is removed too late. Both her husband and her friend Jean, who narrates most of the story, know she is dying when the two of them start an affair. We are not surprised when Mary proceeds to go crazy. A chilling, gripping, well-written book.

Britain

Pre-19th Century

387. BURNEY, Fanny. EVELINA. 1778. N.Y.: Norton, current. $2.95.
Evelina, Fanny Burney's best work, appeared some 30 years after the works of Richardson and Fielding. Critics Utter and Needum suggest, in their book **Pamela's Daughters**, that Eliza Haywood's novel **The History of Miss Betsy Thoughtless** may have been an important influence. Burney wrote a first version of **Evelina** called **The History of Caroline Evelyn** when she was around 13, but family disapproval delayed its re-working and final appearance until Burney was 26. The novel is presented in the form of letters from a 17-year-old woman to her guardian. With a deft hand, Burney exposes the brutality and violence that constantly threatened women and gives us a remarkable sense of the total lack of choice for women at that time.

388. CENTLIVRE, Susanna. THE BUSIE BODY, A COMEDY. 1709. London: Lintot Publishers, 1732. (available only in libraries.)
Not a great deal is known about the early life of Susanna Carroll Centlivre, beyond the fact that her father was a Dissenter and Parliamentarian who had been dispossessed during the Restoration. She, however, came to be known for her plays and her outspoken political views. She favored Protestantism and strongly opposed a Stuart successor to Queen Anne. An enthusiastic Whig, she was denounced by Pope in his Dunciad. Mrs. Centlivre's plays include 14 comedies, 3 farces, a tragedy and a tragicomedy. She died in London in 1723. Critics applaud **The Busie Body** as the most remarkable comedy of intrigue in English. Her contemporary, Richard Steele, wrote in the Tatler, "The plot and incidents of the play are laid with that subtlety of spirit which is peculiar to females of wit, and is very seldom well performed by those of the other sex." The play's main theme is the lack of choice open to women of the period and their many underground forms of rebellion. Fully conscious of what they have to lose, the heroines of the play, Miranda and Isabinda (and their chamber maids) are sharp-witted, fast-moving hustlers. The men appear uniformly boorish or foolish in their various roles as oppressors—father, guardian, suitor or knave. A popular innovation of the play was its use of the character, Marplot, a male busie-body. In 1710, Centlivre wrote **Marplot**, a sequel to her first play. Some critics feel that her best work is **The Wonder, A Woman Keeps a Secret**, written in 1714, also a masterpiece of sardonic wit.

INCHBALD, Elizabeth Simpson (1753-1821). *Born in 1753, Elizabeth grew up in a Catholic family, in a rural area. She received no formal education. She passionately wanted to educate herself and to become an actress. Her first strategic move was to marry a man 18 years older than herself—who could introduce her to the theatrical world of London. In spite of a speech impediment, she acted for 18 years. Another actress, Sarah Kemble Siddons, was a close friend of hers for 45 years. When Elizabeth was 37 she published a novel,* **A Simple Story***, the first to deal with the situation of the Catholic minority. The novel was highly praised by Maria Edgeworth, her contemporary. Best known as a playwright, she was eventually able to cease acting (for which she said she was getting too old) and to make her living by her pen. Her friend, William Godwin, described her as "a piquant mixture of a milkmaid and a fine lady, a charmer whose sparkling talk had to break through the impediment of a stumbling tongue."*

389. _____ **EVERYONE HAS HIS FAULT, A COMEDY IN 5 ACTS**.
1793. Can be found in: **LESSER ENGLISH COMEDIES OF THE 18th CENTURY**. Ed. Allardyce Nicoll, Oxford University Press, World Classics editions, 1927.
Like the other women playwrights who preceeded her, Mrs. Inchbald felt compelled to begin her play with a defiant plea: "Then, drive not, Critics, with tyrannic rage, a

supplicating Fair-one from the Stage; the Comic Muse Perhaps is growing old, Her lovers, you well know, are few and cold. 'Tis time then freely to enlarge the plan, And let all those write Comedies—that can." Mrs. Inchbald's fears were happily unfounded, and the play continued to be revived even into the early 19th century. In keeping with its genre, **Everyone** deals with romantic entanglements. Through its male characters much is said about the status of wives, and through the weak-willed Miss Woolburn, a divorcee, we learn that even in divorce women were in a dependent and inferior position. Although interesting, **Everyone** was an early Inchbald production and lacks cohesion compared to later work.

390. _____ **A SIMPLE STORY**. 1791. N.Y.: Oxford University Press, 1967. $6.25.
One of the more readable 18th century works of fiction, its wit and intelligence give us an idea of the tradition that Jane Austen so brilliantly built on. Often cited as one of the earliest "novels of passion," it was a forerunner to the psychological depth and emotional intensity of the Brontes. Charlotte is supposed to have received her first inspiration for **Jane Eyre** from it, and certain parts of the story also call to mind Emily's **Wuthering Heights. A Simple Story** is, at bottom, a moral tale about the proper education of females, contrasting a willful, spoiled heroine with a properly humble and submissive one.

391. _____ **TO MARRY, OR NOT TO MARRY, A COMEDY IN 5 ACTS**. 1805. London: Longman, Hurst, Rees and Orms Pub. Co. (See: Collection of Farces and Other After Pieces. 7 Volumes, NY Adler, Repr of 1809 edition, Set $722.50.).
Enjoyable especially for its spunky female characters, **To Marry, Or Not To Marry** is full of a witty cynicism about the motives that drive people into marriage. This is probably best expressed by Lady Susan: "The favourite lover of a woman of fashion has the same prerogative as a king—he never dies—there's always an immediate successor." Marriage and "falling in love" are the two things that most of the characters are trying to avoid. There is also a somewhat heavy-handed plot. Lavensforth and his black servant plan to murder Sir Oswin, but this diabolical scheme is foiled through a complicated series of amorous matches and mismatches leading Sir Oswin to shelter Lavensforth's run-away daughter—with whom he inevitably falls in love.

392. LENNOX, Charlotte. THE FEMALE QUIXOTE. 1752. London: Oxford University Press, 1973. $4.50. p.b.
Arabella, like Cervantes' Don Quixote, bases her assumptions about life on the French heroic romances she is fond of reading. Of course, 18th century reality, even for upper class ladies, was very different from the romance, and Arabella's entry into society is marked by a series of comic misadventures. One involves the gardener whom she mistakenly identifies as a disguised prince. Finally, a doctor of divinity restores her to reason and she settles for a conventional marriage in place of her romantic ideals. An amusing and very readable novel.

393. MANLEY, Mary de la Riviere. THE ADVENTURES OF RIVELLA. 1719. New York & London: Garland Publishing, Inc., 1972.
A rebellious upper class woman, Mary Manley wrote plays and political satires. Her rebellion extended into her private life, and she was involved in numerous liaisons and even contracted a bigamous marriage. As the daughter of a lieutenant governor, needless to say her conduct cost her social prestige. Modelled on her own life, **The Adventures Of Rivella** deals in a lighthearted manner with the intrigues a well-meaning, independent, sensual woman finds herself involved in. Manley's frank treatment of female sexuality as an assumed norm of life contrasts with the sexual restraint of 19th century women's fiction. Recommended only for those with a special interest in the period, since it is written in the much-dated style of the 18th century chronicle, predecessor of the novel.

394. RADCLIFFE, Ann. THE ITALIAN. 1796. London: Oxford University Press, 1971. $7.25 h.b. $3.50 p.b.
Inspired by **Mysteries Of Udolpho**, Matthew Gregory Lewis wrote **The Monk**, a fleshy

gothic novel that quite graphically explores what villains do. Mrs. Radcliffe responded by writing **The Italian** as protest against the sexual explicitness of Lewis's novel. Superficially similar to **The Monk** in that the villain is also a monk guilty of unseemly crimes against his family, the preoccupations of the two novelists differ greatly. Radcliffe's Schedoni, who has already committed crimes, wants power and prestige; whereas Lewis's Ambrosio, who already has both, wants sexual gratification. A more compact novel than **Mysteries Of Udolpho**, in **The Italian** Mrs. Radcliffe cuts down on supernatural paraphernalia and landscape description. Harrowing experience brings out strong character in Ellena, at the start of the novel a totally innocent and sheltered heroine. Not easy reading, but we recommend it.

395. _____ **THE MYSTERIES OF UDOLPHO**. 1794. London: Oxford University Press, 1970. $9.75 h.b. $5.95 p.b.
Suspense and sentiment blend in what Mrs. Radcliffe defines as a tale of terror, as opposed to one of horror. "Terror and horror are so far opposite, that the first expands the soul, and awakens the faculties to a high degree of life; the other contracts, freezes, and nearly annihilates them." **Mysteries of Udolpho** is the opposite of Warhol's **Frankenstein**—everything is cloaked and hidden; although as events unravel, supernatural occurrences, like music at midnight, or a corpse behind a curtain, all have rational explanations beneath them. As the novel's heroine, Emily, gradually discovers rational reasons for each supernatural occurrence, she gains control over her fears and power over her male oppressor. Despite frequent swoons, Emily maintains a strong-willed opposition to Montoni's threats. Although Mrs. Radcliffe exaggerates the evils endemic to the Italian character and countryside, Montoni is convincing as a villain obsessed with power for its own sake . . . and as villains go, he seems capable of almost anything. We highly recommend this novel.

396. WOLLSTONECRAFT, Mary (1759-1797). **MARIA, OR THE WRONGS OF WOMAN**. 1797. N.Y.: W.W. Norton, 1975. $1.95.
Better propaganda than literature, Wollstonecraft's novel is nevertheless an important work and well worth reading. Wollstonecraft was perhaps one of the few intellectuals of her time to suggest that the "inalienable rights" men fought for in the French and American revolutions might logically extend to women. Based in part on her own life, this novel is a frame for Wollstonecraft's feminist ideas and an angry, passionate exposition of the injustices suffered by 18th century women. The plot revolves around Maria, a young woman tricked, abused and confined to a mental asylum by her husband. Through her story and that of Jemima, the asylum attendant, Wollstonecraft presents a spectrum of women's oppression from the servant's quarters to the refinements of the middle-class home. Left unfinished by Wollstonecraft's early death, the novel is fragmented and badly flawed by overblown prose and implausible circumstances. But if the credibility of her heroine suffers from melodramatics and an unrealistic burden of tragedy, the issues Wollstonecraft confronts are real enough.

19th Century

AUSTEN, Jane *(1775-1817). The daughter of a country clergyman, Jane Austen was restricted to the narrowest of lives. Her novels do not move beyond the limits of her life; with her light, ironic touch, she paints the day-to day lives of the country gentry of her time. Her largest dramas have generally to do with marriage. (She herself never married.) Her literary excellence is now widely recognized by all but a few smug male critics. What makes her work particularly interesting to us is its healthy realism; her heroines are plausible young women without unnaturally perfect attributes, and the relations between men and women are presented with unvarnished honesty—there are misunderstandings and conflicts of personality, and, underlying it all, the money and class bases of the marriage market. If the idealization of an unreal*  *vision of love is one of the ways in which the novel has oppressed women, Jane Austen was a courageous rebel against this literary tradition.*

397. _____ **LOVE AND FREINDSHIP.** [sic] In **LOVE AND FREIND-SHIP AND OTHER EARLY WORKS.** Folcroft, Pa.: Folcroft Library Editions, $12.50. Written when Austen was only in her teens, though never published until 1922, this is a hilarious parody of the sentimental novel and its absurd conventions.

398. _____ **SENSE AND SENSIBILITY.** 1811. Many cheap editions. This early Austen novel explores the dualism inherent in a society which opposes sense to sensibility, reason to romance, and social form to emotional honesty. Eighteenth and 19th century British mores reflected the philosophical dichotomy of rationalism versus romanticism, and Austen attempts to dramatize the effects of this split on the lives of those whose behavior was measured against such standards. Although Elinor is not all "sense," nor Marianne pure "sensibility," together the sisters may represent the divided self struggling for expression and fulfillment within the walls of prescribed social conduct. It is perhaps Elinor who comes closest to the balance Austen appears to be advocating, in her ability to feel deeply without hysteria and to observe form without hypocrisy. Not as penetrating as **Pride and Prejudice**, but still an enduring Austen work.

399. _____ **PRIDE AND PREJUDICE.** 1813. Many editions. Austen's novel about the marriage market explores marriage for what it was—a career goal most women were raised to fulfill. A woman's stock and trade was her eligibility; and marriage, "the only honorable provision for well-educated young women of small fortune. . ." The women and men in this novel marry for a variety of reasons: physical attraction, fortune, love, and sometimes all three. The romance between upper-class Mr. Darcy and the intelligent, lively Elizabeth Bennet is classic and compelling. Elizabeth is proud and prejudiced against Darcy for a variety of reasons, foremost among them his upper-class snobbishness. Love involves compromise and gradually Darcy bends and Elizabeth's prejudice against him turns to love. Elizabeth's loving relationship to her sister Jane and their mutual endurance of problems arising from a difficult mother and foolish sisters is dealt with perceptively, as are the embarrassments young people suffer at the hands of well-meaning adults interfering in their social lives. Austen's satiric and sound novel reads like a marriage handbook written in fairy tale form; it is practical and romantic simultaneously.

400. _____ **MANSFIELD PARK.** 1814. Many cheap editions. Readers who delighted in the intelligence and independence of Austen's Elizabeth Bennet in **Pride and Prejudice** and the incomparable Emma, can only be dismayed by

Fanny Price. Passive and self-effacing, she triumphs by sitting quietly by, until all the other characters have acted in ways which prove them morally inferior. This was a transitional book, written at the time of **Pride and Prejudice**'s publication, after an apparent ten-year abstention from writing. That Austen was suffering from qualms about her earlier work is apparent from her mockery of the witty Mary Crawford, a character who resembles both Elizabeth Bennet and Austen herself.

401. _____ **EMMA.** 1816. Many cheap editions.
A rich and idle young woman, Emma is resigned to a life of comfortable spinsterhood. Her major pre-occupation is manipulating the lives of the people she associates with. She lives with her father whom she manages so effectively that she is in reality the head of the house. Much more complicated than this smooth domestic arrangement are the situations that arise from Emma's misguided efforts to direct the romantic entanglements of all those around her. In her zest to control the lives of others Emma represses her own feelings—feelings that are awakened by the rational Mr. Knightley. Love and father substitute rolled into one, he is destined from the beginning to win Emma's hand. A study of how middle and upper class women are driven to sublimate the libido into manipulation of people in order to achieve domestic power.

402. _____ **NORTHANGER ABBEY.** 1818. Many cheap editions.
This satirical put-down of gothic novels and their unreal conventions is a healthy and realistic antidote to the popular cult of romantic sensibility. Catherine Morland is a gullible innocent nourished on novels. She yearns for high drama and romance, and instead comes up against the harsh realities of life and, in particular, the marriage market. Even the conventional happy ending is described with tongue in cheek.

403. _____ **PERSUASION.** 1818. Many cheap editions.
Austen's last complete novel, written while she was dying, explores the uncertainties of social order. The heroine, bereft of home, mother and sweetheart, is approaching middle age when her chance for "a second spring of youth and beauty" arrives in the person of a successful navy officer, a one-time suitor whom she rejected eight years earlier. She had been persuaded by family and friends that the man had no prospects, but now he's rich and back looking for a bride who he insists must combine "a strong mind, with sweetness of manner." Can our persuadable heroine make the grade? Or, far more importantly for Austen, has she the resources to grow, become active and find purpose in a world where the old order is in moral collapse?

404. _____ **LADY SUSAN: THE WATSONS: SANDITON**, Ed. Margaret Drabble, London: Penguin Books, Ltd., 1974. $1.75.
Edited and with an excellent introduction by Margaret Drabble, this collection of Austen fragments is well worth reading. A rarity among Austen characters, Lady Susan is a thoroughly unlikable heroine—a flirtatious middle-aged mother contriving to force her daughter into a loveless marriage. In **The Watsons**, Emma, a dependent single woman, reflects upon her limited choices: "Poverty is a great evil, but to a woman of education and feeling . . . it cannot be the greatest.—I would rather be a teacher at a school (and I can think of nothing worse) than marry a man I did not like."

405. _____ and **ANOTHER LADY. SANDITON.** Boston: Houghton Mifflin Company, 1975. $8.95.
Too ill to continue writing, Jane Austen left her last novel a fragment. Recently completed by Another Lady who picks up where Austen left off in the middle of chapter eleven, the novel develops smoothly out of hints dropped by Austen in the opening chapters. It centers around a sensible young woman's romantic adventures at Sanditon, a not-so-popular watering spot. Particularly humorous are the Parker hypochondriacs—two sisters and their brother.

406. HODGE, Jane Aiken. ONLY A NOVEL/THE DOUBLE LIFE OF JANE AUSTEN. 1972. Fawcett, $1.25.
A good (if uninspired) general work on Jane Austen, this book is a sketch of her life and times. Much of Hodge's information is conjecture, built on her knowledge of the

scanty facts available, evidence from Austen's novels, and Hodge's own efforts to read between the lines. She dispels the myths of the pious old maid and the frivolous husband-hunter, and creates a plausible picture of a well-integrated woman who conformed outwardly to the society of her day, but used her irony and her anger as effective tools of her genius in the novels. Hodge is a sympathetic biographer, yet careful to distinguish between truth and supposition. Helpful features include a bibliography, an index, a family tree, and synopses of the novels.

407. BODICHON, Barbara. AN AMERICAN DIARY, 1957-8. Boston: Routledge and Regan Paul Ltd. $10.75.
Unitarian, abolitionist, and feminist Barbara Leigh Smith Bodichon traveled to the United States on her honeymoon in 1857-8; out of the trip came this diary, a collection of her reactions to the southern and New England states just prior to the Civil War. Although her perceptions are predictably tinged with racist and nationalist stereotypes, her style is lively and readable, and she provides us with an Englishwoman's view of slavery and the American people in the 19th century. Included in this volume is a short biography of the author, who was also a painter, a close friend of George Eliot (the model for Eliot's **Romola**), and an extremely vocal activist for women's rights in England.

408. BRADDON, Mary Elizabeth. LADY AUDLEY'S SECRET. 1862. N.Y.: Dover, 1974. $3.00.
Here is a popular "sensational" novel that is a good deal better than one might expect from that genre. The characters have real depth and the plot is logical and absorbing (Thackeray envied Braddon her deft hand with a plot). In this, one of the earliest detective novels, the lazy, rather unwilling detective seeks to find a lost friend and unravel Lady Audley's secret. An obvious villain, Lady Audley is rather fascinating all the same. Her niece Alicia is aggressive, intelligent, and in love with the hero, but she, too, is denied a happy ending. "Too bouncy," says our detective. His heart is won by the only flat character in the book, a passive female object. What were Braddon's feelings about woman's role? She wrote this book to pay her lover's debts. With creditors always at the door, she continued to write a breakneck pace, rearing a whole troop of children at the same time. She was a writer of obvious talent and one can only speculate what use she might have put it to, had her life been less pressured. **Lady Audley** is for readers with an interest in popular 19th century writers and/or detective stories.

409. BRONTE, Anne. AGNES GREY. 1847. London: Oxford University Press, 1976. $5.50.
The novel ranks above the majority of 19th century fiction about governesses and is much under-read. In **Agnes Grey** a governess recounts her experiences first hand. In both the families Agnes works for, she is treated disrespectfully by the children and delegated no real authority over them by their parents. Her position is merely custodial. Agnes Grey smolders in quiet rebellion against the enforced passivity of her lot. Outraged by the acts of cruelty towards animals, she is frequently forced to witness, in one scene Agnes takes militant action. She drops a stone on a nest of birds to prevent her young male pupil from slowly torturing them to death. Many 19th century readers found this scene objectionable on the grounds that it was overly sadistic, and therefore, an unfeminine and unnecessary plot addition. However, as Charlotte Bronte later related to Mrs. Gaskell, this incident actually occurred. Anne Bronte's own experiences as a governess left her with a great deal of hatred for the British class system.

410. _____ THE TENANT OF WILDFELL HALL. 1848. N.Y.: Dutton. $3.95.
Although Anne Bronte was unable to achieve Charlotte's mastery of the novel form or Emily's uniqueness, this novel is worth reading for the perspective it gives on the Bronte milieu and for its own sake. Because the novel's heroine Helen Grahm is both an artist and mother, it is reminiscent of Avis in Elizabeth Stuart Phelps's **A Story of Avis**. Unlike Avis, though, Helen lives independently of husband or lover and partially supports herself and her child by selling her work. She causes a stir by her outspoken theories on the upbringing and education of children. Like other Bronte novels,

Tenant has an oppressive Byronic male figure. We learn that Mrs. Grahm is not a widow, but rather an escapee from a destructive marriage. Anne Bronte describes Helen's middle-class marriage in terms of the power balance which allowed a man to keep his wife in bondage if he so desired. Helen discovers her hatred of this double standard. Unfortunately the novel is flawed by the author's occasional urge to sermonize and by a happily-ever-after ending which brings Helen again to a romantic marriage.

411. BRONTE, Charlotte. THE SEARCH AFTER HAPPINESS. N.Y.: Simon & Schuster. 1969. $3.50.
When the Brontes were children, their play consisted almost entirely of a make-believe game, the elaborate creation of a world—Glasstown—populated by Twelve Young Men (12 wooden soldiers). **The Search for Happiness**, written when Charlotte was only thirteen, recounts the adventures of one of these young men. Henry O'Donnell (Captain Tarry-not-at-Home) leaves his city in search of happiness. he visits strange places, encounters several mysterious persons and one friend, and returns to find happiness exactly where he left it—at home. This is a child's novel with childish flaws in grammar and punctuation, heavily influenced by the books the author had read. But, as Charlotte Bronte was an extraordinary child, so this is an extraordinary story: vivid and brilliantly imaginative. One finds here the origins of later Bronte characters and situations.

412. _____ JANE EYRE. 1847. Many cheap editions.

A powerful and moving story with a satisfying—if too neat—resolution, this book is a sweet indulgence of one's dreams for justice. Jane, an orphan, describes her growth from childhood through maturity, detailing with a very alert sensibility the conditions which work to keep her a dependent. If you've read it before, you may be surprised to find that Rochester is extremely manipulative, even sadistic; and that Jane is stronger, more intelligent, and altogether finer than you remembered. You may realize that the ending is happy not because Rochester's wife has died, but because Jane's economic and social needs are met without Rochester, so she is free to choose him as a lover and friend instead of for survival. If you find yourself unable to make a connection between this story and present reality, read Adrienne Rich on **Jane Eyre** (MS, October, 1973) for a sensitive and timely discussion of the novel.

413. _____ SHIRLEY. 1849. N.Y.: Everyman. $2.95. N.Y.: dutton.
In this overlong, underpolished novel, written at a time of almost overwhelming personal tragedy, Charlotte Bronte attempts to include the working classes through her descriptions of factory workers, framebreaking industrial riots, and economic hierarchy within a Yorkshire community. This social concern, however, is soon overshadowed by the activities of the two central women characters, Shirley Keeldar and Caroline Helstone. Shirley, modeled on Emily Bronte, is active, outgoing, confident, and occasionally seen as androgynous. Her friendship with Caroline is egalitarian and sisterly. Sandwiched in between the melodrama and the limited social commentary are wonderful feminist conversations between Shirley and Caroline. The conclusion, like the beginning, is disappointing and traditionally pat: love conquers all, even industrial unrest.

414. _____ VILLETTE. 1853. N.Y.: Harper and Row, $3.45.
A classic work of women's literature, **Villette**'s Lucy Snowe is in many ways the culmination of all of Charlotte Bronte's sharp-witted, forceful, plain women. This novel, Charlotte's last, was written after Anne, Emily, and Branwell were all dead, a time when she was feeling terribly isolated, often ill. It is based on the period between 1842 and 1844 when Charlotte (and for a year Emily as well) had been both a student

and a teacher at a Catholic girls' school in Brussels. Important themes of the novel include: the demands of her work as a teacher; the importance of work to women; the cultural contrast between Catholic Brussels and her own beloved Protestant England; the contradictions of class in the aristocratic school; and finally, her impossible feelings for a married teacher, M. Heger. Male definitions of women's roles reach Lucy through the perspectives of the two major male characters and the projections of images of women in painting and theater. Lucy's choices of men are limited to a cold, rational doctor who types women as hysterical or trivial, or a fiery but domineering professor who wants simultaneously to mold her and to compete with her. Some positive effects of Lucy's female experience afford her a strong share of intuition, sensitivity to feelings, even a sense of premonition, and the strength to survive. She refuses to accept the usual lot of women, "a great many women and girls are supposed to pass their lives something . . . like a bark slumbering through halcyon weather, in a harbour still as glass—the steersman stretched on the little deck, . . . buried, if you will, in long prayer." But Bronte also gives us an amazing sense of the cost of her character's rebellion: terrible fits of depression, lonely isolation, hypochondria, and nervousness. The ending is similar to **Jane Eyre**, but more extreme—this time the Rochester figure is drowned in a shipwreck and Lucy's work and life really do take precedence.

415. _____ **THE PROFESSOR**. 1857. Everyman Paperback, 1972. $2.95.
Bronte was unable to see this, her first book, in print during her lifetime. Some have hypothesized that publishers rejected it because the essentially simple plot line contained nothing exotic enough for public tastes. Although unique among her novels in possessing a male narrator, one finds introduced here the themes which were to be so important in her later works: the struggle between reason and passion, the physical and spiritual survival of women lacking financial means, and finally, her vision of marriage between equals. Not as polished or elaborate as what was to come after, but satisfying reading in its own right.

416. GASKELL, Elizabeth. THE LIFE OF CHARLOTTE BRONTE. 1857. Baltimore: Penguin, 1975. $3.95.
This is an excellent biography, telling the story of a family whose lives were quite as fascinating as the novels they wrote. Mrs. Gaskell was a personal friend of Charlotte's. There are a few things she had to conceal because she was writing so soon after Charlotte's death and at the personal request of her father; for example, she doesn't mention Charlotte's love for M. Heger. On the whole, however, she was remarkably honest, to the point of provoking a few scandals.

417. GERIN, Winifred. CHARLOTTE BRONTE, THE EVOLUTION OF GENIUS. 1967. N.Y.: Oxford University Press, 1969. $3.95, p.b. $15.00, h.b.
One of the best biographies of Charlotte Bronte. The author has seemingly made use of every piece of available data. Gerin breaks new ground by correcting factual mistakes of earlier biographers, and also by proposing several original (and certainly debatable) hypotheses about the Bronte family. While the writing style is undistinguished, Charlotte Bronte's life is so compelling that one cannot help being swept up in this book.

418. BRONTE, Emily. WUTHERING HEIGHTS. 1847. Many cheap editions.
The powerful and haunting story of the love-hate bond between a willful woman, Catherine Earnshaw, and an exotic, sinister man, Heathcliff. Growing up as brother and sister in isolated Yorkshire moor country, Catherine and Heathcliff develop a kind of primal commitment to each other which is eventually squelched and distorted by family and social pressure. In her article in the June 1973 issue of _Liberation_, Barbara Deming says that Bronte was illustrating woman's dilemma: a woman can either "remain unmarried and undeveloped, or marry and become lost to herself in another sense, the maddened slave." She suggests that we read the book as though Heathcliff were not literally a separate person, but simply—as Cathy herself speaks of him—_herself_: "I am Heathcliff." Unique in its time, it remains so today.

419. GERIN, Winifred. EMILY BRONTE. 1971. N.Y.: Oxford University Press, 1972. $10.95.
Gerin notes in her preface that the scarcity of material and reclusive nature of her subject make a biography of Emily nearly impossible to write. Gerin, who lived in the Brontes' village for ten years and has written biographies of them all, gives as thorough an account of Emily's life as is possible. She emphasizes Emily's choice "to be as God made me" rather than conform to traditional female role models in attitudes, appearance, or behavior. Gerin retells legendary Emily anecdotes and offers interesting speculations on the subjects of Emily's relationshp with her brother, her death, and remaining manuscripts.

420. BRUNTON, Mary. DISCIPLINE. 1814. London, 1837.
Mary Brunton, a Scotswoman, read and worked with her close friend Mrs. Izett and published two novels, **Self Control** and **Discipline**. Jane Austen thought **Discipline** an "excellently-meant, elegantly-written book, without anything of nature or probability in it." By 20th century standards the novel is a sentimental, moralistic, melodramatic tale about a wealthy and spoiled merchant's daughter who develops a sound character only after her father's bankruptcy and suicide render her destitute. The novel is tedious reading. If you plan to read Mary Brunton, we recommend this edition because the Memoir, written by her husband, contains interesting excerpts from her letters and journals.

421. CORELLI, Marie. A ROMANCE OF TWO WORLDS. 1886. N.Y.: Rudolf Steiner Publications, 1973. $2.45.
A popular writer and Queen Victoria's favorite novelist, Marie Corelli writes about two worlds, the spiritual and the material. For readers interested in contemporary spiritualism and occultism or in an 1890s esoteric ambience, the novel is worth reading. In it a nervous, artistic woman begins to have visions after she drinks a mysterious liquid. Her absorption in the spiritual world increases, and she goes to live with Heliobas, a face in her visions, a Svengali-like trip guide in real life; his literally magnetically attractive sister Zara; and Leo, a dog with uncanny psychic powers. All this has its basis in the electrical nature of the universe, and Zara eventually departs this "earthly prison" in an blaze of light (intentionally electrocuted) to be with her spiritual soul mate. The synopsis may seem incomprehensible, but the novel flows smoothly and gives a first-person account of one woman's spiritual adventures.

EDEN, Emily. *(1797-1867). An ancestor of Virginia Woolf's dear friend Violet Dickinson, Emily Eden lived and based her novels in aristocratic London society. In addition to her social comedies, which won considerable fame, Eden also translated verse and published travel memoirs (**Portrait of the People and the Princes of India**, 1844.)*

422. _____ THE SEMI-ATTACHED COUPLE. 1860. Boston: Burnham, 1861.
The characters and situations in this elegant comedy-of-manners are reminiscent of Jane Austen with perhaps a trace of George Eliot. Lady Helen tries to reconcile herself to an unhappy marriage while friends and neighbors look on, offer advice, and struggle with their own romantic tangles. Although the novel falls short of Austen's fine observations, on one hand, and Eliot's broad social vision, on the other, it remains a witty, engaging study of women striving for personal growth within the confines of Victorian high society.

ELIOT, George *(Mary Ann Evans) (1819-1880). She was born and grew up in the prosperous English farming country of the Midlands (the setting for most of her novels) and received what was, for a girl, a good education in those times. In her youth she was a deeply devout convert to evangelical Christianity; later she broke completely with the church, but all her work is influenced by a religious and ethical preoccupation, sometimes weighted by it. Her brilliant mind, wonderful sense of humor, and deep understanding of human nature shine through in all her works. Eliot's fictional portraits of women reflect her own ambivalent longings for both worlds: the traditional, woman as wife, helpmate, mother, and unconventional:*

woman as worker, scholar, man's equal. Much has been made of her relationship with George Henry Lewes, a married man unable to get a divorce, with whom she lived for over 20 years. They always thought of their relationship as a marriage, and the social ostracism which resulted brought Eliot a great deal of pain and self-consciousness. For her, to live with Lewes was not a radical act, simply a courageous one.

423. _____ ADAM BEDE. 1859. Many cheap editions.
In this, her first novel, Eliot presents us with two women whose lives are far less conventional than those of the characters in her later books. Dinah is a Methodist preacher who for many years scorns marriage so that she may be free to live her own life. Hetty has a clandestine affair and becomes pregnant out of wedlock. Yet the consciousness behind this story lacks the ironic comments on "women's role" and the sympathetic understanding of the social pressures to conform to that role, which are found in some of Eliot's later works.

424. _____ THE MILL ON THE FLOSS. 1860. Many cheap editions.
The very quality we first admire in heroine Maggie Tulliver—her passionate impetuous, unconventional nature—inevitably brings about her downfall. Typical Victorian conflicts between feeling and moral obligation serve George Eliot well in developing this tragedy about a sensitive, highly intelligent but provincially bound English girl who inevitably suffers each time her instincts supercede social conventions. Psychologically acute descriptions of Maggie's childhood, her relationships with her idolized brother Tom, pampering father, and insipid mother, as well as Eliot's excellent satirization of parochial English manners contribute to the book's merits. many readers, however, will be disappointed by the plot in which Maggie changes from "ugly duckling to swan" and falls for a charismatic but superficial young dandy.

425. _____ SILAS MARNER. 1861. Many cheap editions.
George Eliot treats several sophisticated issues in this novel about the miserly, bitter Silas Marner and his return from alienation to society. Silas recovers his humanity by raising the child Eppie, found mysteriously on his doorstep one winter's night. The validity of his parental claim is acknowledged despite their lack of blood relationship. Eliot also surprises us by asserting the advanced opinion that a childless couple (Godfrey and Nancy Cass) can still be a happy one. In the manner of a fable, **Silas Marner** counts on fateful coincidence to teach the moral lessons of error, repentance, and rectitude.

426. ELIOT, George. FELIX HOLT, THE RADICAL. 1866. Baltimore, Md.: Penguin, 1972. $4.25.
Among our 19th century British writers, George Eliot stands out for her deep interest in the interplay between people, politics and history. **Felix Holt** is her most deliberate attempt to write a political novel and it stands out today for its treatment of class differences and the relationship between an individual's social class and their life choices. The novel's setting is the election which occurred after the passage of the first Parliamentary Reform Bill of 1832. Felix Holt, a working-class man with much energy and leadership ability chooses to stay with his class rather than "rise up." Through him, Eliot articulates the position that, without education, votes alone will not empower the working class. Also interesting is the character of Mrs. Transome, a woman whose tragedy exists apart from the issues of electoral politics. She provides an outstanding portrait of an aging woman whose intelligence and strength have been denied—and the bitter consequences of this situation. Because the historical setting is complex, the annotated Penguin edition is recommended.

427. _____ MIDDLEMARCH. 1872. Many cheap editions.
Eliot's portrait of an English provincial town on the eve of the first Reform Bill explores the complexities of class society. The spirit of the times is embodied in a large cast of characters, who only half understand the momentous events breaking around them. Society's assimilation of individuals who nourish nonconforming dreams is a recurrent theme of the novel. Dorothea, a would-be reformer, yearns for knowledge and

social action, but settles for marriage as the only path out of the limitations of a conventional woman's role, only to find herself caught in the shadow of a narrow old man. "Many who knew her," concludes Eliot, "thought it a pity that so rare and substantitive a creature . . . should be only known as a wife and mother. But no one stated exactly what else was in her power she ought rather to have done." In the end Eliot does not give Dorothea independence—but a younger, more attractive, and more interesting man to serve.

428. _____ **DANIEL DERONDA.** 1876. Baltimore, Md.: Penguin, 1975. $3.95.

Daniel Deronda and Gwendolen Harleth exchange glances over a roulette wheel, then go their separate ways: he toward political leadership; she toward marital disaster. Eliot was annoyed by critics' tendency to overlook her ideal hero, and today, it's more tempting than ever to skip the flat, unconvincing Deronda episodes, turning instead to Gwendolen. She's a dangerous combination of will and naivete, and her clashes with her sadistic husband, Lord Grandcourt, carry the Victorian novel into new psychological realms. She confesses her inner rebellion to Deronda, who becomes her "moral savior." Despite this, we urge you to read the entire novel for the sake of a skillfully woven story and for Deronda's long-lost mother, a marvelous character who appears near the end and lambasts the patriarchy. "You can never imagine," she tells Deronda, "what it is to have man's force of genius in you and yet to suffer the slavery of being a girl."

429. REDINGER, Ruby. GEORGE ELIOT: THE EMERGENT SELF. New York: Knopf, 1975. $15.00.

"Few women, I fear, have had such reason as I have to think the long, sad years of youth were worth living for the sake of middle age." Thus declared George Eliot at the age of 38, several days before her first novel **Clerical Sketches** appeared. Fifteen years in the making, Redinger's fine Eliot biography is, among other things, an insightful reimagining of the process by which the sorrow and self-destructiveness of Mary Ann Evans were forged into the powerful, compassionate novels of George Eliot. Book by book, Redinger takes us through Eliot's reworking of her unhappy childhood and youth: from **Adam Bede** ("The Book of the Father" Redinger calls it, a romantic recreation of Eliot's own father) to **Daniel Deronda**, which Redinger sees as "The Book of the Mother," an affirmation of motherhood. Redinger also explores the effects of the masculine pseudonym: whether it led Eliot to overprotest her own femininity as well as traditional female roles. "There is no subject on which I am more inclined to hold my peace and learn than on 'The Woman Question'," Eliot once remarked. "It seems to me to overhang abysses, of which prostitution is not the worst." **The Emergent Self**, dedicated to ". . . George Eliot herself, who occasionally has annoyed or disturbed me, but has never bored me," is a remarkable combination of research, imagination, and love.

430. FERRIER, Susan. MARRIAGE. 1818. London: Oxford University Press, 1971. $11.25.

A satire of manners and marriage, the institution of marriage itself is not criticized, although the education of women to frivolity instead of moral and common sense is. Crucial obstructions to an ideal marriage are the interference of parents and the choice between love and money. Although the contrast between upper-class British and middle-class Scottish manners gives rise to some of the most entertaining scenes of the novel, class conflict takes a back seat to the conflicts between mother and daughters. Ferrier's understanding of mother/daughter relationships is timeless, and her portrait of a mother, Lady Juliana, living out her fantasies through her eldest daughter, Adelaide, is outstanding. Of the great variety of female characters, the most memorable is Lady Emily, a spirited and cynical commentator on situations and persons, perhaps, very like the author herself. Often compared to Jane Austen, Ferrier's style is light and Austenesque—although her satire is not as sharp, nor her style of writing as lively.

GASKELL, Elizabeth (1810-1865) *After the death of her mother, Elizabeth Cleghorn Stevenson was sent by her father to live with an aunt in Knutsford. This period she later fictionalized in* **Cranford**. *From a strongly Unitarian family, she married the junior minister of a Manchester Unitarian chapel when she was 22. She had four daughters and a son and not until the death of this only son in 1845 did she begin her first novel,* **Mary Barton**. *Best known for her concern with reform, she was part of the pioneering literary movement that dealt with the problems of working-class life. Although she always abhorred the bluestockings she did begin to believe in certain rights for women. In 1865 she signed the Petition of a Married Woman's Property Bill because she realized that many women less fortunate than herself were subject to husbands who by law could appropriate any of their wife's property or money. Often portrayed as the happy homemaker, Mrs. Gaskell was married to a man who became increasingly cold and distant through the years of their marriage; the conflicts that resulted from this have been largely ignored by critics for the sake of myth. Herself the author of a famous and controversial biography of her friend Charlotte Bronte, Mrs. Gaskell wished that no biography be written of her and deliberately destroyed much material and correspondence about her life.*

431. _____ **MARY BARTON**. 1848. N.Y.: Norton, $2.25; Dutton, $2.50; Penguin, $2.95.
Mary Barton, Gaskell's first novel, provides a detailed and compassionate description of the poor manufacturing population of industrial Manchester in the late 1830s and early 1840s. Multiple hierarchies (master and worker, Chartists and Parliament, men and women, prostitutes and seamstresses . . .) are examined in an economic context—how economic and social conditions affect the poor—and the limitations of choices for women in employment and leisure connote the rigidity of imposed Victorian ethics. The treatises on class alienation and the wide variety of characters (particularly the women) are not sidetracked by the melodramatic and contrived plot.

432. _____ **CRANFORD**. 1853. N.Y.: Dutton, current. $2.95.
Cranford is a delightful and entertaining 19th century novel which could probably be enjoyed by younger readers—especially if read aloud. **Cranford** portrays a community of spinster ladies. Gaskell's characters come across with dignity and pride, and we learn about their attitudes toward marriage, men, sexuality and each other. When Miss Matty loses her annual pittance, her young friend, Mary Smith, tries to

think of how a genteel, timid woman of 58 could possibly survive and make her living. Though we have come to know that under Matty's delicate exterior she is sensible and courageous, Mary realizes that Matty has no self-confidence, and no marketable skill, being suited only for the specialized environment of the middle-class home. In a way the manners and morality of the Cranford ladies could be seen as age-old survival techniques of the oppressed. Attempt to find the 1891, London, Macmillan & Co. edition in the library so you can enjoy the illustrations as you read.

433. _____ **NORTH AND SOUTH.** 1855. Baltimore, Md.: Penguin Books.
North and South was first published in serialized form in Dickens' **Household Words** (Sept. 1854 to Jan. 1855). Many readers today will find the contrived coincidences and subplots of the serial form overdone and annoying. In spite of this the novel is well worth reading. It was cited by Wanda Neff in her **Victorian Working Women** as the "greatest Industrial novel in English," due to the excellent view afforded of Manchester: its class divisions; the poverty of urban textile workers; labor union activity, including the use of the strike, and the retaliation of the owners through blacklisting and importation of Irish scab labor. Gaskell wrote **North and South** as the sequel to **Mary Barton** in order to fill out the viewpoint of the manufacturer (she focuses particularly on Mr. Thornton, a self-made man and integrity personified). Typically, though, she balances her portrait by presenting very sympathetic working-class characters such as Higgins, an independent-thinking mill worker and his daughter Bessy, who is to die from consumption—common to mill workers who constantly inhaled cotton bits in the unventilated factories. The novel's central character is Margaret Hale, a young, middle-class woman who enters a new life in the industrial city after living in the rural south. She is often caught between her friendships and responsibilities to the mill workers and their families and her social ties to the manufacturing class. Sad to say, Gaskell favored a Christian solution of individual cooperation rather than even Parliamentary reform.

434. _____ **SYLVIA'S LOVERS.** 1863. N.Y.: Dutton. $3.95.
A well-done if unhappy tale of a young woman in early industrial England and what happens to her and her relationships with men and her family when she moves off the peasant farm and into the bourgeois village. Don't be put off by the title; Sylvia is not a frivolous young thing stringing men along, but a real person with a changing life and real problems.

435. _____ **WIVES AND DAUGHTERS.** 1866. Maryland: Penguin Books, 1975. $2.50.
When Mrs. Gaskell died, she left this novel unfinished. Hardly a fragment, it is 700 pages long and focuses on three women drawn together by their relationship to one man—his second wife, daughter, and stepdaughter. The domestic concerns of the women are played out against the changing social structure of a traditional English village. The portrayal of a daughter's resentment of and adjustment to her father's second marriage is vivid. Recommended for those who like Mrs. Gaskell.

British 19th century

436. GRAND, Sarah (Frances Elizabeth McFall). **THE BETH BOOK.** New York: D. Appleton and Co. 1897. O.P.

All but forgotten, **The Beth Book** is lengthy and at times heavily written; and yet this tale of the life of a free-spirited woman is so unusually direct (with its heroine eventually becoming a women's movement orator at the end) that it must be highly recommended. Written in the style of an autobiography, the book is, no doubt, a mixture of autobiography and fiction. Opening with a feminist's-eye view of the repeated pregnancy and forced motherhood that was most women's lot, Beth places her own birth in this miserable tradition. Later in the book she says, "I have observed that no woman who marries and becomes a mother can ever again live happily like a single woman. She has entered on a different phase of being and there is no return for her." Some of the best parts of the book come in Beth's adolescence: the exhilerating freedom of a weekly forbidden swim with a gang of neighborhood girls, for example, or Beth's adventures as a schoolgirl in the cramped, oppressed atmosphere of a boarding school for lower-middle class girls. Beth's marriage to a doctor gives rise to a polemic on the evils of British law and custom regarding women. Grand's criticism of marriage is every bit as direct and scathing as that of Anne Bronte in her earlier **Tenant of Wildfell Hall**. It is also of special interest (in spite of melodramatic flaws) to see Beth as an escaped wife struggling on her own in London, and working with other women in the women's rights movement.

437. GREEN, Anna Katharine. THE LEAVENWORTH CASE. 1878. G.P. Putnam's sons.
Presumed to be the first detective novel written by a woman, **The Leavenworth Case** is an overly dramatic but entertaining mystery featuring a rheumatic, ridiculous sleuth named Ebenezer Gryce. Two young women cousins are caught in a quagmire of suspicion when their rich uncle is murdered. Note: this book was published almost a decade before the first Sherlock Holmes. It is no wonder that Anna is "variously called mother, grandmother and godmother of the detective story."

438. KEMBLE, Frances Anne. JOURNAL OF A RESIDENCE ON A GEORGIAN PLANTATION IN 1838-1839. 1969, Repr. of 1864 ed. New edition.
"Charlotte, Renty's wife, had had two miscarriages, and was with child again. She was almost crippled with rheumatism, and showed me a pair of swollen knees that made my heart ache. I have promised her a pair of flannel trowsers. . ." So run the detailed letters of the 29-year-old English actress Fanny Kemble. She vehemently denounced slavery from the bird's-eye view of the "missis" of rice and cotton plantations on two islands off the coast of Georgia. Kemble regularly visited the infirmaries and homes of the slaves. She decried the shacks given to the slaves as "dirty, desolate, dilapidated dog-kennels," the food rations of two meals of Indian corn a day a sub-subsistence, the field work inhumanly excessive, the lashings and sexual coercion for purposes of economic profit and egocentricity disgusting. All this on a "progressive" plantation. In her position of impotence (and alienation from her husband and all the landowners) Kemble zealously distributed flannel, meat, and sugar with concern (and, unfortunately, condescension). Her analysis was that slaves had been ruthlessly beaten into endless humiliation, and that nothing could change until the institution of slavery was destroyed. **Journal** was first published in 1863 to influence British opinion during the Civil War.

LINTON, Elizabeth Lynn *(1822-1898) Born the daughter of a country parson and the youngest of 12 children, Eliza Lynn Linton had no formal education but educated herself, first in her father's library, and later, in the Reading Room of the British Museum. A better journalist than novelist, her fame as a writer was based on intelligence, professionalism, and perseverance rather than on an outstanding creative talent. Ironically, Linton, an aggressive, competitive, self-made journalist herself, idealized the cloying feminine Victorian woman, and even opposed higher education for women, although she had struggled to educate herself. An antifeminist, she dealt with the subject of women's rights most effectively in her nonfiction essays which appeared over a ten-year span in* **The Saturday Review** *under the title "The Girl of the Period." If you want to know more see Anita Colby's* **The Singular Anomaly.**

439. _____ OURSELVES: ESSAYS ON WOMEN. London & New York: G. Rutledge & Sons, 1869. o.p.

A series of essays on the faults women of all social roles—maidens, matrons, ladies, and spinsters—fall prey to. The tyranny of fashion, the uselessness of fine ladies, and the excesses of the emancipated woman are censored, and in a footnote at the end of the book Linton states "that I am not the enemy of my sex because their censor." A successful career woman at a time when it was difficult to be, she advocates rights for women but not organized feminism. Recommended only for those with a special interest in the period.

440. _____ THE TRUE HISTORY OF JOSHUA DAVIDSON, COMMUNIST, 1873. N.Y.: Garland, 1975. $35.00.

This true history isn't; it's a fictional biography of Joshua Davidson, a carpenter, who models his life after Christ's. A Christian Communist organizer finally torn apart by a mob, Joshua believes that, "The modern Christ would be a politician. His aim would be to raise the whole platform of society, he would not try to make the poor contented with a lot in which they cannot be much better than savages or brutes. He would work at the destruction of caste, which is the vice at the root of all our creeds and institutions. He would not content himself with denouncing sin as merely spiritual evil; he would go into its economic causes, and destroy the flower by cutting at the roots—poverty and ignorance . . .. Christianity is not a creed as dogmatized by churches, but an organization having politics for its means and the equalization of classes as its end. It is Communism." Although Mrs. Linton's Christianity is hardly orthodox, this novel, popular in its day, would be better expressed as an essay or a tract in ours.

441. _____ THE GIRL OF THE PERIOD: and Other Social Essays. London: Richard Bentley and Son, 1883. A two-volume collection, reprinted from the Saturday Review. O.P.

Having raised herself by the bootstraps in the profession of journalism, Mrs. Linton believes that other women are capable of the same. She refers to the women's movement of her day as the "shrieking sisterhood," and in her essay of the same name says about it: "One of our quarrels with the Advanced Women of our generation is the hysterical parade they make about their wants and their intentions . . .. The silent woman who quietly calculates her chances and measures her powers with her difficulties so as to avoid the probability of a fiasco, and who therefore achieves a success according to her endeavour, does more for the real emancipation of her sex than any amount of pamphleteering, lecturing, or petitioning by the shrieking sisterhood can do. Hers is deed not declamation; proof not theory; and it carries with it the respect always accorded to success." Generally preaching and condescending toward women, she sympathizes with the aging woman's plight, and her essay "The Habit of Fear," dealing with women's wild paranoia about "housebreakers" should be read along with **Cranford.** Dated and antifeminist, the entire two-volume collection is impossible to get through; however, Mrs. Linton has opinions on a wide range of subjects from boarding houses to the women's movement—some of which still make interesting and lively reading.

442. _____ WITCH STORIES, 1883. N.Y.: Barnes & Noble, 1972. $12.50.

Witch Stories is a collection of case histories of the witch persecutions in Scotland and England. All sorts of people were condemned as witches: young and old, beautiful and ugly, women and men, rich and poor, but the majority were poor, elderly women. "To be skilful in healing was just as dangerous as to be powerful in sickening; . . . and the testimony of the healed friend was the strongest strand in the hangman's cord . . .. This was the saddest feature in the whole matter—the total want of all gratitude, reliance, trustiness, or affection between a 'witch' and her friends." Although the style is undistinguished, the evidence presented in case after case stands as a strong indictment of institutionalized scapegoating.

MARTINEAU, Harriet (1802-1876) *A learned and highly respected bluestocking, Harriet Martineau was fortunate to have grown up in a family of Unitarian dissenters who believed that children of both sexes should receive an education. Though the Calvinistic rigor of their faith caused the sensitive Harriet years of nerve-wracked religious trauma (even into adulthood) she emerged from this early atmosphere a dedicated writer and thinker. At age 19 she published her first article, "Female Writers on Practical Divinity" in a Unitarian periodical. This article caused her brother James (whom she deeply admired) to encourage her to "leave it to other women to sew and darn and you devote yourself to this." The daughter of a manufacturer, Harriet was always a keen observer of social and economic systems. She had a passion for democratic (though not socialist) justice. She was a woman who never stopped evolving and growing. She strongly supported abolitionism, legislative reforms, and new advances in science and medicine. In later years she shocked her religious family and friends with her complete disbelief in their views and in immortality. Because of her vigour and outspoken beliefs, she was always a controversial figure.*

443. _____ **DEERBROOK**. 1839. London: Smith, Elder and Co., 1892.
Deerbrook was Harriet Martineau's only attempt to write a domestic novel. A tremendously disciplined writer, she was anxious for a chance to experiment with purely fictional writing. Her only other full length novel, **The Hour and the Man**, more typically illustrates her political views by fictionalizing the life of Haitian revolutionary Toussaint L'Ouverture. It is more likely that the writing of **Deerbrook** comes directly from Harriet Martineau's need to find an emotional outlet for her feelings about love, marriage, and work relationships between men and women. Taking as her story a dissenting doctor's struggle against bigotry and ignorance, the novel's main theme is the suffering and bondage caused by love between people forbidden to each other by law or morality. "There are sad tales sung and told everywhere of brains crazed, and graves dug by hopeless love, and I fear that many more sink into disease and death from this cause than are at all suspected to be its victims." Harriet had experienced a tragic engagement to a man she loved who suffered a mental collapse and died when she was 24. Strangely, her five-year long illness at Tynemouth began with the writing and publication of **Deerbrook.**

444. _____ **AUTOBIOGRAPHY**. vol. I, 1877. London: Smith, Elder & Co.
Although Harriet Martineau frequently wrote short "tales" to illustrate her popular treatises on economy, politics, and society (a form chosen for its accessibility to the widest possible audience), she is probably best remembered as an essayist and as the author of her several volumes of autobiography. Because she wrote the entire autobiography at age 53, it tends to reflect the wisdom of experience rather than the energy and experimentation of earlier years. Volume I takes us from childhood (for example, going into the origins of her lifelong deafness) to 1834 when she was age 32. We learn about her early writing efforts, which include a story on machine-breaking and fair wages—written 20 years before Charlotte Bronte's **Shirley**. Harriet had a strong head about her career, and in Volume I she takes the defiant, necessary steps to London (at first constantly hungry and overtired with work). We see her eventual success as a much-sought-after literary figure.

445. _____ **AUTOBIOGRAPHY**. vol. II, 1877. London: Smith, Elder & Co.
Volume II opens with Harriet's journey to America in September of 1834, her opposition to slavery, support of American abolitionists and the violent reaction of pro-slavery elements. In 1836 and 1837, after her return to England, Harriet wrote her two books on America and generally continued to push herself. But by 1840 physical problems (uterine displacement and a tumor) brought her activities to a stop and she was forced to retire to her sick room in Tynemouth. After nearly five years of miserable suffering, she was encouraged by friends and driven by need to look into a method of cure developed by Franz Mesmer. We cannot know what effect the practice of mesmerism had on Harriet's real problem, but she was at this time restored to

good health, and with her revitalized energy wrote a book on the subject. Volume II is also interesting reading for insights it provides into Harriet's perceptions of her contemporaries Dickens, Mrs. Gaskell, Charlotte Bronte, Margaret Fuller, Charlotte Elizabeth Toona, and many more.

446. OLIPHANT, Mrs. Margaret. MISS MARJORIBANKS. 1870. Folcroft, Pennsylvania: Folcroft Library Editions. $17.50.
This book is both highly entertaining and interesting as a presentation of social expectations for women in 19th century England. Lucilla Marjoribanks is a woman with an immense amount of energy and ambition—all focused on her desire to run her father's household and rule the society surrounding it. Lucilla manages to have her own way always, without ever encountering severe direct disapproval, because she has an immense respect for societal rules. She uses a sweet, demure manner and subtle manipulative tactics to achieve her goals; a classic example of "feminine wiles." Lucilla is at times direct and undauntable as well. The author's attitude to her heroine seems to be a subtle mixture of wry wit and empathy.

447. PAGET, Violet (pseud. Vernon Lee). **HAUNTINGS,** 1890. Plainview, N.Y.: Books for Libraries. $10.50.
In the moment of the ghost's appearance, the past and present overlap, for Vernon Lee's ghosts haunt the imaginations of people, usually artists and scholars, who are obsessed with the particular past the ghost inhabited in life. They are not white sheets overturning chairs; real people once, they haunt the imagination now, and their reality is made to seem palpable or at least ambiguous to the reader. Venus returns to the modern world in **Dionea**, very much a woman's version of Pater's **Apollo in Picardy**; the overtones are as lesbian as Pater's are homosexual. A summary of these stories does them an injustice by making them seem outlandish or imitative. They are neither—Vernon Lee wrote fine supernatural fiction, and all the stories in this collection are interesting and entertaining.

When Frankenstein's monster was just a gleam in Mary Shelly's eye—Jerusha

448. SHELLEY, Mary. FRANKENSTEIN, OR THE MODERN PROMETHEUS, 1818.
CT: Pendulum Press, 1973. $ .95.
Mary Shelley's first novel is the story of two monsters: an eight foot giant with yellow eyes, and the monster's creator, Victor Frankenstein. The drama centers on Victor's fabrication of a living soul out of inanimate matter, and the subsequent conflict between creator and creation. Victor's sensibility is offended by the physical ugliness of his work, so he runs away from it. The creature, born innocent and loving, becomes a monster when his human needs are frustrated. He rages at Frankenstein for bringing him to life unfit to live it, and vows revenge. A trans-global chase ensues as the two

take turns trying to annihilate each other. Whether or not Percy Shelley supplied the model for Frankenstein, as some speculate, Mary Shelley has drawn an unappealing portrait of the romantic hero. Victor is ambitious, hysterical, egotistical and very much weaker than the women who support and nourish him. Women participate only peripherally in the story, in the dual role of supporters and victims. They exist, as perhaps Mary Shelley felt she existed, to endure tragedy cheerfully and to sacrifice for the men they love.

449. TROLLOPE, Frances. LIFE AND ADVENTURES OF MICHAEL ARMSTRONG, The Factory Boy. (3 volumes). 1840. Oregon: International School Service, 1968. $14.50.
This bitter attack on England's factory system is embedded in a romantic "waif turns wealthy" plot. The horrifying conditions of factory work and Trollope's lively array of characters, from the mill workers to the mercilessly mocked wealthy snobs who control Lancashire County, could make any reader a zealous "reformer." Unfortunately, Mary Brotherton, the tenacious young reformer who saves Michael Armstrong from the drudgery of life in the factories and from the whims of vain manufacturers and opportunists, feels powerless in seeking long-term economic changes, and focuses on the individual "heroes" she has rescued. Trollope was aware that such individual solutions had no effect on the general abuses of work in the mills; in this long and very readable novel, she promotes the passage of the 10-hour reform bill as a potential cure-all. The etchings from the 1840 London edition of **Michael Armstrong** increase the impact and sarcasm of the story.

1900-1950

ALLINGHAM, Margery *(1904-1966). Like her mystery-writing contemporaries, Marsh and Sayers, Allingham chose a gentleman sleuth. But her most entertaining novels concern the mating of her male hero with her own idea of the coming woman.*

450. _____ **SWEET DANGER**. 1933. N.Y.: Penguin, 1975. $1.95.
Albert Campion, famous silly-ass sleuth, meets and joins forces with Amanda Fitton, a feisty 17-year-old. She can do anything in the mechanical/electrical line. She can also take a bullet and save the day when necessary.

451. _____ **THE FASHION IN SHROUDS**. N.Y.: Doubleday, 1938.
Amanda is now an aeronautical engineer. She and Albert make (and break) an engagement in the interest of crime-busting. Val (Campion's sister) is depressing testimony to Allingham's ambivalence about independent women.

452. _____ **TRAITOR'S PURSE**. 1941. Manorbooks, 1975. $1.25.
A bonkered Albert goes amnesiac. Amanda keeps her wits. Together they save Britain and cap "Punch" quotations.

453. ASHFORD, Daisy. THE YOUNG VISITORS. 1919. N.Y.: Doubleday, 1972. O.P.
The author was only nine when she wrote this, but she already had a good many insights into the mechanisms of "coutship" [sic] and social climbing in the "Society" [sic] of her day. A delightfully amusing little book.

454. BAGNOLD, Enid. THE SQUIRE. In **THE GIRL'S JOURNEY.** 1938. N.Y.: Curtis, 1972. O.P.
This short novel is in many ways a moving and positive account of one woman's experience with pregnancy, childbirth, and motherhood. The Squire is a woman in her 40s who is expecting her fifth child. Her husband is away and, with the help of her impressive midwife, the Squire is in full control of the events in her life. These positive aspects of the book may be balanced on the negative side by the upper-class snobbery of the Squire and her lack of empathy with the people who work for her. The novel is recommended for the strong characterization of the midwife and for the Squire's reflections on childbirth and children.

455. _____ NATIONAL VELVET. 1935. N.Y.: Archway, 1971. $ .75.
Where but in juvenile fiction do you find an abundance of heroines whose ambitions are not the pursuit of a man, and whose goal is not marriage? **National Velvet** is both the archetype and the best of the horse stories. Enid Bagnold has an intuitive grasp of girls' fantasies and a gift for rendering the fantasy believable. Unpretty, awkward Velvet Brown lives a dream of horses. Magically she inherits five and wins a sixth, an unpretty, awkward piebald gelding. For the piebald, she decides to enter the Grand National, England's most prestigious and difficult steeplechase. The outcome of the race matters less than the skill, vision, and courage needed for the endeavor. Velvet receives practical help from the hired hand, Mi, and psychic energy and support from her mother, a mountain of a woman who swam the English Channel in her youth. Strong characterizations, particularly of the mother, and the perceptive portrait of family interactions will appeal to all readers.

BOWEN, Elizabeth (1899-   ) is now one of the grand old women of the British and Irish literary scenes. Often in the rarefied atmosphere of her upper-middle class world, the reader might think herself still in the 19th century. Yet Bowen is deeply concerned with the fine detail of emotions, with the morality of personal relations, and with women's lives. A recurrent theme in her work is that of a young woman's loss of innocence; dreams turn into dust, and the limiting confines of the real world must be accepted.

456. _____ FRIENDS AND RELATIONS. London: Jonathan Cape, 1931. O.P.
The style of this book is its primary attraction. It mirrors life in its undeveloped explanations, unfinished remarks, and suggestions left hanging. It is a subtle book; the importance of the characters' commitments and feelings is enhanced by the author's understatement of them. The drama centers around two sisters and the men they have married. Mysterious, rich, it gives one a sense of the little bit of themselves that the characters share with each other, the bulk that remains buried, and the many ways they could relate to one another if they dared.

457. _____ THE HOUSE IN PARIS. 1935. N.Y.: Vintage, 1971. O.P.
The brief meeting of two children in a Paris house serves as the looking glass into the past of four adults. Leopold, a displaced child of the upper class, wants to live with his mother instead of his adopted family. In forcing adults to deal with his presence, Leopold forces them to confront themselves. His existence connects past and present and projects them into an unforeseeable future. Remarkable insights into the interaction of children with each other and their manipulation of adults. A superb characterization of a mostly unseen yet influential dying woman and the different perspectives the two children hold of her. A sensitive, well-crafted novel.

458. _____ **THE DEATH OF THE HEART**. 1939. N.Y.: Vintage, current. $1.95.
Widely considered Bowen's best work. Again, an unwanted child of the upper class searches for love, and in doing so forces those around her to confront themselves. After the death of her mother, the adolescent Portia Quayne is taken into the leisurely London existence of her stepbrother, Thomas. He and his wife Anna do not care about Portia, except as a diversion from their routine. The inability of these two to express their feelings, or really to have feelings, is presented in the context of their privileged, emotionally atrophied lives. The insightful Portia pigeonholes these two and their friends in her diary—discovered by a spying Anna. Bowen writes forceful tales of the emotional deprivation children of the upper classes experience at the hands of adults.

459. _____ **THE HEAT OF THE DAY**. 1948. O.P.
Stella Rodney is a competent, divorced, middle-class woman who must deal with the reality of World War II. War-time dilemmas are brought home to her through her son who is in the Army, and through a man who informs her that her lover is passing secrets to the enemy. The effects of war on everyday life, particularly between men and women, is an important part of **The Heat of the Day**, but the subject matter promises more than this rather superficial book holds. The most sympathetic characters are Louie and Connie, working-class women who help each other survive, and Cousin Nettie, an elderly perceptive woman who lives in a genteel mental institution.

460. _____ **A WORLD OF LOVE**. 1954. O.P.
A bundle of old love letters found in the attic of an Irish country house brings about a crisis among its inhabitants. The two older women there both loved the man who wrote them, and for a moment young Jane falls in love with the dead man, too. This novel is heavy with implication, and a tendency to overdo style at the expense of substance. .

461. _____ **THE LITTLE GIRLS**. N.Y.: Knopf, 1963. O.P.
Three women who were friends at a girls' school come together after about forty years. Bowen's enigmatic story concerns their past relationships with one another and the needs, fears, and expectations that surface when they renew their acquaintance. One of the women asks another if she is a lesbian, which is unusually bold for Bowen. Though the question goes unanswered, the intensity which builds up between these two characters is so gripping that the answer is rendered irrelevant. The style is not as cohesive in this book as in the others listed here, so perhaps **The Little Girls** is not a good introduction to Bowen's work.

CARRINGTON, Dora. CARRINGTON, SELECTED LETTERS AND EXTRACTS FROM HER DIARIES, Ed., David Aarnett (see 1950 to present, British section)

COMPTON-BURNETT, Ivy (1892-1969). _Though still writing in the late 1950s, Compton-Burnett said of herself: "I do not feel that I have any real organic knowledge later than 1910. I should not write of later times with enough grasp or confidence." Her novels are restricted not only in time, but also in scope; her setting is typically the country mansion of an upper-middle-class English family, in which human behavior is perceptively observed and the power politics of the family remorselessly analyzed. These novels are significant both for their intimate insights into family structure in an earlier age and for the enduring clearsightedness of her dissection of characters and relationships. She has a wit and a lack of sentimentality which are in some ways reminiscent of Jane Austen. Two novels recently reprinted in one paperback volume are:_
462a & b. _____ **MORE WOMEN THAN MEN** and **A FAMILY AND A FORTUNE**. N.Y.: International Publications Service, 1971. $8.00.
a _____ **MORE WOMEN THAN MEN**. 1933.
This is set in a girls' school (though the pupils are largely invisible) and dominated by its headmistress, whose character is slowly revealed in the course of a sequence of marriages, deaths, and other events. The novel is of particular interest, among other things, for the way it touches (briefly) on some explicit feminist issues, and for its presentation of homosexual and lesbian relationships.

b _____ **A FAMILY AND A FORTUNE.** 1939. O.P.

A family drama is sparked by the fortune inherited by a bachelor uncle in the household. As the drama unfolds, all the personalities in this extended family reveal themselves.

463. LIFE AS WE HAVE KNOWN IT by Co-operative Working Women, Edited by Margaret Llewelyn Davies. 1931. N.Y.: Norton Library, 1975. $2.95.

Working-class English women describe their lives of many children and many hours of work with little pay, and how the Women's Co-operative Guild (founded in 1883) has affected them. For many women, the Guild was their first opportunity to discuss such issues as minimum wage, divorce laws, suffrage, and to decide how to go about changing these conditions. (This includes the Co-operative societies in which communities run their own stores.) The various firsthand accounts of earning a living at age 8, washing steps for a penny, working in a felt hat factory, and living in a mining village, are clear and conversational. An incisive introduction by Virginia Woolf reveals a middle-class woman's responses to the far-reaching effects of the Guild.

464. DICKENS, Monica. ONE PAIR OF HANDS. 1939. O.P.

The tale of a well-educated upper-class English girl who, searching for something to do, decides to become a cook-housekeeper. She reports entertainingly on her own struggles, the manners of her employers, and life backstairs. Her sense of humor, however, doesn't prevent a sudden reaction against the long hours, the constant grind, and the enforced obedience of her position, nor a disheartening return at the book's end to the original question of what to do with her life, time, and energies.

465. GIBBONS, Stella. COLD COMFORT FARM. 1932. N.Y.: Dial, 1964. O.P.

This is a brilliant, humorous book, a parody of the earthy rustic novel, with some well-aimed sideswipes at the intellectual establishment. It also contains some sharp feminist insights. Flora Poste, orphaned at 19, and possessed of "every art and grace save that of earning her own living," goes to live with relatives on Cold Comfort Farm and promptly proceeds to reorganize the messy lives of her country cousins. Just one example: she takes the hired maid, who is in the habit of falling pregnant every summer when the sukebind is in bloom, and gives her a lesson on birth control.

466. HALL, Radclyffe. THE WELL OF LONELINESS. 1928. N.Y.: Pocketbooks, 1975. $1.95.

When first published, **The Well of Loneliness** was notorious because it was one of the first English-speaking novels written explicitly and sympathetically about lesbians. Virginia Woolf, Vita Sackville-West, and George Bernard Shaw were among the 1940s writers who went to the trial but were not allowed to speak in the book's defense. The book was judged "obscene" and banned in England for 30 years. (It was not banned in the U.S.) The genetic and religious fatalism is conspicuous throughout the story of Stephen Gordon's life. With only her father and her horse as intimate companions, she is considered boyish and "strange" as a child and is then shamefully rejected by her mother. Her enduring love affair with Mary Llewelyn (a co-ambulance driver during World War I) is laden with the albatross of being lesbian (an "invert"), as are the lives of her "inverted" friends. Writing is the only deterrent to a life ridden with oppression and failure. Although the numerous portrayals of lesbians are flat and stereotypic, and the compelling story is soaked in sentiment, the issues of class, race, wealth, work, and women's choices are poignantly exposed. Particularly interesting is Hall's depiction of women's active involvement in World War I.

467. KAYE-SMITH, Sheila. JOANNA GODDEN. N.Y.: E.P. Dutton & Co., 1922. O.P.

Sheila Kaye-Smith seems more wrapped up in the English landscape and the provincial church-going values of a small town than in a sustaining plot and unstereotypic characters. But for all the book's predictability, she has created the audacious and unpredictable Joanna Godden. Joanna decides to run her father's farm in Sussex, England, despite her neighbors' insistence that a man is needed for the job. Her sturdiness temporarily wilts for romance, but she dramatically regains her clearsightedness to make the independent, unprecedented decision to remain unmarried and pregnant. Although not well-developed, Joanna's ambivalent relationship with her sister and with workers on the farm reveal a flexibility and wide spectrum of emotions which her community never sees.

468. LEHMANN, Rosamund. DUSTY ANSWER. 1927. N.Y.: Harcourt, Brace, Jovanovich, 1975. $3.95.

Young Judith lives next door to a large family who intrigue and attract her. After she has started studying at a women's college at Cambridge, she becomes romantically involved in turn with three sons of this family. She also has an intense relationship with a fellow student, Jennifer, until the sinister Geraldine appears. Though dated now, the lesbian content of this book, slight as it is, made it exceptional in its day.

469. _____ **THE BALLAD AND THE SOURCE**. 1945. N.Y.: Harcourt, Brace, Jovanovich, 1973. $3.95.

Sibyl Jardine was in her youth a Victorian beauty, a mother, a rebel, a feminist novelist. The novel opens upon her old age; she is still direct, magnetically charming, and sensitive. Although Sibyl and her past is the novel's focus, the personal history of and interrelationship among three generations of women—grandmother, daughter, and granddaughter—unfolds itself. **The Ballad And The Source**, the woman behind the scandals and myths, emerges as her story is gradually put together by her granddaughter's friend Rebecca. Fascinating is the resolution of conflict between grandmother and granddaughter, as the granddaughter's myth about her mother, who deserted her, crumbles in the face of actual contact with her.

MANSFIELD, Katherine *(1888-1923) Some of Mansfield's best fiction came from memories of her New Zealand childhood, yet, as a restless young artist, she begged her wealthy father to send her to London. There she found herself weighted down by unaccustomed hardships and deteriorating health. Nevertheless, she boldly asserted herself in artistic circles with her exotic lifestyle (she was the model for Gudrun in D. H. Lawrence's* **Women In Love***) and her passion to capture all experience on paper. An impressionistic writer, Mansfield excelled in stream-of-consciousness narrative, leaping from one character to another with consummate grace. Her central theme is the effects of a brutal world on the sensitive, creative woman. Mansfield spent her last months in a commune run by the mystic Gurdjieff; she believed herself to be on the threshold of a healing, visionary style of writing. "We have got the same job," she once told acquaintance Virginia Woolf, "and it is really very curious and thrilling that we should both, quite apart from each other, be after so nearly the same thing."*

470. _____ **STORIES**. N.Y.: Vintage, current. $2.95.

These stories were written between 1908, when Mansfield was 20, and her early death in 1923. Many of them, besides being excellent by literary standards, present perceptive analyses of women's lives and of relations between the sexes. To mention only a few from this collecton of 26 stories: "The Tiredness of Rosabel" shows a shopgirl fantasizing herself leading the life of a rich woman customer; "The Little Governess" encounters a dirty old man on her first terrifying journey to Germany. "Prelude" and "At the Bay" deal with the same cast of characters, a boisterous. insensitive male and a gamut of finely drawn women covering virtually all stages of the female life-cycle.

The Garden Party E.M.

471. KATHERINE MANSFIELD: THE MEMOIRS OF L.M. N.Y.: Taplinger, 1971. $7.95.
"Friendship was to become the roadway of my life," writes memoirist L.M. in this loving account of her long relationship with Katherine Mansfield ". . . just as Katherine expressed herself in writing, so I expressed myself in service." L.M.'s service was immense: for nearly 20 years she dedicated herself to helping Mansfield fulfill her artistic genius, providing total emotional and material support whenever needed. Mansfield's primary allegiance, however, was to her husband John Middleton Murray; their marriage was a stormy, erratic one, and L.M. often had to postpone her own life to go live with Katherine until the next reconciliation. During her final illness, Mansfield, driven nearly mad by Murray's neglect, would turn her anger on L.M., who was always present when needed. Nevertheless, L.M. remained her closest confidant. "In spite of what I have said—and shall say—" wrote Mansfield to L.M., "you have been a perfect friend to me." An intimate portrait of a remarkable, enduring friendship.

472. OLIVIA (Dorothy Bussey). OLIVIA. 1949. N.Y.: Arno Press, 1975. $9.00.
Published anonymously by Dorothy Bussey in 1949, this short novel tells of 16-year-old Olivia's passionate love for her schoolmistress, Mlle. Julie, a love which is apparently reciprocated. The whispered intrigues and intense emotional attachments among the women and girls at a French boarding school serve as backdrop for Olivia's reminiscences about her first love. Although lesbianism is unsatisfyingly linked with excessive jealousy, forbidden desire, and inevitable tragedy, the story itself is absorbing and unique in its serious treatment of schoolgirl "crushes." Bloomsbury buffs may be interested in noting that the author was Lytton Strachey's sister and **Olivia** was dedicated to "the beloved memory of V.W." (undoubtedly Virginia Woolf). From the information available, it would appear that the book is semi-, if not wholly, autobiographical.

473. RENAULT, Mary. PURPOSES OF LOVE. 1939. O.P.
This book is a vivid portrait of an independent young woman slowly drained by the demanding drudgery of her work (nursing) and by an unequal love relationship in which she seeks privacy and relief. The reader may find that the novel's passionate atmosphere distracts them from an appreciation of Renault's realistic grasp of day-to-day relationships.

474. _____ **THE MIDDLE MIST.** 1945. N.Y.: Popular Library, 1975. $1.50.
Naive Elsie, burdened with family guilt and self-centered romanticism, visits her long-lost older sister Leo, a remarkable character who lives with her lover Helen in a houseboat on the Thames and writes cowboy-thrillers for a living. Much of the satire in this witty, yet restrained, novel is directed at straight people who are unable (or unwilling) to recognize a happy lesbian relationship when they see one. **Middle Mist** is

one of the few works in which Renault deals with lesbianism, and, before the appearance of this Popular Library edition, it was one of her least accessible works.

475. _____ **THE CHARIOTEER**. 1959. N.Y.: Bantam Book, 1974. $1.75.
The dilemmas of war and homosexuality are meshed in this novel, much of which is set in an army hospital in England during World War II. The compelling plot centers around Laurie Odell, a soldier injured at Dunkirk. Laurie's perceptions about his sexuality, and his compassion for people's responses and choices are so delicately detailed that his relationships are often deadlocked and unsatisfying. He is the unwitting participant in the jealousy, competition, and violence within the insulated homosexual circles of the army. The women are few and seen only in direct relation to Laurie. The reader may feel frustrated with the incomplete discussions about pacifism, patriotism, and homosexuality, and with the story which seems constantly on the verge of resolution.

RHYS, Jean (1894-   ) _was born in the West Indies, but from the age of 16 lived in England and Europe. Her first works, published in the 1930s, were ahead of their time; it is only with their reissue in the 1960s that they seem to have struck a responsive chord. Typically they feature an unconventional woman leading an unhappy, rootless, adventurous life._

476. _____ **AFTER LEAVING MR. MACKENZIE**. 1931. N.Y.: Harper & Row, 1972. $6.95.
Julia is "a female without the instinct of self-preservation," reflects Mr. Mackenzie, who has just sloughed her off. When his checks stop coming, she is left stranded; she returns from Paris to England and tries to sponge money off relatives and lovers. Her aimless desolation and the way others perceive her are rendered with a brutal lucidity.

477. _____ **VOYAGE IN THE DARK**. 1934. N.Y.: Popular Library, 1975. $1.25.
Anna, at 18, is a chorus girl touring English provincial towns. England chills her emotionally as well as physically, and dreamlike memories of her home in the West Indies keep returning to her. She is picked up by a rich man, kept for a while, then dropped; from then on her life drifts—she moves from lodging to lodging, from man to man, and ends by having a gruesome abortion. Rhys conveys with stark clarity the piercing sadness of this hopeless life.

478. _____ **GOOD MORNING, MIDNIGHT**. 1939. N.Y.: Harper & Row, 1970. $6.95.
Over 40, scarred by life and human cruelty, Sasha returns to Paris for a vacation. The city teems with memories of her earlier life and the marriage that ended unhappily there. She is bitter, defensive, and particularly mistrustful of men; she thinks of drinking herself to death. A young gigolo approaches her and their strange relationship proceeds to a grim ending that will haunt the reader.

479. _____ **WIDE SARGASSO SEA**. 1966. N.Y.: Popular Library, 1975. $1.25.
This is the story of Antoinette, Rochester's first wife (remember—the madwoman in

Jane Eyre?). She tells of her girlhood in Jamaica as a member of the dispossessed and threatened slave-holding class; Rochester narrates part of the story of their early marriage; and she again speaks at the end, where she is locked up in Thornfield Hall. The whole is a brilliant, powerful story of a cruelly abused woman.

480. _____ **QUARTET**. N.Y.: Vintage Books, 1974. $1.65.
"The problem of her existence had got beyond her, her brain had given up grappling with it." Stranded and penniless in Paris after her husband's arrest, Marya Zelli, a downwardly mobile middle-class woman, drifts into a relationship with the Heidlers, a strange and affluent couple fond of refined sado-masochistic mind games. What follows is a sensitive portrait of one of life's losers as Marya, cruelly manipulated and then dropped by Mr. and Mrs. Heidler, is gradually pushed beyond the limits of her pain threshold. As Marya struggles to resist the unhappiness of her life, her world is exposed as one in which people survive like caged animals, each according to his or her capacity for endurance.

RICHARDSON, Dorothy _(1873-1957) was a pioneer in the use of the stream-of-consciousness technique in the novel. An excellent writer with a strong feminist consciousness, she deserves to be rescued from the obscurity into which she has fallen. Her greatest drawback is the length of her novel:_ **Pilgrimage** _is 13 volumes. Twelve volumes appeared between 1915 and 1938, in which year there was also a 4-volume collected edition; a final, incomplete volume was included for the first time in the 1967 re-issue of the collected edition. To summarize the content of_ **Pilgrimage** _does not do the work justice, since its essence lies not in the narrative, but in the exploration of a developing consciousness. Reading it can be an intensely exciting experience; Richardson's prose has the density and intricacy of poetry, and she really gives one the feeling of being inside her heroine, Miriam._

481. _____ **PILGRIMAGE: Volumes 1, 2, 3, 4.** 1938. N.Y.: Knopf, 1967. O.P. Volumes 1 & 2, N.Y.: Pocket Books, 1976. $1.95.
Volume 1 contains **Pointed Roofs** (the 17-year-old Miriam is a governess at a small girls' school in Germany), **Backwater** (after an interlude with her family, Miriam goes on to teach at a school in London), and **Honeycomb** (she is a governess in a wealthy family). In Volume 2 are the two books **The Tunnel** and **Interim**. Miriam finds more independence working in a dentist's office and living in a boarding house in London. **The Tunnel** can be particularly recommended. **Deadlock, Revolving Lights**, and **The Trap** make up Volume 3. Miriam has a romantic involvement with Michael Shatov and goes to meetings of the Lycurgan Society (the Fabians). Volume 4 contains **Oberland, Dawn's Left Hand, Clear Horizon, Dimple Hill**, and the incomplete **March Moonlight. Dawn's Left Hand** is a particularly interesting volume, which covers both Miriam's affair with Hypo Wilson (H.G. Wells in real life) and the intense relationship she has with the young woman Amabel. Towards the end of **Pilgrimage** Miriam, after a succession of unhappy loves, is in the process of moving towards becoming a Quaker.

SACKVILLE-WEST, Victoria _(1892-1962) A writer who has undeservedly fallen into obscurity, Vita was a close friend of Virginia Woolf and was the model for Woolf's Orlando. In addition to fiction, Vita wrote poetry and criticism (see entry number 806, "Works About Literature".)_

482. _____ **CHALLENGE.** 1924. N.Y.: Avon, 1975. $1.50.
This is a melodramatic story of romance, danger, bravery, adventure, and passion, told from a very elite, very male point of view. It gains in interest and lessens in offensiveness by the knowledge that the novel was written in the midst of, and about, a reckless, flamboyant affair between Vita and Violet Trefusis. As an expression of the emotional reality of their relationship, this book will be most interesting to those already acquainted with Vita Sackville-West who wish to know her better.

483. _____ **ALL PASSION SPENT.** 1931. O.P.
A fine novel, presenting women's new-found chance to reconstruct her life when, at the age of 88, her husband's death gives her the leisure to reflect on her life, on the changes that occurred at her marriage, and on her desire to be an artist.

484. _____ **THE DARK ISLAND.** 1934. O.P.
Compelling and sinister, **The Dark Island** cuts through to the guts of psychological survival. Shirin is a willful and introverted young woman who grapples with her need for integrity and power. After years of dull flirtations, marriage, and childbearing, she marries Venn, the young and possessive inheritor of the wild Island of Storn, and discovers that the harshness of life is what really interests her. Power and powerlessness are the vital aspects of Venn and Shirin's relationship. Jealousy, revenge and sadism weave throughout the enigmatic characters, and the only moments of respite involve Shirin's growing intimacy with her secretary, Cristina, the only person she can love.

485. _____ **THE EDWARDIANS.** 1934. O.P.
Set between 1906 and 1910, the novel asks whether people can escape the class into which they have been born. The central character is an upper-class male, and women are used as representatives of other classes rather than described as people in their own right.

486. NICHOLSON, Nigel. PORTRAIT OF A MARRIAGE. N.Y.: Bantam, 1974. $1.95.
A valuable contribution to our knowledge of Vita Sackville-West, this book reveals the art in which Vita excelled—the exploration of her unconventional feelings. She acknowledges not only her lesbianism, but also her feelings of hate, jealousy, pride, and elitism. Composed of chapters she had written which recounted the story of her affair with Violet Trefusis, bits of her journal, and letters, **Portrait** also offers the reader glimpses of Vita's relationship with her husband, Harold, and with Virginia Woolf. Explanatory chapters by her son, Nigel Nicholson, are helpful, though his reasonable, respectable tone can be obnoxious.

SAYERS, Dorothy L. *(1893-1957) Best known for her Lord Peter Wimsey detective stories, Sayers is a fine story-teller and writer. She is one of the few mystery novelists to care enough about her characters to have them change and grow in the course of their sleuthing. Besides her excellent detective fiction, Dorothy also wrote philosophy, theology, criticism, drama, and translated Dante.*

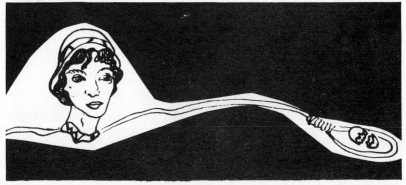

487. _____ **STRONG POISON**. 1930. N.Y.: Avon, 1971. $1.25.
Introduces Harriet Vane, "Bloomsbury Bluestocking," as the alleged murderer. From the very start, Harriet is a complex human and very real woman—most male critics hated her!There are several glimpses of the arrogant quasi-intelligentsia of "Blooms-bury." The grasping men who talk a liberal "equality" game but exploit women with a vengeance are the hardest hit. This mystery is satiric, concise and highly enter-taining.

488. _____ **HAVE HIS CARCASE**. 1932. N.Y.: Avon, 1968. $1.25.
This book had gotten bad press, which is a shame because it's a really fine mystery. Harriet finds a body on a hiking/backpacking trip through the south of England. Here is a disdain of "watering-places" worthy of Jane Austen. All the people seem de-formed, incompetent—comic yet tragic—as if they each stepped out of a Diane Arbus photograph. The gigolo characters are especially fascinating and surprisingly sym-pathetic. Harriet and Peter solve the murder mystery and Peter gets his chivalry thrown back in his face (by Harriet, of course).

489. _____ **MURDER MUST ADVERTISE**. 1933. N.Y.: Avon, 1967. $1.25.
Despite the fact that Harriet Vane is not part of this book, it is still one of Sayers best. Dorothy worked for several years in advertising while launching her writing career. The advertising game was relatively harmless in those pre-"Madison Ave" days, but Sayers still saw quite a few atrocities. This is a very successful satire—a wit-ty but scathing indictment against the business of lying. Equally fascinating is a study of the decadent drug culture of the "bright young people" of the post-World War I England. Dorothy was obviously taking steps to unite the murder mystery and the serious novel. The murderer in this story is one of the most tortured and sympathetic killers you are liable to find.

490. _____ **THE NINE TAILORS**. 1934. N.Y.: Harcourt, Brace Jovanovich, 1966. $1.25.
Again, a masterpiece. Here, Dorothy draws on her memories of her childhood in East Anglia. The character of the "fen" country and its people is strong and clear. And the knowledge she displays on campanology (bell change-ringing) is amazing and shows just how hard she researched these mysteries. The trite problem of uncovering the identity of the murderer is full of irony in this haunting epic of country life and crime. All of the characterization in this book is superb but the character of Hillary Thorpe is especially impressive. She is a gangly adolescent with a sharp mind and a strong will, gutsy but always sympathetic, a real survivor.

491. _____ **GAUDY NIGHT**. 1935. N.Y.: Avon, current. $1.25.
An "Oxford novel" and detective thriller magnificently combined. As an expression of Dorothy Sayers' philosophy, her concern for women, her fervent belief in intellec-tual integrity and as a document of two human beings (Peter and Harriet) trying to build a meaningful egalitarian relationship—this book is a classic! It broke most of the rules of the detective story and half of the rules for straight novels. It is also a brilliant comedy of manners (Harriet wears a dog collar). Strongly recommended for feminists. If you only read one Dorothy Sayers novel, make it this one.

492. _____ **BUSMAN'S HONEYMOON**. 1937. N.Y.: Avon, current. $1.25.
This was the last Dorothy Sayers novel. She called it a "sentimental comedy" with "an intolerable deal of saccharine." Purists will be glad to know that it sports a murder, and an elaborately wrought one at that. It says a great deal about the characters in-volved, a great deal about relationships in general, and a great deal about Dorothy Sayers in particular. Peter's nervous breakdown at the end of the book is a perfect, humane anecdote to the cold-blooded and methodical detectives that abound in 99 per cent of standard American "dick" fiction.

493. _____ LORD PETER. 1972. N.Y.: Harper & Row, 1972. $12.50.
This is "A Collection of All the Lord Peter Wimsey Stories." It is excellent not only because it combines the Wimsey stories from three anthologies, but because of the 'extras' included in the volume. Especially worthwhile is the essay "Sayers, Lord Peter and God" by Carolyn Heilbrun.

TEY, Josephine *(1897-1952) is the "nom de crime" used by Elizabeth MacKintosh, and was the name of her great-great grandmother. Tey's mysteries, although not consciously feminist, are always a delight.*

494. _____ THE FRANCHISE AFFAIR. CA: Berkeley Pub., 1971. $ .75.
Marian Sharpe and her mother are not sweet little ladies and never pretend to be. For this they are attacked by the mindless savagery of a young girl and the misogynist bigotry of their small town. This novel proves that a mystery need not contain a murder to be first-rate!

495. _____ TO LOVE AND BE WISE. 1950. Berkeley, 1975. $ .95.
A talented young photographer is missing and presumed murdered. This superb mystery is highly recommended for feminists, but prepare your sex-stereotyping sensibilities for a healthy shock.

496. _____ MISS PYM DISPOSES, 1946. N.Y.: Berkeley, 1971. $ .95.
Unusual insights into love, justice and class differences in this excellent mystery of murder at a women's athletic college. Lucy Pym is a memorable character and a compassionate, if fallible, sleuth.

497. _____ A SHILLING FOR CANDLES, 1936. N.Y.: Berkeley, 1972. $ .95.
The murder victim seldom plays a major role in a mystery. But as the death (and life) of actress Christine Clay are investigated, she becomes the novel's hero, as does Erica, the sixteen-year-old tomboy instrumental in solving the case.

498. _____ THE DAUGHTER OF TIME, 1951. CA: Berkeley Medallion Books.
A detective story, seeking to solve a crime committed 500 years ago: the murder of the two little princes in the Tower of London. Thomas More, Shakespeare and popular historians since have blamed Richard III, the boys' uncle. But bed-ridden detective Alan Grant has his doubts and sets out to prove otherwise. An original achievement in an overworked genre, this novel helped popularize the British Society for the Vindication of Richard III. Unfortunately, the sexist tough-guy remarks serve no function other than to irritate.

499. WALTON, Evangeline. THE ISLAND OF THE MIGHTY. 1936. N.Y.: Ballantine, 1974. $1.50.
Evangeline Walton took Welsh mythology as her inspiration and produced a fascinating book. She fashioned a real and believable society, quite unlike our own. Like good science fiction, it enables us to see some of our cultural assumptions in a new light. In ancient Druidic Wales, people still understood magic, and paternity seemed, to most, an absurd concept. But Gwydion, Prince of Wales, wants a son of his own to succeed him. He eventually learns that he can't sort one value out of its context. With paternity comes monogamous marriage, the concept of virginity, the act of rape, the need to possess others and the corollary vice of jealousy. Walton thought about sexual politics long before the term existed, and while everyone will not agree with her ideas, they are bound to excite and provoke. (**The Island Of The Mighty** is one in a series of four books).

WOOLF, Virginia (1882-1941). *She was born into the wealthy, educated British upper class. She lived all her life in it and wrote primarily about it. Her perspectives on working-class characters are limited. One of her purposes in writing was to explore the inner lives of her characters, to give these lives as much reality as the more obvious outer ones. Her probing of sex roles and relationships has been appreciated by many women. Yet others complain that her "idle" women are hard to relate to, her style is too sensitive and "over-refined." Others still, intimidated by all this, have resisted reading her at all. If you are one of these, try her. Perhaps you will agree with her critics, or perhaps you will find a writer whose language and images are hauntingly beautiful, and whose depictions of sexual politics are incredibly enlightening.*

500. _____ **THE VOYAGE OUT**. 1920. N.Y.: Harcourt, Brace Jovanovich, 1968. $2.45.
Virginia Woolf spent seven years writing and rewriting this, her first novl. The highly individualistic, lyrical style by which she is known and her skill at weaving together the disparate elements which make up "life" are firmly established in this work. The story centers around four characters: a middle-aged woman, her niece who is just coming into womanhood, and two young men they meet in the microcosmic setting of a South American resort. As relationships develop among these four, they wrestle with problems which are immediate yet timeless: the nature of life, and love; the meaning of friendship, the differences between the sexes. Those who have never read Woolf may find this novel to be a gentle, rewarding introduction to her work. Those who are already familiar with it will discover in here kernels of themes and style which reappear in all of her writing.

501. _____ **NIGHT AND DAY**. 1920. N.Y.: Harcourt, Brace, Jovanovich, 1973. $4.25.
Virginia Woolf's second novel, **Night and Day**, was less successful in its time than **The Voyage Out.** Its style is fairly conventional, and though Woolf's interest in the emotions of her characters and their thoughts on life is apparent in this novel, the prose never really flows as it does in her later works. It is bound by a typical romantic upper class plot, in which, as usual, the person who works for social change (in this case, a feminist) fares badly. The novel does question men and women's roles and the institution of marriage, though rather weakly.

502. _____ **MRS. DALLOWAY**. 1925. N.Y.: Harcourt Brace & World, current. $1.75.
A single day in the life of wealthy Mrs. Dalloway, during which she plans and gives a party. On that day she manages to reflect on most of her life. Particularly moving are her thoughts about her sexuality, followed by her memories of a girlhood passion for Sally Seton, in which she knew "what men know" in love.

503. _____ **TO THE LIGHTHOUSE**. 1927. N.Y.: Harcourt Brace & World, current. $2.25.
The most easy-reading and popular of Woolf's "interior" novels. In it we see the Ramsays: he a self-pitying, conceited intellectual, she the perfect "beautiful woman." Their destructive power is seen through the eyes of Lily, a "spinster" painter. He makes her angry with his poses, then guilty about her anger. But Mrs. Ramsay is living proof that it is possible to live "woman's role": compassionate, self-sacrificing, lovely, and seemingly happy (for only readers have heard Mrs. Ramsay question whether life is worth living). It is she who is the real threat to the self-esteem of Lily, who desires an independent life.

504. _____ **ORLANDO**. 1928. N.Y.: Harcourt, Brace, Jovanovich, 1973. $2.95.
Elizabeth Bowen called this book not a novel but a fantasy. It was an experiment, an attempt to break into a vivid new way of combining fiction and historical reality, and a vision of what this reality was for real men and women. Woolf wanted to escape from the oppressive method of presenting a few cold dates and facts as history. Orlando, the central person of the book, begins as a 16-year-old male in the

Elizabethan era. As the fantasy continues, time spins by, but Orlando's time moves slowly. Towards the end of the 17th century Orlando's sex is changed from male to female, and (s)he experiences the next three centuries as a woman. What we have here is a brilliant portrayal of British history, so much so that we can almost taste the unique flavor of each period. Even more important, we have a vivid picture of how gender molded the existence of the individual in the various periods. Many critics have ignored **Orlando**, as they have tried to ignore equally innovative pieces by Gertrude Stein and other women who dared to experiment with fictional forms to give us women's historical reality.

505. _____ **THE WAVES**. 1931. In **JACOB'S ROOM AND THE WAVES**. N.Y.: Harcourt, Brace, Jovanovich. $2.65.
This is a rich book, but a hard one, not worth reading unless you want to work at it and read it at least twice. It traces, through interior monologues, the lives of six friends, three women and three men—or is it the many facets of a single soul? There is much about the problems of different life stages and the restrictions of male and female roles.

506. _____ **FLUSH**. 1933. N.Y.: Harcourt Brace & World, current. $ .45.
This is the biography of Elizabeth Barrett Browning's dog. It is an amusing tale, containing many insights into the poet's life, but it certainly does not offer the reader any of the stylistic or thematic complexities of Woolf's other works—nor, most probably, was it meant to.

507. _____ **BETWEEN THE ACTS**. 1941. N.Y.: Harcourt, Brace, Jovanovich, Inc., 1969. $2.45.
"All the world's a stage," and perhaps social life is merely a collective dream which can end at any moment on an individual or grand scale. Virginia Woolf killed herself shortly after the novel's completion, and social life nearly reached an apocalyptic end during World War II when this novel was written. The novel touches many themes: the violence of men towards nature; the violence of men towards women, art and society. The annual village pageant is set against the English countryside and recounts English history from its legendary past up to its wartime present. The pageant's

audience is as much in focus as the actors and countryside; they all intertwine, and between the acts the play momentarily falls away to expose the real lives of the spectators, the real history of England. The stripping off of illusion is painful, and like analysis impossible to complete. Critics have noticed the novel's unfinished character, but perhaps, like life, it is left in process. A beautiful last novel.

508. BELL, Quentin. VIRGINIA WOOLF: A Biography. 1972. N.Y.: Harcourt, Brace, Jovanovich, 1974. $3.95.
This account of Woolf's life by her nephew makes fascinating reading, though perhaps a woman biographer would have given Woolf's feminism more serious attention. Bell is good at evoking the atmosphere of Bloomsbury and the intellectual and artistic excitement this avant-garde circle generated. He seems to deal carefully and honestly both with Woolf's mental illness and with the little-known facts of her sex-life, as well as giving some insights into the arduous process of her work as a writer.

Contemporary: 1950-Present

509. BANKS, Lynne Reid. THE L-SHAPED ROOM. 1960. N.Y.: Pocket, 1975. $1.25.
Single and pregnant, June Graham, 27, goes to hide in a shabby London roominghouse. Her tatty L-shaped room changes from exile to sanctuary as the varied people who live in the house take their places in her life. Her reflections on jobs and incidents in her past are a joy to read. The slow development of her first real friendships and loves is a moving accompaniment to her growing acceptance of her pregnancy and herself. The movie of the same title, though not so complex or understanding, is also recommended.

510. _____ THE BACKWARD SHADOW. 1970. N.Y.: Pocket, 1975. $1.25.
Many of the hopes we had for Jane Graham and her new baby in **The L-Shaped Room** are rudely battered in this sequel. Some of her staunchest supporters have died, leaving Jane fully responsible for the support of her small household. The friend with whom she now lives is struck by a tragedy which affects both women, and the man on whom she has staked so much hope and affection falls very short of what she demands. The author very suddenly wraps up characters and plot, leaving us with a less satisfying novel than her first.

BAWDEN, Nina *(1925-   ) An accomplished English writer whose portrayals of family life are piercing, unromantic, and unexpectedly touched by humor. Inadequately recognized in this country, she is also the author of several children's books.*

511. _____ TORTOISE BY CANDLELIGHT. 1963. N.Y.: Ballantine, 1969. $ .75.
The mother of Alice (16), Emmy (14), and Oliver (9) is away. A new couple moves in next door; the wife is recovering from a breakdown. In unfolding the intense relationships that develop among these neighbors, Bawden portrays the world of children with great sensitivity. Emmy in particular emerges clearly with all her passionate devotions and painful embarrassments.

512. _____ A WOMAN OF MY AGE. 1967. N.Y.: Lancer, 1969. $ .95.
Elizabeth, a rather perceptive woman, knows that her middle-aged marriage is held together mainly through force of habit. Although she was raised by two feminist aunts, she married because she was pregnant and she stays with her husband for security and other practical reasons (children, the opinion of others). Any time Elizabeth ventures from her domestic shell, her own guilt and social pressures drive

her back in. A depressing yet realistic novel dealing with the stultifying psychic state of marriage.

513. _____ **THE GRAIN OF TRUTH**. N.Y.: Harper & Row, 1968. O.P.
The chapters of this book are presented in turn from the points of view of three people—Emma, her husband Henry, and her friend Holly.This is skillfully done to show their different perspectives on the world and their lack of understanding of each other. Particularly interesting is the contrast between the two women: Holly is all there on the surface, sexually exuberant, totally frank; Emma is quiet, shy, fantasy-prone, haunted by childhood memories which now surface to lead to a dramatic crisis.

514. _____ **THE BIRDS ON THE TREES**. N.Y.: Harper & Row, 1971. O.P.
This is a depressing and realistic account of the gap between children and well-meaning parents, a constant series of bruises and misunderstandings with an unexpectedly positive ending.

BROPHY, Brigid _(1929-   ) A successful British novelist and critic known for her wit, as well as her enthusiasm for Freudianism and sexual freedom. She is known as a feminist of sorts (for instance, she has said that in men she most admires beauty, in women emancipation from domesticity), but has recently been somewhat critical of the women's movement._

515. _____ **THE KING OF A RAINY COUNTRY**. 1956. N.Y.: Knopf, 1957. O.P.
Nineteen-year-old Susan's first job is working for a hole-and-corner porno bookseller. In one of his books she discovers a naked photograph of a schoolmate, Cynthia, whom she had loved intensely. With her roommate, Neale, she sets out on a romantic quest to find her; the trail leads eventually to Venice, where they find not only Cynthia, but also an older woman, the singer Helena Buchan. An unexpected realignment of relationships brings the romantic quest to a startling end.

516. _____ **FLESH**. N.Y.: Popular Library, 1962. O.P.
Marcus, from whose point of view the story is told, starts off as an unemployed, socially incompetent, and self-effacing Jewish virgin. Then Nancy takes him in charge, marries him, molds him, and, above all, introduces him to a rich world of sexual pleasure. It is a case of Pygmalion with the sexes reversed. Eventually, however, the Marcus Nancy has created moves beyond her control.

517.a. and b. _____ **THE SNOW BALL** and **THE FINISHING TOUCH**. N.Y.: World, 1964. O.P.
a. The Snow Ball is a stylized love story; at a costume ball in an 18th century mansion the heroine, dressed as Donna Anna, meets a stranger dressed as Don Giovanni.
b. The Finishing Touch is a humorous fantasy, plainly modelled on the works of Ronald Firbank; sexual capers among the mistresses and the highly connected pupils of an elite girls' finishing school.

518. _____ **IN TRANSIT**. 1969. N.Y.: Putnam, 1970. O.P.
Pat O'Rooley, sitting in an airport, starts confusing different languages, then forgets what sex (s)he is, and whether homo- or hetero-. This is a _very_ clever book, full of linguistic, literary, and sexual allusions and witticisms.

519. CARRINGTON, Dora. SELECTED LETTERS & EXTRACTS FROM HER DIARIES.
Editor, David Garnett. N.Y.: Ballantine Books, 1974. $2.25.
If Dora Carrington is known at all, it is in the context of the Bloomsbury Group and as an appendage of Lytton Strachey. This book establishes her as a unique personality on her own. As a young artist in London, Carrington came to know many of the writers and painters associated with "Bloomsbury" (Virginia Woolf, Katherine Mansfield, among others), and thus made the acquaintance of Lytton Strachey, the biographer/historian. Her fascination with and devotion to him shaped the course of

the rest of her life (and death—she committed suicide when he died). But to view her solely as a tragic figure who sacrificed herself and her art is to do her a great injustice. Her letters and diaries reveal a strong-willed vital woman who continuously struggled to maintain her own identity against the demands of love and traditional role prescriptions. Her letters, however, are not mere chronicles of yet another female oppressed by patriarchal society. She writes with humor and an ingenuousness which give the reader a real sense of her individuality and liveliness of spirit. The sketches and caricatures she includes with her letters are especially entertaining. A good book for anyone interested in the Bloomsbury Group or the life of an intriguing young woman artist.

520. CARTER, Angela. HEROES AND VILLAINS. 1970. N.Y.: Pocket Books, 1972. $ .95.
This gothic fantasy takes place in a futuristic, war-shattered world inhabited by nomadic Barbarians, who live by their emotions, and Professors, who maintain small pockets of reason within the chaotic wilderness. Marianne, a Professor's daughter, ventures into the jungle, where she is captured by the Barbarians and forced to marry their chieftain, a Heathcliff type. Prehistoric past and post-atomic future merge and become one in Carter's eerie, compelling vision of a nuclear wasteland.

521. _____ SEVERAL PERCEPTIONS. N.Y.: Simon & Schuster, 1969. $4.50.
An engaging novel about an obsessive, suicidal young man's adjustment to his life. Many of his obsessions center around realities—disease, poverty, the Vietnam War. His friends are an interesting assortment: hobo, rock musician, secretary, and prostitute. Carter does not deal with feminist issues, although her women characters are stronger than the men they emotionally support. Although the ending is extreme, her lush style and wry sense of humor make the novel worth reading.

522. _____ THE WAR OF DREAMS. 1972. N.Y. and London: Harcourt Brace Jovanovich, 1974. $6.95. (Originally published in England under the title **THE INFERNAL DESIRE MACHINES OF DOCTOR HOFFMAN.**)
Dr. Hoffman discovers the means of making dreams real and the ensuing libido plague destroys life as we know it—the concepts of linear time, space, and reality vanish. Carter uses the persona of a male narrator to explore male sexual fantasies about women. The novel reads like a collection of dreams, and in the chapter "The River People," the narrator finds himself in a matrilineal world. For those preoccupied with dream, illusionistic space, and reality, this is a unique science fiction novel.

CHRISTIE, Agatha (1890-1976) _The finest and most prolific practitioner of the "pure puzzle" mystery. Her work, although entertaining, seldom shows any depth of characterization or insight into the lives of women._

523. _____ NEMESIS. 1971. N.Y.: Pocketbooks, 1973. $ .95.
The last (and best) Miss Marple mystery. Agatha had now grown into the elderly experience of her "spinster" sleuth—and it shows. Marple's refusal to be nullified by age makes her the hero she never really was before. This makes the book worthwhile despite the revoltingly misogynist opinions expressed on rape.

DRABBLE, Margaret (1939-   ). _Highly thought-of in her native England, she is now gaining notice in the U.S. The literary establishment has praised her unique style; feminist critics add that she portrays female experiences honestly. Her style, often_ deceptively simple and chatty, takes us into her heroines' thoughts, draws us into the flow of their lives. Drabble's women are most often attractive and intellectual, but there is much more to them than that. They are always conscious of where they are in the world, and that "where" is constantly changing. An oft-repeated phrase in Drabble criticism is that her characters "create their own lives;" they make choices, little ones perhaps, and sometimes mistakes, but they always choose. On the other hand, some readers feel that the courses of her heroines' lives are arbitrary and the situations they end up in are often bad; Drabble's great achievement is in showing only-too-human women with a lucid consciousness of their plight. We recommend that you read her yourself and come to your own conclusion.

524. _____ **A SUMMER BIRD-CAGE**. 1962. N.Y.: Belmont, 1971. $ .95.
"I had to come home for my sister's wedding." Sarah begins her story with this grudging sentence when her beautiful older sister, Louise, marries a rich, successful novelist. Gradually chinks appear in the facade of this "perfect" marriage. As the story develops, so does the relationship between the two sisters and each woman's understanding first of herself, then of the other.

525. _____ **THE GARRICK YEAR**. 1964. N.Y.: Belmont, 1971. $ .95.
Emma has found that marriage deprives her of "a whole string of finite things, and many more indefinite attributes, like hope and expectation." Her actor husband now proceeds to uproot her and their two small children to the provinces, making her sacrifice the possibility of a TV announcing job. There, she proceeds to have an affair with the famous producer of the season until events jolt her and her husband into dealing with what has been going on. The novel ends on a note of qualified acceptance: "One just has to keep on and to pretend, for the sake of the children, not to notice."

526. _____ **THANK YOU ALL VERY MUCH**. 1965. N.Y.: Signet, 1969. $ .75.
Here is a positive picture of unmarried motherhood. Although she is shielded from the hardships endured by most women in her position by academic success and family prosperity, Rosamund grows in sensitivity to the world around her and comes to perceive both others and herself with more understanding and compassion. A good book and recommended for single mothers and adolescents.

527. _____ **JERUSALEM THE GOLDEN**. 1967. Harmondsworth, England: Penguin, 1972. $1.25.
A young woman's flight from the narrow restrictions of her lower-middle-class existence to what she perceives to be a "dense, richly complex" life in London. The guilt-provoking claims of the past are represented in her mother, a joyless woman who has buried her own youthful dreams of escape. The "golden" life Clara yearns for is personified by a close and loving, wealthy and intellectual London family. What she envies them most is their ease. She herself can never relax; she has had to work hard for everything and is always self-conscious. Human relationships are difficult for her, but, in the end, the reader and Clara can take heart in her strength, a strength which enables her to work at her life.

528. _____ **THE WATERFALL**. 1969. Harmondsworth, England: Penguin, 1972. $1.50.
Complex in both style and content, **The Waterfall** employs two distinct narrative voices. The first voice, a distanced third-person account of "Poor helpless Jane, abandoned . . . timid . . . bereft" passively drifting into an affair with her cousin's husband, is frequently broken in upon by the second voice—an intense, introspective one—Jane herself struggling to get to the crux of her own needs and desires and to find out how much she herself has engineered her own fate, a fairly happy fate, which includes both personal and artistic fulfillment.

529. _____ **THE NEEDLE'S EYE**. 1972. N.Y.: Popular Library, 1973. $1.25.

Rose Vassiliou, heroine of **The Needle's Eye**, must be one of the best-sketched women in literature. Drabble has lavished love and understanding on this heiress who, unable to cope with her fortune, tries to give it up. Much of the action is seen from the point of view of Simon. Raised poor, and striving for comfort, Simon is like Rose in his inability to move towards his own happiness. A memorable book, more reflective than Drabble's other works.

530. _____ **THE REALMS OF GOLD**. N.Y.: Knopf, 1975. $8.95.

Drabble returns to a light, ironic tone in this story about Frances Wingate, a world-famous archaeologist who, in the course of winning back an estranged lover, uncovers an astonishing network of family ties in her past. Unlike remorseful Rose Vassiliou in **The Needle's Eye**, Frances enjoys worldly success with a minimum of guilt. A personification of the "golden" life envisioned in **Jerusalem the Golden**, Frances is very much in control of her life as Drabble is in control of this amicable, old-fashioned novel. Drabble's asides on the craft of fiction-writing will probably amuse some readers and annoy others, as will the ease with which the less fortunate women characters (an embittered housewife; a deranged lesbian) are brushed aside to make way for the happy ending.

531. DUFFY, Maureen. THAT'S HOW IT WAS. 1962. London: New Authors, Ltd. o.p.

This is the story of Paddy Miller, a girl who grows up all over England (although she calls the East End of London her home), and of Louey, her mother, who is slowly dying of tuberculosis. Paddy tells the story after her mother's death, attempting to put it all down so that she can remember it without distortions. This is a powerful, warm, love story—for these two are fiercely committed to one another. Neither Paddy's love for Evelyn Tysorf, her English teacher, nor her mother's marriage ever really threaten their primary relationship. They struggle with poverty and illness, always finding bright moments together. Nicely written and recommended for its portrait of an unusually supportive mother-daughter relationship.

532. DUNN, Nell. UP THE JUNCTON. 1963. N.Y.: Ballantine, 1967. O.P.

Sixteen short stories about working-class women in London, with some characters reappearing in several stories. Dunn maintains an objective stance, presenting her characters mainly through dialogue and making no judgments. This sometimes makes the book hard to follow (the movie based on it is more coherent). The women work in a factory ("The Gold Blouse"), and at night live it up at parties and in the local pub. Particularly good are "Wedding Anniversary" (the violence of relations between men and women), "The Clipjoint" (B-girls in a nightclub), and "Band on the Common " (the story of a lurid abortion).

533. _____ **POOR COW**. 1967. N.Y.: Dell, 1968. O.P.

A vivid account of the life of a working-class woman in London, sparing none of the details of her ultimately hopeless existence, where snatches of "security" alternate with work as a barmaid and a model while her men are in prison.

534. _____ **FIGES, Eva. EQUINOX**. London: Panther, 1969. O.P.
An extremely well-written account by an English feminist of the slow break-up of a marriage. (Figes is the authof of a serious analysis called **Patriarchal Attitudes**.)

535. FORSTER, Margaret. GEORGY GIRL. 1965. N.Y.: Berkeley Medallion Books. O.P.
George is 27, a "great big strapping girl" with a huge heart and no faith in herself. When a baby enters the picture she flings herself into obsessive maternity at the cost of everything else in her life.

536. _____ **THE BOGEYMAN**. 1965. N.Y.: Ballantine, 1967. O.P.
This book explores the potential horror of the nuclear family. Dad tries to dominate his family with brute strength; the two teenagers spend their time thinking up newer and better ways to drive him insane; the passive and eager-to-please wife and mother is totally broken down by a situation which doesn't even offer her the opportunity to play happy homemaker.

537. _____ **FENELLA PHIZACKERLY**. 1970. N.Y.: Ballantine, 1972. O.P.
Fenella is a spoilt child raised to believe that her beauty will overcome all obstacles. It takes her quite a while to become a real person.

538. GILLIATT, Penelope. ONE BY ONE. N.Y.: Atheneum, 1965. O.P.
A mysterious epidemic strikes London, killing off the population one by one. Polly Talbot is pregnant; her husband, who has volunteered for hospital work, tries to isolate her from the world, and, worst, from him. This is a gripping story of love under terrible pressure, with some brilliantly drawn characters and lovely humorous touches. One might see it in contrast to Camus' **Plague**. This is a woman's view of the plague, a more human and personal view, and one which shows the limits of heroism.

539. _____ **A STATE OF CHANGE**. N.Y.: Popular Library, 1967. O.P.
This book more or less follows the life of Kakia, a Polish woman artist in post-war England, though we never feel really involved with her or any of the other characters. In some ways her lifestyle is delightfully radical, but its radicalism is simply presented as background rather than theme; for instance, although Kakia and Harry's relationship is seen as close to ideal, they somehow never get around to getting married, even after having twins and living together for many years.

540. _____ **COME BACK IF IT DOESN'T GET BETTER**. (English edition: **WHAT'S IT LIKE OUT?**) N.Y.: Random House, 1969. O.P.
Excellent short stories by a skillful writer. A number are remarkable for their presentation of a particular type of independent, eccentric, usually older, woman, towards whom Gilliatt has ambivalent feelings. "Living on the Box" tells of a woman's revenge against her arrogant poet husband; "The Tactics of Hunger" shows how the partners in a couple can become isolated from each other; "What's It Like Out?" presents an old couple being interviewed by an insensitive young reporter. Many of the stories are very amusing, but never at the cost of compassion.

541. HOBBS, May. BORN TO STRUGGLE. 1973. Vt.: Daughters, Inc. 1975. $3.50.
May Hobbs matter-of-factly tells about her life in Hoxton, the East End of London, and the bureaucratic structures which finally convince her to fight back. Born in 1938, she was one of many children to be evacuated during World War II to families who didn't want them. From then on, her life was a series of shoves in which she was given no choices, and in this short autobiography, she cuts through rhetoric and romance to include her opinions of jails, hospitals, schools, factories, homes and unions. No one is spared criticism. Victimized as a night cleaner and as a tenant, Hobbs helped form a union, Cleaners Action Group, and worked with people who were evicted from their homes. Hobbs explains the sense of community in the East End, and provides the details of eking out a living (both legal and illegal) in which cooperation among neighbors is demanded. (Examples: hoisting—shopflifting, jewelry store robbery, bookmaking.)

542. HOBSON, Polly. THE THREE GRACES. London House, 1971. O.P.
Hobson is a master of portraying psychological as well as physical violence in her mysteries. In this story of three sisters, their lives and deaths, she explores heterosexual morality and its crippling effects. One especially ironic scene features a brilliant description of visual rape—with the male (sleuth) shocked to find himself the victim.

543. HOWARD, Elizabeth Jane. ODD GIRL OUT. 1972. N.Y.: Dell, 1974. $1.50.
This is the story of a content, insular middle class couple who have been married for ten uneventful years, when suddenly Arabella, the husband's poor-little-rich-stepsister descends upon them for a visit. First the husband, then the wife, become emotionally and sexually involved with her. Though the plot is somewhat contrived to allow each of them to develop an independent relationship with Arabella, the portrayal of the women sharing love is realistic and positive. Recommended for this view of supportive and loving women. The ending is conventional (probably realistic) and thus disappointing.

JAMES, P.(hyllis) D.(orothy) *is one of the few writers still producing true detective fiction. She adds psychological insight to the classic puzzle.*

544. _____ **SHROUD FOR A NIGHTINGALE.** 1971. N.Y.: Popular Library, 1976. $1.25.
Multiple murder strikes at a nurse training school. In this women's community the lines between victim and villain are seldom clearly defined. These women are complex, believable, and often tragic. The sleuth, Adam Dagliesh, is pale in comparison.

545. _____ **AN UNSUITABLE JOB FOR A WOMAN.** 1972. N.Y.: Popular Library, 1975. $1.25.
James' finest and an excellent mystery for feminist readers. Young Cordelia Gray runs a detective agency, much to the consternation of the "man's world" surrounding her. She proves to be sensitive, humane, yet amazingly tough in solving the murder of a young idealist. The case's conclusion proves that women can obtain solidarity without liking one another.

LESSING, Doris *(1919-   ) grew up in Rhodesia, moving to England in 1949. She is a first-class novelist with a highly developed consciousness of the ways in which sex, race, and class limit people's lives; most of her work is honest and penetrating. Her early novels and stories deftly portray the intricacies of Southern Africa's racist society; above all, virtually all her works offer insights into life as a woman. Her women characters are usually profoundly conscious of the limitations their sex imposes on them, but they struggle to be "free women," reaching for wider horizons of political and intellectual awareness. Despite Lessing's own disclaimers of feminism, many women readers have found strength and inspiration in her works. Since the late 1960s, however, Lessing's worldview has undergone some drastic changes; she appears to have become increasingly influenced by Laingian psychology, religio-mystical theories, and a belief that the world is set on a disaster course.*

546. _____ **THE GRASS IS SINGING.** 1950. N.Y.: Popular Library, 1973. $ .95.
Lessing's first novel is a powerful story exploring the intersection of sexism and racism in the relationship between a white woman and a black male servant in Rhodesia. Mary Turner's marriage to a struggling farmer is a destructive and isolating experience for her. As her will and her pride are slowly eroded, she becomes more and more obsessed with the black man she once struck with a whip, ultimately reaching the limits of degradation for a white woman in the racist society she lives in.

547. _____ **MARTHA QUEST.** 1952. N.Y.: New American Library, 1970. $3.95.
This is the first in a series of five books with the cover title **Children Of Violence**. It starts with Martha as a rebellious adolescent growing up on a farm in Rhodesia in the

late 1930s. She reads voraciously, worries about clothes, fights with her parents. After finishing high school she moves into the town to take an office job, and is swept into a feverish social life; she is sexually initiated, and ends up getting married on the spur of the moment. The dating scene, the parent problems, the first disillusioned experiences of sex will strike responsive chords in many women.

548. _____ **A PROPER MARRIAGE.** 1954. N.Y.: New American Library, 1970. $3.95.
This sequel to **Martha Quest** is the story of Martha's marriage; it ends with her leaving her husband and child. The book raises important questions, touching on nearly all the issues a woman with a family faces today. Both these first two volumes are excellent consciousness-raising material; they are honestly written and deal with experiences common to many women.

549. _____ **A RIPPLE FROM THE STORM.** 1958. N.Y.: New American Library, 1970. $3.50.
In this third volume we see Martha deeply involved in intense political activity with a left-wing group in Rhodesia during World War II. She marries a German communist exile, and ultimately becomes somewhat disillusioned both with him and with politics.

550. _____ **LANDLOCKED.** 1965. N.Y.: New American Library, 1970. $3.50.

This fourth volume of the **Children of Violence** series finds Martha Quest still involved in politics as World War II ends. Her second marriage has disintegrated, and she falls very deeply in love with another man, who eventually dies. The characters in this small Rhodesian town continue to develop. Of particular interest is the awkward, flighty Maisie, who serves as a kind of counterpoint to Martha. Martha's ineffectual but endearing father dies; there is an African strike. At the end of the book, Martha is about to set out for England.

551. _____ **THE FOUR-GATED CITY.** 1969. N.Y.: Bantam, current. $1.95.
In this final volume of the **Children Of Violence** series, the complexity of Martha's life in London is paralleled by increasing complexity in Lessing's own style and thinking. Martha eventually moves beyond politics to venture over the very edges of reality, first in a trip into the area of experience commonly called insanity, and then in a futuristic projection of a nuclear cataclysm. An exhausting but compelling conclusion to the **Children Of Violence** series.

552. _____ **IN PURSUIT OF THE ENGLISH.** 1961. N.Y.: Popular Library, 1975. $1.75.
Lessing recounts her search after her arrival in London for real English people, and in particular for the English working-class. What she finds is a household full of people who are undoubtedly working-class, but striking in their individuality.

553. _____ **THE GOLDEN NOTEBOOK.** 1962. N.Y.: Bantam, 1973. $1.75.
One of Lessing's most complex novels, this is the story of Anna Wulff's attempt to combine the personal, the political, and the artistic in her life, as she records different aspects of her experience in a set of separate notebooks. Lessing drives deep into Anna's mind, exposing many of the problems a modern woman confronts in seeking

to be both a free person and a whole one. In style and structure this book is more sophisticated than Lessing's earlier works; many women see it as the peak of her achievement and have found it one of contemporary literature's richest and most compelling works about women.

554. _____ **A MAN AND TWO WOMEN**. 1963. N.Y.: Popular Library, 1975. $1.50.
A collection of superb short stories, many of them about women. "A Woman on a Roof" explores the reactions of three working men to the sight of a woman sunbathing; "Notes for a Case History" analyzes lucidly the career of a young woman whose only possibility for social advancement is to trade on the "capital" of her looks and her virginity. Many of these stories would be excellent material for use in a course where there is little time for whole books.

555. _____ **PARTICULARLY CATS**. 1967. N.Y.: New American Library, current. $ .95.
For cat lovers, here are Doris Lessing's affectionate memories of the cats in her life.

556. _____ **AFRICAN STORIES**. 1969. N.Y.: Popular Library, 1975. $1.50.
This volume brings together 30 Lessing stories about the land where she grew up. Here we see English colonials, like Lessing's parents, struggling against the forces of this new continent; the women, in particular, are defeated in their attempts to live according to the genteel English standards they know. We catch glimpses of a tough small girl roaming the veld with a rifle, or an awkward adolescent observing the affairs of her elders; this, perhaps, is Lessing herself. From the vantage point of these English settlers, we see the other groups in the country: the Afrikaaners, toughened and coarsened by their longer familiarity with this land; and the Africans, who appear mainly in the role of servants, dark alien figures who defeat the best-meaning efforts of their liberal English mistresses. In only one story does Lessing present a black man directly; this is the long story "Hunger," written deliberately to expose the plight of Africans, and now repudiated by Lessing herself. African women appear only rarely and in marginal roles, as the wives, property, or victims of men, whether black or white.

557. _____ **BRIEFING FOR A DESCENT INTO HELL**. 1971. N.Y.: Bantam, 1972. $1.95.
This novel is . . . a myth? a Laingian picture of schizophrenia? a science fiction story? an astrological explanation of history and politics? Stylistically, it is not on a par with Lessing's best; it tends to run on, reducing even its fans to boredom at certain points. But subject matter is the crux here. People who take astrology seriously, and see a relationship between it and mental health and illness, will be interested in what Lessing is attempting. If one questions whether wars and riots result from "combinations of the planets and the sun—and the moon," whether "the life of humanity is governed elsewhere," then this book may be a little hard to swallow.

558. _____ **THE TEMPTATION OF JACK ORKNEY, AND OTHER STORIES**. 1972. N.Y.: Bantam, 1974. $1.95.
The long title story in this volume seems to sum up Lessing's new viewpoint on the world; it shows a man, rational, radical, and middle-aged, "getting religion" in spite of himself. The story "An Old Woman and Her Cat" is a fine and deeply moving story of an old woman's attempt to survive on her own rather than give up the cat she loves for a place in a housing project. It is the only story in the collection, however, that

presents a woman in the positive and perceptive light that we used to expect from Lessing. Both "The Story of a Non-Marrying man" and "Mrs. Fortescue" present men with somewhat anti-woman perspectives.

559. _____ **THE SUMMER BEFORE THE DARK.** 1973. N.Y.: Bantam, 1974. $1.75.

In this book Lessing is again writing with her familiar critical intelligence about a woman's life. Kate's life has been wholly absorbed with her husband, home, and family of four children. These last are now grown up; in the summer of the story, husband and children are all going away, and Kate is left to face the question of her life. She gets a job, and acquits herself with distinction; she has an affair; she falls ill; for a while she becomes involved with the life of a young woman whose apartment she is sharing. All this takes place against a background of crisis in the world outside and rising fascism in Britain, while through the novel Kate has a symbolic, serial dream. And in the end—what? None of the new roles Kate has tried on has satisfied her, so she simply returns home—to the dark. Despite this bleak ending, the book says much that strikes true about women's lives.

560. _____ **THE MEMOIRS OF A SURVIVOR.** N.Y.: Knopf, 1975. $6.95.

Lessing's latest novel deals once again with themes used in earlier works, particularly **The Four Gated City**. This time catastrophe comes in the form of the degeneration of society to a barbarism which pits human against human until all life is virtually worthless. The "survivor"/narrator is an older woman who watches the breakdown of her own urban community while simultaneously "tuning in" to another world (the future?) on the other side of her apartment walls. Lessing's climax leads us through that wall with the survivors, but there is something unsatisfyingly simplistic in her conclusion. The picture she has painted of a moral/political cataclysm is so depressing that one feels unconvinced that survival is possible. A strange book—in some ways compelling but definitely not Lessing at her best.

561. MEACOCK, Norma. THINKING GIRL. 1968. N.Y.: Avon. $1.25.

A good first novel by an English writer. Lindy Loo starts as the self-consciously masculine partner in a lesbian relationship. When her lover abandons her, she has some ludicrous sexual exploits with men and finally enters a disastrous marriage because her doctor advises it. Through all this, however, she is acutely aware of the discrepancy between her life and her aspirations; her real yearnings are to be a thinker, to understand the world. Meacock's humor does not fail, and her honesty spares nothing. Some particularly entertaining descriptions of sex, expurgated from the first English edition, are totally realistic. The book shows some fine insights into the female condition.

562. MELVILLE, Jeannie. A NEW KIND OF KILLER. N.Y.: McKay, 1971. $4.95.

The latest in a series of mysteries featuring Charmian Daniels, Deerham detective. Charmian temporarily leaves her husband to return to school. While there, she researches the advent of the casual male killer and investigates campus violence and the murder of a close female friend.

563. MITCHISON, Naomi. MEMOIRS OF A SPACEWOMAN. 1962. N.Y.: Berkley, 1973. $ .75.

Mary is a space explorer whose specialty is communicating with alien cultures. She is not a female character stuck in a slot usually filled by males. Her values, understanding and non-interference, differ from those of the galactic warrior. Mary is conscious of her womanhood. She is probably the wish-fulfillment of a female author: she lives in a society where women are expected to have both children and a career. Marriage no longer exists. Unfortunately, most of the details are about "alien" cultures. We learn little about how a society like Mary's might work. **Memoirs Of A Spacewoman** is enjoyable reading, but it is fanciful, not mind-stretching.

564. MORTIMER, Penelope. THE PUMPKIN EATER. 1963. Plainfield, Vt.:Daughters, 1975. $3.50.

This book deals with several dimensions of the female experience, such as learning about life through women's magazines, male brutality, and the importance of children as a means of gaining an identity. The woman that Mortimer has created is considered by men to be merely an excessive breeder; her experiences and real needs have been so trivialized that even she cannot articulate them. Her numerous children (we never know how many there are, and only one has a name and an identity) are a haunting presence throughout the book.

565. _____ MY FRIEND SAYS IT'S BULLET-PROOF. N.Y.: Random House, 1968. O.P.

Muriel has just had a breast removed. "Convinced that no one could ever feel anything for her, sexually, but pity and disgust," she breaks with her lover. The English women's magazine she writes for send her on a journalists' tour of the United States, and in the course of the trip and her two different relationships with men, she comes to accept herself. The book is well-written and perceptive.

566. _____ THE HOME. N.Y.: Random House, 1971. O.P.

A fine book, raising many of the same problems as **The Pumpkin Eater**, though perhaps not as well written. Eleanor is a middle-aged woman whose husband has always had affairs with younger women, and now has left her. She tries desperately to create a home for her adult children who no longer need her as much as she would like them to. In the course of the story her own mother dies, and she feels totally alone in the world. Eleanor has outlived her usefulness, she has lived for the love of a man, but no man can even see her as a person, let alone love her. A good book for consciousness-raising.

MURDOCH, Iris *(1919-   ) An Oxford don in philosophy, her field is the moderns, notably Wittgenstein and the French existentialists. As a most prolific novelist (some 17 books in the last 20 years), her vision is darkly comic, sharply ironic, but usually compassionate. her choreographic plots relate nearly all her wide range of characters with one another in some way (usually directly or implicitly sexual) in each novel. She slights no social class. Though not crisply brilliant, her insights ring true.*

567. _____ A SEVERED HEAD. 1961. N.Y.: Viking, current. $2.45.

The story of some uses and abuses of love in the lives and relationships of six characters. Contemporary London life here is empty and superficial, devoid of passion and conviction of any kind. Because the novel is intended to be comic, stock situations occur frequently and characters are stereotyped. Murdoch's distance from her story somewhat clouds her perception of reality.

568. _____ AN UNOFFICIAL ROSE. 1962. N.Y.: Warner, 1973. $1.25.

A clever, nasty sort of humor pervades this book, which is a depressing story about people trying to possess other people, with few redeeming insights. The characters vary in terms of power: an ineffectual housewife trapped in her own vague "morality" is at one end of the spectrum. At the other extreme is a totally unscrupulous lesbian, who vindictively controls the lives of people in her circle. Not recommended for those who seek a positive rendering of human possibilities.

569. _____ THE UNICORN. O.P.

In **The Unicorn**, as in many Murdoch novels, one household is a microcosm of all society. As governess Marian Taylor becomes involved in the oppressive relationships at Castle Gaze, she and those around her seem to sink ever deeper into a mire of futile attempts at self-determination. The tension between freedom and fatalism builds as the characters struggle to change through individual actions what seems an inevitable chain of events. It's difficult to determine exactly what Murdoch's personal philosophy is, but perhaps, like Marian, she is uncertain "whether the world in which she had been living was a world of significant suffering or a devil's shadow-play, a mere nightmare of violence." The destructiveness and prison-like atmosphere which pervade the book make it somewhat depressing, but nonetheless compelling.

570. _____ **THE RED AND THE GREEN.** 1965. N.Y.: Avon, 1971. $1.25.
A small group of people are all intricately related to each other by both blood and passion. The politics of their relationships are a counterpoint to the politics of Ireland approaching a revolution. The traps that the various women's lives have become are quite truthfully but rather hopelessly depicted.

571. _____ **THE BLACK PRINCE.** 1973. N.Y.: Warner Paperback Library, 1974. $1.75.
Aloof and fastidious, Bradley Pearson wants only to retire to a suitably remote cottage to write his great novel. Instead he finds himself embroiled in the affairs of his family and closest friends, thus plunged into the center of the human drama he would rather glorify in art. What follows is both bizarre and gruesome, but Murdoch renders it all not only believable but dismayingly universal. Her bleak portraits of older women and the indignities and misery inflicted upon them by age will make one wince. Billed as a love story, **The Black Prince** is a convincing and impeccably crafted testament to the ordinariness of injustice, treachery, and petty viciousness.

572. NORTON, Mary. THE BORROWERS. 1956. N.Y.: Harcourt & Brace, current. $1.50.
One of the most imaginative children's books ever written, and certainly enjoyable for adults to read as well. The Borrowers, Homily, Pod, and Arrietty, are tiny people who live in the walls of an old countryhouse in England, taking their furnishings from the smaller items of the household. All mysterious disappearances—of pencils, matchboxes, thimbles—are, Mary Norton tells us, the work of "Borrowers." In this book (to which there are three sequels, **The Borrowers Afloat, Afield,** and **Aloft)** Arrietty, Pod, and Homily match wits for survival against a disbelieving and often dangerous human world. This is a wonderful adventure story, with the young girl Arrietty the bravest, most resourceful character.

573. PEARSON, Diane. THE MARIGOLD FIELD. Phila., Pa.: Lippincott, 1969. $6.50.
This novel, in the tradition of popular historical romances, doubtless contains some accurate insights into the life of the rural poor in England around the turn of the century; these are the people who built the great middle-class Forsyte fortunes. Early scenes dramatize the limitations of their lives: the degrading dependence on a capricious landlord, the lack of birth control. The novel chronicles each individual's search for a meaningful life: "in service" in London, at sea, as postmaster in the village, married, single. The book is remarkable for its perception of the differences among human beings usually lumped together as "the poor," who actually share only their background and their common search for dignity.

▲▲▲▲▲▲▲▲▲▲▲▲▲▲▲▲▲▲▲▲▲▲▲▲▲▲▲▲▲▲▲▲▲▲▲▲▲▲▲

574. _____ **SARAH.** Phila., Pa.: Lippincott, 1971. $6.95.
This sequel to **The Marigold Field** continues the story of a girl from the village who "makes good" and becomes a teacher, not to free herself as her family had hoped, but only to exchange a feudal landlord for a vicious headmistress as the power on whom she is dependent. Given the limitations of her position, she struggles with family obligations, her own sexuality, her competing desires for adventure and stability. These struggles take her far from her origins and towards control of her own life.

575. SHARP, Margery. THE EYES OF LOVE. Boston: Little, Brown, 1957. O.P.
For those who like the clever comedies that British writers seem to excel at, here is a well-done one. What separates this book from the rest of the genre is the portrait it gives us of a little girl, a portrait quite unique in fiction. Martha, the child, is unsentimentally portrayed; she is totally lacking in charm. Stereotypes are so strong that one may get half-way through the book before noticing her talent and integrity. But then it becomes a positive inspiration to watch her maintain her independence in spite of all adult interference, well-meaning or otherwise. Sharp's portrait is doubly interesting because she is the author of numerous children's books.

576. _____ **IN PIOUS MEMORY**. Boston: Little, Brown, 1967. O.P.
The tongue-in-cheek account of a thoroughly adjusted woman left accidentally without a husband, and the scramble that ensues among her male acquaintances as each one, recognizing what a prize she is, views for her selfless domestic services the next time around.

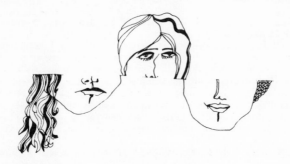

SPARK, Muriel (1918-   ). _She was born in Edinburgh, Scotland. She began her career as a poet, but has achieved recognition primarily for her work as a novelist. The novels, which have established her as one of Britain's foremost writers, are generally satirical, a unique and often brilliant blending of comedy and horror. Spark has also produced a sizable body of critical works, several of them dealing with the Brontes._

577. _____ **THE BALLAD OF PECKHAM RYE**. Philadelphia: Lippincott, 1960. O.P.
A well-written black comedy set in working-class South London. While the plot moves right along, and the laughs keep coming, it is impossible to care about any of Spark's characters, impossible to believe that she herself might. They are types, without depth or complexities. The women are particularly one-dimensional.

578. _____ **THE PRIME OF MISS JEAN BRODIE**. 1962. N.Y.: Dell, current. $ .95.
The highly readable and entertaining story of Miss Jean Brodie, a school teacher at a Scottish private girls' school in the 1930s. Miss Brodie, who considers herself at 40 to be in the prime of life, is a highly unconventional figure at the school and functions as something of a benevolent despot in the lives of six of her students. One of them eventually betrays her, and the story revolves around the how and why of that betrayal. This book is particularly recommended for high school students, since much of the story revolves around emergent adolescent sexuality.

579. _____ **THE GIRLS OF SLENDER MEANS**. N.Y.: Knopf, 1963. O.P.
An assortment of young women living together at the May of Teck Club in end-of-war London, "when everyone was poor." Spark's attitude towards the group of women she has created is detached to say the least, contemptuous to say the most.

580. _____ **THE MANDELBAUM GATE**. 1965. Greenwich, Conn.: Fawcett. O.P.
An exciting suspense novel set in Israel "between the wars." It contains an element of compassion lacking in some of Spark's earlier work, yet lacks their tightness of construction, something of a flaw in the thriller. It is concerned in part with the identity questions of a Catholic convert who is the daughter of a WASP and a Jew. She is conscious that most of the world, having pigeon-holed her as a spinster, never sees her as having a real identity at all. Her relationship with another woman receives a disappointing treatment, coming off finally as comical and unhealthy.

581. _____ **MEMENTO MORI.** 1959. N.Y.: Avon, 1973. $1.65.
The author has assembled a cast of characters who are all over seventy. Each has known the others for at least forty years; each is now, in some way, mentally or physically affected by the process of aging. They are basically an upper-class set—some have led creative lives and achieved a certain measure of fame; others have had their existence defined by inherited wealth—managing a family business or dabbling in philanthropy. Their working class servants, also elderly, provide a different perspective. All receive the same anonymous telephone call: "Remember you must die"; all respond in different ways. Spark has taken the serious theme of mortality, fleshed it out with a lively plot, brilliant characterizaton and just the right touches of humor, and produced a book which is as enjoyable as it is meaningful.

582. STANNARD, Una. THE NEW PAMELA: Or Virtue Unrewarded. N.Y.: Ballantine, 1969. O.P.
A novel in letters by a feminist academic: in the age of the sexual revolution, Pamela struggles against the double standard. The novel seems to be a rather deliberate polemic, and one concentrating on issues that many will consider less than crucial. Still, it should be commended as one of very few attempts to show a self-determining woman consciously trying to change her life.

583. TINDALL, Gillian. SOMEONE ELSE. 1969. N.Y.: Popular Library. O.P.
Joanna has been happily married for four years and has a small son when her husband dies in an accident. After her initial grief she comes to have second thoughts about the husband she idealized; she realizes, too, how much her life was built around his, and faces the problems of restructuring her life alone. This excellent novel does not oversimplify; it captures the texture of life in all its complexity, showing how Joanna changes and grows.

584. _____ **FLY AWAY HOME.** N.Y.: Popular Library, 1971. O.P.
This is the diary of Tonia, an Englishwoman married to a French Jew. She is in the process of reassessing her life; she realizes, among other things, that her husband would have been just a casual lover if she hadn't fallen pregnant. Now, in her search for alternatives, she becomes fired by pro-Israeli sentiments during the Six-Day War, visits Israel, seeks out old lovers, but ends up accepting her bad marriage. Although many of her views and decisions seem conservative, Tonia is a convincing character. The diary form, though some may find it slow going, allows space for reflection, and many perceptive comments are made on such topics as the differences between French and English life and the nature of marriage and motherhood.

585. WEST, Rebecca. THE BIRDS FALL DOWN. N.Y.: Viking, 1966. $5.95.
A well-described tale of a girl raised in England confronting her aristocratic Russian heritage and knowing fear and deception at the same time. Limited in interest perhaps by its single-minded concentration on the upper class.

586. _____ **THE FOUNTAIN OVERFLOWS.** 1966. N.Y.: Avon Books, 1974. $1.95.
Set in turn-of-the-century London, this story of the unusual Aubrey family is strangely absorbing. The mother, a former concert pianist, struggles to educate her musically gifted children and keep the family from poverty as her somewhat unpredictable journalist husband gambles away their income. The adult world, in all its mystery and contradiction, is seen through the eyes of the children, in particular the daughter, Rose, who narrates. Her memories of her childhood and the strength and intelligence of her sisters, cousin, aunt and mother reveal a self-sufficient female family network. Although not an outstanding work, the subtle feminist undertone and the positive images of young girls growing up together are enough to keep one reading to the last page.

International

Africa

19th Century

OLIVE SCHREINER (1855-1920) was born in South Africa, the ninth child of German/English missionary parents. She, however, abandoned all belief in God at an early age; it was in books that she sought spiritual and intellectual enlightenment. While still quite young, she began making up her own stories, and, at the age of 19, she took a position as a governess, and began work on **The Story of an African Farm**, her best known novel. In 1881 she left Africa for England, and two years later the book was published there under the pseudonym, "Ralph Iron." It became an international bestseller, and Olive Schreiner had become a literary celebrity in London. Even at the height of her popularity, however, she continued to live alone in boarding houses, often suffering great mental anguish and physical distress caused by a chronic asthmatic condition and the drugs she took to relieve it. Finally, to ease both her asthma and her depression, she returned to Africa. There she devoted many years to political activities, particularly women's rights. Her nonfiction work, **Woman and Labour**, was regarded by many as "the bible of the women's movement." She also married during this time but refused to give up her own name; her husband added her name to his. Their marriage was apparently based on a solid friendship/love. In 1913 Olive moved back to England alone—there she remained until before her death in 1920, publishing occasional pacifist articles and allegories.

Olive Schreiner

587. _____ **THE STORY OF AN AFRICAN FARM**. 1883. Gloucester, Mass.: Peter Smith. $5.00.
This book is a neglected feminist classic. First published in 1883, it is the story of two female cousins who grow up in the 1860s on an isolated farm in South Africa. Of the two, Em is more conventionally "feminine," resigned to (and even content with) her future as a wife and mother. Lyndall is the rebel; restless and intellectually inquisitive, she leaves the farm to attend boarding school for four years. Upon her return, she speaks to Em and another childhood friend, Waldo, about the narrowness of women's prescribed role: "I am not in so great a hurry to put my neck beneath any man's foot; and I do not so greatly admire the crying of babies." Lyndall steadfastly refuses to "be bound" to any man, even to the lover whose child she bears. She remains uncompromised and uncompromising to the end. Lyndall's struggles and pain were no doubt Olive Schreiner's as well, and **The Story of an African Farm** became the fictional vehicle for her passionate feminism. The novel is at times rhetorical and sentimental, but somehow this is part of its charm. Interspersed throughout are passages filled with profound insights into childhood, art, life, death, and the liberation of the human spirit.

588. _____ **DREAMS**. 1890. Select Books, 1971. $3.50.
This is a collection of the allegories which Olive Schreiner wrote on a variety of subjects: life, death, love, art, truth and wisdom. Her vision of a future society based on love, freedom, and equality between the sexes permeates the book. The stories, some only a page or two in length, have an ethereal, fairy-tale quality, suggested by

the title itself; yet each is solidly based in the author's political commitments to pacifism and feminism. Included in this collection is the beautiful "Life's Gifts," a poem/allegory which concisely and powerfully expresses Olive Schreiner's feminist convictions.

589. _____ **LETTERS**. S.C. Cronwright-Schreiner, ed. Westport, Conn.: Hyperion Press, 1975. $26.50.
Although this is a pretty mutilated and censored collection, there's a lot of interesting reading in it. The editor (her husband) goes to the extent of contradicting her in comments he inserts into the middle of her letters. Many of Schreiner's most interesting letters were written to Havelock Ellis, with whom she had a long and close relationship.

590. _____ **FROM MAN TO MAN**. 1927. N.Y.: Harcourt, Brace, Jovanovich (Johnson Reprints) $31.50.
This was Olive Schreiner's last book, left uncompleted at her death. It has neither the cohesion nor the overall charm of **African Farm**, though there are some similarities between the main women characters: each is a defiant yet inevitable victim of an oppressive patriarchal society. All but one of the male characters are portrayed as total villains, and the lack of alternatives available to the women is driven home again and again—to an almost excruciating degree of pain and melodrama. **From Man to Man** needs editing and revision, but for anyone interested in Olive Schreiner, it contains some of her angriest feminism, as well as long tracts against war and racism.

1900-1950

591. AIDOO, Ama Ata. NO SWEETNESS HERE. 1969. N.Y.: Anchor, 1972. $1.95.
Eleven excellent short stories by a Ghanaian woman who writes perceptively about Africa in transition, the lingering effects of colonialism, and the lives of African women. The story "Everything Counts" raises the issues of physical appearance and wig-wearing through a woman university teacher who teaches "Little frightened lost creatures from villages and developing slums who had come to this citadel of an alien culture to be turned into ladies." "In the Cutting of a Drink" tells with new vividness the classic story of the country girl who goes to the city and ends up as a prostitute. Motherhood is a recurrent theme, for single as well as married women in "Something to Talk About . . ." Aidoo has developed new and distinctive stylistic techniques; she uses not only dialogue but also occasional chorus effects, as well as interior monologue; all is rich in African idiom. This may make her seem a bit unapproachable to some, but her work repays the effort.

GORIMER, Nadine (1923-   ) _A white South African woman. She has been much published in_ **The New Yorker**, _and her work is characterized by control of structure and exquisite craft. She is deeply opposed to the racism of South Africa, and some of her works are now banned in her homeland. When it comes to politics between the sexes, Gordimer appears to be striving for an androgynous ideal; she presents men as sensitively as she does women and sometimes seems too accepting of the male point of view._

592. _____ **THE LYING DAYS**. N.Y.: Simon & Schuster, 1953. O.P.
This first novel tells of a girl's coming to womanhood. Childhood in a South African mine town, dreamy adolescence while World War II rumbles in the distance, the sweetness of first love, political arousal in radical student circles, a grand love affair which turns sour after robbing the narrator of all her own career aspirations—all are tenderly, vividly evoked against the backcloth of the strange, blind, brutal society that is South Africa.

593. _____ **A WORLD OF STRANGERS**. N.Y.: Simon & Schuster, 1958. O.P.

When Toby comes from England to work in South Africa, he is not simply apolitical, but anti-political; he wants to lead a private life. His friendship with a black man eventually makes him decide to stay in this country where all people are strangers to one another. In Toby, Gordimer has created a completely plausible male narrator and one she apparently means her readers to like; yet feminists will be deeply disturbed by his casual and cruel sexism: "for me, the exoticism of women still lay in beauty and self-absorbed femininity. I would choose an houri rather than a companion. No doubt what I had seen in the nasty woodshed of childhood was a serious-minded intellectual woman."

594. _____ **FRIDAY'S FOOTPRINT: Twelve Stories and a Novella.** N.Y.: Viking Press, 1960. O.P.

Many of these stories explore the class gradations in small-town white South Africa. "Little Willie," for instance, shows how a small girl has internalized these class distinctions. Other stories touch on the themes of marriage ("Friday's Footprint") and infidelity ("A Style of her Own," "Our Bovary").

595. _____ **NOT FOR PUBLICATION**. N.Y.: Viking Press, 1965. O.P.

The 16 stories in this volume include many of exceptional interest to women and to those interested in South African politics. To mention only a few: "A Company of Laughing Faces" and "Tenants of the Last Tree-house" deal brilliantly with adolescent girls; "Good Climate, Friendly Inhabitants" shows how a shallow, racist white woman is saved by a black man; "Something for the Time Being" contrasts the political attitudes of a white woman who can afford to be liberal and a black woman whose day-to-day survival is threatened by her husband's political involvement.

596. _____ **THE LATE BOURGEOIS WORLD**. N.Y.: Viking Press, 1966. O.P.

This novel portrays the dilemma of a white woman, Liz, who deeply sympathizes with the black struggle, while both the establishment and the forces of the resistance bar her from real participation. The woman grew up among people aspiring toward a ruling-class lifestyle. An upper-class, self-styled revolutionary becomes the father of her boy, and later, becomes her husband. She learns that the affluence of the whites is based on the hunger and oppression of the majority. Her husband Max's suicide opens the book: faced with prison, he had betrayed his "cause" and the people he worked with. In the end, Liz's relationship to black activist Luke is a useful tool. She finally becomes conscious of the implications of her activity, and realizes that she is working for her own liberation indirectly.

597. _____ **LIVINGSTONE'S COMPANIONS**. N.Y.: Viking, 1971. O.P.

These 14 stories show Gordimer in absolute control of her craft. "A Third Presence" tells the lives of two sisters, one pretty, and one with "a sad Jewish ugliness," who live out lives not totally expected of them. "Otherwise Birds Fly In" presents an intense friendship between two women who end up in very different situations. To select from the riches in this volume, however, can only be arbitrary.

598. _____ **SELECTED STORIES**. N.Y.: Viking, 1976. $10.00.

This collection, drawn from 25 years of story-writing, is a marvelous introduction to Gordimer's fiction. Readers can watch the author's political vision grow in depth and complexity from the early "Is There Nowhere Else Where We Can Meet?"—about a white girl's dawning awareness of black humanity and oppression—to the more recent "Some Monday For Sure"—a first-person account of a black guerrilla's flight into a free African state to train for the liberation of South Africa. As always, Gordimer's depiction of women's lives is superb. In "The Gentle Art," a young

woman gets so caught up in the excitement of a crocodile hunt that she fails (refuses?) to perceive that the white colonial woman's role is to stay behind and keep the home fires burning. Gordimer takes a dim view of conscientious liberals in "Which New Era Would That Be?" in which a brisk young woman infuriates a black man with her overbearing "understanding" of his plight. An outstanding story is "A Chip of Glass Ruby" about a courageous Indian mother who starves herself in prison to protest against apartheid, much to the bewilderment of her husband, who can't see how the degradation of black Africans extends to the total human community. Put this remarkable book on your must-read list.

599. ,JABAVU, Noni. DRAWN IN COLOR: African Contrasts. 1960. International Publications Service. $6.25.
Noni Jabavu is a black South African woman. Her Xhosa family, however, was an exceptionally prominent and highly educated one, representing a miniscule minority among black South Africans; she herself was educated in England and married an Englishman. In this book she tells how she returned to South Africa for the funeral of her murdered brother and then traveled to Uganda to visit her unhappily married sister. Uganda, at this point due to be granted independence, distressed her in many ways, not least in its treatment of women. This book offers interesting insights into tribal society in transition, though Jabavu's pro-Western viewpoint has definite limitations.

600. NWAPA, Flora. EFURU. 1966. N.Y.: Humanities Press, current. $2.25.
In West Africa, storytelling is the basic way of spreading news, teaching history, and linking people with their ancestors. Flora Nwapa, an East Nigerian woman, describes the intimate life of Efuru with storytelling ease. Efuru is seen as an exceptional woman who is pushed to the limits of her generosity by two careless and deceptive men (her husbands). Rituals, legend, and verbal expressions blend into the emotions and daily life of the villagers to give an accessible glimpse into African culture. Two important themes are the significance of childbearing for women and death.

Asia

1900-1950

SMEDLEY, Agnes. PORTRAIT OF CHINESE WOMEN (see American section 1900-1950)

1950-present

JHABVALA, Ruth Prawer (1927-   ) *is an outstanding writer, almost unique in world literature, and unfortunately unrecognized in the United States. Born in Germany, she was educated in England, and, after marrying an Indian, went to live in New Delhi in 1951. Her works are almost all set in India and often deal with the clash of East and West. One wonders if it is her expert control over language and form, or whether it is the sheer intelligence of her observations which transforms the written page into a living world where people speak their greedy, stupid, clever, lively, wise, deceitful, loving or malicious minds, and are clearly illuminated and sympathetically but unsparingly understood.*

601. _____ **AMRITA**. N.Y.: Norton, 1955. O.P.
One of Jhabvala's happiest novels, full of exciting, vivid characters, with a compelling succession of events and a perfect denouement. We become partisans, hope for conclusions, cheer on characters and events, and are not disappointed in the slightly unexpected and much hoped-for ending.

602. _____ **THE NATURE OF PASSION**. N.Y.: Norton, 1956. O.P.
A good Jhabvala novel about a family crowding against each other, misunderstanding each other and themselves, wanting the impossible, quarrelling, scheming, falling in love, and happening—occasionally and by accident—to understand each other and themselves. The Indian setting, rather than distancing the story, somehow has the effect of bringing near and making acceptable to us insights that we might otherwise reject as hitting too close to home.

603. _____ **GET READY FOR BATTLE.** N.Y.: Norton, 1962. O.P.
Entertaining in the reading, incomplete at the conclusion. In this novel of a diverse Indian family where incompatible ambitions threaten a tenuous peace, we are intrigued into the lives of characters who are too quickly drawn to become the vivid companions a full-length novel demands.

604. _____ **A BACKWARD PLACE.** N.Y.: Norton, 1965. O.P.
The author treats a recurrent theme in her work, the Westerner in India—her motives, her way of life, the effect that India ultimately has on her. Here are three Western women, easily recognizable but not stereotypes. There is the Bohemian, depending on others, living off everyone except herself. There is the hard-bitten, aging European courtesan, seeing herself always as some man's mistress, losing confidence in herself and her future, longing to return to Europe but afraid of the recognition that may find her there. And then there is Judy, a loving, trusting woman, married to an Indian, as impulsive as she is wise. Unlike some of the author's earlier novels, this is not a story with a happy ending; we leave our characters pursuing the lives we have watched them leading, and we know (perhaps more clearly than we would be willing to see in our own society) what the consequences of such lives are likely to be.

605. _____ **TRAVELERS.** 1972. N.Y.: Harper & Row, 1973. $6.95.
In this unusual novel it is as if the author were so eager to show us the crowds of India that she widens the focus as far as she can. Is this the tale of three English girls come to study with a guru, or of a young Englishman's affection for an Indian boy, or of Asha, the rich, aging, passionate widow, with her loneliness and her fears? The focus is too wide to explore any one character satisfactorily. Each flickers vividly into life and remains part of a larger landscape illuminated also by others. All these characters converge briefly in a chance meeting on a dusty Indian plain, then each goes on alone.

606. _____ **LIKE BIRDS, LIKE FISHES.** 1963. N.Y.: Norton. O.P.
Jhabvala's development of the short story is exceptional. This is her first volume of collected stories. All but one of these tales is set in India; they are stories of daily life, romance, discovery, renunciation. Each situation is ordinary; each is perfectly illuminated and developed, completely with a penetrating understanding which haunts us long after we have forgotten the details.

607. _____ **A STRONGER CLIMATE.** N.Y.: Norton, 1968. O.P.
This collection, while possessing all the virtues of the earlier **Like Birds, Like Fishes**, brings Jhabvala's withering understanding closer to home. Each story is an encounter between the East and our own culture. Here is an unattractive English secretary, a priggish aging Dutchman, a retired English schoolteacher, a young bride from the West—all major characters, and all a recognizable part not only of our culture, but of ourselves.

608. _____ **AN EXPERIENCE OF INDIA.** N.Y.: Norton, 1972. O.P.
This third volume of stories is prefaced with a personal comment by the author in which she states that she has lost her perspective; India has overwhelmed her. And so with these stories. Without losing one bit of control or clear-sightedness, we feel a loss of distance, or of joy. There is no longer detachment; the wife drifts helplessly from safety, the widow is unredeemably unprotected; it is inevitable, slightly bitter, no longer alleviated by distance. As the author confesses herself overwhelmed by India, by the end of this volume the reader, though moved, is somewhat overwhelmed also.

609. MARKANDAYA, Kamala. NECTAR IN A SIEVE. 1954. N.Y.: Signet, current. $1.25.
The simply-told story of a peasant woman's life in India—an arranged marriage at 12, hard work, children, a constant battle against the forces of nature and of human exploitation. Markandaya is probably the Indian writer best-known in the U.S.; this is unfortunate in some ways, as her attitude tends towards sentimentality and an

unquestioning acceptance of certain realities of a woman's life in India. For more sophisticated and complex novels about India, the reader is advised to try the works of Jhabvala and Rau.

610. RAU, Santha Rama. REMEMBER THE HOUSE. N.Y.: Harper & Row, 1956. $7.95.
Baba is from a protective, wealthy, educated Bombay family. Her mother has left to study with her guru. She herself seeks adventure and, now that she is of marriageable age, contemplates a marriage outside her accepted community. The revelations of the strong position of women within the Indian family and a well-written plot make this study in accident and self-discovery an unusually rewarding novel.

611. VIET NAM WOMEN'S UNION. THE MOUNTAIN TRAIL. Hanoi, 1970. (Available from the Ho Chi Minh Bookstore, Montreal, or the Red Book, 91 River St., Cambridge, MA 02139.)
Seven short stories about the lives of women in war-torn Vietnam. We see a woman army surgeon, women gunners, women in the Volunteer Youth. A nurse stays to tend a critically ill baby instead of saying goodbye to her fiance leaving for the front. A husband resents his young wife's promotion to the vice-chairmanship of their co-op, but comes eventually to accept it. The human details of day-to-day life are richly informative; the strength, spirit, and commitment of these women are an inspiration. Unfortunately the translation is poor, at times very awkward.

Australia

1900-1950

612. RICHARDSON, Henry Handel (Henrietta). THE END OF A CHILDHOOD N.Y.: Somerset, 1934. $15.50.
This is a collection of pieces by an Australian writer. Highly recommended are the eight stories grouped together under the title **Growing Pains: Sketches Of Girlhood**. Although there are no recurring characters, the stories can be seen as a sequence, building up gradually an atmosphere of girlhood friendships, interwoven with the fear and distrust of growiing up, of men, and of sex; this culminates in a pretty clearly lesbian episode in the final story. All the stories, however, will be evocative of many women's experiences; any one could serve as a good discussion-starter to touch off memories of girlhood.

1950-present

613. HAZZARD, Shirley. PEOPLE IN GLASS HOUSES: Tales of Organization Life. N.Y.: Knopf, 1967. O.P.
These excellent short stories, set in what are clearly the offices of the United Nations, can be described as caustic comments on bureaucratic life, but then one misses the warmth, the sadness, the sympathy, the joy with which the stories and characters are presented. Miss Shamsee, the secretary who has a brief affair with an official, wonders if he thinks of her when he sees her initials typed lower-case; two friends, perhaps lovers, rarely see each other, since their offices are on different elevator banks; there is the spiteful head secretary, the mediocre division head. The list goes on, showing us with great humor and sympathy people's lives as they are bent and misshapen by the forces of bureaucracy and organization life.

asdfg;lkjhaqswdefrft;plokijujyazsxdcfvfb;.l,kmjnjbas

614. _____ **THE BAY OF NOON.** 1970. N.Y.: Pocket Books, 1972. O.P. A slow, thoughtful novel, painting a visual and emotional picture of a woman's growth to adulthood. The physical settings is Naples, a year of work away from the scenes of childhood—remote, highlighted, having a mood all its own. The emotional setting is the beginning of a woman's awareness and independence. The emotional time and physical place coincide, each heightening the other, and we are left with a vivid sense both of Naples and of the first struggles towards independence.

STEAD, Christina (1902-   ) _"We often fall for people who are enigmas to us," Christina Stead recently observed ("Christina Stead: AN Interview," by Joan Lidoff, Aphra, Vol. 6, nos. 3 & 4). Stead herself presents an enigma to feminist readers: outspokenly scornful of the Women's Liberation Movement ("Women should have rights. But Women's Lib is nonsense. What put me off is throw away their bra. What would I do without a bra, I should like to know!"), she nevertheless depicts vividly and with great feeling the constricted lives of married and single women. The eldest child of a large family, Stead saved up her meager wages until she was 26 to travel to Europe and then to America, where she lived during World War II. Many of her stories are set in the eastern United States; even_ **The Man Who Loved Children**, _a highly autobiographical novel drawn from Stead's childhood in Sydney, takes place in and around Washington, D.C. During the 1950s Stead was suspected of belonging to the Communist Party; all of her books were allowed to go out of print, including_ **House Of All Nations** _(1938), which had once been acclaimed as the greatest financial novel ever written, and no new titles appeared for 12 years. Fortunately, since 1960 a Stead revival has been underway, and the old titles are gradually being reissued. Stead has since returned to Australia where she still writes prolifically. Her last novel,_ **Miss Herbert** _(N.Y.: Random, 1976. $8.95.), is the saga of an English beauty who wants to "play by the rules" and at the same time be independent._

615. _____ **THE MAN WHO LOVED CHILDREN.** 1940. N.Y.: Avon, 1972. $1.95. This is a portrait of a family you will never forget. Sam Pollit is a complete egocentric, apparently adored by his six children, whom he sees as mere reflections of his own ego. Henny, his wife, has been transformed into a careworn shrew, aged prematurely by too many births, too little money, and a growing hatred for her husband. She lives on tea, aspirin, solitaire, and tirades. Their children are caught between them. Louie, the ugly duckling adolescent daughter, is a poet who takes the decisive action on which the dramatic denouement hinges. Scenes, characters, dialogue, the world of childhood, are vividly captured by a superbly skillful and sensitive writer.

616. _____ **THE PUZZLEHEADED GIRL.** N.Y.: Holt, Rinehart and Winston, 1965. O.P. "We have an instinct [to] look after the weak, an instinct which betrays us to them," remarks a character in one of these four puzzling novellas. Our fascination with the "weak," the enigmatic and the doomed is the dominant theme. "The Rightangled Creek: A Sort of Ghost Story" concerns a haunted house and the residents who try, in vain, to live there. The other stories deal with haunted people: Honor Lawrence, "The

Puzzleheaded Girl," drifts in and out of the lives of four staid lawyers and their wives, causing them to face the panic and emptiness within themselves. The heroines of "The Dianas" and "The Girl from the Beach" seem wayward innocents abroad but are really cunning survivors, much to the dismay of their would-be knights-in-shining-armor. Witty, near-surreal portraits of Americans whom Stead no doubt encountered during her stay in the U.S. in the late 1930s and 1940s.

Canada

1900-1950

Ojibwa Indian women with their birch-bark canoe.

617. CARR, Emily. KLEE WYCK. 1941. Toronto: Clarke Irwin, 1971. $1.75. (No current U.S. edition.)
Emily Carr was an outstanding Canadian painter and writer. **Klee Wyck**, like much of her work, memorializes the culture of the coastal tribes of British Columbia. It is a collection of short pieces. Some, like "Sophie" and "Wash Mary," give us a feeling for Native American women's lives. Others, like "Skedans" and "Tanoo," are portraits of abandoned villages—told simply, they give a powerful feeling of a great culture being lost. And there are chapters like the exquisite "Canoe" which capture the land itself, the shores and forests of British Columbia. Carr brought to her writing an exacting standard of craftsmanship; she went over and over a sentence, "peeling" unnecessary words, replacing an unclear word with a more precise one. She had a painter's eye; her vivid imagery has caused her prose to be compared to poetry.

1950-present

618. ATWOOD, Margaret. THE EDIBLE WOMAN. 1969. Toronto: McClelland and Stewart, 1973. $2.75.
One option women have today is to make ourselves into marketable objects. This is workable only if one can accept being consumed. Thoroughly "normal," absolutely "delicious," Marian McAlpin finds that she cannot. She becomes "nutty." Horrified at her own edibility, she can no longer eat. This wonderfully funny novel is a fine

example of feminist humor. In fact, one of the things that pulls Marian through to the very positive conclusion of this book is her own sense of humor. Nobody should miss reading **The Edible Woman.**

619. _____ SURFACING. 1972. N.Y.: Popular Library, 1974. $1.50.
The narrator's father has disappeared from the remote Quebec island where he lived alone. With a lover and a couple of friends casually interested in making a film she goes to seek him. On the island the four characters unfold while the narrator's past looms larger. This is a very well-written novel whose heroine is involved in the kind of epic quest which literature has hitherto reserved for male heroes. Her quest is not only a physical one against forces of nature; it is also an interior voyage into her own mind which allows her eventually to surface with a whole spirit.

620. BLAIS, Marie Claire. MAD SHADOWS. 1959. (No current U.S. edition.) Toronto: McClelland and Stewart, 1971. $1.75.
A difficult book to describe. The subject matter is almost unrelievedly grim, yet there is something lyrical about the spare, poetic style. Indeed, one of the main themes of the book is the conflict between beauty and ugliness. The story focuses on: a brother, the "beautiful beast," handsome but mentally an idiot; a sister, sensitive but ugly; a mother who worships her son's beauty while refusing to recognize his idiocy, and whose own beauty is now being destroyed by cancer of the face. It will not be to everyone's taste to wander among Blais' mad shadows, where mind and body seem hopelessly split and love appears impossible, but, for some, the reading of this book will be a powerful experience.

621. _____ A SEASON IN THE LIFE OF EMMANUEL. 1966. N.Y.: Grosset and Dunlap, 1969. $1.95.
Blais paints a bleak picture of a large, impoverished French Canadian family living in rural Quebec. But underlying all is an affirmation of human dignity and strength. Gran-mere Antoinette is the bulwark of the family—for her, living has been a succession of disasters, yet she remains committed to life. Jean Le-Maigre is a sensitive child who sees the misery all too clearly, but at times he can transcend it and see the poetry, also. Blais' work is a curious mixture of grotesquerie and beauty. This is one of her best books.

622. _____ **THE MANUSCRIPTS OF PAULINE ARCHANGE**. N.Y.: Farrar, Straus and Girous, 1970. $5.95.

Pauline is a tough, nervy girl of the streets, a typical little hoodlum, who lives in wretched poverty in a French Canadian town. Pauline, beneath her hardness, is different—a sensitive, verbal child who observes everything and feels compelled, at age eight, to write it all down. A fictionalized autobiography, the book is memorable both for the story it tells, in Blais' beautiful prose, of one girl's live from ages five to ten, and for the author's reflections on what happens when the story one wishes to write is one's own.

623. ENGEL, Marian. SARAH BASTARD'S NOTEBOOK. 1968. Don Mills, Ontario: Paperjacks, 1974. $1.50.

Novels about female academics are fairly rare, about Canadian female academics even rarer. We meet Sarah (age 30, Ph.D. and lecturer at a Toronto university) when, no longer able to see the point of her work, she is ready to resign. She muses over her past, trying to make sense of it. Her thoughts about women and about Canadian culture are particularly interesting. It's a meditative book; there really isn't a plot and there's not much dialogue. Engel starts briskly enough, but the writing tends to become somewhat convoluted and confusing, during the final third of the book.

624. _____ **THE HONEYMAN FESTIVAL**. Toronto: Anansi, 1970. $2.95. (N.Y.: St. Martins Press, 1972. O.P.)

Min is in her mid-thirties and enormously pregnant with her fourth child in as many years (her Lippes Loop failed her). For those interested in literary treatments of women and women's bodies, Engel does a superb job with the physical details of late pregnancy. Waiting for her child to be born, Min recalls her past: her childhood in southern Ontario, her twenties spent in Europe as the mistress of the then aging, now dead film director: Honeyman. She frets about her future—all she can envision is arrest by the Toronto police for failure to keep her house clean. Min's mother, Gertude, is never long out of her thoughts; she and her lifelong companion, Alice, are intertwined in Min's mind with the European couple: Stein and Toklas. An introspective book, the novel is more cohesive than her earlier work.

625. _____ **ONE-WAY STREET**. 1973. Don Mills, Ontario: Paperjacks, 1974. $1.50.

A strange mood lingers with this book—a mood of blending isolation, abandon, and decay. Audrey, the main character, is an adventurous Canadian woman, most recently living in London, who vacations on the Greek island where her estranged homosexual husband is now living. Audrey becomes involved in diverse aspects of island life: the artists' scene, business interests, society, and the geographical climate itself. She experiences a sort of private struggle for autonomy and self-awareness which is never fully explained or resolved. Her complex personality is compelling yet inaccessible; readers will find it hard to make sense of the plot's development.

626. GALLANT, Mavis. A FAIRLY GOOD TIME. 1970. N.Y.: Popular Library, 1973. O.P.

One morning Shirley's French husband leaves their Paris apartment. As time passes, it gradually becomes clear that he isn't coming back, and Canadian-born Shirley is left on her own in Paris. Incompetent as she is herself, other people keep turning to her for help and drawing her into strange situations. The humor of this book softens its story of a rather helpless victim surviving as best she can.

627. _____ **MY HEART IS BROKEN. EIGHT SHORT STORIES AND A NOVELLA**. Don Mills, Ontario: Paperjacks, 1974. $1.75.

Mavis Gallant is a writer who never wastes a single word. She has an eye for detail and a talent for characterization that enable her to compress, into a single story, a fuller world than many authors give us in a complete novel. Her stories deal with people (mainly women) who have left home in search of "Something Better". Canadian expatriates hunger for art in Paris, or elegance on the Riviera finding, instead, the seediness and loneliness of exile. One character sums up the plight of all:

"She knew that when you run away from home you are brave, braver than anyone but then you have nowhere to live." These are sad, bitter stories, tinged with humor.

628. HARVOR, Beth. WOMEN AND CHILDREN. Canada: Oberon Press, 1973. $3.50.
This collecton was published in Canada by a small press. It's a book which may be hard to find, even for Canadians—but try. The stories are collage-like creations of character, mood, and place rather than traditional, plot-oriented pieces with a beginning, middle and end. Quite a few focus on the same woman: a housewife and painter in her mid-thirties, with two children (sometimes three) and a husband she no longer feels close to. She is politically active—involved in the anti-war movement, a member of a women's consciousness-raising group. In "A Day at the Front, A Day at the Border," her suburban C-R group has an all-day meeting with a Marxist woman from Toronto. Drawing on the real drama and tension of the consciousness-raising experience, this is a wonderful story which never becomes polemical. Other stories in this volume deal sensitively with widows and with adolescent girls.

629. HEBERT, Anne. THE TORRENT. 1963. (No current U.S. edition.) Montreal: Harvest House, 1973. $2.50.
A brilliant collection of novellas and short stories. Each piece depicts poverty and injustice in the world. The stories spring from a Catholic background, though they are not in any sense pious. Indeed, they depict a world seemingly without grace. The entire collection could be taken as an anguished "why?" directed at God. Most of the stories deal with characters maimed in childhood, but the collection is given wholeness by the final entry. "The Death of Stella" is a compassionate portrait of a poor and ignorant mother who cannot understand her bright and sensitive daughter. This collection cannot be too highly recommended.

630. _____ KAMOURASKA. 1970. N.Y.: Crown, 1973. $5.95.
Canadian paperback: Don Mills, Ontario: Paperjacks, 1974. $1.75.
Hebert attempts, in this novel, "to shatter the hourglass of time." She is highly successful during the first half of the book, when the lives of a respectable matron and the passionate young woman she once was keep intruding on each other. Unfortunately, by mid-novel the story has metamorphosed into an extended flashback which is at times tedious and repetitious. This tale of a woman who felt that survival was possible only if she "buried alive" her true self is flawed, but still interesting. Hebert asks again her questions about love and cruelty, grace and survival.

LAURENCE, Margaret. *(1926-   ) She was born in a small Manitoba prairie town, spent two years in Africa in the 1950s, and went through an expatriate period, living in England during the 1960s. She has recently returned to Canada. All her writing is about women's lives: what she gives us is "a feeling of flesh and blood immediacy, a feeling that this is what it was like to be this particular person with all the complexity that implies, all the irrelevancy and paradoxical quality of life itself." In contrast to portrayals of the frustrated single girl and the "mad housewife" common in contemporary literature, Laurence gives us a character not unlike herself: a creative, competent, independent woman. Laurence is regarded as a major writer in Canada, where most of her books are available in paperback. In the United States she has been well received critically, but has not gotten the general notice she deserves.*

631. _____ A JEST OF GOD. N.Y.: Knopf, 1966. $5.95. O.P. Toronto: McClelland and Stewart, 1973. $2.25.
Rachel Cameron is a 34-year-old school teacher. She loves children, but her life is an endless processon of "grade twos"—new each fall, gone each spring to metamorphose into bigger kids. She is a virgin—masturbating guiltily, fearing lesbian advances from her only woman friend. Trapped in the Manitoba prairie town she always planned to leave, caring for her demanding semi-invalid mother, hating everything about her life, she is afraid to change because she does not want to seem foolish. When she finally does make a fool of herself, it is liberating, and she begins to change. Laurence's

portrait of this painfully self-aware woman is close to perfection. Rachel could so easily have been a stereotype; instead, she is real, vivid, unique. (It might be interesting to compare this book with Howard's **Bridgeport Bus**)

632. _____ THE FIRE-DWELLERS. 1969. N.Y.: Knopf, $5.95. O.P. Toronto: McClelland and Stewart, 1973. $2.50.
Stacey Cameron MacAindra is the older sister Rachel always envied—for her ease, her prettiness, her escape from the prairie, her husband and four children. But as a 39-year-old housewife in suburban Vancouver, Stacey has the same hopeless sense of being trapped in a role she has no desire to play. After 16 years, she can no longer communicate with the husband she married for love. The marriage is believable, both husband and wife portrayed as complex human beings. Stacey drinks a bit too much. Her hips will never be as slim as they used to be. With her children she swings back and forth between resentement and guilt, and Laurence brilliantly enumerates all the tiny cares that can make motherhood such an overwhelming burden. Despite some excess plot baggage, **The Fire-Dwellers** is an emotionally involving book.

633. _____ THE STONE ANGEL. 1964. (Current Canadian paperback; Toronto: McClelland and Stewart, $1.95.
Hagar Shipley, age 90, tells her story. Laurence has gotten inside the head of Hagar to such an extent that the reader actually experiences her—the senility which makes her forgetful, the failing body she cannot believe in ("only the eyes were still hers"), the humiliating dependency—she can no longer even dress herself. Hagar rages against it all; she is, as her 65-year-old son says with anger and tenderness, "a holy terror." Dying, although she does not at first realize it, she recalls her whole life. The first half was spent in a small town on the Manitoba prairie, the rest in cities she never quite understood. Her stern Scots pioneer background gave her a will and pride which enabled her to survive, but it also formed an armor through which she could not break to achieve the give-and-take of love. Not enough can be said about Margaret Laurence's achievement: she has woven past and present together in a thoroughly believable way, and she has made powerful and ultimately lovable a character whose experience of aging is not shared, is, in fact, probably feared by most readers. The book could be read and compared with two other classics about aged women dying: Olsen's "Tell Me a Riddle" and Cather's **My Mortal Enemy**.

634. _____ A BIRD IN THE HOUSE. 1970. N.Y.: Knopf, $5.95. O.P. Toronto: McClelland and Stewart, 1973. $2.25.
This is a collection of eight stories, all about Vanessa MacLeod growing up in Manawaka, Manitoba, (the town all Laurence's heroines grew up in), during the 'Depression. Laurence's strongest talent is as a novelist, giving us a feeling for the totality of a life—for these bits and pieces just don't add up to that. **A Bird In The House** will probably appeal most to fans, readers who have already become involved with the citizens of Manawaka through the novels. One story, hovver, is outstanding in its own right. "Horses of the Night" is a brilliant piece about a young boy who has his hopes destroyed by the economic devastation of the Depression and his spirit broken by the brutality of World War II.

635. _____ THE DiVINERS. 1974. N.Y.: Bantam, 1975. $1.95.
The quest in **The Diviners**, a book by a writer about a writer who is seeking wholeness and integration, is the same one Lessing undertook in **The Golden Notebook**. Snapshots, memorybank movies, innerfilms and mythic retold tales, rather than different colored notebooks, are the devices used. Morag Gunn wants to come to terms with all the roles she has assumed in her personal relationships—daughter, wife, single mother, lover, friend. Morag seeks to understand her country's history: she is haunted by Catharine Parr Traill, omnicompetent pioneer and writer; she experiences a mental dialectic between white and Indian myths, as she tries to comprehend Canada's dispossession of its native peoples. She makes a "pilgrimage" to her ancestors' Scotland to understand what of their land is in her. At the heart of it all, Morag Gunn is a writer, and the book is full of revelations about what it means to be a writer and what it means to be a woman who writes. Laurence's perspective is

strongly feminist, and the book ends (as so many novels by Canadian feminists seem to) on a positive, one could even say triumphant, note. This alone is reason enough to read **The Diviners**. But the book has more: it makes one laugh and cry. Its characters do not go away once the book has been closed.

636. MUNRO, Alice. DANCE OF THE HAPPY SHADES. 1968. N.Y.: McGraw-Hill, 1974. $6.95. (Canadian paperback—Toronto: McGraw-Hill, Ryerson, current. $3.95.)
A wonderful collection of short stories. While the settings are the small towns and small farms of southern Ontario, there is something about them that will probably seem familiar to anyone who has ever lived somewhere in rural North America. "Boys and Girls" is a brilliant feminist story of a little girl who realizes that "a girl was not, as I had supposed, simply what I was, it was what I had to become." In "Red Dress—1946" one frightened, awkward adolescent has her social life "launched". Munro remembers and understands the adolescent years and her stories are especially recommended for high school classes.

637. _____ LIVES OF GIRLS AND WOMEN. 1971. N.Y.: Signet, 1974. $1.25.
A truly outstanding book, both for its literary quality and for its feminist insights. "Autobiographical in form but not in fact," it tells of a girl's growing up in a small Ontario town. Della's mother has strong convictions and a passion for education; she is an agnostic and a feminist in her own eccentric way: "There is a change coming in the lives of girls and women," she says, "but it is up to us to make it come." To her mother's distress, teenage Della does get "distracted" over a man, but in the end rejects him to "get started on my real life." In the background are a whole cast of vividly-evoked local characters, mainly female, and all rich, multi-dimensional human beings. This novel is highly recommended.

638. _____ SOMETHING I'VE BEEN MEANING TO TELL YOU. N.Y.: McGraw-Hill, 1975. $6.95.
The grace and beauty of Munro's prose style and the depth of understanding she brings to her characters combine to make this second story collection outstanding and rewarding. These are stories of people facing difficult times in their lives; confronting private truths vaguely recognized and long ignored. Munro approaches her characters with warm, ironic, honest compassion, mingling humor and melancholy in near perfect balance. Most of the stories focus on women; two sisters bound together through a lifetime of guilt and longing; a young girl facing the sexual divide for the first time; a married woman recognizing the source and depth of her anger against men; a middle-aged woman trying to unravel the contradictory threads of emotion that tie her to her mother. Munro shows us the person behind the face displayed to the

world. She explores those moments, moments of action and the silent moments in the mind, that take everyday life beyond the ordinary. Her stories are a continual revelation, bringing that shock of recognition when one sees reality stripped of rationalization.

ROY, Gabrielle (1909-   ) Along with Anne Hebert and Marie-Claire Blais, she is one of the major female writers to have come out of French Canada. Unlike them, she was not born in the geographical heart of French-Canadian culture, Quebec. Roy grew up on the prairies in St. Boniface, a French suburb of Winnipeg, Manitoba. Her writing differs from her sister authors, too. They are experimental stylistically, while Roy prefers traditional forms. They focus on the darker aspects of life, exploring poverty, suffering and human cruelty. Roy, on the other hand, is more like one of her own characters: "Such was (her) power. She disposed people to become aware that they had reasons for being happy."

639. _____ **WHERE NESTS THE WATER HEN**. N.Y.: Harcourt and Brace, 1951. O.P. Toronto: McClelland and Stewart. $2.25.
Luzina Tousignant lives alone with her family on a small island in northern Manitoba, miles from any neighbors. Here she has a new baby every year. Finally, she has so many children that she is able to successfully petition the government for a school just for them. Her persistent quest for education is the main focus of the book. Luzina is an appealing character, but Roy's portrayal of her is somewhat two-dimensional. The author indicates, but quickly brushes past, conflicts. Left unexplored are Luzina's feeling that her life might have been better if she had not had so many babies, her pain when the very knowledge she had sought for her children separates them from her.

640. _____ **STREET OF RICHES**. 1957. N.Y.: Harcourt and Brace. O.P. Toronto: McClelland and Stewart. $2.25.
In **Street Of Riches**, Roy gives us 18 somewhat fictionalized, somewhat autobiographical sketches of life in a large French family in St. Boniface, in the early part of the 20th century. "The Gadabouts," a piece about her mother, is outstanding; it is recommended for teachers looking for short readings about different kinds of women's lives. Maman, after bearing nine children and leading a most restricted life, announces one day that she wishes to be free. With her youngest child, she departs on a journey across Canada; she decides not to ask her husband's permission preferring to imagine that he gave it. Despite an occasional tendency toward sentimentality, this is a pleasant collection. Roy loves story-telling and the book is full of interesting anecdotes.

641. WATSON, Sheila. THE DOUBLE HOOK. 1959. Toronto: McClelland and Stewart. $1.75.
An innovative book with a difficult but lovely style, **The Double Hook** is a symbolic story of a small isolated Canadian community. The individuals who comprise it are aloof, trapped in their self-sufficiency, though their lives are intertwined as far as their roots, families, and physical proximity. A dramatic act by one person sends ripples of reaction through the community, touching each person differently. This is what the novel describes—the process of changing, the breakdown of isolation as the people come together to really live in community with one another. We strongly suggest that you read the introduction after reading the novel. It is rather pedantic and leaves nothing for the reader to discover.

642. WILSON, Ethel. SWAMP ANGEL. 1954. Toronto: McClelland and Stewart, current. $1.95.
This novel intertwines the stories of two strong women. Middle-aged Maggie Vardoe runs away from a boorish, insensitive husband to start life anew managing a fishing camp in northern British Columbia. She leaves behind her friend, elderly Mrs. Severance, a former juggler and vagabond, who is nearing the end of her life. Although the book contains powerful and beautiful descriptions of the British Columbia countryside and wildlife, it doesn't tout nature as an escape. "I suppose," said Mrs. Severance, "that you thought . . . once out into the fresh air everything would be easy. My dear sap, it never is." This is an enjoyable, basically upbeat book.

France

Pre-19th Century

LaFAYETTE, Marie Madeleine Pioche de la Vergne (1634-1693).

"I am so convinced that love is a bothersome thing," wrote Mademoiselle Marie-Madeleine at the age of 19, "that I am glad that I and my friends are exempt from it." Nevertheless a year later her family married her off to an elderly nobleman, the Comte de LaFayette from Auvergne, one of France's dreariest and most remote provinces. After several years of marriage, husband and wife agreed that Madame LaFayette would live separately in Paris. There she became the center of Parisian literary circles as well as the biographer and friend of Henrietta of England. Toward the end of her life, Madame LaFayette served as a diplomatic correspondent. Her novels include **Zayde** *and* **La Comtesse de Tende**, *although* **La Princesse de Cleves** *remains her masterpiece.*

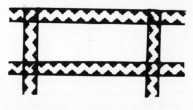

643. _____ THE PRINCESS OF CLEVES. 1678. Included in **SEVEN SHORT FRENCH NOVEL MASTERPIECES.** (Andres Comfort, ed.) N.Y.: Popular Library, current. $ .95.

The seeming irrelevance of both the setting, the elegant, intrigue-ridden French court of the 16th century, and the central conflict, whether a woman's purity is worth preserving at any price, makes this a difficult story to get into. But read on. The characters of the central triangle are superbly drawn, and the mother-daughter relationship is fascinating. A surprise anti-happy ending makes it clear that the author had deep reservations about the viability of both the institution of marriage and romantic relationships between men and women. **The Princess of Cleves** is generally recognized by critics as the first French psychological novel. Before (and, unfortunately, in many works long after) novelists focused on romantic adventure; characters had no consistent personality and changed at every turn to meet the needs of plot. Madame de LaFayette not only made her story flow naturally out of her characters' personalities, but also examined these personalities in considerable detail. The modern psychological novel has travelled a long way from her austere classical style, but Madame de LaFayette is, nonetheless, its grandmother.

de STAEL, Germaine (1766-1817) Mme. de Stael was one of the most dramatic personalities in French history. Brilliant, intense, flamboyant, and compulsively literate, she managed to dominate cultural and political life in Europe, particularly France, during the turbulent years of the French Revolution and Napoleon's rule. After her suitable marriage to a Swedish diplomat, Baron de Stael, Germaine ran Europe's most glittering salon, moving her headquarters around Europe and entertaining the continent's intellectual and social elite. Her sexual affairs were always manic and torturous; and she continued to dominate her lovers long after the affairs were over. DeStael's feminist ideology was concerned with the right of women to be themselves, and much of her writing condemns society for refusing that right. Germaine never did decide if incompatibility between the sexes could be resolved. When she died from a stroke at age 51, Mme. de Stael managed to have born four children; written volumes of correspondence, criticism, essays, and assorted other prose; entangled herself in endless political affairs including exile from Paris by Napoleon; and stimulated most of the intellectual activity in Europe during her lifetime. yet in spite of this frenetic output, there existed a vacuum in her life, for Mme. de Stael preferred worldly chaos to self-exploration. "What I love about noise is that it camouflages life," she once said, revealing a woman of public genius mostly unhappy as a private individual.

644. _____ **CORINNE, or ITALY**. 1833. Boston, N.Y.: Thomas Crowell & Co. O.P.
If you can plod through the awkward translation by Isabel Hill, it may become obvious why **Corinne** was important to such writers as George Eliot, Harriet Beecher Stowe, George Sand, Kate Chopin, Margaret Fuller, and Elizabeth Barrett Browning. Mme. de Stael presents the dilemma of the "woman of genius" in all its misery and glory. Corinne is the exceptional woman: independent (in finances as well as thought), spontaneous, and revered throughout Italy as a poet and musician. Corinne's passion for Oswald Lord Nevil is irreconcilable with her autonomy and public fame; cultural values imposed on women force her to choose between her career and her romance. her tragedy is revealed through sentimentality and bitterness. **Corinne** was published upon Mme. de Stael's return from Italy, and is as much a series of essays on Italian literature, art, history, religion, and landscape as it is of the particular characters and social values of late 18th- early 19th century England and Italy.

GEORGE SAND (Aurore Dupin) *(1804-1876) George Sand is unfortunately known more for her life than her literary achievements. Her famous lovers (Chopin, Musset,*

etc.), her male attire and penname, and her unconventional life style have dominated all other information about her work and life. Hailed by her contemporaries as one of France's greatest writers, she wrote more than 80 novels, plays, essays, which were read throughout Europe and America. In Paris, where she moved after leaving her husband at age 27, she became the only woman to play a major role in various artistic and political groups there. In the 1830s and 1840s, her social reform novels and essays had a revolutionary impact which deeply affected the French people. Later, during the revolution of 1848, she wrote countless circulars and pamphlets explaining socialist/ communist ideals, and even started her own newspaper, **La Cause du Peuple.** *Her personal life was often turbulent, but she never stopped writing her novels, through them questioning the moral and political framework of society. Today, in this country, her translated works are generally unavailable, even in libraries, and it is assumed that she was a poor writer. An incomprehensible fate for the books which Heinrich Heine said "set the world on fire, lighting many a prison where no cheer ever entered."*

645. _____ **INDIANA**. 1831. N.Y.: Howard Fertig, Inc., 1975. $14.00.
In this first novel about a sensitive young woman of Creole blood unhappily married to a boorish older man in France, the author points to the frustrations of women both in marriage and in love affairs with unworthy men. Indiana, the heroine, has resigned herself to a crude marriage until she meets the passionate and unscrupulous Raymon, who almost causes her destruction. It is her loyal cousin Ralph who finally restores her senses and with whom she returns to live peacefully in their childhood home in the West Indies. Surprisingly well-written and engrossing despite its exalted views of love and martyrdom, the novel represents Sand's own views of being repressed by societal roles for women. As she states in the preface; "I wrote **Indiana** with a feeling, not deliberately reasoned out, to be sure, but a deep and genuine feeling that the laws which still govern woman's existence in wedlock, in the family and in society are unjust and barbarous."

646. _____ **CONSUELO** (3 vols.) 1842. George Barrie & Sons, 1900.
Consuelo, one of George Sand's major novels, is an absorbing piece of historical fiction with a woman as the main character. Set in 18th century Italy, Germany, and Austria, it chronicles the adventures of Consuelo, gypsy by birth, "cantrice" by profession. In Consuelo, Sand has created a strong-willed, independent heroine, who never compromises herself to lover or enemy. The story itself has elements of both legend and fairytale, and the mingling of fiction and history is well-balanced. the writing style, though not concise, is clear and fast-moving, and all in all, the novel is thoroughly enjoyable.

647. _____ **THE COUNTESS OF RUDOLSTADT**, Francis G. Shaw, trans. Two volume sequel to **CONSUELO**. William D. Ticknor and Co., 1846. O.P.
The further adventures of Consuelo, whose marriage to the Count of Rudolstadt at his

deathbed leaves her widowed and haunted by a memory. These final episodes in the life of Consuelo become more of a romance than an adventure story, and the sentimental "happy ending" is rather drawn-out and overdramatized. However, of real interest in these volumes are the sections devoted to Consuelo's introduction to and participation in "les Invisibles," an underground revolutionary group devoted to "liberty, equality, and fraternity." Sand displays great revolutionary fervor in the long passages concerned with utopian ideals and the tyranny of the rich and powerful. These are fascinating to read, especially in light of the fact that they were written sometime between the French revolutions of 1830 and 1843.

648. _____ **THE COMPANION OF THE TOUR OF FRANCE**. N.Y.: William H. Graham, 1847.
Written in the years prior to the French revolution of 1848, this book was the most controversial of George Sand's "social consciousness" novels. Originally refused publication, it directly addressed the issues of poverty and oppression, and the main character, Pierre Huguenin, a woodworker, became the inspiration for Walt Whitman's "poet of democracy." The first half of the book is somewhat tedious, but the second half contains passages which are positively inspired. Pierre's words reveal Sand's belief in the revolutionary strength and wisdom of the French people. Though in need of editing, **Companion** is interesting because it contains a variety of characters whose reality is timeless and because it provides the reader with a great deal of information about George Sand's political perspective.

1900-1950

COLETTE, Sidonie Gabrielle (1873-1954). _Although generally acknowledged as one of the greatest French writers of the 20th century and one whose candid style has had a lasting effect on French literature, Colette's works are still ignored in far too many of the French courses taught in American schools and universities. Her writing is of particular interest to women because of its superb, delicate probings into the nature of love and sex, from a perspective at the same time peculiarly French and most definitely a woman's. Colette herself was bisexual and wrote quite openly about her own sexuality and what she called her "mental androgyny" (i.e. the conflicts and pleasures that were hers because of her awareness of the "female" and "male" parts of her personality)._

649. _____ **CLAUDINE AT SCHOOL**. 1900 as **CLAUDINE A L'ECOLE**. N.Y.: Farrar Straus & Cudahy, 1957.
Colette's first book, an account of life in a country girls' school, is based on her own recollections, but with "spice" added at the direction of her husband, Willy (who was actually identified as the book's author). It is difficult to tell how much of the narcissism and pervasive sensuality (mainly between women) of these schoolgirls is "spice;" certainly the book provides a striking contrast to English books of the same period. Claudine herself is a rebellious and, on the whole, likable character.

650. _____ **CLAUDINE IN PARIS**. 1901 as **CLAUDINE A PARIS**. N.Y.: Farrar Straus & Cudahy, 1958. O.P.
At 17, Claudine has moved to Paris with her eccentric father, and starts to meet intriguing new people. Her cousin Marcel proves to be more "girlish" than she; the cousins entertain each other with tales of their passions for members of the same sex. In the end, however, Claudine falls in love with Marcel's father, Renaud.

651. _____ **CLAUDINE MARRIED.** 1902 as **CLAUDINE AMOUREUSE**, later as **CLAUDINE EN MENAGE**. N.Y.: Farrar Straus & Cudahy, 1960. O.P.

Though married, Claudine retains a youthful spontaneity. On a visit to her old school she is overcome with nostalgia, and a powerful attraction to the pretty schoolgirls. Back in Paris, she is captivated by Rezi, a lovely society lady; Claudine's husband, Renaud, aids the progress of this affair like an indulgent father. Claudine is distressed when she discovers that he too has been having an affair with Rezi , but eventually forgives him.

652. _____ **THE INNOCENT WIFE.** 1903 as **CLAUDINE S'EN VA**. N.Y.: Farrar & Rinehart, 1934. O.P.

This fourth and last Claudine novel is narrated by Annie, who functions as a dependent child and slave in relation to her husband. When he goes away, she is "like a useless mechanical toy that has lost its key," until she meets the sophisticated, exciting, intelligent Claudine, who makes her aware of the possibilities of a more independent lifestyle. Finally Annie leaves her husband. The book is an exciting tale of one woman's transformation.

653. _____ **THE INNOCENT LIBERTINE.** 1904, 1905 (two volumes). British Penguin, 1972. O.P.

At 14, Minne builds a romantic fantasy around the figure of a notorious gangster. In the second part of the book she is a young wife seeking sexual fulfillment in the arms of several lovers.

654. _____ **THE VAGABOND.** 1910. (Translated by Enid McLeod) N.Y.: Farrar, Straus & Giroux, 1974. $2.95.

Renee Nere is the vagabond, a recently divorced young woman who supports herself as a mime in music halls. As she attempts to reconcile her needs for both independence and companionship, Renee faces a classic dilemma. The novel offers an unromanticized portrayal of her struggle for autonomy. (Those who have read Agnes Smedley's **Daughter of Earth** or Ellen Glasgow's **Barren Ground** may observe similarities in the conflicts experienced by the three "heroines.") Colette writes with a remarkable economy of words; her descriptions are graphic yet intensely evocative. The mood is stark. Day by day Renee wakes up and goes to bed confronted with real, basic issues. She is determined to be fully herself; she desires love and the protection that is part of it; she must come to terms with loneliness. Her moments of delight, just like those of despair, threaten to change her life dramatically. We get a sense, however, of the energy and courage inherent in Renee's matter-of-fact acceptance of living.

655. _____ **CHERI** and **THE LAST OF CHERI**. 1920. Baltimore: Penguin, 1974. $1.95.

A middle-aged courtesan, Lea, takes as a lover Cheri, the beautiful teenage son of a friend. She keeps him for several years. Colette describes with infinite delicacy and sympathy the bond between the older woman and the young man.

656. _____ **THE LAST OF CHERI**. 1926. Baltimore: Penguin, 1974. $1.95.

The bond between Cheri and Lea persists through World War I and six years of Cheri's marriage. Lea grows into a fat old woman, but it is Cheri who is destroyed.

657. _____ **THE PURE AND THE IMPURE**. 1932 as **CES PLAISIRS**. N.Y.: Farrar Straus & Giroux, 1967. $4.75.

An exceptionally interesting collection of pieces on love and sexual relationships which Colette herself thought her best book. There is the woman who simulates ecstatic orgasm for the sake of her sick young lover; there are male Don Juans, with their violent hostility towards women; there are homosexual men, and lesbians as well.

658. _____ **MY MOTHER'S HOUSE** and **SIDO**. 1953. N.Y.: Farrar, Straus, 1975. $2.95.
These sensitive reminiscences paint a charming picture of the author's childhood in a provincial French village, and in particular, of Colette's remarkable mother, Sido. Twice married, the mother of two sons and two daughters, Sido was happiest while tending the plants and animals in her garden and sharing with her family her love of nature and her often irreverent views of social conventions. Sido's vitality, intelligence, and wit inspired Colette throughout her life; in this somewhat idealized portrait, however, the possessive restraint with which Sido dominted the family is not fully acknowledged.

659. _____ **THE TENDER SHOOT and other stories**. N.Y.: Farrar Straus & Giroux, 1959. O.P.
A collection of marvellously crafted short stories. One deserving special mention is "Gribiche," the story of an actress's death from a home abortion, and the ripples of terror this sends out among the other women in the cast as they recognize their common peril.

660. _____ **EARTHLY PARADISE: Colette's Autobiography Drawn from the Writings of her Lifetime**. N.Y.: Sunburst, 1966. $5.95.
Childhood scenes in the country, three marriages, a lesbian interlude, episodes on the stage and in Paris literary society. These are beautifully-written vignettes of a fascinating life.

661. _____ **BREAK OF DAY**. 1961. N.Y.: Farrar, Straus, 1975. $2.95.
Growing out of Colette's self-examination in middle-age, this poetic, reflective work describes her efforts to live self-sufficiently, without the entanglements of love. She finds nourishment in the natural beauties of her house in Provence and in the company of friends, reducing her needs to simple pleasures and daily writing. Here Colette balances sensuous, atmospheric passages evoking life in the country with more analytical sections reviewing her past life and her current wish to be a woman alone.

1950-present

BEAUVOIR, Simone de. (1908-   ) _Simone de Beauvoir is one of the outstanding figures of the French intellectual scene. For over three decades, she has been at the forefront of major literary, philosophical, and political movements in France and other countries. Her non-fiction work_ **The Second Sex** _(See "Works About Literature") remains one of the classics inspiring the women's movement internationally. Her relationship with Jean Paul Sartre, her life-long friend and companion, has never prevented her from being a strikingly independent woman. Fiction offers few portraits of successfully autonomous women to compare with that which she gives in her autobiography. Recently she has written_ **The Coming Of Age** _(N.Y.: Warner, 1973. $2.25.) a non-fiction work compassionately exploring the condition of another oppressed group, the aging. In the past few years she has come to identify strongly with the current feminist movement in France._

662. _____ **SHE CAME TO STAY**. 1943. N.Y.: Dell, 1954. O.P.
Closely based on an episode in her own life, de Beauvoir's first novel is the story of a menage a trois where the young Xaviere comes to threaten the relationship between Francoise and Pierre, arousing profound emotions and jealousy. The intensity and complexity of the feelings the three have for one another, particularly the two women, make this an especially dense and passionate book.

663. _____ **THE BLOOD OF OTHERS**. 1945. N.Y.: Bantam, 1974. $1.75.
Written during the Nazi occupation of France, this novel graphically depicts the agonizing choice faced by those French citizens remaining in Paris: resistance or

collaboration. De Beauvoir's characters confront the dilemma in classic existential terms; that is, to act or to abstain from acting, action being synonymous with involvement, intimate experience of the Other. It is interesting to follow the development of Helene and Jean from the polarities of sexually-stereotyped behavior to the point when the "blood of others" becomes real for each. As the daily horrors of fascism penetrate to the core of their separate existences, Jean and Helene learn together the necessity of both love and action. A well-written, deeply involving book.

664. _____ **THE MANDARINS.** 1957. Fontana Modern Novels, 1972. O.P.
This is the book that won Simone de Beauvoir the Prix Goncourt. It is a fictionalized account of the overlapping spheres of politics and art in post-World-War-II France. Those who have read the third volume of her autobiography, **Force of Circumstance**, will recognize the raw material from which de Beauvoir created the events and characters in **The Mandarins**. The role of the French intellectual in rebuilding the country after the Liberation is depicted in detail through the personal relationships, political conflicts, and journalistic and/or fictional creations of the men and women in the novel. The personal and political are nicely interwoven, and the central women characters are of particular interest as they exemplify everything from self-sufficiency to self-abnegation to cynical, unfocused rebellion. For character development and fluidity of narrative and dialogue, probably the best of the author's published fiction.

665. _____ **MEMOIRS OF A DUTIFUL DAUGHTER.** 1958. N.Y.: Harper & Row, 1974. $3.95.
This first volume of Simone de Beauvoir's autobiography describes her Catholic girlhood and how she freed herself from it. One is both amazed at how much she remembers from those early years and fascinated by the details of her adolescent thoughts and experiences. The book ends in 1929, when she has become a brilliant student and has met Jean Paul Sartre.

666. _____ **THE PRIME OF LIFE.** 1960. N.Y.: Lancer, 1973. $1.95. O.P.
The second volume covers the years from 1929 to the liberation of Paris in World War II. It chronicles with extraordinary candor de Beauvoir's continuing intellectual and emotional development. The events of her personal life—her teaching, writing, travels, love affairs, and politics—are interspersed with descriptions of external circumstances (particularly the Nazi invasion) which changed her whole mode of existence during those years. Of the four volumes, this one is probably the most vibrant and thoroughly enjoyable to read.

667. _____ **FORCE OF CIRCUMSTANCE.** 1963. N.Y.: Putnam, 1965. O.P.
This third autobiographical volume runs from World War II to the date of its publication, the author's 55th year. She describes in detail her world travels (Cuba, China, etc.), her political commitment to the Algerian liberation struggle, and her disillusionment and disgust with France and its imperialist and right wing politics. As always, her personal reactions to the world and her experience of it make absorbing reading. The epilogue contains an unflinchingly honest and moving discussion of aging, death, and her own life as a whole.

668. _____ **A VERY EASY DEATH.** N.Y.: Warner, 1973. $1.25.
In this short supplement to the author's four-volume autobiography, she describes the last few weeks of her mother's life and her own responses to death and the experience of dying. A probing and intensely personal account of a painful period in de Beauvoir's life.

669. _____ **ALL SAID AND DONE.** N.Y.: Warner Books, 1975. $2.25.
On the whole, the latest volume of Simone de Beauvoir's autobiography is less personal and compelling than the others. She focuses mainly on places, people and events outside of herself, and her sometimes dry reportage can become tedious,

especially if one has not read the books, seen the films, or visited the places she talks about in the first part of the book. More fully developed are later chapters dealing with her trips to Japan, Russia, and the Middle East as well as her reactions to political events between 1962 and 1971. Her first-hand accounts of the May-June 1968 events in France and the 1967 International Tribunal, which brought American action in Vietnam to trial, are particularly interesting. Of special note, for those eager to read of the changes in her feminism since **The Second Sex**, is her discussion of radical feminism vs. socialist feminism, especially in relation to the women's movement today in France and the U.S.

670. _____ **THE WOMAN DESTROYED**. 1967. N.Y.: Putnam, 1969. O.P.
Three excellently crafted stories about women experiencing crucial or critical periods in their lives. In "The Age of Discretion" a successful writer and left-wing intellectual faces age and approaching death with fear, uncertainty, and courage. The short but intense "Monologue" presents a woman, blamed by the world for her daughter's suicide, raving bitterly. The title story, written in diary form, is especially compelling: slowly a woman reaches full awareness of the extent of her husband's infidelity and plumbs the depths of pain and introspection.

671. DURAS, Marguerite. FOUR NOVELS. 1965. N.Y.: Grove Press, current. $1.95.
These unique short works, written over the period 1955-1962, linger with the reader through mood more than content. Their theme is personal isolation and the frustrations of those searching for love. Each suspenseful novel unfolds a brief encounter in which certain estranged individuals achieve intense moments of awareness together, then retreat back into their trance-like existences. In **Moderato Cantabile**, the most famous story, Anne Desbaresdes returns to the same bar each day for a week to meet a strange man who witnessed there, as she did, a woman killed in mercy by her lover. Anne and the man, Chauvin, are drawn together through their shared experience of the event, yet neither can consummate their attraction. **The Square** describes a 20-year-old servant girl, wishing for a husband so that her miserable life will change, who talks one afternoon on a park bench with a middle-aged salesman who expects life never to change. Likewise, the plots of **10:30 On A Summer Night** and **The Afternoon of Mr. Andesmas** are confined to a few hours in which several dispossessed characters temporarily break out of their passive alienation through moments of intimate contact. There are no happy endings in these elusive stories. These early works by Duras sustain an emotional pitch flowing between nightmare and ecstasy, unlike the colder, abstract style which develops in her writing.

672. _____ **HIROSHIMA MON AMOUR**. 1961. N.Y.: Grove Press, current. $2.95.
The tragedies of love and war mingle retrospectively in this poetic screenplay for the film by Alain Resnais. A French actress comes to Hiroshima to make a film on Peace and meets a Japanese architect in the summer of 1957. They share one night and day together as lovers before she must return to Paris; during that time she relives a youthful affair during the Occupation in France, when her German lover was shot and she was outcast by her family and town. Both her girlhood affair and the war have passed into oblivion, yet the horrors of both draw the lovers profoundly together. Duras makes a powerful political statement while portraying a brief, intense romantic encounter.

673. _____ **THE RAVISHING OF LOL STEIN**. 1966. N.Y.: Grove Press, current. $ .95.
A youthful trauma—desertion by her fiance for an older woman—haunts Lol Stein unconsciously through adulthood. Marriage and motherhood become rituals that merely excuse her from noticeable suffering. Ten years later she returns to the town of her betrayal and begins to relive her rejection by voyeuristically experiencing the affair of her girlfriend Tatiana and Tatiana's lover. It is through the lover's eyes that Lol's obsession unfolds, until he himself becomes involved with her sickness. The story has a stifling quality; dialogue is often incoherent and the characters'

detachment from life is unsettling. Duras creates a sharp though slow-moving sexual tension among the trio that is never relieved.

674. _____ **DESTROY, SHE SAID**. 1970. N.Y.: Grove Press, current. $1.25.
Written with screenplay directions in mind, this experimental French "new novel" reflects Duras's increasing ideological concerns with language, destruction, and revolution. Communication among two men and two women at a secluded French country resort breaks down before they are able to achieve intimacy—if that possibility exists at all. Disturbed and alienated from social conventions, they interact ambiguously with one another out of love and hate combined. Their dialogues are surreal and disjointed, with each character observing the action in addition to being observed. This lack of any point of view or protagonist is disconcerting, as is the harsh manner in which they interrelate.

675. GIROUX, Francoise. I GIVE YOU MY WORD. Boston: Houghton Mifflin, 1974. $8.95.
France's first Minister for Women reflects on her experiences as one of 20th century Europe's most important women. Her career includes film directing and scriptwriting, reporting, imprisonment by the Gestapo for Resistance activities, and launching the French magazines **Elle** and **L'Express**. Giroux writes of her failed marriage, raising a son out of wedlock, and of her involvements with friends and lovers, as well as her professional struggles. Giroux considers the women's movement to be "the most profound revolution that highly developed societies will have to contend with—that and the highly charged question of sharing the power of decision." Giroux's lucid memory, her enormous energy and intelligence make this autobiography a fascinating individual and social document.

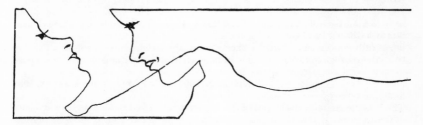

676. LEDUC, Violette. LA BATARDE. N.Y.: Farrar Straus & Giroux, 1965. O.P.
"A woman is descending into the most secret part of herself and telling us about all she finds there with an unflinching sincerity, as though there were no one listening," writes Simone de Beauvoir in her foreword to this book. It is an absolutely fascinating autobiography of an extraordinary woman, covering the years from her birth in 1908 to the end of World War II. Born illegitimate, Violette Leduc was convinced all her life of her own ugliness. Her first loves were for women; later there was an unhappy marriage, and finally an unfulfilled passion for the homosexual author Maurice Sachs. Meanwhile, she worked in menial clerical jobs in the world of publishing and film production, moving on the fringes of Paris literary and intellectual society. By the end of the book she has started her first novel.

677. _____ **THE WOMAN WITH THE LITTLE FOX**. 1966. N.Y.: Dell, 1968. O.P.
Here are three stories about the lives of three women: Mademoiselle, an old woman, dying of starvation and neglect, who gives love, tenderness, and sensuality to a discarded furpiece; Clarisse, a middle-aged woman who tenderly cares for a dead man's body, fantasizing that he is only sleeping; and Clothilde, a young woman overwhelmed by her new longings. Leduc portrays the pains and deprivatons which these women suffer so forcefully that the reader may wish to put the book aside, yet the beauty of her prose compels one to continue.

678. _____ **THERESE AND ISABELLE**. N.Y.: Dell, 1967. O.P.
The 95 short pages of this book describe one day in the lives of two French schoolgirls in love with each other. The sex is embedded in a context of deeply felt emotion. Real life problems and frustrations impinge even on the sex scenes, thus removing the book from the arena of unreal, idealized, mechanical gratification typical of pornography. The book deals positively with the potential of female sexuality.

679. _____ **MAD IN PURSUIT**. N.Y.: Farrar, Straus & Giroux, 1971. $8.95.
This sequel to **La Batarde** spans the years 1945-1949, during which Leduc published her first novels and got to know several famous literary figures, including Nathalie Sarraute, Jean Genet, and Jean Cocteau. Foremost, however, was Simone de Beauvoir, who helped her from the beginning and for whom Leduc developed an intense passion. She also fell in love with a male homosexual again; both loves were unrequited, and much of this book is filled with the anguish of a tormented woman.

680. MALLET, Francoise. THE ILLUSIONISTS. 1951. N.Y.: Arno. $10.00.
Taking the theme of a 16-year-old French school girl's initial lesbian relationship with her father's mistress, Mallet has written an enjoyable, though somewhat shallow and predictable novel. the story is weakened by the masculine role playing and sadism of Tamara, the older mistress. Fortunately, the book also has its more positive side: Helene, the young woman, matures through her relationship and leaves childish daydreaming behind. She learns to take control of her life. The novel has some tender and sympathetic moments in spite of its flaws. Originally published in France as **Le Rampart Des Beguines**, the novel was republished in the U.S. in its hardcover edition as **The Illusionists** and in paperback as **The Loving And The Daring**. Its author is not to be confused with Francoise Mallet-Joris, a better-known contemporary French writer.

681. MALLET-JORIS, Francoise. CORDELIA AND OTHER STORIES. N.Y.: Farrar, Straus & Giroux, 1965. O.P.
Beautifully conceived and written short stories, often ironic, always subtly perceptive, set both in contemporary France and in some vivid and unsentimental European past.

682. _____ **THE WITCHES**. 1968. N.Y.: Farrar, Straus & Giroux, 1969. $6.95.
This volume contains the stories of three women who lived in the late 16th and early 17th centuries. Two of them were burned as witches, and a third wavered between sainthood and witchhood in the eyes of her society until she was finally found to be "possessed" by evil spirits. Mallet-Joris has researched her subject thoroughly; these accounts are based on case histories of actual women. She is most interested in the psychological, or pathologocial, aspects of the witchcraft phenomenon. The book is expecially recommended for its insights into this grim chapter of Herstory.

683. _____ **THE PAPER HOUSE**. N.Y.: Farrar, Straus & Giroux, 1971. $6.95.
The two remarks people most often make to this author are: "I do admire you, the way you manage to write with four children," and: "It must be so convenient having a faith" (Mallet-Joris is a recent convert to Catholicism). This collection of anecdotes about her children, her Spanish maids, and the other tribulations of her day-to-day life show her as a sensible and humane woman, if not the dazzling example of "freedom and femininity" that the front cover claims.

684. NIN, Anais. LADDERS TO FIRE. 1946. Denver: Swallow Press, current. $2.25.
A novel that describes the relationship between two women with great depth and understanding in Nin's controlled, evocative use of language.

685. _____ **HOUSE OF INCEST**. 1958. Chicago: Swallow, current. $1.25.
A good introduction to Nin's fiction in that it incorporates many of the stylistic and

thematic elements of her other novels and short stories. **House of Incest** is a prose-poem which takes the reader alternately into the realm of the subconscious (a subterranean dream of oneness) and into a surrealistic, nightmare world of sterility and isolation. In the final section, it is an intuitive, female vision which seems to provide the hope for the future. This is a rich, multi-layered book. It may not interest the casual reader enough to spend time interpreting its complexities; nevertheless, the beauty of Nin's language and imagery should be sufficient incentive to read it at least once.

686. _____ **A SPY IN THE HOUSE OF LOVE**. 1959. N.Y.: Bantam, 1974. $1.65.
The story of a woman, Sabina, who is not whole, whose life is fractured into different roles. The extraordinary achievement of this book is the power with which it communicates Sabina's feelings, be they swaggering control or paralyzing anxiety.

687. _____ **THE DIARIES OF ANAIS NIN**. Five volumes. N.Y.: Harvest Books, 1966, 1968, 1969, 1972, 1974. $2.85 each.
Anais Nin is typical of many women in having poured a great deal of creative energy into the chronicling of her own life. For years, friends, therapists, and colleagues argued that this was a terrible waste. The enthusiastic personal and critical response to the diaries when they were finally published served both to vindicate her own effort, and to direct those searching for a female culture to examine the diaries of other women. Nin's diaries record her personal struggles as a woman and an artist. The earliest volumes are intensely preoccupied with self, and many find them the most rewarding. In volumes 3, 4, and 5, the author turns more of her attention to the world around her. Many women who feel that they are feminist have been disappointed by her writing, being particularly alienated by her view of "woman's role," and a subtle sort of snobbery which springs, perhaps, from her wealth. Still, many others have found the diaries rewarding reading. Some identify strongly with the author; others, while disagreeing with her answers, have been impressed by the quality of her struggle.

---

688. SAGAN, Francoise. BONJOUR TRISTESSE. 1955. N.Y.: Popular Library, 1974. $ .95.
Written by Sagan when she was 18 years old, this is a sensitive and perceptive look into the mind of a young woman as she becomes an adult, with good insights into female and male sexuality. Cecile's relationship with her father's lover (a sophisticated, mature woman in her 40s) is typical of the love-hate relationship that many women have with their mothers. The sweet and bitter words and feelings between these two women are probably the most important part of this startling first novel.

689. _____ **A CERTAIN SMILE**. N.Y.: Dutton, 1956. O.P.
Sagan's second novel is about a young female university student who has an affair with an older man which becomes more involved than either had intended. The most interesting part of the novel, though, is the relationship which develops between Dominique and her lover's wife. Dominique doesn't want to hurt this woman whom she loves like a mother, and Francoise in turn cares greatly for her, though she is jealous of her, as she says, "physically."

690. _____ **THOSE WITHOUT SHADOWS**. (Tr. from French by Frances Frenaye.) 1957. N.Y.: Popular Library, 1974. $ .95.
A glum picture of Parisian high society, in which the ambitious people are voracious, unfeeling monsters, and those without ambition aimlessly search for someone to love. It presents the quest for happiness in all its pitifulness. The book is short, the characters are believable, if superficial; it is not really an offensive book, but one wonders why it was written.

691. _____ **THE WONDERFUL CLOUDS**. 1962. N.Y.: Popular Library, 1974. $ .95.

Josee and Alan live in a hell which they themselves have created—their marriage. Alan wants to possess Josee totally; he must know precisely every detail of every affair she has had and might have. He even hires detectives to watch her sitting in the park. Josee thinks that Alan is obscene, yet she cannot bring herself to leave him. Some unknown fear forces her to stay with her husband. Rebellion, for her, consists of sleeping with other men whom she doesn't especially like and telling Alan the details. Anyone who is interested in an analysis of the destructive potential of marriage will appreciate this book.

692. _____ **LA CHAMADE**. N.Y.: Dutton, 1966. O.P.

This is the story of Lucille, a woman in her early 30s, who gladly accepts the security of living with a wealthy middle-aged businessman, Charles, until she falls passionately in love with Antoine, a young man of modest means. The fact that Antoine would rather see Lucille in the hands of a quack than have her former lover's money pay for a safe abortion greatly lessens Lucille's feelings for him. Finally, she decides that riding in buses and eating in cheap restaurants is too high a price to pay for a waning romance. So she returns to the "love" and financial security which Charles has always been willing to offer her.

693. SARRAUTE, Nathalie. TROPISMS. 1957. (Tr. by Maria Jolas). N.Y.: Braziller. $2.95.

The author's attempt to repudiate traditional literature resulted in this classic example of the French "new novel" or experimental form. Unfortunately, the book is all style and no content. Twenty-four brief sketches or prose poems present cinematic glimpses of banal situations in everyday Paris; the anonymous male and female characters are trivial rather than substantial, and their unredeemed lives assert nothing beyond surface realities. Dialogue consists of empty chatter in which "tropisms," or subtle, unconscious reactions to surrounding conditions, emerge. Such austere, highly technical writing cannot help but task the reader, however interesting or unconventional such writing may be. Its value, according to critic Wylie Sypher, lies in the fact that Sarraute "listens to our babble and learns that it is our way of avoiding silence."

SARRAZIN, Albertine *(1937-1967) spent most of her short life as a thief and prostitute or in prison, where these two books were written. She died after an operation at the age of 29.*

694. _____ **ASTRAGAL**. N.Y.: Grove, 1967. $ .95.

Nineteen-year-old Anne leaps from a prison wall to freedom, breaking her ankle in the process. Julien, himself a professional thief, comes to her assistance, and she falls in love with him, forgetting the woman she loved in prison. They survive precariously; she reverts to prostitution and crime, he is imprisoned.

695. _____ **THE RUNAWAY**. N.Y.: Grove, 1967. $1.25.

This much longer book documents life in a French prison. Anick is a hardened criminal, and toughly cynical about the world. She recounts the struggle for day-to-day survival in a women's prison—the tenacious clinging to standards of appearance, the bartering of petty luxuries, the friendships, loves, and rivalries among inmates. Anick herself is above all sustained by love for her man Zizi, who was arrested with her, and by endless plans for escape.

696. WITTIG, Monique. LES GUERILLERES. 1971. N.Y.: Avon, 1973. $1.65.

Though Wittig calls her book a novel, it is obviously an attempt to break into a new form. On several pages we find only a circle, the "vulval ring," symbol of female wholeness and affirmation; on others, only a litany of women's names. For the rest, the book is made up of short, seemingly unconnected paragraphs, many of which read as delightfully as poems. We can, with an effort, trace the outline of some kind of sequence of events; the book is clearly about a futuristic society of strong women and a battle they wage. The women glorify the female genitals, and the fine positive female sexual imagery is enough in itself to make the book worthwhile. Interwoven into the text there is also a feminist mythology, ingeniously constructed from the myths of several cultures.

Thanks to that compass, she could navigate from sunrise to sunset. "Monique

Jerusha

Germany

1900-1950

697. SEGHERS, Anna. (Notty, Reiling Radvanyi). REVOLT OF THE FISHERMEN OF SANTA BARBARA. 1929. (Tr. from German by Jack and Renate Mitchell). Berlin: Seven Seas Publishers, 1960. O.P.
In this first novel Seghers writes about a group of fishermen who strike in an effort to raise their wages to a sustenance level. Though women are minor characters in her work, her powerful style and her emphasis on workers' struggles against oppressors make her fiction compelling. Here she portrays a man who incites others to rebel, and shows us his indecision, his fatigue, and his desire to forget his cause, as well as showing us his heroism. Seghers incorporates humor and pathos into her story, and her characters linger long after the book has ended.

698. _____ **THE SEVENTH CROSS**. (Tr. from the German by James A. Galston.) Boston: Little, Brown & Co., 1942. O.P.

In 1942, after severe difficulties in smuggling herself, her husband, and her manuscript to America, Anna Seghers saw the first publication of **The Seventh Cross**. It tells the story of seven German men—political prisoners who have escaped from a Nazi concentration camp shortly before the war. Seghers builds a suspenseful plot which holds one's interest, and her details are excellent. The reader gains a sense of the history of the German people— both the humanity and the years of waste and war. Seghers' story is extremely brutal in its reality: the Gestapo is presented in its full horror. Yet as we learn the fate of each of the seven escapees, we see how many lives they have unsuspectingly changed, and the novel crystallizes into an essentially positive statement. This book is worth searching for in your local library.

699. WEIRAUCH, Anna Elisabet. THE SCORPION. 1908. N.Y.: Arno. $10.00.
In her late teens Metta Rudloff falls passionately in love with Olga Rado; persecution and tragedy follow. The presentation, though clearly sympathetic to lesbianism, is detached and straightforward, without sensationalism, moralizing, or emotionalism. There is a sequel called **The Outcast.**

700. WINSLOE, Christa. CHILDREN IN UNIFORM. Adapted from the same play, **MAEDCHEN IN UNIFORM**. English adaptation by Barbara Barnham. London, 1932. O.P.
Set within the confines of a Prussian girls boarding school, this German play explores the effects of repression on the female psyche, and the overtones are overtly sexual and political. Much has been written and filmed about boys' schools, the custom of fagging and homosexuality, but very little of this genre pertains to lesbians. The filmed version of this play, **Maedchen In Uniform**, (Leontine Sagan, 1931) was withdrawn from the theatres by Nazi propaganda minister Goebbels. The interconnection between sex and politics makes this an important work, particularly as so very few plays or films treat lesbianism in such a sensitive and subtly erotic fashion, and none that we know of perceive the repression of lesbianism as one symptom of an authoritarian state.

1950-present

701. BEDFORD, Sybille. A LEGACY. 1956. N.Y.: Meridian, 1960. O.P.
Francesca tells her family history, taking us back into 19th century Europe and a world of wealth and gracious living Two German families, one Jewish, urban, prosperous, the other Catholic, rural, aristocratic, are united by marriage; their members lead cultivated, eccentric lives, moving around Europe, surviving marriages, intrigues, scandals. There are a couple of strong women characters who have a close relationship. Bedford is superb at evoking the overwhelming richness of this doomed world; this first novel brought her considerable acclaim.

702. _____ **A FAVORITE OF THE GODS**. N.Y.: Simon & Schuster, 1963. O.P.
The history of three generations of upper-class women: Anna, the New England heiress who marries an Italian prince in the late 19th century; their daughter Constanza; and Flavia, the product of Constanza's brief marriage to an Englishman. Flavia, in her late teens in the 1920s, tells their story. A mystery centers round Anna's

reasons for leaving the prince after 20 years of marriage. Anna's past reaches into the future in the influence she has over the young Flavia.

703. _____ **A COMPASS ERROR**. 1968. N.Y.: Knopf, 1969. $5.95.
This is a sequel to **A Favourite Of The Gods**, starting where the first left off and carrying through to their conclusion earlier hints about the shaping of Flavia's life; much of the background material of the earlier book is recapitulated. The young Flavia is alone in Provence while her mother is off on a secret trip with a lover. It is Flavia who initiates her love affair with an older woman, Therese; then she falls in love with another woman, the beautiful Andree. Drama and intrigue follow.

704. WOLF, Christa. THE QUEST FOR CHRISTA T. 1968. (Tr. by Christopher Middleton.) N.Y.: Delta, 1972. $2.25.
This intense, philosophical novel traces the personal growth of an enigmatic young woman, Christa T., from adolescence through her untimely death from leukemia at age 35. Narrated by the author, a former schoolmate, it is a fictitious characterization based on letters, diaries, and unfinished sketches by Christa T., struggling to express herself. The prose is often abstract and difficult, yet not without passages of beauty and imagination. Due to its subtle political overtones, the book was forbidden publication for two years and then, in 1968, released in a limited edition. When published in West Germany in 1970, the story became a best seller.

Ireland

Pre-19th Century

705. MAVOR, Elizabeth. LADIES OF LLANGOLLEN. 1972. N.Y.: Transatlantic, 1971. $10.00. Penguin Books, Canada. $2.50.
In 1778, two Irish women, Eleanor Butler (39) and Sarah Ponsonby (23) eloped. After being caught and separated twice, they left their homes with the begrudged blessing of their families to seek a cottage in which to live. They finally settled in Llangollen Vale, Wales. A scholarly account of their lives together, this book is mostly fact and very cautious conjecture. Whether or not the two women were lesbians is not an issue to Mavor; she describes their relationship as a romantic friendship—a fairly common relationship in its time in which women were deeply committed to each other, often flirtatious with other women, forsaking marriage to devote themselves to "higher" pursuits—study, the arts, or works of charity. Besides supplying us with a valuable addition to women's heritage, the book is a heartwarming account of two women who fought to live a life of their own design.

19th Century

EDGEWORTH, Maria (1767-1849) *Maria Edgeworth is best remembered for her tales of Irish life, especially* **Castle Rackrent** *and* **The Absentee**, *while her novels of fashionable society are largely forgotten. She was the daughter of a wealthy Irish landowner, and the oldest of his nineteen children by four wives—two of them sisters. Maria, as eldest, was to assume the role of her father's "apprentice" (or secretary) as he set about disseminating his theories of moral and educational reform. Maria's own writing career was strongly affected by him (most critics feel adversely) as he took an active role in rewriting or infusing a didactic message into her works. Many of her works were written in collaboration with him. Edgeworth, surrounded by the families* *and children of siblings and servants, never married. She lived to a hearty 82 and outlived her contemporary Jane Austen by 32 years.*

706. _____ **CASTLE RACKRENT**. 1800. N.Y.: Norton. $1.65.
At the time of its publication, author undisclosed, **Castle Rackrent** became a unique success. This short novel portrays the decadence and the eventual ruin of a clan of Irish landlords in the middle of the 18th century. It was one of the first novels to successfully employ an observor-narrator speaking in a regional dialect. It is also seen as a first of a type of 'sociological-historical' novel: Sir Walter Scott cited Maria Edgeworth as his model; and Ivan Turgeniev recorded in his journal that his image of Russian workers had been inspired by her portrayal of the Irish peasant. Edgeworth shows the downward course of her gentry (through the eyes of her narrator, Thady Quirk) with relentless comic precision. Interspersed are tragic accounts of the women of the upper class: for example, Lady Catheat's seven years of imprisonment in her room at the hands of her husband. Probably because Maria Edgeworth wrote this book in secret, it was one of her few books free from her father's customary rewriting. The book still makes enjoyable reading today.

707. _____ **THE ABSENTEE**. 1812. N.Y.: Dutton Everyman, 1972. O.P.
The Absentee is written in the same amusing, fast-moving style that made Edgeworth's earlier **Castle Rackrent** such a success. However, several aspects of the book may trouble today's reader. First there is an overlong romantic plot in which the hero, Lord Colambre, judges his true love, Miss Nugent, not on the basis of her own virginity and purity (which would be bad enough), but on the basis of the proven premarital virginity and purity of the entire line of women from whom she has descended. Second, Edgeworth used the book as a vehicle for the idea that social class is destiny, an idea she very much believed in. This philosophy blames not the class and economic system for people's crime or ignorance, but rather the fact that some of the aristocracy have reneged on their divine duty of looking after the lower classes. These villains are aristocrats who have taken off for London and chosen absentee methods of caring for their Irish estates.

708. WILDE, Lady Jane. ANCIENT LEGENDS, MYSTIC CHARMS AND SUPERSTITIONS OF IRELAND. 2 volumes. Boston: Ticknor and Co., 1887. O.P.
Lady Wilde is a teller of tales, and she makes these ancient Irish legends come alive: cats talk, saints work miracles, the fairies sing. In the British Isles during the late Victorian era, many women writers were interested in old folk myths; Wilde stands

BANSHEE.

out among them as a skillful and witty stylist. If you enjoy mythology and Irish culture, you will probably enjoy these two volumes; Lady Wilde was also a poet, publishing under the name Speranza; her son, Oscar Wilde, reportedly drew inspiration from her work.

1950-present

LAVIN, Mary (1912-   ) *Mary Lavin was born in Massachusetts, but has spent most of her life in Ireland, the source and subject of nearly all her fiction. Widowed young, Lavin wrote prolifically while tending her daughters and invalid mother. "I believe," she says of those early years, "that the things that took up my time, and even used up creative energy that might have gone into writing, have served me well. They impose a selectivity that I might not otherwise have been strong enough to impose upon my own feverish, overfertile imagination." Today Lavin is one of Ireland's foremost authors, and her fiction appears regularly in* **The New Yorker** *and various U.S. small press publications. Two Lavin novels (both out of print) are* **The House on Clewe Street** *(1945), about an upper middle class Irish family, and* **Mary O'Grady** *(1950), about the unhappy marriage of a Dublin woman.*

709. _____ **COLLECTED STORIES**. Boston: Houghton Mifflin, 1971. $8.95.
Lavin has a sharp eye and ear for the harsh realities of lives passed in quiet desperation in a rigid, puritanical society. Many of these stories deal with wasted lives and with the might-have-been that haunts loveless marriages and burdens the unmarried with nostalgia and longing for death. But all isn't grimness in this collection: Lavin has a wonderful sense of the beauty of rural Ireland, and the comic stories included here often turn her death-appeal themes upside-down. In "A Visit to the Cemetery," for instance, two girls daydream about prosperous marriages that will insure their interment in a more fashionable graveyard than the one in which their mother lies buried. "Happiness," a moving, clearly autobiographical tale, tells of a widow's life-long will to joy and how she teaches her skeptical daughters that happiness is largely the result of a determined struggle against the attractions of death.

710. MOYES, Patricia. SEASON OF SNOWS AND SINS. N.Y.: Holt, Rinehard & Winston, 1971. $5.95.
As always, the rich are eager to sacrifice the lives of the poor. In this satisfying whodunnit, three women tell their versions of the death of a young ski-instructor.

O'BRIEN, Edna *(1932-   ) is an Irish writer who writes consistently about women. The women in her novels usually lead passionate and slightly crazy lives which revolve mainly around love and sex. they are generally women of working-class origins—no aura of privilege and the intellectual life here, just damp memories of rural Ireland—who live trapped within the boundaries of typically female experience. O'Brien describes their experiences and emotions with total frankness, in a delightfully fresh and vivid style. Her anti-Catholicism and emphasis on sex have brought her strong disapproval in her native Ireland.*

711. _____ THE COUNTRY GIRLS. 1960. Baltimore: Penguin, 1975. $1.95.
The tale of an Irish girlhood. Caithleen's childhood ends abruptly when her mother drowns and their farm is sold to cover her alcholic father's debts. She and her irrepressible but tyrannical friend Baba leave for the life-denying austerity of a convent school, from which Baba's ingenuity eventually succeeds in getting them expelled. They go on to Dublin—a boarding-house, work in a grocery store, sexual adventures. The book is at once funny and sad, and is narrated with marvellous deftness.

712. _____ GIRL WITH GREEN EYES. 1960. Baltimore: Penguin, 1975. $1.95.
The continuing tale of Caithleen and Baba in Dublin is mainly concerned with Kate's impassioned infatuation with Eugene, a married man much older than she is and a film director. Despite her outraged father's attempts to carry her back home, she moves in with him. Obviously the power relations between the innocent country girl and this prestigious man are grossly unequal.

713. _____ GIRLS IN THEIR MARRIED BLISS. 1964. Baltimore: Penguin, 1975. $1.95.
This third novel about Kate and Baba begins with them afraid "that we'd die the way were were—enough to eat, married, dissatisfied." Kate is soon enough thrown out by the cold and jealous Eugene and faces a desperate solitude. Baba, as always, comes out on top when her *nouveau riche* builder husband agrees to accept another man's child.

714. _____ AUGUST IS A WICKED MONTH. N.Y.: Simon & Schuster, 1965. O.P.
After a year's celibacy, Ellen's first sexual encounter arouses dormant longings, and she sets off for a holiday in the south of France. She has barely tasted the adventure she sought when she hears of her small son's death while on vacation with his father. Immobilized, she stays on in this bizarre and exotic atmosphere for the rest of an incongruous vacation.

715. _____ CASUALTIES OF PEACE. 1966. N.Y.: Ballentine, 1970. O.P.
"There's madness in love," says Willa. A strange marriage has left her, at 27, not only a virgin, but terrified of love. Patsy and Tom, technically her servants, have a much blunter and more down-to-earth attitude towards love and sex. When Patsy tries to leave the fiercely possessive Tom for another man, the lives of these three turn into a fiasco.

716. _____ A PAGAN PLACE. 1970. O.P.
This book shows O'Brien developing beyond her earlier achievements. It is a magnificently realized account of a girl's growing-up in Ireland. the perceptions of childhood are recreated with a vivid immediacy; we sense the irrationality of the world, and the hazards of a life where sin and damnation lurk around every corner. Among later events are the pregnancy of the protagonist's sister, who goes bad in the big city, and her own sexual initiation at the hands of the local priest. The book ends with her setting off to join a convent.

Israel

1950-present

717. DAYAN, Yael. NEW FACE IN THE MIRROR. 1959. N.Y.: Signet, 1960. O.P.
The author, daughter of Israeli General Moishe Dayan, wrote much of this novel during her two-year military service which begain when she was 17. Its detached sophistication and sexual boldness bring to mind the equally precocious Francoise Sagan. Probably autobiographical, the book speaks in the first person of young soldier Ariel Ron, the attractive, intelligent, and utterly coldhearted daughter of Israel's foremost military hero. Only death and her father frighten her; she is a young woman afraid of love yet obviously needing it. After failing with several lovers, she finally meets a man who can match her: a middle-aged diplomatic advisor who conquers 18-year-old Ariel with his selfless love. Despite her metamorphosis into a loving person, she is hardly sympathetic or even pitiable. Disappointingly, the book has little Israeli culture other than its emphasis on discipline as a virtue.

718. SENESH, Hannah. HANNAH SENESH: HER LIFE & DIARY. 1972. Schocken, 1973. $2.75.

Hannah Senesh, an Israeli national heroine, was a young Hungarian emigrant to Israel who was executed by the Nazis for her underground Zionist activities during World War II. Her courageous efforts to rescue captured RAF pilots and her fellow-Jews by parachuting into occupied Hungary and then organizing the resistance there are recorded in this volume of diaries, letters, and testimonies by people who knew her. As a young girl in Hungary, Hannah Senesh's poetry and prose showed the mark of creative ability. When she emigrated to Palestine at the age of 28 she worked steadfastly to build the land on behalf of Zionism and the Jewish people. After her capture and subsequent murder, she became revered in Israel for her heroic efforts. Her writings are deeply moving.

Italy

1900-1950

719. DELEDDA, Grazia. THE MOTHER. 1923. (Tr. by Mary G. Steegman.) GA: Berg, 1974. $7.95.
The anguish of Paul, the parish priest of Aar, his mother, and Agnes, his lover, is studied in excruciating detail amidst the poverty and beliefs of a mountain village in Sardinia (the island off Italy of Deledda's birth). The reader follows two days of the conflicts of mother and son during which they separately question his choice of the priesthood, trying to understand why and how divine love is superior to earthly love. Deledda portrays the psychological vacillations with delicacy and intensity (some of it may seem thick with melodrama) but readers may be left squinting with curiosity about the villagers, their folklore and way of life. Deledda received the Nobel Prize in 1926.

Japan

Pre-19th Century

HEIAN JAPAN The Heïan period in Japan (800-1150) is one of the most fascinating and contradictory eras in history. On the one hand, it was an intensely feudal era, with the nobility (about a tenth of a percent of the population) living in luxury and the masses of peasants in abject poverty. On the other hand, the court women were accorded a degree of legal and social freedom unknown anywhere until present times. It was the golden age of Japanese literature, producing the country's greatest literary geniuses, comparable only to Shakespeare or Homer in the West. They were Murasaki Shikibu and Sei Shonagon, and both were women.

If the genius of Murasaki and Shonagon, as well as that of the many other lesser but still brilliant court ladies, was attributable in part to their relative freedom, it was equally a result of their oppression. Court ladies were expected to write for the enjoyment of the Empress and of their lovers, but their intellects were not considered suitable for the scholarly Chinese language in which the men wrote—much as their contemporary Western male intellectuals chose Latin over their vernacular languages. Murasaki learned Chinese as a girl, studying with her brother, but tried to keep it secret at court for fear of ridicule and censure. The women wrote in their natural language and blossomed; the men wrote artificial, turgid Chinese, read today only by scholars of the era.

Lady Murasaki's true name is actually unknown, the name she is known by is that of the heroine of her great novel **The Tale Of Genji**. Shonagon's masterpiece is her **Pillow Book**, a witty and often devastating compilation of observatons about the court life around her.

Interestingly and not surprisingly, a Shakespeare-Bacon type of controversy has arisen around Murasaki's authorship of **Genji** by some scholars who claim the work must have been written by a man. Other scholars dismiss the claim as groundless, and rooted only in male arrogance.

MURASAKI, Shikibu, Lady (Born 978 AD[?]) Japan's first and perhaps greatest novelist was born into a minor literary branch of the powerful Fujiwara clan, a family that seized supreme political power during the Heian period. As a child, Murasaki shared her brother's Chinese lessons and became so adept at this rough, "unladylike" language that her father once exclaimed, "If only you were a boy, how proud and happy I should be!" Later, as lady-in-waiting to the Imperial empress, the young widow Murasaki tried to conceal her formidable, "unsuitable" grasp of the classics. The empress, however, admired her companion's genius and the two women were soon reading forbidden Chinese verse together "very secretly, in odd moments." This and the writing of her six-volume **Tale of Genji** occupied most of the novelist's time, for, unlike her vivacious court rival Sei Shonagon (see below), Murasaki was bored and revolted by rigid court etiquette and by the flirtations forced upon her during the drunken festivities that she was often obliged to attend. "You're none of you in the least like Genji!" she once complained of her suitors. "So what should Murasaki be doing here?"

720. _____ **THE TALE OF GENJI.** (Written between 1001 and 1015) N.Y.: The Modern Library, 1960. $5.95.

The world's first psychological novel, **Tale of Genji** is often likened to Proust's **Remembrance of Things Past** because of its concern with passing time and the impermanence of human endeavor. Price Genji, "The Shining One," is an enchantingly beautiful aristocrat whose adventures are chronicled in this realistic, yet subtle, account. Genji seduces just about every woman he encounters, a habit which complicates his life and the novel itself. "If only I had some large convenient building," he muses, "where I could house these friends of mine and be able to keep my eye on them and on any babies that might chance to get born, how much simpler life would be!" So onward he goes, graciously wooing all kinds and classes of women. After his death, his descendants encounter similar romantic snarls and look back nostalgically to Genji's reign. Murasaki had many strong friendships with the other women at court; consequently, the female characters in her novel emerge with a depth and poignancy equal to that of Genji. The reader is left with a strong impression of the trials of life (even in this rarified upper class life) in a polygamous society where the practice of marriage politics took precedence over personal feelings.

721. MORRIS, Ivan. THE WORLD OF THE SHINING PRINCE. N.Y.: Alfred A. Knopf, 1972. $8.95.
This is a rich, informative guide to Lady Murasaki's **Tale of Genji** and to her aristocratic world of refined aesthetics and exquisite sensibilities. Deftly, Morris fills in the details that Murasaki considered "unfit for a woman's pen": the economic and political aspects of Prince Genji's kingdom. The role of women in Heian Japan is discussed, and there is a fascinating chapter on Japan's ancient cult of beauty and the perfumed, emotional male ideal that set the social and cultural tone of Murasaki's age. Morris also gives us a glimpse of a world which no sheltered court lady could have been able to write about: peasants and labourers, the largest part of the population and the only economically productive class in Japan at that time. "The terms . . . that were commonly applied to them," writes Morris, "originally connoted 'doubtful, questionable creatures' and carried the implication that they were not really people at all."

722. THE CONFESSIONS OF LADY NIJO. (Tr. by Karen Brazell.) Garden City, N.Y.: Doubleday, 1973. $2.95.
These memoirs of a 13th century Japanese court lady are fascinating to read. The explicitness of class differences and the overt subjugation of women, the classic attention to detail in dress, poetry, and decor, the many differences between 13th century Japan and modern-day America are intriguing, as are the similarities. The fact that we can become familiar with, and share many of the feelings of this woman, who lived seven centuries ago in Japan, will mean a lot to most readers. Lady Nijo's spirit and sense of humor are important, and Karen Brazell does an excellent job of explaining less obvious points to the modern, English-speaking reader.

723. SHONAGON, Sei. THE PILLOW BOOK. (Tr. & ed. by Ivan Morris.) N.Y.: Penguin, 1971. $3.25.
Sei Shonagon served as lady-in-waiting to the Imperial Japanese empress at the end of the 10th century. She wrote during the Heian period of feminine vernacular literature which produced not only Murusaki's **Tales of Genji** but many poems and diaries, mostly by court women, enabling us to imagine how upper-class Japanese women lived a thousand years ago. **The Pillow Book** comprises anecdotes, observations, and opinion about ritual palace life, revealing Shonagon to be a gifted, articulate woman with an impressionistic eye for intrigue and atmosphere. Certainly her delicate prose will appeal to those interested in Japanese literature, as will the instructive material on classic women's roles in Japan. Nevertheless, her arrogant judgments of what pleases and displeases her and her scorn for the lower classes will alienate modern readers, as will the haphazard narrative style which detracts from the work.

Latin America

1900-1950

QUEIROZ, Rachel de *(1910-   ) Much of her writing is set in her homeland, Brazil's arid, conservative Northeast. Her novels, plays and journalistic essays deal mainly with the emergence of the Brazilian proletariat and with the changing status of women in a highly patriarchal, often feudal, society. A Trotskyite, Queiroz was expelled from the Communist part in the late 1930s and now designates herself an "independent socialist." Her early, as yet untranslated novels* **O Quinze (The Year Fifteen**, *1930) and* **Caminho de Pedras (Rocky Road**, *1937) concern prostitution and marriage and, like her masterpiece* **As Tres Marias (The Three Marias**, *1939) focus on the defiance of social norms by strong, loving women. Today Rachel de Queiroz works mainly as a literary critic and a translator, having translated works of Jane Austen, Edith Wharton and Pearl Buck into Portuguese.*

724. _____ **THE THREE MARIAS**. 1939. Austin, Texas: Univ. to Texas Press, 1963. O.P.

A moving, simply-told story of one young woman's years in a South American convent school and her later adventures in cosmopolitan Brazil of the mid-1920s. The school represents choices available to women of various social levels, but as we follow Maria Augusta and her companions into the "real" world, we see how limited these choices are in a society marred by brutal class and sex bias where the slightest departure from a role of exemplary purity can lead a woman to disaster. Most of the schoolgirls fall quickly into their roles: mother, nun, pious spinster. Only Maria Augusta rebels, asking herself, "Why get out of school, why be a woman after all, if life is going to be the same and if growing up has not delivered me from childhood?" She escapes her sleepy backlands home to the big city. Although the story ends in

The Three Marias

a nostalgic, disillusioned mood, one feels this woman will always be trying to escape the sheltered, childlike existence which is the lot of so many women.

1950-present

BOMBOL, Luisa Maria *(1910-   ) Born in Vina del Mar, Chile, her first stories appeared in the great Argentine literary periodical* **Sur (South)**, *which was founded by Victoria Ocampo. Bombol's very lyrical prose hovers somewhere between dream and reality, a style known in Latin America as "el realismo magico"—magic realism.*

725. _____ "The Tree" short story in **CONTEMPORARY LATIN AMERICAN SHORT STORIES**. Pat McNees Mancini, ed. Greenwich, Conn.: Fawcett, 1974. $1.75.

While attending a concert, a naive young woman is borne off into her past by Mozart's childlike melodies. During this reverie, she gradually comprehends the events that led her to reject a marriage based on resignation and false serenity. A lovely, poetic tale.

726. JESUS, Carolina Maria de. CHILD OF THE DARK. N.Y.: Mentor Book, 1962. $1.25.
The story of one woman's struggle to feed herself and her children in the *favela*, the shanty-town slum of Sao Paulo, Brazil, **Child of the Dark** intimately details the desperate effects of hunger and poverty. Every day Carolina walks the streets picking up paper and heavy scrap metal, selling it and buying small amounts of rice and beans. Carolina's bitter comments on her neighbors and greedy Brazilian politicians and bureaucrats relieve the drudgery of her tale, though her lack of compassion for other *faveladoes* whose hopelessness drives them to liquor and violence, is frustrating. Her simultaneous hatred of contemptuous middle-class people and yearning for a brick house is a conflict never resolved, especially since the reader has no access to Carolina's life after 1960. The publication of this diary enabled Carolina and her family to move out of the *favela*.

LISPECTOR, Clarice (1925-   ) *En route from the Russian Ukraine, Lispector's parents paused just long enough to bring her into the world then on they went to Recife and Reio de Janeiro, where their precocious daughter grew up on Katherine Mansfield, Virginia Woolf, and reams of contemporary Brazilian literature, all the while writing stories and plays of her own. At the age of nineteen, she was a law school graduate, wife of a Brazilian diplomat whose travels took her all over the world, and author of a very successful first novel, **Far From the Savage Heart** (not yet available in English.) An existentialist writer, Lispector explores life's absurdity and the conflict between sincerity and role-playing. Interior monolog and stream-of-consciousness techniques are her main vehicles in the short stories, many of which deal with the fears and self-discoveries of women and—occasionally—of animals, as in her engaging tale "The Chicken" in* **Family Ties.**

727. _____ FAMILY TIES. 1960. Austin: Univ. of Texas Press, 1972. $5.75.
What are the ties that bind people together against an indifferent, hostile world? For Lispector's characters—be they a hypersensitive daughter, an alcoholic mother, or a bitter grandmother—psychic survival means sealing oneself up in a state of "happy unconsciousness," making oneself "hollow" and anonymous since society is too tenuous for anyone to "risk becoming her true self which tradition will not protect." Nevertheless, these thirteen stories are illuminated by lightning flashes of consciousness which not only reveal the character to herself, but also expose the rich "horrible" world lying just beneath the surface of a declining civilization. Lispector's prose is gentle and fluid. Her characters wander through peaceable landscapes: through orderly homes and elegant restaurants and along the well-swept paths of public gardens and zoos only to find themselves suddenly, unexpectedly, "at the end of the line," perceiving the inadequacy of their roles as everything from loyal wife to objective scientist. A remarkable collection.

New Zealand

1900-1950

MARSH, Ngaio (1899-   ) *A New Zealand woman with a noted career in theatre as well as the writing of superlative detective mysteries.*

728. _____ ARTISTS IN CRIME. 1938. Berkeley, 1971. $ .95.
Sleuth and policeperson Roderick Alleyn meets and is immediately smitten with
noted painter Agatha Troy. Troy is talented, intelligent, and extremely humane. When
Alleyn solves a murder at Troy's art school and sends one of her students to the
gallows, she does not (thank heaven) find it an endearing act.

729. _____ FINAL CURTAIN. 1947. Berkeley, 1973. $ .95.
a noted thespian is murdered while Troy finishes up portrait of same. Alleyn (now,
you guessed it, her husband) comes home after three years of war-work to solve the
crime and sit by the fire with Troy. Rather nice . . . and never dull.

730. _____ CLUTCH OF CONSTABLES. N.Y.: Little, Brown & Co.,
1969. O.P.
Might be called Troy's Case, and is worth reading for that reason. On a short cruise,
alone, troy becomes involved in an art-smuggling (and murder) plot. Alleyn turns up
eventually to clean up the crime, but the focus is on Troy.

731. FRAME, Janet. FACES IN THE WATER.
1961. N.Y.: Avon, 1971. $ .95.
Faces In The Water is different from most literary
explorations of the theme women and madness,
because it focuses on the life of a chronic mental
patient. What happened to Istina Mavet before
she came to the hospital, what her life might be
if she left, are questions which do not concern
the author. We are given an unforgettable picture
of life in the back wards, where one and a half
doctors care for a thousand women, where bored
and frustrated nurses provoke patients into fights
and fits, where there is a permanent, pervasive
fear of electro-shock therapy and lobotomy,
where hope rarely exists. New Zealander Janet
Frame is a brilliant stylist; her poetic images
vividly and concretely describe the mental
patient's experience.

graphic: Liz Schweber

Portugal

1950-present

**732. BARRENO, Maria Isabel; Maria Teresa Horta; and Maria Velho da Costa. THE
THREE MARIAS: NEW PORTUGUESE LETTERS**. 1975. N.Y.: Bantam, 1976. $2.25.
This is the feminist book that was seized for "public indecency" by the Portuguese
government in 1972, when the women who wrote it were arrested and brought to trial.
When the facist regime was overthrown in 1974, charges against the Marias were
dropped and **New Portuguese Letters** was lauded in Portugal and abroad. The
collectively-written work blends passion with politics, deriving inspiration from the
17th century letters of a young Portuguese nun who was seduced and abandoned by a
French cavalier. Alternately erotic and theoretical, the book can be tedious with too
much aimless passion and narcissism. It is, however, brilliantly eloquent on the
subjection of women, who like nuns, are "sacrificed, self-sacrificing, without a life of
[their] own, sequestered from the world" The original 17th century letters by Mariana
Alcoforado are included at the end.

Russia/Soviet Union

19th Century

733. ENGEL, Barbara Alpern and **Clifford N. Rosenthal** (editors/translators).
FIVE SISTERS: WOMEN AGAINST THE TSAR. N.Y.: Alfred A. Knopf, 1975. $8.95.
The five "sisters" are Vera Figner, Vera Zasulich, Elizaveta Kovalskaia, Praskovia
Ivanovskaia, and Olga Liubatovich, and each dedicated her life to revolutionary
action in late 19th century Russia. Moved by a profound sense of moral and political
outrage, they left security, safety, and economic privilege to work in the factories or
fields and plot the overthrow of a Tsarist society. This book contains the edited
memoirs of these women, who were called by some the "Moscow Amazons." Whether
printing revolutionary papers, tunneling to lay mines to assassinate the Tsar,
organizing workers for "economic terrorism," or staging hunger strikes in prison, they
never stopped fighting against oppression with courage and almost superhuman
strength. Their memoirs are fascinating and truly inspiring to read. Good background
information in the foreword by Alix Kates Shulman.

734. VOYNITCH, Ethel. THE GADFLY. 1897. N.Y.: Pyramid, 1972. $1.25.
The Gadfly has been a perpetual best-seller in Russia ever since its first printing there,
twenty years before the revolution; it has recently enjoyed extraordinary popularity in
China. The author, an Anglo-Irish communist married to a Polish revolutionary, wrote
what is basically a romantic adventure story with the usual 19th century trappings:
mistaken identities, long-lost lovers, menacing spies. Voynitch departed from
convention when she made her heroes and heroines political radicals involved in the
Italian revolutionary movement of the 1830s and 1840s. Unfortunately, the political

dialogues are few and far between, and character exploration is generally sacrificed to a fast-paced plot. Voynitch may have been indirectly protesting women's usual role in radical movements when she made her most brilliant revolutionary a woman who spends her days correcting proofs for her far less intelligent male comrades.

1900-1950

735. KOLLONTAI, Alexandra. THE AUTOBIOGRAPHY OF A SEXUALLY EMANCIPATED COMMUNIST WOMAN. 1926. (Included is "The New Woman." 1920). N.Y.: Schocken Books, 1975. $2.95.
Alexandra Kollontai rushes through this short, dense outline of her life. She drily enumerates her activities and conflicts with the Soviet government (she was the only woman member of the first Bolshevik cabinet in 1917) and elaborates on what was her original focus, the "abolition of the slavery of working women." Kollontai's matter-of-fact tone is softened as she briefly describes her disgruntling bourgeois childhood, and as she laments how women's work is often weakened by dependent and destructive involvements with men. Her uncompromising political activities make evident why she was a thorn in the sides of many prominent men (including her quasi-allies, Lenin and Trotsky). As Germaine Greer indicates in the foreword, Kollontai modified her criticism of the Soviet government in the early 1920s, perhaps for her dedication to the party, perhaps for self-protection. Iring Fetscher's afterword fills in what Kollontai's caution left out: it is a substantial compilation of Kollontai's opinions about worker control, antiauthoritarian socialism, and sexual emancipation. A good introduction to her other works.

Scandinavia

1900-1950

DINESEN, Isak [Karen] *(1885-1962) Karen Dinesen married her cousin, Baron Blixen, in 1914 and left her home in Denmark to run a coffee plantation with him in East Africa. The marriage was unhappy, and left her afflicted with venereal disease. After their divorce in 1921, she kept up the plantation on her own, writing to bring in money. In 1931 she was forced to sell and return to Denmark. Knowing the unhappiness in her life—a father's suicide, unhappy loves, incurable disease—one sees her haunting gothic stories as less fantastic then they may at first appear. Yet in spite of the tragedy which dogged her, Dinesen retained an indomitable spirit and an eagerness for life. She wrote in both Danish and English, and deserves her high repute as a superb writer.*

736. _____ **SEVEN GOTHIC TALES.** 1934. N.Y.: Vintage, 1972. $1.95.
Physically, these stories are mainly set in 19th century Europe, and their classic background is aristocratic. The realm they take us to, however, is essentially other-worldly, a strange, fantastic place rich in myths, symbols, and echoes. One is reminded, perhaps, of Bergman movies, which combine the same haunting atmosphere with penetrating psychological insights. Though most are narrated from a male viewpoint, several feature strong and striking women or touch on the theme of ambiguous sexual identity.

737. _____ **OUT OF AFRICA.** 1937. N.Y.: Vintage, 1972. $2.45.
Written like poetry or music, these short stories recount Dinesen's life in Africa. they

are also interesting for the information they give about life and customs among the women of Africa from the viewpoint of a white upper class woman.

738. _____ **WINTER'S TALES**. 1942. N.Y.: Vintage. $2.45.
Beautifully written gothic stories in the same genre as **Seven Gothic Tales.**

LAGERLOF, Selma *(1858-1940) holds the distinction of being both the first woman to win the Nobel Prize for literature in 1909 and the first woman to be elected to the Swedish Academy. One of the major Swedish novelists of the 20th century, her works were at one time popular in the United States; a good deal of her writing was translated into English, and still remains accessible to us through libraries.*

739.a, b, and c. _____ **THE RING OF THE LOWENSKOLDS**. N.Y.: Doubleday, 1939. O.P.
A brilliantly-plotted trilogy set in the 18th and 19th centuries.
a. THE GENERAL'S RING. 1927. The chronicle of the Lowenskolds opens with a marvelously complex ghost story. It is told as though a master teller of tales were entertaining her companions before the great hearth. This introduction to a lost art makes satisfying reading apart from the rest of the trilogy.
b. CHARLOTTE LOWENSKOLD (1928) and **c. ANNA SVARD** (1931) are so interrelated that it is impossible to fully enjoy one without the other. Charlotte is a "lady" from a poorer branch of the great family, Anna a peasant peddler girl who knows real poverty. They have in common that they are both strong, brave, capable women, and they they both suffer a great deal because of their love for one of the most selfish bores in literature. Lagerlof has absorbed some of the sexist biases and many of the class prejudices of her society; she is by no means a feminist; yet in these books she shows deep sympathy and respect for her female characters and a more than superficial understanding of some of the oppressions they must endure. These works are of special interest to women who wish to understand something of women's lives in another century and another culture. Lagerlof is such an extraordinarily skillful writer and her plot is so engrossingly clever that the reader can expect to be sitting up late at night.

740. _____ **THE TREASURE**. 1904. Vermont: Daughters, Inc., 1973. $3.00.
As June Arnold says in the foreword, "**The Treasure** is an opposite fairy tale, presenting Prince Charming as he really is: an orphan girl is cleaning fish and foreseeing her life of poverty; a man well-dressed in seductive splendor woos her and offers her . . . foreverafter. There is only one catch: she must betray her sister." In love with her foster-sister's murderer, Elsalill chooses not to betray her sister. The cost is her life. A fairy tale of female culture, the intuitive perceptions of women triumph. Only after the body of Elsalill is given to the women of the town to bury does the frozen sea free the ship that harboured the murderers. One is left with the after feeling that the intuitive strength of women rather than the logic and physical strength of men is responsible for over-powering the murderers.

UNDSET, Sigrid *(1882-1949) ranks as one of the greatest Scandinavian writers of the 20th century. Born in Denmark, she lived the greater part of her life in Norway and wrote in Norwegian. Her work falls into two general categories: "modern" novels and medieval stories. She won world fame in the early 1920s with **Kristin Lavransdatter**, a three-volume work set in the 14th century. In 1928 she was awarded the Nobel Prize for literature.*

741. _____ **THE FAITHFUL WIFE**. N.Y.: Knopf, 1937. O.P.
A startlingly modern story about the disintegration of a "comrade marraige." There actually were people attempting to share housework in Norway in the 1920s. The experiment fails here because the faithful wife (daughter of a feminist) enjoys idealizing and waiting on her husband. The husband, too, is trapped by role stereotypes. Though he truly loves his wife, her independence and self-confidence

alienate him. Jealousy, fidelity, sexuality, the future of the family are all issues raised by the book; they are explored rather than finally resolved.

742. _____ KRISTIN LAVRANSDATTER. 1920-22. N.Y.: Knopf, 1951. $10.00.

Start reading **Kristin Lavransdatter** on February 10th, or whenever the winter doldrums hit you. This epic in three volumes can provide weeks of comfortable escape. Set in 14th century Norway, it focuses on the life of one woman, Kristin Lavransdatter. Readers looking for portraits of women in non-traditional roles will be disappointed, however. Although various secondary characters include nuns, woman doctors, and witches, Kristin herself is defined by men. She is the daughter of Laurans, wife of Erlend and mother of seven sons. Still, she remains consistently strong in her actions and her will, and ultimately stands free of them all. Colorful, detailed and grand of scale, **Kristin Lavransdatter** presents the human experience as a tapestry: incidents are vivid as they occur, more meaningful as one begins to see them in relation to other incidents, and only fully understood when the tapestry is completed.

743. _____ FOUR STORIES. N.Y.: Knopf, 1959. O.P.

All the stories are set in small-town Norway at the turn of the century. Three focus on women trapped in loveless and self-sacrificing lives. Another common theme is the struggle for survival which forces many of the characters into jobs which are both alienating and insecure. But what is also important about these stories is that they are beautifully written. Reading, one is absorbed in the characters' lives and problems, and they remain to haunt one long after the book has been put down.

Spain

1950-present

743b. FOREST, Eva. NOTES FROM A SPANISH PRISON. 1975. Berkeley: Moon Books, 1976 (Co-published by Random House). $6.95.

In September, 1974, Marxist Eva Forest was imprisoned without trial by the Spanish political police for her alleged involvement in the assassination of Prime Minister Carrero Blanco. While awaiting trial at Yserias Prison, Forest has undergone torture and lengthy solitary confinement. This *ad hoc* book, a journal of letters composed to her children, gives a portrait of a courageous woman struggling to hang on to her sanity under maddening circumstances and—at the same time—encourage her children to work for "a better world where a human being can really be a human being." At this time (Oct., 1976) Eva Forest still awaits trial. If convicted by the military court, the law will require that she be executed within 12 hours. A world-wide campaign has been launched to support Eva Forest and her co-defendants. For further information contact Amnesty International; 200 W 72nd Street; New York City, New York 10023.

Anthologies

CADE, Toni. THE BLACK WOMAN. (See Works About Literature.)

744. CAHILL, Susan, ed. WOMEN AND FICTION. N.Y.: Mentor, 1975. $2.25.
A rich, wonderful assortment of modern short stories, many of them suitable for high school readers. Some of the stories may be familiar ("I Stand Here Ironing" by Tillie Olsen, "Revelation" by Flannery O'Connor). Others are anthologized here for the first time ("The Gifts of War" by Margaret Drabble and Julie Hayden's "Day-Old Baby Rats"). A wide range of classes, ages, and occupations are represented. The apologetic introduction wastes space explaining that "the house of fiction has never been a comfortable place for idealogues" (read feminists).

745. EDWARDS, Lee R. and DIAMOND, Arlyn. AMERICAN VOICES, AMERICAN WOMEN. N.Y.: Avon Books, 1973. $1.95.
In this outstanding anthology are collected short stories and excerpts from novels by eight little known and rarely reprinted American women writers. The selections span the 19th and 20th centuries and represent a cross-section of American life, from New England to the southern and midwestern states. The reader will discover an abundance of strong women characters: Elizabeth Stuart Phelps' "Avis" attempts to develop skill as an artist amid constant demands from her husband and children; Mary Wilkins Freeman's "New England Nun" opts for independence and solitude rather than endure the clumsy intrusions of men; and Angela in Jessie Fauset's **Plum Bun** struggles to survive and prevail in a white world set against her every effort. Especially recommended, both for feminist content and stylistic excellence, are Susan Glaspell's "A Jury of Her Peers" and Dorothy Canfield Fisher's "A Drop in the Bucket." For those who wish to read further, references to other works by and about the authors are included in the biographical sketches preceding each selection. As a whole, the book reflects careful research and editing which make the end product absorbing and pleasurable reading. Edwards and Diamond have made a real contribution to the resurrection of our female literary past.

746. EXUM, Pat Crutchfield. KEEPING THE FAITH: WRITINGS BY CONTEMPORARY BLACK WOMEN. N.Y.: Fawcett, 1974. $1.75.
In this diverse collection of criticism, poetry, autobiography, and fiction, black women speak and write about their lives and about the stereotypes which have consistently represented black women in literature. Exum provides readers with full and varied portraits of black women. Some writers appear in print here for the first time. The fiction section, which includes writers like Toni Cade Bambara, Alice Walker, and Toni Morrison, is a standout; and Paule Marshall's discussion, "The Negro Woman in American Literature," should not be missed.

747. GOULIANOS, Joan, ed. BY A WOMAN WRITT; LITERATURE FROM SIX CENTURIES BY AND ABOUT WOMEN. 1973. Baltimore, Maryland: Penguin, 1974. $2.45.
Here is an essential anthology for anyone interested in the history of women's literature. Drawing on many forms: diaries, letters, tracts, essays, as well as poetry and fiction, Goulianos and her co-editors have brought into print many writers previously found only in rare book rooms. The first selection is from the early 15th century, and pre-19th century writings make up half the book. The 19th and 20th century writers are primarily ones who are not well known today. This is a rich work of restoration; with 20 writers included, the fascinating surprises that await the reader are too numerous to detail here. All the writers in this anthology are English-speaking; it is hoped that we will soon have similar collections of the translated works of non-English-speaking women.

748. GUY, Rosa., ed. **CHILDREN OF LONGING**. N.Y.: Holt, Rinehart & Winston, 1971. $3.97.

An exciting collection of writings by young black men and women about their lives and hopes for the future. Guy has collected her material in the North and South and in cities as well as rural areas. She prefaces the various sections with her notes about how she came to put the book together and her experiences in doing it. The young writers speak for themselves: they are strong, powerful, bitter at times, and full of creative energy and anger. These stories have been largely unrecorded before, and we owe a large debt to Rosa Guy for putting this book into print.

749. HAINING, Peter, ed. **THE GENTLEWOMEN OF EVIL. RARE SUPERNATURAL STORIES FROM THE PENS OF VICTORIAN LADIES.** N.Y.: Taplinger, 1967. $8.95.

Gentlewomen is the best anthology in its category. It brings us both the ventures into the supernatural of the "literary" writers like George Eliot and Elizabeth Gaskell, and some of the very finest efforts of the "popular" writers like Mary Elizabeth Braddon and Mrs. Oliphant. It is interesting to note that the adoption of a male personna by almost all the authors excludes the use of the traditional gothic formula of a helpless woman menaced. Devotees of the supernatural story looking for further reading are referred to the ghost stories of Edith Wharton and Selma Lagerlof.

750. _____ A CIRCLE OF WITCHES. AN ANTHOLOGY OF WITCHCRAFT STORIES. N.Y.: Taplinger, 1971. $8.95.

All the authors in this anthology are women, and most of them are not generally known or accessible to us. The book is divided into sections of fact and fiction. The witches of both sections are portrayed either as persecuted innocent women or practitioners of black magic. Much of the writing seems tedious today and, for this reason, the collection will not have the popular appeal of the preceding one. Still, a good deal remains interesting. Lady Wilde's Irish witch tales are witty, psychologically perceptive, and written in an engaging and lively style. "The Enchanted Woman" by Anna Bonus Kingsford is recommended to readers concerned with myths and dreams in women's writings.

751. KATZ, Naomi and Nancy Milton, ed. **FRAGMENT FROM A LOST DIARY AND OTHER STORIES. WOMEN OF ASIA, AFRICA AND LATIN AMERICA**. 1973. Boston: Beacon Press, 1975. $3.95.

Although the editors originally intended a compilation of modern third-world literature, they were so struck by the quality of the stories about women's lives, they decided to focus on women. This probably explains why only a third of these stories are actually written by women. The cultural jump required can make some selections difficult to get involved in, at least initially. The style ranges from spare, understated, oriental naturalism to the explicit rhetoric of revolutionary cultures like Vietnam and Cuba. As a book, this anthology has a power and wholeness which come from careful arrangement; each piece has been thoughtfully placed to reinforce or contrast with those next to it. The collection deals with the lives of blatantly oppressed women (those who are bought and sold as wives, concubines, or slaves); transitional women often torn between old ways and new; and modern women who find themselves with more alternatives and a new set of problems. One comes away from this book with an expanded understanding of the realities of third-world women's lives.

752. MANLEY, Seon & Gogo Lewis, ed. **(a) LADIES OF HORROR, TWO CENTURIES OF SUPERNATURAL STORIES BY THE GENTLE SEX**. N.Y.: Lothrop, Lee & Shepard, 1971. $5.95. **(b) GRANDE DAMES OF DETECTION, TWO CENTURIES OF SLEUTHING STORIES BY THE GENTLE SEX**. N.Y.: Lothrop, Lee & Shepard, 1973. $5.95. **(c) MISTRESSES OF MYSTERY, TWO CENTURIES OF SUSPENSE STORIES BY THE GENTLE SEX**. N.Y.: Lothrop, Lee & Shepard, 1973. $5.95.

This is essentially a lightweight series, marred by the inclusion of too many second-rate stories. Still, Manley and Lewis (two sisters) have an obvious enthusiasm for women writers and for the contributions they have made to these genres. Readers interested in mystery and suspense stories are likely to find quite a few writers they will want to pursue further. Clemence Houseman's finely detailed long story "The Werewolf" (in **Ladies Of Horror**) will interest those concerned with the mythic in women's writings for its Diana figure who must ultimately be a monster. Edith Wharton's chilling ghost story (in **Mistresses Of Mystery**) will lead many to seek out her other writings in this form. **Grande Dames Of Detection** is the most satisfying collection.

753. MOFFAT, Mary Jane and **Charlotte Painter**, eds. **REVELATIONS: Diaries of Women.** 1974. N.Y.: Vintage, 1975. $2.95.

The eloquent voices of these women diarists confirm our faith in the evocative powers of language as well as in the literary talents of women. So intense, so vivid are the emotions and ideals they express that one wishes many had the chance to write more than private journals. The women anthologized, from all ages and backgrounds, include both famous and obscure names. We share George Sand's ravings toward her unresponsive lover; Mary Boykin Chestnut's poignant descriptions of the Civil War and its tragedies; Virignia Woolf's agonies over the creative writing process. Also extremely interesting are the entries of such women as Sophie Tolstoy, Anna Dostoevsky, Alice James, and Dorothy Wordsworth who lived in the shadows of men but who could find partial fulfillment through diary-keeping.

754. MURRAY, Michele, ed. **A HOUSE OF GOOD PROPORTION: Images of Women in Literature.** Simon & Schuster, 1973. $3.95.

This collection of poems, stories, and novel excerpts takes a look at the ways women have been regarded in literature over the past two centuries. Thematically, it progresses through a woman's life—from little girl and virgin through the "Women in Love," the independent woman, wife, mother, and on through old age. The individual selections are well-chosen: chapters from Tolstoy and Chekhov on the wife; Tillie Olsen and Colette on the mother; Anne Sexton on women lost—her poem "Consorting with Angels." But perhaps the book tries to do too much—with so many brief varieties of American and foreign, older and contemporary, male and female writers. It might be best appreciated if the reader absorbs one section at a time, rather than trying to race through the numerous selections and thus lose their common motifs. The highlight of the work is Michele Murray's exceptional introduction and comments introducing each chapter.

●●

755. ROTTER, Pat, ed. **BITCHES AND SAD LADIES: An Anthology of Fiction By and About Women.** 1975. N.Y.: Dell, 1976. $2.25.

A "bitch" is an aggressive woman striving for independence and autonomy, and a "sad lady" a female who is as much a victim of her own passivity as of repression by men. Thirty-five finely crafted short stories by Joyce Carol Oates, Edna O'Brien, Anne Sexton, Tony Cade Bambara, Ursula LeGuin, Grace Paley, Rosellen Brown, and others depict women at various stages between bitch and sad lady—often with shocking, unusual, or even violent possibilities. Doris Betts paints a vivid picture of the anger, pain and joy of childbirth. Gail Godwin reflects on the resentment some mothers may feel toward their children. In Sybil Claiborne's satire, a sexually aggressive woman patronizes men as sex objects, while in a perverse twist by Julia O'Faolain, a young woman enslaves her rigid Italian husband in their basement. This collecton will enthrall readers with its experimental style and structure as well as with its compelling heroines. The female characters think, feel, and act in ways mostly unacceptable to traditional literary standards for women. The book can't be recommended highly enough.

756. SARGENT, Pamela, ed. **WOMEN OF WONDER, SCIENCE FICTION STORIES BY WOMEN ABOUT WOMEN.** N.Y.: Vintage, 1975. $1.95.

Science fiction has its roots in social criticism; an author can take a current condition and postulate a future logical extreme. SF stories can portray societies where sex roles have been redefined or eliminated, where institutions like marriage and the family have been transformed, where technology serves human needs. This excellent collection introduces us to the potential that exists for women writers and readers in what has generally been viewed as a pulpy, male, escapist genre. The chronological arrangement of the stories shows that, while speculative possibilities have always existed for women in science fiction, a growing feminist consciousness has enlarged their use. The long introductory essay by Sargent provides a fine historical background on women as writers of, and characters in, science fiction. Interested readers will get many leads on where to go for further reading.

757. _____ MORE WOMEN OF WONDER: Science Fiction Novelettes by Women about Women. N.Y.: Vintage, 1976. $1.95.

A companion to **Women of Wonder**, this collection includes examples of the SF novelette, a form which, unlike the SF novel, is not compelled to resolve its theme. It "is satisfied with the problem dramatized, not solved," the single case standing for many. Adolescence is the theme of the two most baffling novellas: Joanna Russ's "The Second Inquisition" is a surrealistic tale about a young girl's attempts to transcend the limitations of small-town America with the help of a mysterious black amazon "visitor"; Kate Wilhelm's "The Funeral" presents a chilling vision of a society where youth is enslaved by the vampiristic will of adults. A wide variety of time-settings is represented in this collection: Joan D. Vinge's "Tin Soldier" posits a future in which women dominate by virtue of their superior adaptiveness to the rigors of space travel, while C.L. Moore delves into medieval lore to give us a remarkable warrior-heroine in the exotic "Jirel Meets Magic."

758. SINGER, Frieda. DAUGHTERS IN HIGH SCHOOL. Plainfield, Vt.: Daughters, Inc., 1974. $3.80.

This anthology contains poetry, short stories, and essays by high school women from all over the U.S. The book is divided into six parts (The Unknown, Roles, The Male Protagonist, Questioning Relationships, and Walk Tall, Daughter), and each section presents a broad range of perspectives on female adolescence in the 1970s. In their writing, these young women grapple with their lives and the world at large in ways that make their personal concerns relevant to all women, of all ages. An excellent book for high school English or creative writing classes.

759. SULLIVAN, Victoria and James Hatch. PLAYS BY AND ABOUT WOMEN. 1973. O.P.

This anthology contains plays by Alice Gerstenberg, Lillian Hellman, Clare Boothe, Doris Lessing, Megan Terry, Natalia Ginsberg, Maureen Duffy, and Alice Childress. The plays were written between 1913 and 1969; the collecton attempts to provide a sampling of women's views on women during the 20th century. From opponents in the scramble for men, to allies against men, to struggling through less-than-perfect relationships with men—these plays cover many of the changes women are experiencing. Alice Childress's "Wine in the Wilderness" stands out as the most positive—it is a beautiful affirmation of black women. This is a good collection, although none of the plays deal positively with friendship between women.

760. WASHINGTON, Mary Helen, ed. **BLACK-EYED SUSANS. CLASSIC STORIES BY AND ABOUT BLACK WOMEN.** Garden City, N.Y.: Doubleday, 1975. $2.95.

The ten stories in this anthology are, with one exception, by well-known black women authors. Each is so well-written that it is impossible to single one out for special praise. For those wishing to explore any of the authors in greater depth, there are excellent bibliographies on each one, including all their published books, poems, stories and articles, plus works of criticism about them. The organization of the collection around several major topics (physical appearance, mother daughter relationships, the disappointment of romantic love, black women's feelings about white women) provides direction for those interested in a comparative, thematic approach to black women's writings.

Delano. "A Moment off from Chopping Cotton." Georgia, 1941.

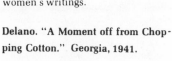

761. WASSERMAN, Barbara Alson, ed. **THE BOLD NEW WOMEN.** 1966. Greenwich, Conn.: Fawcett, 1970. O.P.
A good collection of pieces by contemporary women writers. The first section, "The Inner Eye," brings together some excellent fictional descriptions of women's sexual experiences; the editor comments that "a sexual experience for most women is never just a sexual experience but a clutch on the universe." The remaining two sections are composed of examples of the new, personal journalism, at which so many women excel.

762. WOMEN: FEMINIST STORIES BY NINE NEW AUTHORS. N.Y.: Eakins Press, 1972. $2.50. O.P.
When is fiction feminist? Most of the stories in this book do not move beyond documenting women's oppression; they do not show women coming to consciousness of that oppression, let alone breaking out of it. The title aside, these are fine stories, exploring the lives of a wide range of women, including black women, Italian women, a Greek woman, and a 19th century kitchen maid. All but one were first published in *Aphra* magazine, bringing to light so many new women writers.

Works About Literature

763. ATWOOD, Margaret. SURVIVAL. A THEMATIC GUIDE TO CANADIAN LITERATURE. Toronto: Anansi, 1972. $3.25.
This rich book, by the Canadian poet and novelist, offers many insights into Canada's literature and history. If you plan to read some of the Canadian authors listed in this bibliography, you will also want to read **Survival.** Readers with a special interest in Atwood, herself, will find that her critical writing illuminates the specifically Canadian aspects of her own poems and novels. Feminist critics looking for models should also take a look at Atwood's thematic approach. It is interesting both for how it has been written: it is, as the author says, a "personal statement" and a "political manifesto;" and for what it has been written about: there is a whole chapter on images of women in Canadian literature, but perhaps even more interestingly, Canada itself is seen as playing a part in world politics which bears many similarities to the traditional social role of women. **Survival** has been written with love and care, humor and passion.

764. BASCH, Francoise. RELATIVE CREATURES: Victorian Women in Society and the Novel. N.Y.: Schocken Books, 1975. $3.95.
Wives, mothers, single, working-class, and fallen women—their positions in society are contrasted with their images in the Victorian novel. Among the novelists considered are the Brontes, Dickens, Thackeray, Gaskell, and Eliot. Although marred by a poor translation, it is a good combination of literary criticism and social history, important because it puts our image of Victorian women within its proper social context. Useful bibliography.

765. BAZIN, Nancy Topping. VIRGINIA WOOLF AND THE ANDROGYNOUS VISION. Rutgers University Press, 1973. $9.00.
An intriguing and convincing interpretation of Virginia Woolf's novels. Bazin believes Virginia was trying to achieve the "razor edge of balance between two opposite forces"—the feminine (eternal, significant, and whole) and the masculine (transitory, meaningless, and formless). She bases her theory upon Virginia's life as well as her work. Her conclusions about her life are impossible to verify, but her analysis of the books themselves is not really dependent upon such psychological guesswork. It is thorough, well-written, and not so academic as to be inaccessible to the casual reader.

766. BEAUVOIR, Simone de. THE SECOND SEX, 1949. N.Y.: Vintage, 1974. $2.95.
Beauvoir's monumental exposition of woman's past and present is a true foundation stone of contemporary feminism, examining social, cultural, historical, biological, psychological, mythical concepts that have shaped women's destinies in western culture. In terms of literature, she considers the images of women present in the works

of five authors: Montherlant, Lawrence, Breton, Claudel and Stendhal. She places her analysis within the framework of each author's total world view, and the critiques are sharp, penetrating and sometimes angry. Throughout the book, Beauvoir draws often on literature to illustrate her arguments. Whatever limitations age has placed on this work, no one else has given us as detailed, thorough and thoughtful an analysis of woman's place and how we got there. Mine it for its ideas, information and inspiration.

767. BLAKE, Fay M. THE STRIKE IN THE AMERICAN NOVEL. N.Y.: The Scarecrow Press, Inc., 1972. $8.50.
Fay Blake glibly traces the novelists' use of strikes and political climates from pre-Civil War America through 1945. The historical context is sketchy and generalized, but the 70-page annotated bibliography at the end is abundant in both information and opinions.

768. CADE, Toni. THE BLACK WOMAN. N.Y.: Signet, 1974. $1.25.
A solid and well put-together collection of political, historical, and critical essays by black women. The collection also includes short fictional and biographical pieces and poems by Nikki Giovanni, Kay Lindsey and Audre Lorde. In her introduction, Cade says, "there have been women who have been able to think better than they've been trained and have produced the canon of literature fondly referred to as 'feminist literature,' Anais Nin, Simone de Beauvoir, Doris Lessing, Betty Friedan, etc. And the question for us arises, how relevant are the truths, the experiences, the findings of white women to black women?"

769. CALVERTON, V.F. SEX EXPRESSION IN LITERATURE. N.Y.: Boni & Liveright, 1926. O.P.
V.F. Calverton was the pseudonym of George Goetz who edited a leftist quarterly called *Modern Monthly* in the 1930s. As an independent Marxist and an outspoken critic of the Stalin trials of the late 1930s, Calverton was a target of severe censure in party circles. In **Sex Expression In Literature**, Calverton's critical goal was to explain changing attitudes toward sex in English literature in terms of the changing social and economic conditions of the various classes. The chapters on Restoration Drama, the Sentimental Comedy and "The Immoral Revolution" of the 1890s are especially interesting as background for those researching the women writing and living in these periods.

770. CANTAROW, Ellen. "The Radicalizing of a Teacher of Literature." *Change: The Magazine of Higher Learning*, Vol. 4, No. 4, May 1972.
Cantarow says "our particular responsibility as teachers of literature is to act on the humanizing knowledge art can give us to construct our students new, revolutinary ideas of culture, and to construct with them outside the classroom both an active socialist movement and culture." Cantarow graduated from Wellesley and Harvard, and it was from her experience there that she began to realize the contradictions involved in being a female in a male-dominated culture. "In graduate school I began vaguely to realize that the gender of the critical mind (of literature, art, etc.) was masculine and that to be a 'critic' I would have to neuter my understanding."

771. CHURCHILL, Allen. THE IMPROPER BOHEMIANS. N.Y.: Ace Books, Inc., 1959. O.P.
Churchill tells about the ups and downs of life in Greenwich Village in the years when it was referred to as "The Coney Island of the soul" and "New York's Left Bank." he lightheartedly traces the standards and stereotypes from 1912 to 1932, zeroing in on particular personalities (Mabel Dodge, Edna St. Vincent Millay, John Reed, George Cram Cook, Margaret Anderson, Eugene O'Neill) and also recalling the generalized effects of World War I, the Depression, and Prohibition. The anecdotal gossip approach makes for entertaining reading, but the emphasis on sexual rumors is tiresome and highlights the incompleteness of the book. (For example, lesbianism is not mentioned.)

772. COLBY, Vineta. THE SINGULAR ANOMALY. N.Y.: New York University Press, 1970. $3.95.
A lively, expertly documented study of those "singular anomalies"—British women authors—during the Victorian period. Eliza Lynn Linton, Olive Schreiner, Mrs. Humphrey Ward, John Oliver Hobbes (Pearl Craigie), and Vernon Lee (Violet Paget) were all highly read and acclaimed writers of the 19th century who used prose for public instruction and edification. Forbidden the pulpit, university lectern, or seat in Parliament, they acceptably wrote in private and produced best-selling didactic works. As women they achieved the power of reformers, educators, and polemicists through the more subtle vocation of literature. Vineta Colby sensitively portrays the tempestuous personal lives of these authors as well as providing insightful criticism of their books. For anyone intrigued by Victorian popular culture in addition to women's history, **The Singular Anomaly** is enthusiastically recommended.

773. CORNILLON, Susan Koppelman, ed. IMAGES OF WOMEN IN FICTION: Feminist Perspectives. Bowling Green, Ohio: Bowling Green University Popular Press, 1972. $4.00.
A collection of critical essays on literature from a feminist perspective. Among other interesting items, the volume includes the first version of this bibliography.

774. DAMON, Gene, Jan Watson, and **Robin Jordan. THE LESBIAN IN LITERATURE: A Bibliography.** 2nd edition. Available from Box 5025, Washington Station, Reno, Nevada 89503, 1975. $10.00.
A comprehensive listing (96 pages) of titles with coding systems to indicate: 1) whether there are major, minor, or repressed lesbian characters, and 2) the quality of the lesbian content. A large majority of titles are coded "T" for trash, but there is plenty of good stuff, too. They'll probably be hard to find in local libraries.

775. DEEGAN, Dorothy Yost. THE STEREOTYPE OF THE SINGLE WOMAN IN AMERICAN NOVELS. Columbia University, N.Y.: King's Crown Press, 1951. O.P.
This dry, scholarly book makes its horrifying point with little emphasis: based on the literature from the late 18th century to 1935, Deegan concluded that there is virtually no admirable single woman to be found in American literature. She based her study on the Dickinson Lists of American fiction and defined single woman as a woman over thirty who has not married and is not planning to marry. Deegan exposed the huge gap between fact and male writers' presentation of the single woman, as revealed in the very different, positive picture that emerged from sociological studies of the time. The implications of Deegan's findings are profound. This careful study is very well done and very hard reading.

776. DWORKIN, Andrea. WOMAN HATING. N.Y.: E.P. Dutton & Co., Inc., 1974.
Dworkin explores the institutionalized and universal social phenomenon of woman hating. She examines the cultural history behind women's victimization in patriarchal cultures everywhere. The connections between fantasy representations of women (fairy tales and myths) and the reality of women's social oppression (witch burning and foot binding) is perceptively explored. The author urges an end to patriarchally defined and culturally reinforced, as opposed to biologically determined, sex differences between people.

777. ELLMANN, Mary. THINKING ABOUT WOMEN. 1968. N.Y.: Harcourt Brace Jovanovitch, 1970. $2.65.
Essentially a criticism of the sexism that pervades literary culture, though Ellmann would probably not use the term "sexism" herself. there are chapters on "Sexual Analogy," "Phallic Criticism," "Differences in Tone" (between male and female writers), and "Responses" (of women writers to experience). A wide range of writers, from the 19th century to the 1960s, get critical jabs from Ellman's acid pen, and women are by no means exempt. Ellman is difficult to read: her style and arguments are often convoluted and her witticisms occasionally irritating. If you can get through this, she makes some extremely thought-provoking points.

778. FIEDLER, Leslie A. LOVE AND DEATH IN THE AMERICAN NOVEL. 1960. N.Y.: Stein & Day, 1975. $4.95.
An important criticism of American male novelists. The book deals with their immaturity, that is, their inability to deal with their sexuality or their relationships with women, and their obsession with death.

779. FIRESTONE, Shulamith. THE DIALECTIC OF SEX. 1970. N.Y.: Bantam, current. $1.25.
This book presents a brilliant and provocative general feminist analysis. Perceptive and informative discussions of the family (especially interesting is her history of the treatment of children); Freudianism; the Left and the interconnections between economic, racial and sexual revolution; and love, culture and romance make this basic theoretical reading.

780. FOSTER, Jeannette. SEX VARIANT WOMEN IN LITERATURE. N.Y.: Vantage, 1956. Baltimore: Diana Press, 1976. $8.00.
A scholarly and comprehensive study of women portrayed in literature who might be considered to be lesbians, from Sappho to the 20th century. There is some speculation on the sexual orientation of certain women writers, too. The book is an excellent source of reference; Foster's sympathy shows through the scholarly apparatus.

781. GAGEN, Jean Elizabeth. THE NEW WOMEN: Her Emergence in English Drama 1600-1730. N.Y.: Twayne, 1954. O.P.
This is a study of female characters in English plays and their relationship to real women over the period studied. Particular attention is paid to education and the figure of the learned lady as she emerged following Renaissance theories on the education of women.

782. GLOSTER, Hugh M. NEGRO VOICES IN AMERICAN FICTION. N.Y.: Russell & Russell, 1965. $15.00.
An excellent study of black writers since their first work in the antebellum era to about the end of the Depression. The works of Pauline E. Hopkins, Frances E. Watkins Harper, Sarah Lee Fleming, Jessie Fauset, Nella Larsen, and Zora Neale Hurston are discussed. Gloster sets them in a framework of the political and social position of blacks and the movements of each era.

783. GORNICK, Vivian, and Barbara K. Moran, eds. WOMAN IN SEXIST SOCIETY: Studies in Power and Powerlessness. 1971. N.Y.: Signet, 1972. $1.95.
A fine collection of essays, ranging over many of the disciplines in which feminist research and analysis has been carried out; the field of culture is particularly well represented. Some pieces discuss the historical position of women in literature and art; others begin to develop ideas about how women should re-define themselves, and create a new art. In her essay, "Women and Creativity: The Demise of the Dancing Dog," Cynthia Ozick says, "art must belong to all human beings, not alone to a traditionally privileged segment." Other literary essays include Vivian Gornick's "Woman as Outsider," Wendy Martin's "Seduced and Abandoned in the New World," and Elaine Showalter's "Women Writers and the Double Standard." Together these essays make a contribution to a growing body of feminist criticism.

784. HEILBRUN, Carolyn. TOWARD A RECOGNITION OF ANDROGYNY. N.Y.: Harper & Row, 1973. $2.95.
In the three essays which make up this book, Carolyn Heilbrun traces androgyny as an ideal expressed in literature since its beginnings. The first essay deals with evidence of and reaction to androgyny from the Greeks, through the Judeo-Christian tradition, the Medieval and Renaissance periods, and finally, to the emergence of the novel. The second essay deals with women as presented in the novel; and the third essay concentrates on the Bloomsbury group. Her ideas are sometimes sketchily presented, but what she does say is both fresh and solidly supported, from her discussion of Oedipus to her comments on Virginia Woolf. Heilburn continues Millet's discussion of Lawrence and comments on writers as dissimilar as Heloise, Shakespeare, Defoe, Jane Austen, Hawthorne, Wilkie Collins, Dorothy Sayers, and Joyce. If Heilbrun is disappointing, it is in her insistence on disassociating herself from the women's movement. She writes of androgyny as our "future salvation," but her apparent tolerance of present conditions subtly denigrates the value of action to effect this change.

785. HINKLEY, Laura L. LADIES OF LITERATURE, 1946. Plainview, N.Y.: Books for Libraries Press. $14.50.
This book is not as bad as the title sounds. It contains information about Fanny Burney, Jane Austen, Charlotte and Emily Bronte, Elizabeth Barrett Browning, and George Eliot.

786. JESSUP, Josephine Lurie. FAITH OF OUR FEMINISTS. N.Y.: Biblo & Tannen, 1950. $5.50.
This book contains criticism and reviews of the works of Ellen Glasgow, Edith Wharton, Willa Cather. It is uninspired; the author's standard seems to be simply to find women characters who exceed men in strength.

787. KLEIN, Viola. THE FEMININE CHARACTER: History of an Ideology. 1948. Chicago: University of Illinois Press, current. $2.95.
"The hypothesis of this study is the view that the social and cultural situation at any given time is expressed in ideologies and reflected in all products of the human mind: in art, in science, in literature." Klein analyzes a long novel by a Dutch author covering three generations—1) before the industrial revolution, when the female characters were completely subjected, 2) the late 19th century and the beginnings of emancipation, and 3) before World War I. It is an extremely interesting study.

788. LAKOFF, Robin. LANGUAGE AND WOMAN'S PLACE. N.Y.: Harper and Row, 1975. $2.25.
This first booklength sociolinguistic exploration of sexism in language deals with women's speech as compared to men's and convincingly demonstrates that two separate languages, reflecting male and female role differences exist. Separate but unequal, language is indicative of women's social role. Social change, Lakoff concludes, must precede linguistic change.

789. LANE, Margaret. PURELY FOR PLEASURE: A Collection of Literary-Biographical Essays. N.Y.: Knopf, 1967. O.P.
Lane is not an obvious feminist, but she clearly has a special interest in women. Apart from a number of essays on women writers (three on the Brontes, three on Elizabeth Gaskell, two on Beatrice Potter, one on Jane Austen, and one on the little-known Flora Thompson, who wrote the story of her childhood in poor, rural England in the late 19th century), this volume includes several essays which deal with other little-explored areas of life and literature. An entertaining and perceptive book about topics men would not think important enough to write about.

790. LAWRENCE, Margaret. SCHOOL OF FEMININITY. 1936. PA: Richard West, 1973. $10.00.
This study of women writers will be fascinating and helpful to those deeply involved in rediscovering women's fiction. Lawrence includes 45 authors: she touches on Sappho, leaps to Mary Wollstonecraft, then painstakingly makes her way through the centuries to Virginia Woolf. Some of the authors she discusses were still writing at the time this book was written; for these and many others the data was not all in, so Lawrence is safest to read about authors you know. What is most dated about her are her Freudian assumptions about women and her analysis of the psychological motivations of whole groups of writers. Yet, once a reader has learned the grain of salt rule with Lawrence, her knowledgeable appreciation of so many and such varied writers is worthwhile. She occasionally has surprising little rays of insight into the future (now), usually preceded by the phrase, "well, the feminists say . . ." Lavish with her personal opinion, which she rarely distinguishes from fact, she is, nevertheless, a lively voice of the 1930s, making a very real contribution to women's literature.

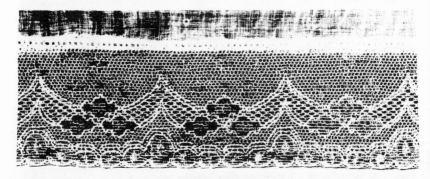

791. LESSING, Doris. A SMALL PERSONAL VOICE. 1974. N.Y.: Vintage, 1975. $2.45.
Written between 1956 and 1973, these essays, reviews and interviews with Lessing present a fascinating collage of her opinions and ideas. The essays and reviews range over diverse subjects, each distinguished by Lessing's remarkable ability to fuse emotional understanding and political consciousness into a cohesive vision. The three interviews included are fragmentary, but offer revealing insights into Lessing's attitudes toward her craft, her society and herself. Perhaps the most intriguing piece in the collecton is "Preface to the Golden Notebook." Written for a 1971 paperback edition, the essay details Lessing's views on the social and political functions of the novel and the factors—especially in education—that influence (and too often limit) our perceptions of literature.

792. MacCARTHY, Bridget G. WOMEN WRITERS: Their Contribution to the English Novel. 1946. Folcroft, PA: Folcroft Library Editions. $20.00.
A very valuable and comprehensive piece of work. Volume I covers the work of women from 1671 to 1744, while Volume II deals with later women writers from 1744 to 1818. Highly recommended for both its factual and its interpretive material.

793. McCARTHY, Mary. ON THE CONTRARY: Articles of Belief. N.Y.: Noonday, 1962. O.P
A collecton of critical essays written between 1946 and 1961. Twelve fall under the heading "Politics and the Social Scene," three under the heading "Women" (the brilliant essay "Tyranny of the Orgasm," a discussion of women's magazines, and one on "The Vassar Girl"), and six under "Literature and the Arts." Among these last, "The Fact in Fiction" and "Characters in Fiction" can be recommended as excellent general discussions of the novel.

794. MARCUS, Steven. THE OTHER VICTORIANS: A Study of Sexuality and Pornography in Mid-Nineteenth-Century England. 1964. N.Y.: Basic Books, 1974. $10.95.
An extremely interesting study of the underside of Victorian life that the novelists ignored, the sizable sub-culture that wrote, sold, and read pornography. There is a perceptive analysis of **My Secret Life**, the sexual memoirs of a wealthy Victorian gentleman; a concluding chapter discusses the unreal fantasies pornography deals in, or what Marcus calls "pornotopia." Marcus draws interesting contrasts between pornography and literature.

795. MARKALE, Jean. WOMEN OF THE CELTS. London: Gordon Cremonesi Publishers, 1975. $17.95.
Markale explores the position of women in Celtic society through an analysis of Celtic mythology, and compares and contrasts her social position with the contemporary woman's. Celtic society, unlike our own, emerges as one in transition between matriarchal and patriarchal cultures. Celtic culture conflicted with Christianity and was driven underground; yet, the remnants of Celtic gynocracy are reflected in Celtic mythology and medieval romances. Although the connection Markale tries to forge between the Celtic woman's somewhat egalitarian social position and the contemporary woman's is tenuous and hardly feminist, the book is worth reading for those with a special interest in matriarchy/gynocracy, medieval literature, and Celtic mythology.

796. MAUROIS, Andre. SEVEN FACES OF LOVE. 1944. Plainview, N.Y.: Books for Libraries Press. $13.50.
Maurois discusses the differences between concepts of love embodied in seven French works of fiction: the 17th century **Princess of Cleves**, by Madame de La Fayette, the 18th century **Nouvelle Heloise** and **Liaisons Dangereuses.**

797. MILLET, Kate. SEXUAL POLITICS. 1969. N.Y.: Avon, 1973. $2.25.
Millet first explains her theory of sexual politics, by which she means all male-female power-structured relationships, then gives examples from literature to illustrate her theory and trace some changes in attitude over the past century and a half. A solid chapter on the 19th century draws on the works of several writers; in the 20th century, D.H. Lawrence, Henry Miller, Norman Mailer, and Jean Genet are examined at length.

798. NEFF, Wanda. VICTORIAN WORKING WOMEN. 1929. N.Y.: AMS Press. $8.50.
Between 1820 and 1850, new economic structures were evolving. An increase in the urban population, an emerging "middle class", and greater proportions of women and children working outside the home were all outgrowths of the British Industrial Revolution. But the Victorians still maintained their crystallized notion that women's capacities were exclusively as potential mothers, and the woman who worked was an affront against nature and the protective instincts of man." It is between these shifting walls that Wanda Neff traces the history of labor legislation and how it affected

women as textile workers, paper mill workers, dressmakers, governesses, and finally, as idle wives of the middle class. The text is filled with references to women who were writers and political activists, such as Harriet Martineau, Charlotte Elizabeth Tonna, Elizabeth Gaskell, Frances Trollope, Anna Jameson, and has an expansive (though, like the book, not easily available) bibliography.

799. NIN, Anais. THE NOVEL OF THE FUTURE. 1968. N.Y.: MacMillan, 1970. $1.95.
In the first chapter of this book of literary criticism, Anais Nin quotes Carl Jung: "Proceed from the dream outward . . . ." This directive becomes the basis of much of what she has to say about literature, her own and others'. For her a dream is the "source of creation," and the novel of the future is a combination of prose and poetry, conscious and subconscious awareness, dream and waking, what is and what could be. "It is the function of art to renew our perception," says Nin, and in this book she discusses in detail how she has tried to do this in her fiction and diaries. She includes her reactions to other artists and their work, including several little-known women writers: Marianne Hauser, Maude Hutchins, Anna Kavan, Marguerite Young, and Djuna Barnes. Essential reading for Nin enthusiasts and even for those who find her egotistical or narcissistic, a provocative and woman-oriented view of literature.

800. OLSEN, Tillie. "Silences—When Writers Don't Write." *Harper's*, October 1965. Also in Susan Koppelman Cornillon, ed. **IMAGES OF WOMEN IN FICTION**, Bowling Green, Ohio: Bowling Green University Press, 1972.
A very interesting article, discussing the many things that prevent women from writing and from developing into serious writers.

801. PAPISHVILY, Helen Waite. ALL THE HAPPY ENDINGS. Port Washington, N.Y.: Kinnikat Press, 1956. O.P.
A study of the popular novels ordinary women wrote in the 19th century and how these books helped women at home develop "survival techniques" that are still considered part of female culture now. It contains much helpful information.

802. RIDEOUT, Walter. THE RADICAL NOVEL IN THE UNITED STATES 1900-1954.
N.Y.: Hill & Wang, current. $1.95.
A critical history of the radical and socialist traditions in American literature, showing the interrelations between literature and society. Reference is made to several women who wrote in the early socialist or realist tradition, such as Caroline H. Pemberton, who wrote **The Charity Girl** (1901) and Rebecca Harding Davis, who wrote the story "Life in the Iron Mills" in 1861 (see entry).

803. ROGERS, Katherine. THE TROUBLESOME HELPMATE: A History of Misogyny in Literature. Seattle: University of Washington Press, current. $3.95.
A historical survey of both direct and indirect manifestations in literature of hatred, fear, or contempt for women, from Biblical and classical times to the 20th century.

804. RUBENIUS, Aina. THE WOMAN QUESTION IN MRS. GASKELL'S LIFE AND WORK. 1950. N.Y.: Russell and Russell, 1973.
This excellent critical work explores Elizabeth Gaskell's attitude toward women and women's issues. Rubenius marks changes in Gaskell's thinking after her first success as a writer, when she journeyed abroad alone or with her daughter. She began to meet and form friendships with many people involved in the Women's Rights movement. Shifts in her thinking about working women (prostitutes, needlewomen, etc.) are relatively easy to document: while Gaskell had condemned all factory work for women in **Mary Barton**, by the time she wrote **North and South** she was able to accept the fact that women preferred the higher wages of factory conditions. Harder to grasp is the transition in Gaskell's thinking about the position of middle class women, both married and unmarried, though Rubenius shows how she did grapple with this.

805. RULE, Jane. LESBIAN IMAGES. N.Y.: Doubleday, 1975. $ .95.
Lesbian Images offers a look at the work of writers who have loved women and written about it. Rule begins with a very personal introduction, then goes on to two strong chapters in which she discusses the beginnings of taboos against homosexual and lesbian love and the attempts to police it—from the church fathers to modern-day psychiatrists. She devotes twelve chapters to specific women writers from Radclyffe Hall through Maureen Dufy, and ends with two chapters on recent fiction and non-fiction. Very upfront about herself personally and politically, Rule combines love and knowledge of her subject to give us a solid book which supports both lesbianism and literature. Her remarks about the authors and their works contain researched details, and are carefully selected to introduce readers to these writers. Now try finding them in your local libraries and bookstores.

806. SACKVILLE-WEST, Vita. APHRA BEHN, The Incomparable Astrea. 1928. N.Y.: Russell & Russell, 1970. $7.00. Folcroft, PA: Folcroft Library Editions, 1975. $10.00.
An unusual critical work. Written in a simple, flowing style the book is scholarly while giving a living, personal portrait of the "incomparable Astrea." One of Vita's purposes in writing the work is to rebut critics, such as the esteemed Ernest Bernbaum, who theorized that little of the information reported about Aphra was actually authentic—including works attributed to her. Vita is convincing in her arguments; she digs up and authenticates old facts, lovingly rereads the major works. Many parts of Aphra are considered: the child in the colonies, the young wife and widow, the government spy, debtor in prison, controversial playwright, and novelist.

807. SCHRAUFNAGEL, Noel. FROM APOLOGY TO PROTEST: THE BLACK AMERICAN NOVEL. Deland, Florida: Everett/Edwards Inc., 1973. O.P.
Dealing primarily with the change in political focus in the novels of black writers between 1940 and 1970, Schraufnagel's book is convincing and well documented. A growing tradition of work reflecting the black experience had begun to accumulate before and through the Harlem Renaissance period; this tradition eventually crystallized into protest with the appearance of Richard Wright's **Native Son**. The 1940s and 1950s was to witness a broadening of the fictonal image of black protest, sometimes hedged with accommodation or assimilation with white society. In the 1940s period, Schraufnagel deals very perceptively with the work of women: Ann Petry's **The Street**, Dorothy West, Felice Swados, Odella Wood and Zora Neale Hurston's last novel, **Seraph on the Suwanee**. For the 1950s to 1970s, Gwendolyn Brooks, Ann Petry's **The Narrows**, Carlene Hatcher Polite, Margaret Walker, Louise Meriwether, Paule Marshall, Kristin Huner, Rosa Guy and Sarah Wright are included. The book culminates with a description of militant protest in mid- and late-1960s novels. For additional information on the women of the 1940s, Carl Milton Hughes' **The Negro Novelist: A Discussion of the Writing of American Negro Novelists 1940-50**, gives a sense of the decade though the author resorts to occasional sexist remarks and is less helpful than Schraufnagel.

808. SHOWALTER, Elaine. "Women Writers and the Female Experience." In **NOTES FROM THE THIRD YEAR: Women's Liberation**, available from Box AA, Old Chelsea Station, N.Y. 10011, 1971. $1.50.
". . . feminine experiences have not been fully explored, or honestly expressed by women writers . . . women have, in fact, been kept from their own experience by a double critical standard, by a double social standard, by external censorship, and, most dangerous, by self-censorship—which is sometimes exercised in self-defense, more frequently in self-hatred."

809. SONTAG, Susan. AGAINST INTERPRETATION. N.Y.: Delta, 1966. $1.95.
Although Sontag does not concern herself with the art of women (rarely dedicating an essay or even a passing reference to women artists), she is conscious of the irrelevance of much of today's literary criticism. She feels that too often the dissection of a work's content has been used to isolate and reduce the power of the artist's work. She argues in "Against Interpretation" and "On Culture and the New Sensibility" that "art today is a kind of instrument for modifying consciousness and organizing new modes of sensibility." these essays are thought-provoking, though maddening for Sontag's apparent assumption of a 98% male art world.

810. TOMPKINS, J.M.S. THE POPULAR NOVEL IN ENGLAND 1770-1800. 1932. Lincoln, University of Nebraska Press, 1961. $1.50.
This very excellent study focuses primarily on lesser known writers between the years

1770-1800. Tompkins especially emphasizes the work of women and the role of the female novelist. She analyzes a group of writers who are completely unknown today—women who wrote for economic survival, to sell to a popular market, or to find some outlet for opinions and views they could express nowhere else. Tompkins places these writers in the context of another group of women (themselves long overlooked by a male literary tradition) whose work women are now re-examining with new interest: i.e., Fanny Burney, Elizabeth Inchbald, Maria Edgeworth, Ann Radclyffe, Charlotte Lennox. Tompkins is highly sensitive to the tone of these women's work and the life experiences from which 18th century women wrote. As she says, "these women writers had taken note of all the stupidities, all the selfishness and clumsy notions of conceit with which for centuries their sex had been affronted."

811. SPACKS, Patricia Meyer. THE FEMALE IMAGINATION. 1975. N.Y.: Discus Books, 1976. $2.45.
"What are the ways of female feeling, the modes of responding, that persist despite social change?" is the question in this critical work on women writers. Using literary and psychological analysis rather than political interpretation, Patricia Spacks looks for those themes which have occupied women writers from the 17th century to the present. Autobiography, fiction, diaries, and essays by some 80 authors include Jane Austen, Elizabeth Gaskell, George Eliot, Virginia Woolf, Ellen Glasgow, Kate Millett, Sylvia Plath, Edith Wharton and Mary McCarthy. The text is scholarly and assumes a wide literary background; it is not an introductory book about women writers. Such motifs as power and passivity, adolescence, the artist as woman, and female altruism derive from the author's experiences as well as from the works she investigates.

812. UTTER, Robert Palfrey and **Gwendolyn Bridges Needham. PAMELA'S DAUGHTERS.** 1936. N.Y.: Somerset. $23.50.
A study of "changing fasions in heroines" since Richardson's 18th century **Pamela**. Much of the work is concerned with trivia and Utter takes pleasure in putting down women novelists, but there is a great deal of very useful information.

813. VIOLETTE, Augusta Genevieve. ECONOMIC FEMINISM IN AMERICAN LITERATURE PRIOR TO 1848. Orono, Maine: University Press, 1925. O.P.
Violette examines the feminism in the writings of Thomas Paine, Sarah Grimke, Margaret Fuller, Emerson and others—in short, "any American writers who evinced any positive interest in the extension of legal and political privileges to women." She ends the study in 1848, as she feels that this year marks the beginning of the organized suffrage movement in the United States.

814. WALLACE, Ada. BEFORE THE BLUESTOCKINGS. London: Allen, 1929. O.P.
A study of the lives of educated Englishwomen from the Restoration to the end of the first third of the 18th century.

815. WATT, Ian. THE RISE OF THE NOVEL: Studies in Defoe, Richardson, and Fielding. 1957. Berkeley: University of California Press, current. $2.50.
This book gives some excellent background on economic and social conditions in the 18th century, linking the rise of the novel to the social setting. There is a good chapter on love and the novel with insightful information on the changing position of women.

816. WOMAN: An Issue. Lee R. Edwards, Mary Heath, and Lisa Baskin, eds. Boston: Little, Brown, 1972. $3.75.
A collection of writings about women. The issue includes several literary essays, as well as short stories and poems.

817. WILLIAMS, Ora. AMERICAN BLACK WOMEN IN THE ARTS & SOCIAL SCIENCES: A BIBLIOGRAPHY SURVEY. N.J.: Scarecrow Press, 1973. $6.00.
"Called Matriarch, Emasculator and Hot Momma. Sometimes Sister, Pretty Baby, Aunti, Mamie and Girl. Called Unwed Mother; Welfare Recipient and Inner City Consumer. The Black American Woman has had to admit that while nobody knew the trouble she saw, everybody, his brother and his dog felt qualified to explain her, even to herself." (Maya Angelou) Ora Williams attempts to dispel the stereotypes about the

black woman with this substantial bibliography of over 1000 entries, dating from 1746 to 1972. The lists are divided into sections which include reference works, biographies, anthologies, fiction (for young readers, too), music, and painting. It now rests with us to find these works in the deficient collections of black writers in libraries and bookstores. It would be a difficult but welcome task to add annotations to a bibliography of such diverse women.

818. WOOLF, Virginia. A ROOM OF ONE'S OWN. 1929. N.Y.: Harcourt Brace & Jovanovich, current. $1.95.
A fine essay dealing with the socio-economic factors that prevent women from writing. It includes historical data, literary criticism on Jane Austen and the Brontes, and thoughts on the stylistic differences between male and female writers.

819. _____ THREE GUINEAS. N.Y.: Harcourt, Brace & World, 1966. $1.95.
Three separate requests for charitable contributions of one guinea each trigger Woolf's lyrical feminist analysis of the reasons why women should withdraw their support from oppressive male-controlled social institutions. It is a very angry reaction to and analysis of women's position in a technocratic patriarchal society; yet, as a political tactic women's total withdrawal from the system could have resounding effects, like an end to war. Woolf's feminist analysis, unlike much feminist analysis by and about middle-class women, does not overlook the connection of sexism and capitalism, even for the middle-class woman: "we, daughters of educated men, are between the devil and the deep sea. Behind us lies the patriarchal system; the private house, with its nullity, its immorality, its hypocrisy, its servility. Before us lies the public world, the professional system, with its possessiveness, its jealousy, its pugnacity, its greed. The one shuts us up like slaves in a harem; the other forces us to circle, like caterpillars, head to tail, round and round the mulberry tree, the sacred tree, of property. It is a choice of evils. Each is bad. " Essential reading.

Graphic Credits

Artists contributing original material:

(Number indicates the Bibliography entry number that the graphic illustrates.)

Baron, Cynthia and Elizabeth Marshall. Drawing of Christina Stead, 750.

Korin-Hornstein-Arnoldi, Harriet (Jerusha). 7; 33; 37; 55; 114-116; 138; 155; 165; 187; 213; 240; 250; 327; 333; 412; 448; 474; 529; 598; 600; 619; Borders p154; 696; 743b; 767; 779; 790; 800; Drawings p205; Drawing p207; Drawing p208; Drawings p211.

Maio, Kathi. 22; 220; 450; 487.

Marshall, Elizabeth. 25; 45; 108; 118; Drawing of Zora Neale Hurston; 125; 128; Drawing of Meridel LeSeuer; 143; Drawing of Gertrude Stein; 244; 280; 466; 470; Drawing of Vita Sackville-West; 555; Drawing of Olive Schreiner; 638; 643; Drawing of George Sand; Drawing of Colette; 698; Drawing of Mary Lavin; 718; 724; 763.

Pearl. 394.

Senesac, Lorene. 819.

Vitagliono, Maria. Drawing of Louisa May Alcott; Drawing of Kate Chopin; 83; 87; 433; Drawing of Agatha Christie.

Additional Graphics: Bibliography entry number follow graphic credit in parenthesis.

Alisa. From **THE NEW WOMAN'S SURVIVAL CATALOG** by Kirsten Grimstad and Susan Rennie, 1975. (266).

Barnes, Djuna. Drawing reprinted from **COME!** N.Y.: Unity Press. (61).

Bishop, Isabel. "Office Girls." (90).

Broadside Press; 12651 Old Mill Place; Detroit, Michigan. **FAMILY PICTURES** by Gwendolyn Brooks. (198).

Brown Brothers. **HEALTHRIGHT**, Vol. II, Issue 4, Summer 1976. (138).

Cadden Wendy. Drawing from **YESTERDAY'S LESSONS** by Sharon Isabel. Oakland: Women's Press Collective, 1974. (256).

Catlett, Elizabeth. "Homage to My Young Black Sisters," sculpture: photograph from **SEVENTEEN BLACK ARTISTS** by Elton C. Fax. N.Y.: Dodd, Mead & Co., 1971. (385).

Congress of Racial Equality/UPI. Photograph from **OUR FACES/OUR WORDS** by Lillian Smith. N.Y.: W. W. Norton & Co., 1964. (Pg. 89).

"Cranford Society at Tea." From 1853 edition of **CRANFORD** by Elizabeth Gaskell. (432).

Delano. "A Moment off from Chopping Cotton," Georgia, 1941. Photograph from Library of Congress. (760).

Eck, Diana L. Photographs. (602 and 751).

Flynn, Elizabeth G. **REBEL GIRL**. N.Y.: International Publishing Co., 1955. (97).

HARDHITTING SONGS FOR HARDHIT PEOPLE by Alan Lomax, Woody Guthrie, and Pete Seeger. N.Y.: Oak Publications, 1967. "Photograph of strikers." (67 and 68).

Heaton, H.R. "Friendly Banshee." Drawing from **IRISH WONDERS** by D.R. McAnally, Jr., 1888. (708).

Johnson, Frances Benjamin. Photograph of "Women Working in a Cigar Box Factory, 1910" from **A Talent for Detail: The Photographs of Miss Frances Benjamin Johnson, 1889-1910.** N.Y.: Crown Publishing, Harmony Books, 1974. (463).

Kollwitz, Kathe. "The Mothers," 1921. (71).

Lange, Dorothea. "Ex-Slave With A Long Memory," Alabama, 1938. (379).

Lee, Russell. "Lafayette, Louisiana, 1938." F.S.A. (307).

M.I.T. Historical Collections. "Women in Lowell School of Design, circa 1885." Photograph, (pg. 199).

Mount, Martha Jane. Drawing from **Women and Literature: An Annotated Bibliography of Women Writers**, 2nd edition by the Sense & Sensibility Collective, 1973. (676).

Royal Canadian Geographical Society. Photograph, circa 1939, from **Patterns of Canada;** William J. Megill, editor. Toronto: Ryerson Press, 1966. (617).

Schumann, Nikki. "Duality of Consciousness." Drawing. (504).

SECOND WAVE: A Magazine of the New Feminism—Box 344, Cambridge A; Cambridge, MA 02139. (A special thanks to **SECOND WAVE MAGAZINE** for use of the following graphics):
Horowitz, Janet: Vol. 1, No. 3, (469).
Marshall, Elizabeth: Vol. 3, No. 4, (International, Japanese section).
Natti, Susanna: Vol. 3, No. 3, (550).
Newman, Beth: Vol. 3, No. 3, (757).
Schweber, Liz: Vol. 2, No. 3, (731).
Segaloff, J.: Vol. 1, No. 3, (Muriel Spark Biography entry) and Vol. 2, No. 3, (pg. 212).

Siegel, Anita. Cover artist of **FIVE SISTERS: Women Against The Tsar**, edited and translated by Barbara Alpern Engel and Clifford N. Rosenthal. N.Y.: Alfred A. Knopf, Inc., 1975. (733).

Student Nonviolent Coordinating Committee. From **THE MOVEMENT**, text by Lorraine Hansberry, N.Y.: Simon & Schuster, 1964. (807).

Vitagliono, Maria. Drawing from Susan Saxe Defense Committee Newsletter. (pg. 206).

Author Index

Subject Index

Abortion 112, 153-155, 202, 216, 221, 244, 268, 287, 332, 380, 477, 509, 532, 538, 564, 623, 626, 635, 659, 669, 676, 692, 724, 761

Adolescence 2, 3, 44, 65-66, 74, 76-77, 117, 151, 154, 163, 176, 180, 182-184, 186, 189-190, 195-196, 199, 203, 206-207-209, 221-222, 224, 238, 241, 244-245, 247, 251, 253, 255, 268, 288, 290, 292, 294, 297, 300, 305, 307-308, 311-312, 314, 320, 328, 332, 340, 343, 363, 366, 370, 372, 375, 424, 429, 458, 468, 472, 474, 481, 490, 497, 511, 514, 515, 527, 531, 536-537, 547, 556, 560, 564, 578, 586, 587, 590, 592, 595, 612, 614-615, 621, 628, 633-638, 640, 649-650, 664-665, 676, 678, 680, 688, 702, 704, 709, 711, 716, 724, 727, 748, 758

Alcoholism 63, 275, 299

African Background 194, 254, 373, 546-550, 553, 556, 587-588, 590-600, 737, 751

Aging—See Middle Age, Old Age

Appearance 26, 38, 42, 54, 60, 70-71, 121, 128, 141, 185, 203, 232, 251, 261, 265, 272, 299, 307, 314, 319, 366, 372, 432, 446, 537, 559, 565, 591, 595, 597, 618, 620, 632, 654, 676, 722, 756

Arts, Women and the 3, 12, 18-19, 28, 37, 50-51, 55, 72-73, 76, 87, 95-96, 106, 110, 117, 119, 122, 124, 141, 157, 160, 174-175, 181, 184, 186, 188, 196, 199, 204, 208, 215, 219, 228, 230, 236, 243-244, 246, 250, 263, 265, 269, 278, 283, 287, 289, 296, 303-304, 310, 317-318, 332, 338, 340, 350, 357-358, 407, 410, 429, 466, 474, 483, 503, 506, 508, 519, 527, 539, 553, 581, 586, 617, 628, 635, 644, 646-647, 654, 659-660, 662, 664, 666-667, 669, 676, 679, 683, 687, 728-730, 745, 747, 753, 799, 816

Asian Background 156, 601-611, 672, 720-723, 751

Autobiography 30, 40, 44, 95, 97, 106, 112-113, 119, 122, 138, 155, 160, 181, 183-184, 204, 208, 213, 218-219, 230, 243, 245-246, 251, 256, 288, 296, 304-305, 310, 363, 407, 444, 471, 519, 599-660, 665-669, 675-676, 679, 683, 687, 717-718, 722, 733, 737, 753, 758

Biography 17, 57, 96, 161, 406, 416-417, 419, 429, 508, 806

Birth Control 191, 221, 465, 548, 573, 624

Black Characters from a white perspective 4, 10, 14, 45, 49, 83, 133, 136, 139, 149, 159, 177, 194-195, 198, 209, 230, 244, 276, 292, 294-295, 323, 327, 337, 343, 368, 373, 382, 391, 438, 479, 546, 556, 590, 592-593, 596, 598, 745

Black Culture 10-11, 14, 26-27, 50, 57, 84, 120-122, 183-184, 190, 194, 198, 213, 230, 240-241, 255, 263-264, 297-300, 305, 307-308, 334-335, 341, 375-379, 385, 591, 599-600, 746, 748, 751, 760, 762, 768, 816

Black Writers 7, 26-27, 86-88, 120-123, 128-129, 183-184, 190, 198, 209, 213, 230, 240-241, 243, 255, 263-264, 297-300, 305, 307-308, 333-335, 341, 360, 375-379, 385, 591, 599-600, 726, 745-746, 748, 751, 760, 762, 768, 816

Catholic Background 9-14, 29, 34, 157, 191, 252, 254, 288, 311, 314, 349, 390, 580-581, 629-630, 639-640, 665, 683, 708-709, 711-713, 716, 719, 724, 732, 734

438, 445, 465, 467, 474, 484, 546-547, 556, 573-574, 587, 591, 598, 609, 611, 619, 621, 631, 633-635, 637, 641-642, 705, 709, 711, 716, 719, 737, 742, 745

Russian/Soviet background 332 , 733-735

Science Fiction 228, 247, 260, 279, 280, 284, 301, 352-353, 448, 499, 520-522, 560, 563, 756-757

Separations 55, 96, 187, 190, 202, 216, 232, 235, 263, 283, 285, 287, 289, 304, 313, 361, 378, 528-530, 534, 548, 550, 566-567, 599, 625-626, 642, 713-715, 741

Sexuality 12, 14, 54, 58-60, 70, 73, 101, 109, 112, 128, 135, 145, 148, 151, 153, 158, 175-176, 182, 186-187, 190, 192, 195-196, 200, 216, 219, 221, 223-225, 226, 228, 234-235, 249, 263-265, 268, 279, 287, 289, 292-294, 297, 306, 308, 310, 316-317, 319-320, 332, 336, 337-338, 340, 349, 353, 361, 366, 387-388, 393, 412, 418, 456, 467, 472, 474, 474, 482, 486, 495, 500, 502, 504, 513, 515-516, 518-520, 525-528, 542-543, 547, 548, 554-554, 561, 565, 567, 569, 573, 574, 582, 600, 605, 631, 635, 637-638, 653-655, 657, 662, 671-673, 676-678, 685, 688-691, 711-716, 719, 732, 735, 758, 761, 771, 779

Short Stories 6, 8, 10-11, 13-17, 25-25, 33-34, 39, 42-43, 60, 62, 65, 72-73, 82, 102, 137, 148, 154, 156, 173, 193, 200, 207, 215, 228, 247, 260-261, 274, 285, 301, 311, 316-318, 320, 323, 327, 329-330, 335, 342, 367, 372, 377, 382, 442, 447, 470, 532, 540, 554, 556, 558, 588, 591, 594-595, 597-598, 607-608, 611, 612-613, 616, 627-629, 634, 638, 640, 659, 670-671, 677, 681, 703, 708-709, 725, 727, 736, 738, 743, 745-747, 749, 750-752, 754-758, 760-762

Sickness 30, 38, 85, 121, 130, 140, 144, 164, 171, 182, 193, 228, 234, 239, 243, 272, 299, 315, 327, 340, 349, 378, 386, 443, 445, 473, 500, 510, 526, 531, 538, 565, 574, 581, 697-698, 704, 745

Single Women 3-4, 8, 14-15, 21, 28, 31-32, 41, 51, 56, 58, 62-63, 75-76, 90, 94, 98, 122, 135, 140-141, 154, 158, 160, 171, 176, 182, 190, 193, 196, 201, 208, 215, 223, 230, 233, 251-252, 258, 260, 264, 278, 287, 289, 304, 306, 337-338, 349, 356-358, 360, 371, 387, 403-404, 412, 424, 423, 428, 432-446, 474, 476-478, 481, 501, 503, 526-527, 530-531, 535, 543-544, 565, 569, 574-575, 578-580, 587, 616, 619, 623, 625, 631, 635, 654, 661, 663-664, 690, 705, 709, 722, 724, 743, 745

Sisters 2, 241, 398, 399, 435, 467, 524, 542, 591, 638, 716

Slavery 7, 26, 45, 83, 149, 379, 407, 438, 443, 445

Southern Background 7, 9-13, 16, 26, 27, 34, 45, 49-50, 67-68, 82-83, 95-96, 100-106,
100-106, 120-123, 136, 139-140, 149, 164, 180, 182-183, 186-187, 196, 214, 217,237, 250-251, 263-264, 266, 276, 292-295, 305, 321-323, 343, 368, 376-379, 382, 384, 438, 745, 748

Suicide 58, 176, 297, 521

Supernatural/Ghost Stories 46, 102, 258, 394-395, 421, 447, 749, 750, 752

Translations—French 620-622, 630, 639-640, 644-650, 652-683, 688-696

Translations—German 697-700, 704

Translations—Italian 719

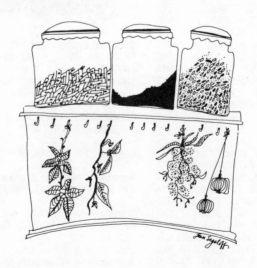

Women and Literature is a member of COSMEP

Perfectly Princess

Blue
Princess
Takes the
Stage

by Alyssa Crowne

illustrated by Charlotte Alder

Scholastic Inc.

New York   Toronto   London   Auckland
Sydney   Mexico City   New Delhi   Hong Kong

For my sister, Katherine,

aka "Princess Superstar."

ISBN 978-0-545-20851-2

Text copyright © 2010 by Pure West Productions, Inc.
Illustrations copyright © 2010 by Scholastic Inc.

12 11 10 9 8 7 6 5 4 3 2 1   10 11 12 13 14 15/0

Printed in Jiaxing, China   68
Designed by Kevin Callahan
First printing, October 2010

Contents

Contents

Chapter One

The Lucky Blue Ribbon

"Oh, I am a magical princess!
And I live in a magical place . . ."

"Emma Harrison! Are you singing again?" asked Mr. Parker.

A few kids laughed. Emma looked up from her math paper. She must have started singing while she was doing her subtraction problems. She wasn't supposed to sing in class. But sometimes she couldn't help it!

"Sorry, Mr. Parker," Emma said. "I have an audition today."

Monica Sanchez shook her head. "We're not doing *addition*, we're doing subtraction," she said.

"I said 'audition,' not addition," Emma replied. "It's when you try out for a part in a play. We're doing *Princess Lyrica and the Choral Kingdom* at Miss Lisa's School of the Arts. I'm trying out for the part of Princess Lyrica." She sat up very straight in her chair.

"But you already go to this school," Monica said, looking confused. "How can you go to two schools at the same time?"

"I go to Miss Lisa's after school on Tuesdays and Thursdays," Emma explained. "It's not like regular school. We learn how to sing and dance and act."

"Emma is good at all of those things," chimed in Victoria, Emma's best friend.

Emma smiled. Ever since she could remember, she dreamed of becoming an actor. And this was going to be her big chance! She started going to Miss Lisa's just a few months ago. Miss Lisa put on three plays every year, and this was Emma's very first one.

"Well, good luck, Emma," said Mr. Parker. "But please practice your song outside the classroom, okay?"

Emma nodded. She would try! "Okay, Mr. Parker."

Just then, the bell rang. Emma almost jumped out of her seat. She couldn't wait to get to the audition!

Emma and Victoria ran down the hall,

out the front doors, and right to Emma's mom's car. Emma's little sister, Sydney, was strapped into her car seat.

Mrs. Harrison gave the girls a big smile as they climbed into the car. "Are you ready for your audition?" she asked.

"Yes!" Emma said confidently. "I practiced the song over and over. And I'm wearing my lucky blue dress. *And* my lucky blue ribbon."

Emma looked at her reflection in the rearview mirror. The blue dress matched the color of her eyes exactly, and the blue ribbon was tied in her curly blonde hair.

"I just *know* I'm going to be Princess Lyrica!" Emma said. "It's the perfect part for me. I love princesses!"

"I know you'll get it, too," Victoria said. She frowned. "I just hope I get a cool part. I'm not a very good singer."

"You *are* a good singer," Emma told her. "Plus, you're the funniest kid in the school. Miss Lisa even says so."

Two-year-old Sydney tugged at the ribbon in Emma's hair.

"Pretty! Pretty!" Sydney said.

"Don't touch it!" Emma cried. "Mom, Sydney's messing up my ribbon!"

Emma looked in the mirror again. Now her ribbon had a smear of jelly on it from Sydney's fingers.

"It's ruined!" Emma moaned. "I won't

get the part if my lucky ribbon looks like this."

"Calm down, Emma," Mrs. Harrison said, giving a little smile. "It's not ruined. Besides, you'll get the part because you're a good actor, not because of a ribbon."

Emma glared at Sydney. "Just don't touch it anymore!"

"We're here, thank goodness," Emma's mom said with a sigh. She pulled up in front of Miss Lisa's. "Good luck, girls. I'll pick you up later."

"Don't say 'good luck,' Mom," Emma said. "Miss Lisa says that's *bad* luck. Say 'break a leg.'"

Mrs. Harrison looked horrified. "I will not say that! I don't want you to break your leg."

Emma rolled her eyes. "It's just a saying, Mom."

Mrs. Harrison leaned over the front seat

and gave her a kiss. "I'll just say I love you. Okay?"

Emma smiled. "Okay, Mom. Love you, too."

Emma and Victoria left the car and walked up the path to Miss Lisa's School of the Arts. The school didn't look like a regular school. It was a big old house with a porch that went all the way around. The inside didn't look like a regular school, either. There were no desks or books or chalkboards. Instead, there was a room with big mirrors on the walls where they practiced dancing and acting. There was a music room with a piano. Another room was filled with racks and racks of costumes.

Inside, Emma and Victoria found the other students in the music room. Emma's friend Adam was practicing a dance move. Kelly Chang was playing the piano and singing the princess song.

"Oh, I am a magical princess!
And I live in a magical place . . ."

"Wow, she sounds good," Victoria whispered to Emma. "But not as good as you," she added quickly.

Miss Lisa came into the room, and everyone got quiet. The owner of the school was short and thin, with brown hair tied in a ponytail. She wore a long black skirt and a black leotard. Emma always thought Miss Lisa looked like some kind of beautiful fairy. But her voice was loud and powerful.

"Good afternoon, students!" she said. "Please take your places. It's time for the auditions to begin!"

Chapter Two

The Big Audition

Emma sat down on the shiny wood floor with the other students.

"As you know, today you are auditioning for a role in *Princess Lyrica and the Choral Kingdom*," Miss Lisa said. "There are several speaking parts, and a big chorus. If you don't get a speaking part, you will still get to perform in the play."

It's nice that everyone gets a part, Emma thought. But she didn't want just any part.

She wanted to play Princess Lyrica so badly!

"When I call your name, please come to the front of the room and sing the song you have practiced," Miss Lisa said. "I'll tell you when to stop."

Emma had already read the whole script of the play. It was about the Choral Kingdom, where everyone loved to sing. But then a mean witch named Malvira used magic to steal all of the music from the kingdom. Princess Lyrica went on a magical journey to find the witch and get the music back.

Princess Lyrica was definitely the best part in the play. Most of the girls were going to try out for that part, except Victoria. Victoria was trying out for the part of Princess Lyrica's magic unicorn.

When Miss Lisa called her name, Victoria got up in front of the other

students. Miss Lisa nodded and started
playing the unicorn song on the piano.
Victoria sang along.

"March, march, march!
We're marching through the woods.
Follow my trusty horn . . ."

Victoria was right—she wasn't a very
good singer! But she marched up and down
the room as she sang. She pranced like a
unicorn. She twirled around. Everyone
started to giggle.

While Victoria was marching, she
accidentally tripped
over Adam's feet.

Splat! She fell and slid
across the floor.

"Oh, no! Are you okay?"
Adam asked.

Victoria gave a big
smile. She held her arms
out wide.

"Ta-da!" she cried. "I, um, I did that on purpose!"

Everyone laughed. Miss Lisa stopped playing the piano.

"Great energy, Victoria!" she said. "Adam Lenos, you're up next."

Adam sang the unicorn song, too. But he didn't fall down. While some other kids took their turns, Emma practiced her song over and over in her head.

Finally, Miss Lisa called her name.

"Emma Harrison!"

Emma took her place at the front of the room. It felt like little butterflies were flapping their wings under her skin. She closed her eyes for a second and tried to stop being nervous. When she opened them, Miss Lisa nodded. The song started.

"Oh, I am a magical princess . . ."

As Emma sang, she imagined she was Princess Lyrica. She could almost feel the crown on her head, and the long dress brushing against her ankles. She wasn't just pretending to be a princess—she *was* a princess.

When Emma finished the last note of the song, everyone clapped.

"Wonderful, Emma!" Miss Lisa said. "That was a real treat."

Emma could feel her smile stretching all the way across her face. She walked back

to her space on the floor and sat down. Other girls sang the princess song, too, but she wasn't really listening.

Miss Lisa said she was wonderful! Emma was sure she got the part. She was a perfect princess!

Emma closed her eyes again. She imagined herself onstage, wearing a sparkling blue gown. A glittery crown rested on her head. She walked to the front of the stage and took a bow.

The crowd went wild. They clapped and cheered. They stood up. Somebody even threw a bouquet of beautiful blue flowers onstage!

Emma opened her eyes. She had dreamed of moments like this before. But now, finally, her dream was going to come true!

Chapter Three

Princess Practice

Emma could hardly wait until Thursday. That was the day when Miss Lisa would announce who got which parts in the play. Emma wasn't nervous, just excited. She was sure she was going to play Princess Lyrica!

All day Wednesday, Emma kept daydreaming about being onstage. Mr. Parker had to call her name twice to get her attention.

After school, Emma hurried through

her homework. Then she went up to the bedroom she shared with Sydney. Emma's half of the room was painted blue, her favorite color. Sydney's half was painted pink. Emma wished her *whole* room could be blue.

Emma marched to where Sydney was playing with her baby doll on the floor.

"Come on, Sydney," she said. "Let's play a new game. It's a princess game!"

"What princess game?" Sydney asked.

Emma wanted to practice being a princess so she could be the best Princess Lyrica ever. She went to her toy box and took out a silver princess crown. It had blue jewels on it.

Sydney grabbed for the crown. "Pretty!"

Emma quickly put the crown on her own head. "No, the crown is for me. I am

Princess Lyrica. You are my loyal servant."
She stood tall, looking very royal.

"I want to be princess!" Sydney said,
pouting.

"Being a servant is a very important
job," Emma told her little sister.

Sydney frowned. "No!"

Emma thought for a minute. She needed
Sydney's help if she was going to practice.
She went back to her toy box and pulled
out an old pink dress with silver glitter all
over it. It didn't fit Emma anymore, but it
was the perfect size for Sydney.

"Servants get to wear pretty dresses.
See?" Emma said. She slipped the dress
over her sister's head.

Sydney beamed. "I'm a princess!"

Emma sighed. "No, you're my servant.
I am a princess, and this is my throne."

She put her desk chair in the middle of
the room and sat down. Then she closed her

eyes. She imagined herself in a beautiful blue gown. She was Princess Lyrica, ruler of the Choral Kingdom!

"Servant! Please fetch me the royal teddy bear," Emma said, opening her eyes and pointing.

Sydney trotted over to Emma's bed and picked up her teddy bear. Then she brought it to Emma and dropped it on her lap.

"Excellent!" Emma said. "Now Princess Lyrica is thirsty. Please fetch me a juice box!"

"Okay!" Sydney said. She ran out of the room. A few minutes later, she came back with two juice boxes. She gave one to Emma. Then she sat on the floor and slurped down her apple juice.

"Servant, it is not time for your break yet!" Emma said.

But Sydney was already tired of the game.

"Thirsty," she said.

"But we have to go find the wicked witch, Malvira!" Emma told her.

Sydney shook her head. "That's scary." She picked up the baby doll and put her in her stroller. Then she wheeled it out of the room.

"Fine! I'll just let someone else be my servant!" Emma yelled after her.

But there was no one else. Emma took off her crown.

When she got the part, she would ask Victoria to practice with her. Victoria was better than Sydney, anyway.

The next day, Emma wore her lucky blue ribbon to school. Her mom had washed off all the jelly stains.

In class, Emma could hardly sit still. She was just so excited inside. Today she would get the part of Princess Lyrica!

"Emma Harrison, are you bouncing up and down?" Mr. Parker asked during reading time.

"Sorry, Mr. Parker," Emma said.

When the school bell rang, Emma and Victoria raced to Mrs. Harrison's car.

"My, you girls are excited!" Emma's mom said.

"I'm going to get to be Princess Lyrica today," Emma said. "I just know it!"

"Emma, you might not get the part you want," her mom said gently. "You might not even get a speaking part at all. I don't want you to be sad if that happens."

"I won't," Emma promised. But that was because she didn't believe her mom. She *had* to get the part of Princess Lyrica.

They reached Miss Lisa's School of the Arts a few minutes later. Inside, everyone was buzzing with excitement. Miss Lisa walked in, holding a piece of paper.

"Everyone please sit down," she said. "I am going to announce the actors who have speaking roles in *Princess Lyrica and the Choral Kingdom*."

Victoria held Emma's hand as Miss Lisa began reading the names. She started out with the smallest parts.

Kids clapped and cheered when their names were called.

"The role of Mischief the Cat goes to Victoria Baron," Miss Lisa said.

"Meow!" Victoria shouted happily.

"But I thought you wanted to be the unicorn," Emma whispered.

Victoria shrugged. "It's okay. The cat doesn't have to sing."

Miss Lisa called out some more names.

She was getting near the end of the list. Emma felt more and more excited. She knew Miss Lisa was going to call her name any minute now.

Miss Lisa looked right at her. Emma took a deep breath. This was it!

"The role of Malvira the Witch goes to . . . Emma Harrison," Miss Lisa said.

Emma couldn't believe her ears! She didn't clap or cheer. She didn't say anything at all.

Miss Lisa looked up from the paper and smiled. "And finally, the role of Princess Lyrica goes to Kelly Chang."

"Yay!" Kelly cheered. A bunch of kids clapped.

Emma was shocked. She jumped to her feet.

"Miss Lisa! There must be some mistake!" she cried out.

Emma the Witch?

"**Emma, please sit down,**" Miss Lisa said.

"But I think you read the names wrong," Emma insisted.

"I did not!" Miss Lisa said sharply. "We will talk about this after class, Emma. Right now, I want us all to learn how to sing the opening number."

Emma slowly sat down.

"Oh, Emma, I'm so sorry!" Victoria whispered.

Emma didn't say anything.

She still couldn't believe it. She wasn't going to play Princess Lyrica. Instead, she was going to play a nasty old witch!

Emma took the lucky blue ribbon from her hair and stuffed it into her pocket. It wasn't lucky at all!

Miss Lisa asked everyone to stand up. She passed around sheet music for the opening song. It was called "We Love Music."

"This is the first song in the play," said Miss Lisa. "The people of the Choral Kingdom sing about how much they love music. Everyone is in this number." She paused and looked down at the sheet. "Actually, Emma and Victoria aren't in this song. The witch and her cat don't appear until later, but you girls can sing along as we practice."

"Fine," Emma mumbled.

Miss Lisa played the song on the piano.

Usually, Emma sang nice and loudly. But now she sang very softly. What did it matter?

Princess Lyrica had a special part in the song, and Emma had no part at all.

That should be me! Emma thought.

The group practiced the song a few times. Then Miss Lisa clapped her hands. They were done for the day.

Everyone ran up to Kelly.

"Congratulations!"

"You'll make a great princess, Kelly!"

Emma didn't say anything. She leaned against the wall and looked down at her shoes.

Adam and Victoria walked up to her.

"Sorry you didn't get to be the princess," Adam said. "But the witch is a good part."

"No it isn't," Emma said flatly.

"Isn't it great that Adam gets to play the

27

unicorn?" Victoria asked, trying to cheer up Emma.

"I guess," Emma replied. Adam looked hurt. "Sorry," Emma added. "It's really good that you got the part."

"Don't be sad," Victoria urged. "I get to be your cat! We'll be onstage together. Won't that be fun?"

Emma shrugged. Victoria and Adam were happy and excited. But Emma didn't feel that way at all.

Then Miss Lisa tapped Emma's arm. "Let's talk," she said.

Emma followed her to a quiet corner of the room.

"I know you wanted the part of Princess Lyrica," Miss Lisa began.

"It's the *only* part I wanted!" Emma said sadly. "If I have to be a witch, I don't want to be in the play."

Miss Lisa looked surprised. "I thought

you were an actor, Emma,"
she said. "A real actor
would never turn down
a juicy role like this one."

"Really?" Emma
asked. She wasn't so sure.

"Of course," Miss
Lisa said. "I chose you
to play Malvira because it is a very
important role. The audience will have
to believe that the Choral Kingdom is in
danger. Only a very good actor will be
able to convince them of that."

Emma hadn't thought of it that way.

She sat quietly for a moment. "Then I
guess I shouldn't quit," she finally said.

Miss Lisa smiled. "I'm glad to hear
that!"

Emma smiled back. "Don't worry, Miss
Lisa. I'm going to be the best witch ever!"

"I think you'll be a wonderful witch," said

Chapter Five

Too Scary for Sydney

"I think you'll be a wonderful witch," said Emma's dad. Emma's family was eating spaghetti at the round kitchen table.

"I agree," said Emma's mom. "You'd be great in any role, Emma. You're a very good actor."

"That's exactly what Miss Lisa said!" Emma told her. "I *have* to play the witch. It's an important part."

"Well, I can't wait to see the show," said Mr. Harrison. "Just don't forget your parents when you're famous, okay?"

"Of course I won't!" Emma replied, rolling her eyes. She turned to her little sister. "Will you help me practice after dinner?"

Sydney had tomato sauce all over her face. She nodded.

After dinner was done, Mrs. Harrison washed the sauce off of Sydney's face. Then the two girls went to their room.

Sydney pulled the sparkly pink dress out of the toy box. "Princess!" she cried.

"No, we're not playing princess," Emma

said. "I'm a witch, and you're my evil servant."

Sydney scowled. "I want to wear the dress!"

"All right," Emma said, sighing. "Wear whatever you want."

Sydney held up her arms so Emma could help her put on the dress. Then Emma looked around the room. She couldn't wear her princess crown this time. What would a witch wear?

She spotted the small pink blanket that Sydney slept with. It wasn't a witchy color, but it would have to do. She put the blanket around her shoulders.

"My blanket!" Sydney wailed.

"I'm just borrowing it," Emma said. "It's my witch's cape, see?"

Emma hunched her shoulders. She pointed at Sydney. Then she talked in a scary voice.

"I am the witch, Malvira!" she said.
"Fetch me my broom, servant!"

Sydney stared at Emma for a moment.
Then she burst out crying.

"Waaaaaaaaaaaah!"

"Sydney, stop it!" Emma said, shushing
her.

That only made Sydney cry harder.

Mr. Harrison poked his head into the
room. "Girls, what's going on?"

Sydney stopped crying long enough to
answer. "Emma scared me!"

"I'm supposed to be scary," Emma pointed out. "I'm practicing to be a witch!"

Mr. Harrison picked up Sydney. "All right, Syd. Let's go get a drink of water," he said. He looked at Emma. "Maybe you should practice being a witch by yourself."

"Okay," Emma said with a frown. She sat on the edge of her bed.

Malvira might be an important part, but it was a scary part. Everyone would like Princess Lyrica. Nobody would like Malvira the Witch.

Nobody would clap and cheer when she took a bow. Nobody would stand up. Nobody would give her flowers. Kelly would get all the flowers and applause.

Emma fell back on her bed and stared up at the ceiling. Her side of the ceiling was painted blue with silver stars and planets.

They helped her fall asleep at night. They helped her think, too.

She couldn't quit the play! If she did, Miss Lisa would think she didn't really want to be an actor. But she couldn't play Malvira, either. She wanted everyone in the audience to like her!

Just then, a little thought came into Emma's head. Right now, Malvira was a scary witch. But she didn't have to be . . . did she?

Chapter Six

The Worst Costume

For the next few days, Emma thought about how she could fix the part of Malvira the Witch. Emma and Victoria practiced their lines together every chance they got. When Tuesday came, they were ready for the first rehearsal.

Miss Lisa gathered everyone in the old barn behind the school. The barn had a big stage in the back and lots of seats for an audience. There was a piano right in front of the stage.

"All right, everyone," Miss Lisa called out cheerfully. "Please get onstage if you're in the opening number."

Emma and Victoria sat in the seats and watched the others. Kelly was wearing jeans and a shirt with a blue heart on it. She didn't look like a princess, but onstage she acted just like one. Emma listened carefully this time when Kelly sang her solo.

"Wow, she's really good," Emma whispered to Victoria.

Miss Lisa clapped her hands when the number was over.

"Nice job, Kelly. Next, we need Emma and Victoria for Malvira's first scene," she said. "Kelly and Adam, please go to the costume room and try on your costumes."

Adam waved to Emma as he passed by. "I wish I could watch your scene," he said.

"That's okay," Emma replied, grinning. "I'll sing loud enough so you can hear me."

Emma and Victoria climbed up on the stage, and Miss Lisa told them where to stand.

"You're in Malvira's cottage," she said. "Malvira is putting a magic charm on her vacuum cleaner so it will suck up all the music in the kingdom."

"Right," Emma said. "I memorized the script already."

She was pretty sure Miss Lisa looked impressed.

One of the boys from the school wheeled the vacuum cleaner onstage. Emma stood behind it and wiggled her fingers over it.

"I am Malvira, and there's nobody meaner. I'm putting a spell on my vacuum cleaner!" she said in her scary witch voice.

"Excellent!" cried Miss Lisa. "Now you and Mischief the Cat dance around the vacuum as you cast your spell."

Emma and Victoria really got into the dance. Emma waved her arms in the air and twirled around. Victoria pranced with her hands in front of her like paws.

Then Victoria tripped over the vacuum cleaner cord. She didn't fall, but the vacuum tumbled off the stage with a clatter.

Victoria blushed. "Sorry!"

"Victoria, you're a cat. You are graceful. Like this," said Miss Lisa. She walked up on stage and danced a circle on her tiptoes.

"Got it," Victoria said with a nod.

After the vacuum cleaner dance, Emma sang her song. It was called "I Hate Music." Emma did her best to look mean and scary while she sang. She knew it meant that people might not like her. But she wanted to do a good job for Miss Lisa. Besides, acting like a witch was kind of fun!

Maybe I don't have to fix the part of the witch after all, Emma thought.

"Good job," said Miss Lisa when Emma was finished. "You and Victoria can report to the costume room now."

Emma jumped off the stage and ran down the aisle, with Victoria close behind. She loved the costume room! Miss Sylvia was in charge. She was a round lady with lots of red hair piled on top of her head. She made all of the costumes for Miss Lisa's school.

But when Emma walked into the costume room, she froze. Kelly was trying on her princess costume. It was light blue with puffy sleeves and a long, beautiful skirt covered in silver sparkles. It was exactly like the princess dress Emma had imagined for herself!

Kelly spun around. "Miss Sylvia, this is beautiful!" she sighed.

"You look just like a princess," Victoria said.

Emma thought so, too. But she didn't say it out loud.

Adam galloped up to Emma, wearing a white unicorn costume. It looked kind of like white pajamas. He wore a unicorn head on top of his head. There was an opening for his eyes, nose, and mouth underneath the unicorn's nose.

"What do you think?" Adam asked. "I've never been a unicorn before."

"It's nice," Emma said, trying to sound like she meant it. But all she could think about was Kelly's beautiful princess dress!

Miss Sylvia winked

at Emma. "Wait until you see your witch costume, Emma. It's perfectly terrifying!"

Miss Sylvia went into the closet of colorful costumes and came back with a long, black robe on a hanger. It was straight and plain and boring. She held a black cone-shaped hat in the other hand.

"You must try it on," she insisted, handing Emma the costume. "And wait until you see the nose. It's the best part."

"Nose?" Emma asked. She didn't like the sound of that. At all.

Miss Sylvia dug through a nearby box. She pulled out a long, green fake nose with bumps on it. "See? It's perfect!"

Emma did not think it was perfect. She thought it was ugly!

There was no way she was going to wear that costume. But how could she convince Miss Sylvia to change it?

Victoria was getting impatient to see her costume. She reached up on a high shelf. "Miss Sylvia, I think I see my cat ears," she said.

Miss Sylvia looked alarmed. "No, dear, that box is full of —"

Victoria tapped the box, and it fell off of the shelf. Colorful feathers rained down on the costume room.

"— feathers!" Miss Sylvia finished.

"Sorry," Victoria said sheepishly.

Emma looked down at her witch robe. It was covered with feathers! It actually looked kind of pretty.

Miss Sylvia touched her hair, and feathers flew out of it. Everyone laughed—even Emma.

She wasn't happy about her witch costume at all. But finally had an idea about how to fix things. . . .

Chapter Seven

Emma Makes
Some Changes

That night at dinner, Emma put the first part
of her plan into action.

"Mom, I need help with my costume
for the play," she said.

Mrs. Harrison looked surprised.
"Really? Isn't Miss Sylvia making it?"

"I said I would help," Emma fibbed.
"She has a lot of costumes to do."

Mrs. Harrison nodded. "What do you

need? A black robe and a witch's hat?"

Emma shook her head. "Not black. Blue."

Emma's mom looked thoughtful. "I think we can use one of your old blue princess costumes, if that's okay."

Emma nodded. That's just what she had been thinking. "Remember that lacy tablecloth with the spiderwebs we used on Halloween? Maybe we can put that over the blue—to make it a little scary."

"No scary!" Sydney cried.

"Just a little scary," Emma promised. "But mostly pretty."

"I'll get right on it," Mrs. Harrison said, and Emma smiled. Part one of her plan was under way!

* * *

Emma tried out the second part of her plan at the next rehearsal. She waited until they were practicing the last scene of the play.

Kelly, Adam, Emma, and Victoria were all onstage. Princess Lyrica and her unicorn had just reached Malvira's cottage. In the script, Princess Lyrica asked for the vacuum cleaner, but Malvira wouldn't give it to her. So Princess Lyrica sang a song. Malvira decided she liked music after all, and she gave up the vacuum cleaner.

That's what was in the script. But Emma had another idea.

"Malvira, please give us your vacuum

cleaner so we can return music to the land," Kelly said.

"No! Never!" cried Emma.

"Then I will sing you a song," said Kelly. Miss Lisa started to play the piano. But Emma interrupted before Kelly could start singing.

"You don't need to sing a song!" Emma cried. "I am not really Malvira the witch. I am Emmaline, your long-lost twin sister—and I am a princess, too! I will give music back to the land!"

"Cut!" Miss Lisa yelled. Everyone looked confused. "Emma, what was that all about?"

"It's a better ending," Emma said, grinning proudly. "It's much more interesting than the old ending. Don't you think?"

Miss Lisa put her hands on her hips. "No, I'm afraid I don't," she said. "The

play is fine just the way it is. Please stick to the script from now on."

"Okay," Emma muttered. "If you're sure."

"I am very sure," said Miss Lisa. She sat back down at the piano, and Kelly began to sing.

Emma scowled. Suddenly, it was very easy to pretend that she was a mean old witch. Right now, she hated music. She hated princesses. She hated the whole play!

Chapter Eight

Malvira's Dance

That weekend, Victoria and Adam came over to Emma's house to practice. But Emma didn't feel like practicing. Instead, they all sat at the kitchen table, munching on some popcorn Emma's dad had made.

"It's a dumb play," Emma complained. "I can't wait until the next play. That one will be much better."

"I like this play," Adam said, shrugging. "It's interesting. And the songs are good."

"That's what you think," Emma muttered.

"Hey!" Adam was insulted. "You're not being very nice."

"Emma's upset because she's not Princess Lyrica," Victoria said matter-of-factly. Emma glared at her. "Well, you are."

"It's not fair!" Emma moped. "Princess Lyrica is the best part."

"I think the unicorn is the best part," Adam said.

Victoria giggled. "No, the cat is the best part!"

Emma did not giggle. "The witch is a good part, but she's too scary. Nobody will like her or clap for me," she said.

Victoria's eyes got wide. "Is that why you changed the script?"

Emma nodded. "But Miss Lisa said I can't change my lines anymore. It's not fair."

"I think people will clap for you," Adam said. "They'll clap if you do a good job. They don't care if you play a mean witch."

"Sydney cares," Emma said. "I made Sydney cry when I was practicing."

"Sydney cries at everything," Victoria pointed out. "There will be other people there, not just little kids. They won't cry."

Emma thought about that for a minute. "I guess you're right," she said. "Still, it's more fun to play a beautiful princess than an ugly old witch. I love princesses!"

"Well, *I* wouldn't want to play a princess," Adam said.

Emma laughed. She stood up. "Maybe we can practice that dance at the end," she said, feeling better.

"Yay!" Victoria cried. "I love to dance!"

The three friends went into the backyard and started to dance. As they jumped and wiggled around the yard, Emma got an idea.

Miss Lisa said she couldn't change the script. But Emma could change some other things instead. . . .

At the next rehearsal, Emma waited until the end of the play to try out her idea. Kelly started to sing Princess Lyrica's last song.

"Give us back our music,
Music is the best . . ."

Behind Kelly, Emma began to dance. She leaped like a ballerina. She whirled and twirled. She spun in circles.

Miss Lisa stopped playing the piano. "Emma! What are you doing?" she asked.

"Well, the song is supposed to make Malvira like music," Emma said. "So I thought it could make her dance, too."

Miss Lisa frowned. "Emma, I asked you not to change the script."

"But I didn't," she protested. "I didn't make up any new words. I'm just dancing!"

Miss Lisa shook her

head. "Emma, you have to stop this. No more changes, okay?"

Emma nodded. "Okay." But she didn't feel okay. None of her ideas were working!

After rehearsal, Kelly walked around with invitations for everyone.

"I'm having a cast party after the play," she said. "Everyone's invited."

Emma imagined how she would feel the night of the play. Kelly would get flowers and everyone would love her. But nobody would love Emma.

Thinking about it made Emma mad.

"I hope you can come, Emma," Kelly said, giving her an invitation.

"I don't think I can," Emma lied. "I'm going to another party that night."

"What other party?" Kelly asked.

"It's none of your business," Emma said loudly. "I just can't go, okay?"

Kelly looked sad and walked away.

Right away, Emma felt bad. She liked Kelly. She didn't mean to hurt her feelings!

Next to her, Adam shook his head. "Emma, I think you're turning into a wicked old witch!" he said.

He was right. Emma didn't feel nice inside. She felt mean—just like Malvira.

Chapter Nine

The Magic Apples

That night, Emma stared at the stars and planets on her ceiling.

She didn't want to be mean — she wanted to have fun! She wasn't going to get to be Princess Lyrica. She wasn't going to get to make Malvira nice. If she wanted to be in the play, she'd have to do what Miss Lisa asked. And more than anything, she wanted to be in the play.

The next morning, Mrs. Harrison had a surprise for Emma. Her witch costume was hanging in the kitchen when Emma came downstairs for breakfast.

The long, blue dress had lacy black spiderwebs all over it. Emma's mom had even sewn silver spiders onto a black witch's hat. The costume looked really cool!

"Oh, Mom, it's beautiful!" Emma cried, hugging her.

"I think so, too," Mrs. Harrison said. "I'll bring it to the dress rehearsal on Tuesday, okay?"

"Okay," Emma said. Then she remembered. Miss Lisa had told her not to change anything else. How would she feel about the new witch costume?

✷ ✷✷ ✷

On Tuesday, Emma changed into her costume in one of the small rooms at Miss Lisa's school. Nervously, she stepped into the hall.

Miss Sylvia saw her first. Her green eyes got big.

"Why, Emma, that's lovely!" she said. "Did you make that costume?"

"My mom did," Emma said proudly.

"I'll have to ask her to help me with the next play," Miss Sylvia said.

Just then, Miss Lisa walked up. She wasn't as happy as Miss Sylvia.

"What is this?" she asked, looking at Emma curiously.

A small group of kids gathered around. Emma took a deep breath.

"I know you didn't want me to make any more changes," she said. "But I had already asked my mom to make me a new costume. Isn't it nice?"

Miss Lisa studied her for a minute. "Well, it *does* look witchy. But where's your nose?"

Oops! Emma had forgotten all about the long green nose.

Miss Sylvia held it up. "Right here," she said.

"I don't think I should wear that," Emma said quickly. "It's hard to sing with the nose on. Besides, it's unfair to people with big noses. Just because someone has a big nose, that doesn't make them mean."

"But the nose makes you look scary," Miss Lisa said.

To Emma's surprise, Kelly spoke up. "Emma doesn't need a fake nose to be scary, Miss Lisa. She's already good at acting scary onstage."

Emma smiled

at Kelly. It was really nice of Kelly to stand up for her!

"You're right," Miss Lisa said, nodding. "The costume is fine the way it is. Now everyone take your places for dress rehearsal!"

Emma couldn't believe it. She was going to get to wear her blue costume in the play!

She joined the rest of the kids as they gathered in the barn. The stage looked just like a magical kingdom, with fake flowers and big mushrooms everywhere. There was even a fake tree with magical apples. But the apples weren't real, either—they were made of foam.

"Dress rehearsal is very important," Miss Lisa explained. "We need to pretend that we have an audience here. If you make a mistake, keep going. We're going to perform the play from start to finish."

Everyone took their places and the rehearsal started. It all went very fast! Emma felt like a whole different person in her costume. She sang and danced and cackled even better than before.

Soon, they reached the part where Malvira and Mischief the Cat take the magic vacuum cleaner to the Choral Kingdom. Emma dragged the vacuum cleaner while Victoria danced ahead. Victoria wore a cute cat costume with a tail and pointy ears.

Victoria turned around and said her line. "Malvira, we're almost there!"

Then she kept dancing—backward. She forgot to turn around! Victoria knocked into the tree of magic apples. The apples fell off and bounced all over the stage!

Victoria looked shocked. Then she started to giggle. Emma tried hard not to laugh. She knew they were supposed to keep going with the play. But she couldn't help it!

Luckily, Miss Lisa was laughing, too.

Then Emma had an idea. "Mischief, clean up those apples now!" she said in her witch voice.

Victoria nodded and started chasing after the apples.

"Good job, Emma," Miss Lisa called out, and Emma smiled.

It was fun being in the play, no matter what part she had!

Chapter Ten

Blue Flowers for Emma

"Mom? Are you ready yet?" Emma called out.

"I'm getting Sydney dressed!" her mom called back. "She won't let me put on her tights."

Normally, Emma would have been mad at Sydney. But she was too excited. It was the night of the play!

She ran into the room she shared with Sydney. Mrs. Harrison finished pulling on Sydney's tights, and the little girl jumped down from the bed. Emma was surprised to see that Sydney was wearing a pretty blue dress, even though she *always* wore pink.

"That's a nice dress, Sydney," Emma said.

"Just like you!" Sydney cried.

"Isn't that sweet?" Mrs. Harrison said. "She wants to look like her big sister."

Emma smiled at Sydney. Sometimes it wasn't so bad having a little sister.

Emma turned to leave, but then she spotted something on her dresser — her blue ribbon. She picked it up.

Maybe it was a lucky ribbon after all. She slipped it into her pocket.

"Come on, ladies! We need to get our star to the theater!" Mr. Harrison called from downstairs.

They all hurried to Miss Lisa's school. There were tons of cars parked on the street outside. Emma started to feel a little bit nervous. A lot of people were coming to see the play!

Emma kissed her parents good-bye and went to the costume room to get changed. Adam was putting on his unicorn head. Kelly was next to him, dressed in her princess costume.

Emma walked up to Kelly and took the blue ribbon from her pocket.

"This is for you," she told Kelly. "For luck. Plus, it goes with your dress."

Kelly smiled and took the ribbon. "Thanks! Blue is my favorite color."

"Mine, too," said Emma.

Kelly tied the ribbon around her wrist. "It's too bad you can't come to the party tonight."

"Actually, I can, if you still want me to," Emma said shyly.

Kelly's face lit up. "Great! See you then."

"Emma Harrison, please get into your costume!" Miss Sylvia called from across the room.

Emma quickly got dressed. She was trying not to feel nervous, but tiny butterfly wings flapped under her skin again, just like when she auditioned. This was no dress rehearsal. This was the real thing!

"Places, everybody!" Miss Lisa called out. "You're going to be wonderful!"

The cast walked onstage for the opening number, and the curtain went up. Emma and Victoria waited backstage for their first scene.

"I'm so nervous!" Victoria whispered.

"Me, too," Emma whispered back, squeezing her friend's hand.

"What if I knock over the tree again?" Victoria worried. "Or the vacuum cleaner? Or if I fall off of the stage?"

"You won't," Emma promised her. "And if you do, we'll just pretend like it's part of the play."

That made Victoria feel better. The two girls held hands while they waited for the song to finish. Then they heard the crowd clap.

"Okay, we're on!" Emma said.

The rest of the cast left the stage, and Emma and Victoria walked on. All the seats in the barn were filled with people. Emma started to feel scared.

Then she remembered—*she* was the scary one! She was Malvira, the wicked witch. Emma raised her arms above the vacuum cleaner.

"I am Malvira, and there's nobody

meaner. I'm putting a spell on my vacuum cleaner!"

With that, Emma forgot about all of the people in the audience. She sang and danced. She acted mean and scary.

Victoria stopped being nervous, too. Best of all, she didn't trip over anything!

Just like at dress rehearsal, the play went by fast. Before Emma knew it, the whole cast gathered onstage to sing the last song together. When they were done, the audience clapped and cheered.

The curtain closed. Everyone ran backstage. It was time for the curtain call!

The curtain opened up again. The members of the chorus came out and took a bow. Victoria and Adam came out together and bowed, too. Then it was Emma's turn.

She ran out onstage. She couldn't believe it. Everyone was clapping!

Emma looked out into the audience. Her mom and dad were standing up and cheering. Then Sydney ran down the aisle. She was holding some pretty blue flowers. She reached up as far as she could to hand them to her big sister.

It was just like Emma always dreamed. It didn't matter if she was a princess or a witch. She was an actor!

I can't wait until the next play! Emma thought.

Make It Yourself!
Cast Party Cupcakes

These fun cupcakes would be perfect for Emma's cast party — or any party for princess lovers!

Emma's Blue Princess Cupcakes

Make vanilla cupcakes using your favorite recipe. Use a few drops of blue food coloring to turn white frosting blue. Frost each cupcake, and then put one yellow M&M in the center of the cupcake. Surround the yellow piece with six blue M&M'S to make flower petals. Add two green leaf-shaped jelly candies to either side of your flower for a finishing touch.

It's a cupcake any princess would be proud to eat!

Victoria's Kitty Cat Cupcakes

Make chocolate cupcakes using your favorite recipe. Frost them with chocolate frosting. Use two green M&M'S for the cat's eyes and a red one for the nose. Cut a chocolate-covered peppermint patty into triangles and use two triangles for each cat's ears. Place them near the top of the cupcake, above the eyes. Add whiskers and a smiling mouth with a tube of black cake-decorating gel. A purrfect treat!